Praise for *Hearty Country Cooking*

"A reference work that will be of immeasurable value to every cook and student of culture who cares about the region and its people. . . . An exemplary model of the best and most useful of food books."

—John Egerton, author of *Southern Food*

"Chockablock with information . . . As practical as it is informative, the book constitutes a mini-encyclopedia of mountain ways of living, past and present, revealed through the culinary habits of one of our most valuable and delightful regions."

—Betty Fussell, author of *I Hear America Cooking*

"Once in a while, a cookbook surfaces with a true ring to it . . . *Hearty Country Cooking* is such a book."

—Antonia Allegra, Editor in Chief of *Napa Valley Appellation*

"Way beyond being just a cookbook . . . Written with joy, sensitivity, and an awareness of today's nutritional needs."

—Ethel G. Hoffman, author and President of the International Association of Culinary Professionals

"Great scope and more Appalachian recipes than I have seen together before. *Hearty Country Cooking* includes standards . . . but also creative country seat 'aspiring' dishes."

—Loyal Jones, author, humorist, retired professor, and former director of the Berea College Appalachian Center

HEARTY Cooking COUNTRY

HEARTY
Cooking
COUNTRY

Savory Southern Favorites

MARK F. SOHN

with a foreword by John Egerton

 ST. MARTIN'S GRIFFIN ❧ NEW YORK

HEARTY COUNTRY COOKING: SAVORY SOUTHERN FAVORITES. Copyright © 1996 by
Mark F. Sohn. Foreword copyright © 1996 by John Egerton. All rights reserved.
Printed in the United States of America. No part of this book may be used or reproduced
in any manner whatsoever without written permission except in the case of brief
quotations embodied in critical articles or reviews. For information, address St. Martin's
Press, 175 Fifth Avenue, New York, N.Y. 10010.

Illustrations copyright © 1996 by L. P. Berman

Grateful acknowledgment is given for permission to reprint previously published material
from the following works:
From *More Than Moonshine: Appalachian Recipes and Recollections*, by Sidney Saylor
Farr. Copyright © 1983 by Sidney Saylor Farr. Reprinted by permission of the
University of Pittsburgh Press.
From *The Cookie Cookbook*, by Darlene Kronschnabel. Copyright © 1977 by Darlene
Kronschnabel. Reprinted by permission.
From *Hill Country Cookin' and Memoirs*, by Ibbie Ledford. Copyright © 1991 by Ibbie
Ledford. Reprinted by permission of Pelican Publishing Company, Inc.
From *Shuck Beans, Stack Cakes, and Honest Fried Chicken*, by Ronnie Lundy.
Copyright © 1991 by Ronnie Lundy. Reprinted by permission of Grove/Atlantic, Inc.
From *Mountain Cooking*, by John Parris. Copyright © 1978 by John Parris. Reprinted
by permission of Asheville (N.C.) Citizen-Times Publishing Co.
From *Head o' W-Hollow*, by Jesse Stuart. Published in 1936. Reprinted by permission
of The Jesse Stuart Foundation, Inc., P.O. Box 391, Ashland, KY 41114.

Library of Congress Cataloging-in-Publication Data

Sohn, Mark F.
  Hearty country cooking.
Mark F. Sohn.
    p.   cm.
  Includes bibliographical references and index.
  ISBN 0-312-19461-7
  1. Cookery, American.   2. Cookery—Appalachian Region. Southern.
I. Title.
TX715.S678117   1996   96-20436
641.5974—dc20   CIP

First published in the United States under the title *Mountain Country
Cooking* by St. Martin's Press

First St. Martin's Griffin Edition: November 1998

10 9 8 7 6 5 4 3 2 1

HEARTY
Cooking
COUNTRY

To the cooks of this region

who share their foods and talk

with me about recipes

■ ■

Contents

Acknowledgments

THE CHALLENGE OF this work was made possible when Sarah Jane Freymann of the Stepping Stone Literary Agency sold my proposal to St. Martin's Press. I thank Sarah, my agent, and Jennifer Weis, my editor.

I also thank my wife, Kathy, for not only letting me control the kitchen but also for editing this material. I thank my children, Laura and Brian, for eating and critiquing a continuous stream of new recipes.

For seven years now, the *News-Express* and my "Images" editor, Nancy Goss, have provided me with a public forum—a sort of workshop—for many of these recipes. Without the excitement of this forum and of the dynamic cooks of this region, my thoughts would not be on paper.

Finally, I received valuable proofreading assistance from my friend Ernestine Collins Meade and my daughter, Laura.

Foreword

ONE OF THE great standard cookbooks of the South is *Southern Cooking*, written in 1928 by Henrietta Stanley Dull—Mrs. S. R. Dull to her readers and to just about everyone who knew her. She was for many years the editor of what was then called the home economics page—today's food section—of the *Atlanta Journal*. Mrs. Dull was a recognized voice of authority on her chosen subject, and readers throughout the region came to depend upon her comprehensive knowledge.

Southern Cooking has remained in print for nearly seventy years. Its continuing usefulness is largely explained, I think, by its no-nonsense approach to presenting recipes. Mother Dull was not one for idle chit-chat; she was direct and to the point, and she knew what she was talking about. If you read her book, you soon learned to trust her judgment and simply do exactly as she said.

Mark Sohn's *Hearty Country Cooking* reminds me strongly of Mrs. Dull's *Southern Cooking*. Here is a wealth of information about food in the Appalachian mountain region, a virtual encyclopedia, presented in clear and direct language. This is more than just a cookbook—it's a reference work that will be of immeasurable value to every cook and student of culture who cares about the region and its people.

It is one thing to compile a book of recipes; it is something else altogether to assemble and organize a comprehensive body of knowledge and then to put it into a readable and usable form. This is the Sohn approach. Not only will you find the familiar Appalachian fare here—the greens and beans, the corn and potatoes, the standard meats and hot breads, the cobblers and pies and cakes—in addition, you'll learn about such authentic and exotic dishes as chocolate gravy, dry-land fish, fried ramps, poke sallet, dilly beans, baked cushaw, sorghum butter, pawpaw custard, sassafras apple syrup, black walnut cake, Christmas rocks, and hard-times coffee, to name only a few.

And, going far beyond Mrs. Dull, *Hearty Country Cooking* offers a glossary of regional food terms, a valuable list of mail-order sources, and a good bibliography. All in all, Mark Sohn's book is an exemplary model of the best and most useful food books. As a serious student of American cultures, he has always paid close attention to what the people around him liked to eat. And, as a serious cook since his boyhood in Oregon, he has learned to prepare and enjoy the regional foods of whatever culture he shares.

Now, after twenty years in the mountains of eastern Kentucky, he has brought us *Hearty Country Cooking*, and all of us who love the mountains, the South, regional culture, and this food will be forever in his debt. The wise and encyclopedic Mrs. Dull surely would have been impressed too, had she lived to see this straightforward production. As we drift further and further into the brave new world of contemporary foods—from the take-out chains to the fern bars and nouvelle cuisine restaurants—the preservationist works of such people as Mark Sohn will continue to grow in importance and stature.

—John Egerton, author of *Southern Food: At Home, on the Road, in History*

Introduction

STACK PIES AND stack cakes, shuck beans and soup beans, cushaw pie and poke sallet: These are Appalachian foods. From Georgia to Maryland and including the Shenandoah, Blue Ridge, Great Smoky, Cumberland, and Allegheny Mountains, the Appalachian Mountain System is a chain with deep valleys, small farms, and rugged people. Within this region you'll find monuments of geography such as the Shenandoah and Great Smoky Mountains National Parks and monuments of culture such as the Greenbrier of White Sulphur Springs, West Virginia, Boone Tavern of Berea, Kentucky, and the Biltmore House and Gardens of Asheville, North Carolina. Like these monuments, the region has produced a unique food tradition.

The food of Appalachia is based on staples—sorghum, dumplings, beans, pork, greens, corn, and potatoes. With these staples, we prepare specialties such as Corn Bread Salad, Buttermilk Biscuits and Sausage Gravy, Tomato Dumplings, Pinto Bean Pie, and Corn Relish. Some regional dishes of Appalachia are virtually unknown in the United States. Narrow valleys, lush vegetation, and severe isolation have come together in these mountains to stimulate a style of country cooking without parallel.

While the old-timers who created this cuisine used a pinch of this and a handful of that, now for the first time, you can enjoy precise, modern, tested, and easy-to-follow recipes that preserve the flavor and heritage of Appalachian foods. Using fresh ingredients, modern kitchen equipment, and health conscious alternatives, *Hearty Country Cooking* collects a region's food memories and presents creative new recipes that exemplify current trends in mountain cooking. It traces the development of recipes from their origins in old Europe to their display at community dinners.

The recipes and stories here are a synthesis of those loving, creative, and resourceful Appalachian cooks of the 1930s, 1940s, and 1950s who would not let you leave the kitchen until you had eaten. They are the recipes of a gregarious people who have lived in, by, and under the tight mountains and narrow valleys that form the spine of this region. Now you can recreate authentic, home cooked mountain food.

Appalachia is enjoying a rebirth of its native food legacy. With *Hearty Country Cooking* you can be part of a fast-moving renaissance of authentic food and honest home cooking. For the first time you can enjoy a region-wide, heritage-oriented Appalachian cookbook, one that focuses exclusively on the unique food of the central and southern areas of the region.

Many Appalachian foods are strikingly different from foods of the South. Southern food includes Louisiana bayou, Creole, plantation, Ozark, Florida-Spanish, and low Charleston. Southern coastal regions are as diverse as the Maryland Shore and the Gulf Coast. Southern food also includes the foods of religious groups such as the Kentucky Shakers and

North Carolina Moravians. In one volume, Southern cookbooks represent mountain and coastal, African-American, Spanish, and Cajun, often leaving the reader confused about distinct subregions within the South. *Hearty Country Cooking* defines for the first time the common foods of an uncommon region.

THE APPALACHIAN REGION covered by this book includes parts of nine states: West Virginia, Ohio, Maryland, Kentucky, Virginia, Tennessee, North Carolina, South Carolina, and Georgia. Also known as the Appalachian Highlands, this system of mountains includes a number of smaller ranges: the Shenandoah, Blue Ridge, Great Smoky, Black, Cumberland, and Allegheny Mountains.

In the 1930s and 1940s, mountaineers were largely dependent on the forest and soil. On garden plots at the base of severe mountains, people grew much of what they ate. This closeness to the land, coupled with a low-budget lifestyle and severe isolation, was the source of our food legacy. It is a tradition that emphasizes mountain-grown food: pork, tomatoes, nuts, apples, beans, corn, and potatoes.

In the 1920s, some families purchased very few foods, perhaps just sugar, salt, and coffee. What they couldn't grow or buy, they gathered or hunted: In the forest, they picked morels and shot squirrels. In the springtime, they picked garden greens and wild greens. From fields and stream banks, they collected chickentoe, poke, watercress, dock, and rape. In the fall, they shelled pecans and broke into black walnuts.

More recently, perhaps just thirty years ago, mountain cooking was a mixture of old and new, mountain-grown and off-the-radio. Because cooks of the 1950s and 1960s wanted to please their families, they tried new foods such as pot pies and yeast dinner rolls alongside traditional favorites such as Fried Cabbage, Fried Mush, and Soup Beans.

Today, mountaineers, like people everywhere, are passionate about food. We continually sift, sort, and modify traditional recipes, and occasionally we create new ones. New recipes emerge from our food legacy. Two examples of this are Corn Bread Salad and Spicy Orange-Sugared Pecans. Some foods in this book could be cooked anywhere in the United States. But look closely: The sugar cookies are made with black walnuts, and the chocolate chip cookies contain dried apples.

Our dumplings are Slick Dumplings. From these we prepare Tomato Dumplings, Bean Dumplings, likker dumplings, kraut dumplings, and of course, Chicken and Dumplings.

Our dry beans are pinto beans, and from these we make Soup Beans, Pinto Bean Pie, and Pinto Bean Chili. We cook our green beans with salt pork, or we mix them with potatoes and onions.

We serve fresh corn roasted on the cob and fried with pepper; we make corn into Succotash, Custard Corn Pudding, and Corn Relish. With gritted corn we make gritted corn bread. We use shelled corn for hominy and hominy grits. We grind dry corn into meal, and with meal we make Corn Bread Dressing, Skillet Corn Bread, and, of course, Hush Puppies and Buttermilk Corn Bread. With sprouted dry corn we make mush, and mush becomes moonshine. With popped corn we make Peanut Popcorn Candy.

With precious pork we make Barbecue, Cracklings, Red-Eye Gravy, Sausage Gravy, and souse. When we don't eat sorghum as Hot Sorghum, we use it to make Sorghum Bread Pudding, Sorghum Pecan Pie Bars, and Sorghum Butter. From our hills, we gather and cook with morels, persimmons, poke, and pawpaws.

Our native Appalachian nuts—we use them for pies, cakes, candy, and cookies—are making a comeback, and they include hickory nuts, beechnuts, butternuts, black walnuts, and, of course, the always present pecans.

Capitalizing on the intense flavor of dried apples, we make Dried Apple Stack Cakes and Stack Pies. With dried apples we also make Dried Apple Applesauce and Fried Apple Pies. Our special cakes include the Black Walnut Cake, Jam Cake with Caramel Frosting, Prune Cake with Buttermilk Glaze and Country Whipped Cream, Savage Mountain Pound Cake, and Holiday Pumpkin Roll.

I SOMETIMES MODIFY traditional recipes to reduce fat, saturated fat, sugar, or salt. I increase fiber and complex carbohydrates. I omit frosting and reduce eggs. Why?

My Healthy Choice Alternatives will help our traditional foods become accessible in today's diet-conscious food climate. However, in order to preserve our food legacy, I first present recipes the way they were cooked, before fat became a sin. I can't change tradition. The Healthy Choice Alternatives, rather than detract from our recipes, enhance them. By making recipes accessible to health-conscious people, we help preserve our food traditions. If we do not prepare and enjoy our special foods, they will be lost.

My solution to the conflict between diet and tradition is sometimes a compromise, sometimes an improvement. For example, the Kraut Slaw recipe calls for mayonnaise. In the Healthy Choice Alternative, I suggest using a fat-free mayonnaise substitute, and I believe this makes the recipe more accessible. Because the sauerkraut so dominates the salad, the use of a fat-free mayonnaise substitute is barely noticeable. For another example, the Corn Bread Salad recipe calls for two cups of mayonnaise. In the Healthy Choice Alternative, I suggest replacing the mayonnaise with two cups of nonfat sour cream, and I believe this too makes the recipe better. Other examples include Corn Relish with half the sugar, and Sweet Potato Casserole without any pecans and minus the butter-crumb topping.

Unlike so many recipe authors who make extreme claims about the joy of low-fat and less-sweet foods, I suggest that my alternative recipes may not be as smooth or as tasty as the original. Alternatives are compromises. My reduced-fat or reduced-sugar recipes, however, are not so changed that the original recipe is lost.

IN DEVELOPING THE recipes for this book, I have tried to keep the number of spices and the overall number of ingredients to a minimum. This practice is both historically accurate and convenient for today's cook. You, the creative cook, will add ingredients. I do. I use spices or ingredients that I like and have on hand. For example, when I make the Chicken Stew, I may add mushrooms, paprika, and parsley. When I make Country-Fried Steak, I add fresh garlic and hot peppers.

The difficulty ratings are based on technique, number of ingredients, number of steps, time required, and equipment needed. A "Very Easy" recipe calls for one or two ingredients and should take less than five minutes to prepare. The fifteen very easy recipes, like a Baked Potato, are often very popular, as well.

A recipe rated "Easy" has fewer than five ingredients and is cooked with common equipment in one step. I may rate a recipe with six or seven ingredients "Easy" if it does not call for cooking. The seventy easy recipes in this book include Pan-Fried Chicken, Shuck Beans, Boiled Poke, and Lemon Curd.

The most common rating in this book is "Moderate." A recipe rated "Moderate" has fewer than ten ingredients and may be cooked in two steps or uses two cooking methods. Two cookies that are moderate in difficulty are Apricot Unbeatables and Black Walnut Sugar Cookies.

Recipes rated "Difficult" take more than an hour to prepare, usually have more than ten ingredients, and may require some special skill or equipment. I rate Country-Fried Steak and Fried Pork Chops difficult, as both recipes include a batter and gravy.

I use a rating of "Very Difficult" for four recipes that combine more than one complete recipe. As I learned in Paris, French chefs add one layer onto another layer and even another to form a single dish. The dish is a number of cooked items put together to form a complex whole. Country cooks don't use many "Very Difficult" recipes, but two examples— recipes that I am proud of—are my Sassafras-Caramel Granola Cookie Dessert and Chocolate Peanut Butter Cream Pie.

Difficulty Ratings

Rating and Example	Number of Ingredients	Time and Steps
Very Easy: Corn on the Cob	1 or 2	5 minutes or less, 1 or fewer cooking steps
Easy: Cucumber Salad	less than 5	1 cooking step, common equipment
Moderate: Black Walnut Cake	less than 10	2 steps, 2 cooking techniques, 30 minutes
Difficult: Bean Dumplings	11 or more	2 or more steps, special skill/equipment, 1 hour
Very Difficult: Chocolate Peanut Butter Cream Pie	11 or more	combines 2 recipes, special skill/equipment, 1 hour or more

In the mountains, we are sometimes isolated from population centers, and yet we are usually close to family and friends. Topography has forced us to live in string towns that fill the narrow valleys. Our hollows are deep; our creeks are long. Where topography is severe, we build houses along the creek, not up the side of a mountain.

Our families are strong, and we frequently gather together. If we don't gather for a meal, we share the cooking. On any day of the week, we may make a large dish, pass it next door, drive it to church, or carry it to a ball game. Eating is a social event, and large recipes reflect the fact that we eat in groups. In this book I offer both large and small recipes. Small recipes reflect our small, modern families, and large ones our traditions.

One

Mountain Country Breakfasts

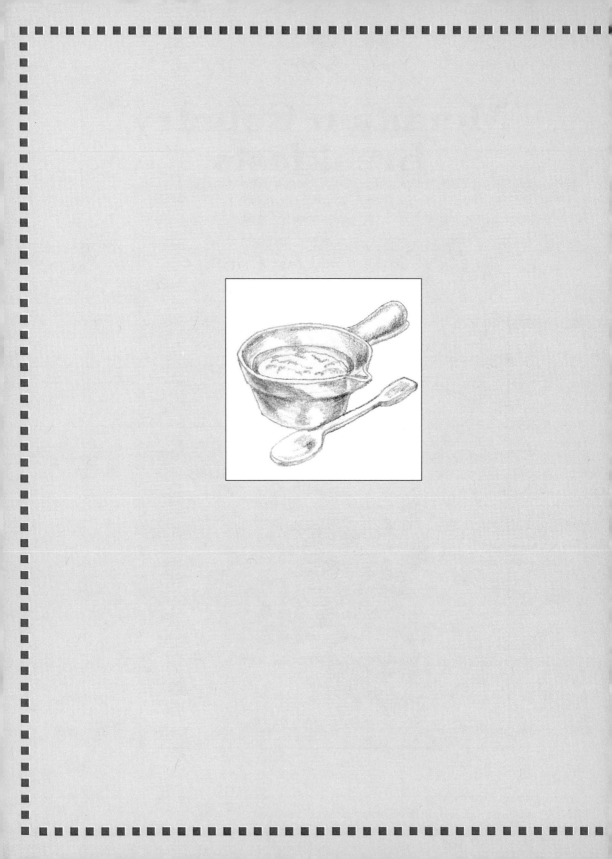

Fried Apples *(Fat-Free Fried Apples)*

Country Breakfast Grits

Fancy Cheese Grits Casserole

Red-Eye Gravy *(Country Ham and Red-Eye Gravy)*

White Sausage Gravy *Potato Gravy*
(Breakfast Gravy, Morning Gravy, and Biscuits and Gravy)

Chocolate Gravy

Sugar Syrup

Breakfast Menus

CONSIDER YOUR USUAL breakfast menu. Do you serve hash brown potatoes or home fries? Pancakes or waffles? Fried apples or fried green tomatoes? Sugar syrup or hot sorghum? Or, perhaps, none of the above? Is there a proper breakfast? A mountain breakfast? A modern breakfast?

People may argue about what to serve for an old-fashioned mountain breakfast, but on one issue everyone agrees: Fifty to seventy-five years ago, mountain people ate gigantic breakfasts. Over the last seventy-five years, however, our lives and our breakfasts have changed.

I have observed three phases in the evolution of mountain country breakfasts. First, seventy-five years ago, just after the railroads pressed their steel tracks into mountain coal fields, breakfast was really big. The cook loaded the table with bacon, sausage, and pork chops—all at the same meal. If they were saving the pork chops for another day, they served ribs, back bones, fried chicken, or country ham. With this they often ate fried potatoes or hash browns, buttermilk biscuits, breakfast sausage gravy, homemade blackberry jam, grits or hominy, and eggs, eggs, eggs. To top it off, they may have eaten apple or pumpkin pie, milk, juice, and coffee. These foods, which they called *victuals*, stuck to the ribs and supported outdoor labor until the mid-day lunch.

In the 1950s, breakfasts got smaller. We traded toast for biscuits, the pie disappeared, and bacon, sausage, or ham often stood alone with eggs. Hot cereal or sweet potatoes sometimes managed a place on the table. We served milk, juice, and coffee, and perhaps hot or cold cereal.

In recent years—the fat-fighting nineties—country cooks, like others, reserve eggs and bacon for special occasions. We worry about cholesterol. We cover dry cereal with skim or low-fat milk, we microwave a frozen bagel, or we lower a toaster pastry into the toaster. No time for hot cereal. No eggs. No pork chops. No cooking. It's often an on-the-go breakfast.

If you want a break from this daily hustle, this drive-thru, stand-up, speeded-up, and thoughtless routine, you can make the time, and you can find a place for an old-fashioned country breakfast.

Country Breakfast Menus

Once in a while, on a special vacation day or perhaps New Year's Day, the Fourth of July, or Labor Day, you have a crowd to serve. Enjoy breakfast with family or friends. It's a meal; it's a party. The table is full of dishes. Select from the following Country Breakfast Menus.

Breakfast One

Fried Apples, Fried Potatoes, fried eggs, bacon or sausage,
Buttermilk Biscuits, fresh butter, Hot Sorghum, and Pear Honey

Breakfast Two

Gingerbread-Apple Upside-Down Cake, Sausage Casserole, Fried Mush, fried eggs, Fried Green Tomatoes, Buttermilk Corn Bread, Sorghum Butter, and mixed fresh fruit

Breakfast Three

Dried Apple Applesauce, Biscuits and Gravy, scrambled eggs,
pork chops,
Country Breakfast Grits, and fresh-squeezed orange juice

Breakfast Four

Highlander Double-Crust Apple Pie with Raisins or
Dried Apple Stack Cake,
Sweet Potato Biscuits or Highlander Dinner Rolls, fresh fruit, and coffee

Breakfast Five

Red-Eye Gravy with Country Ham, Angel Biscuits, Cushaw Bread,
Fried Potatoes, toast, eggs, juice, fruit, and Sorghum Pie

Fried Apples
(Fat-Free Fried Apples)

*T*he confusing thing about fried apples is that they are never fried—fried apples are braised. They are not candied or glazed, and you do not caramelize the sugar or thicken it with long, slow cooking. Candied apples, glazed apples, and caramelized apples are entirely different.

Using a cast-iron skillet, mountaineers steam-fry their fried apples, seasoned with bacon or sausage grease, butter, margarine, or lard. As you braise them in the skillet, much of the moisture evaporates, which heightens the apple flavor. But be careful—if you choose a soft apple or if you cook them too long, they will get mushy, like applesauce.

Fried apples are so popular that in mountain markets you can buy them canned and ready to eat. One brand name is Luck's and another is Lucky's. They are called "country style," and they are a mindless substitute for my Fried Apples.

You can easily make your own fried apples with any full-flavored, in-season cooking variety, such as June apples, Granny Smiths, McIntoshes, Winesaps, Jonathans, or Rome Beauties. Years ago, the apples of choice for frying were green June apples, firm and sour. Few dried or canned June apples.

Traditional country cooks prepare their apples with pork flavoring. They fry the apples in a pan of bacon grease, the drippings from pork sausage, or several sticks of margarine. Others use just a little grease, perhaps two tablespoons for six cups of apples. Some add lemon juice, and others add brown sugar or sorghum.

Most cooks fry their apples at low heat on the stovetop in a covered cast-iron skillet, a method that releases moisture and melts the sugar. Because apples release liquid after they start to cook, I like to cook them covered first and then uncovered, which helps to evaporate juices. Some varieties are dry and need to be braised in a little water. But do they need shortening? Do you need to flavor them with bacon grease or butter? You can melt the sugar by adding water or orange juice, or perhaps by adding the sugar when the apples are half cooked. For my fat-free fried apples, I use the microwave oven and I omit the pork flavoring. The microwave oven is fast, and it preserves the apples' light color. With my procedure you'll end up with great apple flavor and extra syrup.

Some of us eat them every day. Fried apples are a sweet breakfast fruit, a lunch-plate vegetable, and a low-calorie dessert. We fry them in a skillet and we flavor them with bacon drippings.

This side dish is as mountain as biscuits, gravy, grits, and country ham. When she was young and attending Douglas Long Girl Scout Camp in

Guilford County, North Carolina, my wife, Kathy, ate fried apples for breakfast, with pork sausage. The chef at Shakertown, in Pleasant Hill, Kentucky, serves fried apples with other breakfast fruits in large buffet trays. In some cookbooks you'll even find fried apples listed as a vegetable!

STEPS In a small mixing bowl, combine the sugar, cornstarch, and cinnamon, stirring until the cornstarch is fully distributed.

Arrange the apples in a casserole dish, and cover with the sugar mixture. Cover, and microwave on high for 5 minutes, or until the sugar is melted. Stir and cook, uncovered, another 4 minutes, or until the apples are soft through to the center. They should be fork tender. Stir and serve.

HEALTHY CHOICE ALTERNATIVE Traditionally we fry apples with bacon grease, or dot them with butter, or cover them with whipping cream. Or perhaps as I do in this recipe, we eat them fat free!

Serve these warm for breakfast, with pork chops, country ham, sausage, gravy, grits, eggs, biscuits, and Hot Sorghum. Add orange juice, milk, and coffee.

For lunch serve as a side dish or a vegetable, with pork, ham, or fried chicken. It also makes a wonderful light seasonal supper dessert, topped with whipped cream and garnished with a maraschino cherry.

INGREDIENTS
1 cup sugar
1/4 cup cornstarch
1/2 teaspoon cinnamon
3 cups peeled and sliced Granny Smith apples
3 cups peeled and sliced Rome Beauty apples

YIELD 8 servings

Country Breakfast Grits

We use the short and simple term *grits* for the ground hominy grits our mills make from white corn hominy.

Consider the differences among old-fashioned, quick, and instant grits. While this recipe calls for old-fashioned grits that cook for twenty to thirty minutes, our mountain markets today sell two other kinds of enriched and precooked grits: Quick grits cook in five to seven minutes, and instant grits "cook" as soon as you stir them into boiling water.

Old-fashioned grits are stone-ground, whole kernel grits such as Callaway Gardens Speckled Heart Grits. Having undergone less processing, the old-fashioned grits are more robust, fuller, coarser, and less smooth than quick grits. I buy stone-ground hominy grits from Callaway Gardens, listed in Mail-Order Sources, page 343. Serve alone as a hot cereal with fresh cream or butter and sorghum, or serve as a side dish with bacon, eggs, toast, and jelly.

STEPS In a medium saucepan, bring the water to a boil and whisk in—don't dump them in all at once—the grits gradually. Then add the butter and salt.

DIFFICULTY Easy. With five ingredients and one cooking step, these grits are easy to prepare.

INGREDIENTS
4 cups water
1 cup old-fashioned grits
1 tablespoon butter
1 teaspoon salt
Milk or water, as needed

YIELD 6 servings

Mountain Country Breakfasts

Reduce the heat to a low simmer and cook, covered, for 20 minutes. Add water or milk as needed—the grits should have the stiffness of mashed potatoes. To avoid sticking, stir often.

HEALTHY CHOICE ALTERNATIVE This dish is an example of healthy old-fashioned mountain country cooking. If you need to, you may reduce the salt and butter.

Fancy Cheese Grits Casserole

DIFFICULTY Moderate. With seven ingredients and two cooking steps—boil, then bake—this recipe is moderate in difficulty.

In this two-step process, I enrich grits with eggs and cheese and then bake them in a casserole. As I whisk in the chunks of butter, the grated cheese, and the eggs, I can almost see the flavor emerging from the pan. As soon as I have them mixed, I draw my tongue across the stirring spoon, checking for salt and savoring the combination corn and cheese. With these grits, you'll have a trace of our southern mountains in your kitchen. Serve for breakfast or brunch, as an accompaniment to any seafood or main dish, or serve in place of potatoes with pork or chicken.

INGREDIENTS
3/4 cup quick-cooking grits
1 1/2 cups milk
1 1/2 cups water
1 teaspoon salt
1/4 cup butter
3 eggs
1 1/2 cups (6 ounces) grated Cheddar cheese

YIELD 6 servings

STEPS Preheat the oven to 375°F. Grease a 1 1/2- to 2-quart casserole dish.

Boil the grits, milk, water, and salt 5 to 7 minutes. When the water is absorbed and the grits have the consistency of applesauce, stir in the butter, eggs, and 1 cup of the cheese, stirring until fully mixed and the cheese has melted. Add salt to taste.

Pour the mixture into the casserole dish and bake for 25 to 30 minutes, or until the casserole is puffed up through to the center. Remove from the oven and garnish with the remaining 1/2 cup of cheese.

HEALTHY CHOICE ALTERNATIVE For a healthy alternative, omit the egg yolks and use fat-free cheese.

Red-Eye Gravy
(Country Ham and Red-Eye Gravy)

This is as Southern as Andrew Jackson, who some say gave the gravy its unusual name. It is a broth or strong bouillon, made with country ham and water. If you know a French dip or beef *au jus*, you know something about red-eye gravy.

HEARTY Cooking COUNTRY

Red-eye gravy is low in calories and fat, and making it takes almost no skill: Forget the milk, cream, or egg yolks. Forget the flour. Forget the grease. Red-eye gravy is made from the drippings that remain in the bottom of a skillet after frying country ham. Simply pour some liquid—any liquid—into the skillet. If coffee is perking on the stove, pour some in the frying pan. If you are drinking a Pepsi, add some. And water does the job too. Boil it and, using a spatula, deglaze the pan, scraping the bottom until it is clean.

Did our seventh president name this gravy? Perhaps. Some say he taught a drunken red-eyed cook to prepare the gravy. Others say that during the Jackson presidency, red-eye gravy was a favorite at the White House. Some cooks say they see a "red eye" in the middle of the pan when the gravy is ready. Others think of the bone in the center of the slice of ham as an eye.

To me, there is nothing red about this gravy, and I have yet to see an eye in the pan!

DIFFICULTY Very easy. With two ingredients and one step, this recipe is very easy.

STEPS In a skillet over medium to high heat, brown the ham on both sides, allowing 2 to 3 minutes per side. Place the ham on a serving plate. Add the liquid to the frying pan, and bring to a boil. Using a spatula, loosen particles from the pan and scrape until clean. Stir, boil 3 minutes, and serve. If there is a lot of fat, pour it off and discard.

For a classic country breakfast, serve with Country Breakfast Grits, Buttermilk Biscuits, scrambled eggs, and Fried Apples. For a special treat, offer Angel Biscuits and a mountain honey: honey locust, sourwood, or linn (basswood) honey.

INGREDIENTS
½ to ¾ pound country ham slices
¾ cup black coffee, Pepsi, or water

YIELD ⅔ cup gravy and enough ham for 4 servings

White Sausage Gravy
Potato Gravy (Breakfast Gravy, Morning Gravy, and Biscuits and Gravy)

*W*e make this gravy in the grease and drippings left from fried bacon or sausage patties. We derive the name of the gravy from the source of the pan drippings. For example, if we make this gravy after we fry sausage, the gravy is sausage gravy. If we make it after we fry potatoes and serve it over potatoes, the gravy is potato gravy. The same is true for fried green tomatoes, hamburgers, squirrel, or raccoon.

To keep the gravy white, I don't brown the flour, and I use white pepper.

DIFFICULTY Easy. With five ingredients and one step, this recipe is easy.

STEPS In a cast-iron skillet over medium heat, fry the sausage, breaking it into small pieces. When the sausage is no longer pink, add the flour, and stir until

INGREDIENTS
1/3 pound pork breakfast
   sausage
1/4 cup all-purpose flour
2 cups milk plus more
   as needed
1/2 teaspoon salt
1/2 teaspoon ground
   white pepper

YIELD 4 servings

mixed. The oil from the sausage must absorb all the flour. Add oil if needed.

Whisk in the milk, salt, and pepper. When the milk comes to a boil, cook 1 minute, or until the mixture resembles pancake batter. If the gravy is not thick, continue to cook over low heat for 5 to 15 minutes, stirring every few minutes.

Remove from the heat and reheat just before serving. If the gravy gets too thick, add milk.

HEALTHY CHOICE ALTERNATIVE Omit the sausage and make the gravy with a cold roux. Omit the salt, adding it at the table as needed.

To serve, split a biscuit, turn it center-side-down on a warm plate, and cover with gravy. Serve with sausage, fried potatoes, eggs, and orange juice. Serve beside sunny-side-up fried eggs and mix the two together as you eat. Later in the day, at lunch or dinner, serve over Southern Fried Chicken, Country-Fried Steak, or Ham Biscuits.

Potato Gravy After frying potatoes, prepare White Sausage Gravy and serve it over potatoes. Or, replace the sausage with 1/4 cup bacon grease or safflower oil, and proceed as above.

Chocolate Gravy

DIFFICULTY Easy.
With five ingredients and
one step, this recipe is
easy to prepare.

This gravy, once served by isolated Highlander families as a treat for children, is now a treat for adults. Why? Because while adults have fond memories of chocolate gravy, children don't know it. They don't see it advertised on TV, and they can't buy it at McDonald's.

When I first heard about this sauce, the name did not appeal to me. Later when I tasted its smooth chocolatey sweetness, when I lifted it with butter and biscuit to my mouth, when I first smelled the chocolate and saw it shine, then its flavor filled my chocolate-craving taste buds and it entered my long-term memory. I will never forget that moment. As badly as an itinerant preacher seeks converts, I want you to taste this gravy!

Our elderly mountain cooks make chocolate gravy with canned "cream," a product that manufacturers call evaporated milk. To this "cream," they add enough water so the gravy will flow and spread, but not so much that it runs over the plate. You, too, want your chocolate gravy thick enough to stay on a biscuit, but thin enough so that you don't have to spread it with a knife. Chocolate gravy is a milk and flour–based sauce, a white sauce or a béchamel. It is low in fat—spoon for spoon, it has fewer calories than butter, cream cheese, chocolate sauce, marmalade, or strawberry jelly—and it is low-cost and easy to prepare. It is thick, full, smooth, and chocolatey. And when this gravy is cold, it can be used as a cake filling—it softens as it warms.

STEPS In a medium saucepan, combine the dry ingredients: sugar, flour, and cocoa. Mix fully. Mix until the lumps of flour and cocoa are gone. Gradually mix in the milk. Bring the mixture to a boil, simmer 1 minute, and stir in the vanilla. Remove from the heat.

HEALTHY CHOICE ALTERNATIVES Reduce the sugar to ½ cup and use skim milk.

To serve, break a biscuit open and lay the two halves on a breakfast plate. Ladle Chocolate Gravy over the biscuit and top with a pat of butter. Eat with a knife and fork.

INGREDIENTS
1 cup sugar
¼ cup all-purpose flour
¼ cup European-style cocoa
2 cups milk
1 teaspoon vanilla
Biscuits, as needed

YIELD 6 servings

Sugar Syrup

I studied cooking in Paris, France, not Paris, Kentucky. Looking back at the pages of my cooking school notebook from June 19, 1987, I found a recipe for sugar syrup: "Boil 150 grams of sugar and 0.2 liters of water for 5 minutes. Stir in ½ glass of Grand Marnier. Mix thoroughly and brush the syrup on layers of a genoise." We were making a birthday cake.

Here in the mountains we make a different sugar syrup, thick with sugar and alcohol-free. It is a sauce of convenience. Years ago in the southern Highlands, mountaineers often had trouble getting supplies, or perhaps they could not afford pancake syrup. On these occasions they melted sugar in water and poured it over biscuits or pancakes.

Today, for pure sweetness, you too can make sugar syrup with white sugar, brown sugar, or scrapped maple sugar. Our traditional choice was white sugar.

If you make this as I suggest, using ⅔ cup water, the syrup will be fairly thin, and it will stand for an hour without forming crystals. When crystals form, reheat it, and it will again be smooth and crystal free. If you make it with less water (⅓ cup), it will be thick, but you have to serve it quickly—without constant heat, this version will turn back to sugar!

DIFFICULTY Very easy. With two ingredients, this recipe is easy.

STEPS In a saucepan over medium heat, combine the sugar and water, stirring until the mixture boils and turns clear. Boil an additional 10 *seconds*. If your syrup gets cold and turns to sugar, reheat.

Serve over pancakes, waffles, corn griddle cakes, or French toast, but don't use this on ice cream.

INGREDIENTS
2 cups sugar
⅔ cup water

YIELD 2 cups, or 8 servings

Two

Breads

CORN BREAD, DUMPLINGS, BISCUITS, AND ROLLS

Corn Bread:
Staple of the Mountains

I DIDN'T GROW up near the Blue Ridge or Smokies, and I didn't grow up eating corn bread. During my childhood in Oregon, our bread was made with flour and yeast. My first experience with corn bread was at the Hotel Soaper in Henderson, Kentucky. I was sixteen, having breakfast with my father. Like I remember my first girlfriend, I remember my first corn bread: sticks made with yellow cornmeal, nicely browned, a bit sweet, and served in a basket under a cloth napkin. They were fresh, crusty, and steaming hot. We ate them like we would biscuits, with butter and jelly. I never forgot.

Long before Columbus arrived in the Americas, Native Americans baked corn into bread. Corn bread has evolved with our culture and tastes. At the beginning Native Americans made a bread they called suppone. Their corn pone, or batter, was a combination of cornmeal, water, grease, and salt. Later we made ashcakes, hoecakes, griddle cakes, and dodgers, some with flour and some without.

Some people in the mountains view corn bread as a gift from God. It compares to the manna that sustained the Israelites for forty years in the desert. When mountaineers grew their own corn, they made corn bread three times a day. Through the Great Depression, coal booms and busts, mountain isolation, and still today, corn bread nourished. It is still a staple, a daily food. It is the staff of life, a primal joy.

Corn bread is a quick bread made with ground cornmeal, leavened with baking soda and buttermilk or with baking powder. Its varieties include puffy corn fritters, gritted bread, crusty corn bread, fried corn pone, jalapeño corn bread, Mexican corn bread, and quick corn bread. To this, add recipes for hush puppies, johnnycakes, and corn dodgers. Other varieties suggest ingredients: hot-water corn bread, mayonnaise corn bread, crackling bread, and buttermilk corn bread. Still others, muffins, dumplings, sticks, griddle cakes, ashcakes, and skillet corn bread—tell us about how they're cooked.

Corn pone is the early Native American corn bread batter, which they called *apone* or *apan*. A pone—a round loaf or piece of baked corn bread—is baked in a cast-iron skillet and served in wedges. A pone can also be a small round corn bread cake—a biscuit-size and shaped individual serving of corn bread. Using thick batter, you can shape small pones between the palms of your hands and bake them on a cookie sheet. You can also drop thick batter into a stew pot for dumplings, called cornmeal dodgers. If the corn pone is thin, you can pour it on a griddle and make griddle cakes, hoecakes, johnnycakes, or cornmeal pancakes.

Corn picked fresh from the garden, but too old to eat from the cob, is grated to make gritted corn bread. Not as dry as corn bread made with meal, gritted corn bread develops crust more easily, and its center is more like pudding. The flavor of fresh corn seems to linger in the bread.

When eating out, I've found that large establishments serve a soft, thick, crumbly, yellow corn bread, baked in large sheets and cut into squares. The top and bottom are soft, and the edges are center-cut. This corn bread is as weak an excuse for mountain corn bread as it is crustless. Institutional corn bread is so soft that you can't spread a pat of butter over it without it breaking into pieces.

This style may please some, but it is not mountain country. It is too tender and too sweet. Institutional corn bread, which is more like cake than any of my recipes, has little trace of corn-meal and little trace of old-fashioned brash mountain country spirit. Mountaineers that I know serve corn bread as wedges, sticks, or muffins.

Mountain corn breads range from three-fourths of an inch to four inches thick. Thinner bread cooks more quickly, has more crust, and can be reheated in a toaster. Because we consider crust more desirable than center, take note: You can increase the crust-to-center ratio by adjusting the size of the recipe to fit your pan, using a larger pan, or baking the batter in two pans. To me, an ideal thickness is one inch, which gives a nice balance between crust and crumb, or the center of the corn bread.

Corn bread centers range from crumbly to substantial. As corn bread batter gets richer and the corn more refined, the crumb becomes more tender. The addition of oil and eggs to the batter adds tenderness. Many corn breads are so rich that they crumble. I prefer a more primitive, more substantial, and less rich bread, one with a tougher crumb. I like the bread to tear, and so I reduce or eliminate the eggs and oil.

Corn bread crusts have three parts: top, bottom, and edge. A thick and crunchy crust is a forceful counterpoint to a soft center. When baked in a heavy cast-iron skillet in a 450°F oven, corn bread should emerge crusty brown on top and crunchy golden brown on the bottom. For a crispy, crusty edge, heat the oil and skillet over high heat on the stovetop until just below its smoking point, pour in the batter, and bake. To achieve the desired crusty brown bottom, place the oven rack in its lowest position. To brown the top, move the pan up under the broiler. I do this using two oven racks, placing one low and the other high.

Try to handle your corn bread so that it does not get soggy. To do this, serve it as soon as possible after you take it from the oven. Gripping the handle of your cast-iron skillet, you should be able to jiggle a baked pone in the pan. Flip it onto a cooling rack and then back onto a cutting board. Then hear it crunch as you cut through the crispy top and hardened bottom with a big-wheeled pizza cutter or a 12-inch chef's knife. Return it to the cooling rack or place it uncovered on an absorbent cloth in a basket. Left in the pan, sealed in plastic, or covered with foil, your crusty corn bread will soften, and you'll lose the crunch. Remember, a thin and crusty corn pone is your goal.

We argue about the correct way to eat corn bread. Do we dip, break, or crumble the wedges? Do we use forks, fingers, or spoons? I have heard these discussions from people that dip and people that crumble. Even within families we argue about corn bread wedges and corn bread crumbles.

For flavor, or perhaps convenience, some crumble the bread. Others hold their wedges between the thumb and index fingers and dip. Around our table, those who hold their wedges fuss at the crumblers for being messy; the crumblers argue back, sopping up every delicious bit of their bean likker (pot liquor) and enjoying each bite.

Dipped or crumbled, spoons or fingers, the traditional corn bread experience includes buttermilk, pot likker, wild greens, and soup beans. I try to prepare enough pot likker to wet the corn bread, and I find the pleasure is the same whether I dip or crumble.

U.S. Highway 23, the north-south route that winds its way from Portsmouth, Ohio, to Kingsport, Tennessee, is dotted with a fast-food chain called Dairy Cheer. At Dairy Cheer stores during the winter you can get a lunch special of corn bread muffins, soup beans, and diced onion. This lunch special is a balanced meal, an art form, an Appalachian tradition, and a form of honest cooking. I suggest serving corn bread with main dishes such as Country-Fried Steak, Five-Hour Stew, Pot Roast, Roast Pork, and Southern Fried Chicken. For old-fashioned mountain eating, I like a wedge of corn bread with Wilted Lettuce and buttermilk. This makes a complete meal, and so do Soup Beans, Simple Corn Bread, and Chow Chow. For a feast add Fried Potatoes and a thick slice of onion. This combination moves me like a day with clear blue sky. Corn bread and soup beans are a feast for the eyes, a meal for the spirit.

In mountain tradition, even leftover corn bread is never wasted. Feed it to the chickens. Use it for bread pudding, Corn Bread Dressing, or Corn Bread Salad. I drop my Thin Corn Bread into a toaster or use the toaster oven to reheat thicker pieces. Avoid reheating in your microwave oven—microwave ovens steam food, and steam softens the crust.

In the recipes below you'll find the wide range of options popular in the mountains—thick or thin, tough or tender, sweet or savory, rich or low in fat, full of goodies like bacon, cheese, and cracklings, or blissfully plain.

Through its evolution the old Native American corn pone has changed to include flour, baking powder, eggs, bacon grease, butter, vegetable oil, buttermilk, yogurt, and sugar. To the batter we have added creamed corn, diced green peppers, red hot peppers, onions, and diced ham. We bake corn bread in the oven, fry it in oil, and boil it in water. Corn breads reflect our cooking habits from the Smokies to the Blue Ridge.

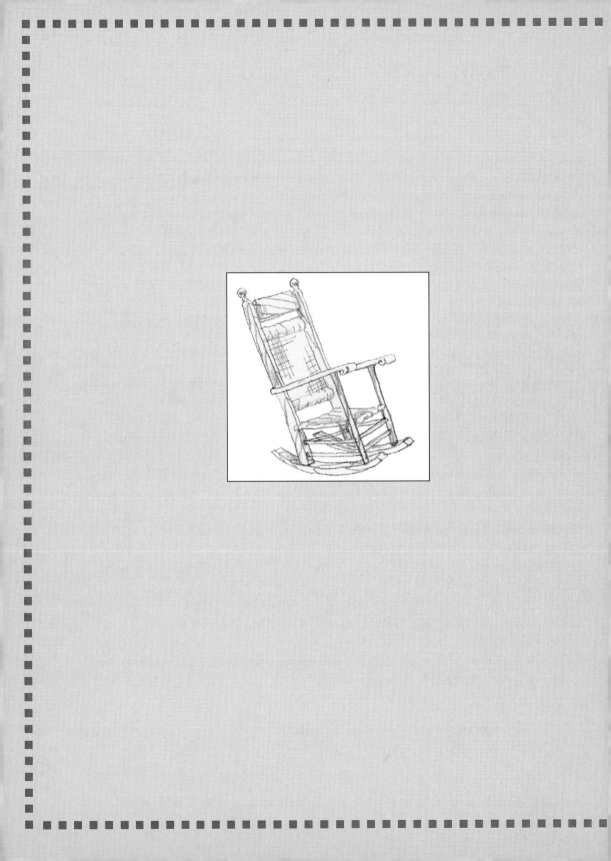

Simple Corn Bread
Quick Kernel Corn Bread and Thin Corn Bread

*S*imple. Quick. Thin. Not fancy or complicated. This recipe represents the good that comes from old-style mountain cooking, and it appeals to my search for unadorned corn bread. Today, some cooks refine their corn bread with eggs, sugar, and oil, but the recipes for Simple, Quick, and Thin Corn Bread save you time and calories. They are healthy, old-style, and modern all at once.

STEPS Preheat the oven to 450°F. Drop the grease into a number 8 (10-inch) cast-iron skillet, and heat it over high heat on top of the stove until the grease just starts to smoke.

As the skillet gets hot, stir the milk into the cornmeal mix. Pour and scrape the batter into the smoking grease. Place the skillet in the oven and bake for 20 minutes, or until the corn bread is brown on the bottom and edges. Broil the top for 1 minute, if needed.

HEALTHY CHOICE ALTERNATIVE For starters note that this batter does not contain oil or eggs. For the buttermilk, I use nonfat buttermilk. For the grease, substitute 2 teaspoons of safflower oil, or replace the grease with nonstick cooking spray.

Crumble in a bowl and pour buttermilk or pot likker over it. Cut into wedges and serve.

Quick Kernel Corn Bread
To the above batter add 1 cup whole kernel corn. Bake for 25 minutes and broil to brown the top.

Thin Corn Bread
Use 1 cup cornmeal mix and 1 cup buttermilk. Bake in a 10-inch cast-iron skillet for 15 minutes and broil to brown the top. The pone will be 3/4-inch thick, crisp, and crusty, and thin enough to reheat in a toaster.

DIFFICULTY Easy. With three ingredients, one mixing bowl, and a trusty cast-iron skillet, this recipe is easy. The pone will be 1-inch thick.

INGREDIENTS
1 tablespoon bacon grease or other oil
1 1/2 cups self-rising cornmeal mix
1 1/2 cups nonfat cultured buttermilk

YIELD 4 to 6 servings

Mountain Country
Corn Bread
Corn Sticks

INGREDIENTS
1 1/2 cups self-rising
  cornmeal mix
1/2 cup bread flour
1/2 cup stone-ground
  cornmeal
1 teaspoon salt
1/2 teaspoon baking
  powder
2 eggs
2 cups nonfat cultured
  buttermilk

YIELD 10 servings

This corn bread is a light, low-calorie, quick bread. Not like a muffin, not sweet, and not tender like cake, this is pure country-style corn bread. It is less coarse than the breads above, but it still tears rather than breaks. The stone-ground cornmeal poured in the skillet and over the top gives the crust a robust texture.

STEPS Place the oven baking rack at the top of the oven and preheat the oven to 450°F. Grease the bottom of a heavy 12-inch cast-iron skillet and preheat the pan in the oven or on the stovetop.

In a large mixing bowl, combine the self-rising cornmeal, flour, 1/4 cup of the stone-ground cornmeal, the salt, and baking powder. Make a well in the center of the dry ingredients, and using a hand whisk, mix in the eggs. Add the buttermilk and stir until mixed.

Remove the skillet from the oven and sprinkle the bottom with half of the remaining stone-ground cornmeal. Pour the batter into the skillet and sprinkle the top with the remaining cornmeal. Bake for 30 minutes or until the corn bread pulls away from the edge of the pan. If the top is not brown, broil it for 1 1/2 minutes.

Remove the corn bread from the oven and turn it out of the skillet onto a wire rack to cool. Cut into wedges and serve.

HEALTHY CHOICE ALTERNATIVE Many traditional country cooks use 1/4 or even 1/2 cup of bacon grease in the bottom of the skillet. I use a nonstick cooking spray. The only source of fat and cholesterol in this recipe are the two egg yolks, and if you like a tougher crumb, you may eliminate them.

Serve in or with Soup Beans, Fried Potatoes, Wilted Lettuce, and buttermilk.

Corn Sticks Use two large cast-iron corn stick pans. Bake for 20 minutes, or until the edges are deep brown and the top is golden or even spotted with brown.

Buttermilk Corn Bread
Skillet Corn Bread

This corn bread tastes of buttermilk, a constant favorite of mountain cooks. We either bake skillet corn bread in the oven, as I direct below, or fry it on the stovetop. If you fry it on the stove, divide the recipe between two skillets so it won't be too thick.

DIFFICULTY Easy. With five ingredients, this batter is easy to prepare.

STEPS Preheat the oven to 450°F. Grease a heavy 10-inch cast-iron skillet. Sprinkle the stone-ground cornmeal on the bottom and place the pan in the oven.

In a large mixing bowl, combine the self-rising cornmeal and the salt. Make a well in the center and whisk in the egg and the buttermilk. Pour the batter into the hot skillet.

Bake for 30 minutes, and brown the top under the broiler for 1 minute. Remove from the oven and turn the corn bread out of the skillet onto a wire rack to cool. Cut into wedges and serve.

INGREDIENTS
2 tablespoons stone-ground cornmeal
2 cups self-rising cornmeal mix
1 teaspoon salt
1 egg
2 cups buttermilk

YIELD 10 servings

HEALTHY CHOICE ALTERNATIVE Omit the salt—the self-rising cornmeal contains salt. In place of the bacon grease, use nonstick cooking spray. Notice that the recipe does not have any added oil.

Skillet Corn Bread To the above recipe, add 1 1/4 cups cracklings. Bake as muffins, sticks, or a pone and adjust the baking time according to your pan size.

Tender Corn Bread

In her book *Shuck Beans, Stack Cakes, and Honest Fried Chicken*, Ronni Lundy catches our attention when she says, "If God had meant for corn bread to have sugar in it, He'd have called it cake." I suspect that Ronni grew up south of the Mason-Dixon line.

DIFFICULTY Moderate. With eight ingredients, this batter is moderate in difficulty.

Adding oil and sugar to the recipe for Buttermilk Corn Bread makes it tender and cakelike. Replace the white cornmeal with yellow, and you are baking a corn bread popular north of the Mason-Dixon line. Many in the southern mountains despise thick, sweet, tender, yellow corn bread, but you'll find recipes like this one common in the north and quite available farther south.

STEPS Preheat the oven to 450°F. Pour the grease into a heavy 10-inch cast-iron skillet. Sprinkle with the stone-ground cornmeal on the bottom and heat the pan in the oven.

INGREDIENTS

1 tablespoon bacon
 grease
2 tablespoons stone-
 ground cornmeal
2 cups white or yellow
 self-rising cornmeal
 mix
1/4 cup sugar
1/3 cup safflower oil
2 eggs
1 cup buttermilk
1 cup water

YIELD 10 SERVINGS

In a large mixing bowl, combine the self-rising cornmeal and the salt. Make a well in the center of the dry ingredients and whisk in the eggs. Add the buttermilk and water and stir until well mixed. Remove the hot skillet from the oven and add the cornmeal batter.

Bake for 30 minutes, and brown the top under the broiler for 1 minute. Remove the corn bread from the oven and turn it out of the skillet onto a wire rack to cool. Cut into wedges like a pie, and serve hot, with butter.

HEALTHY CHOICE ALTERNATIVE Omit the salt—the self-rising cornmeal contains salt. Grease the pan with nonstick cooking spray. If you omit the oil and sugar, you'll be back to the Buttermilk Corn Bread.

Serve hot with butter. Serve with Soup Beans or Turnip Greens.

Stone-Ground Yellow Corn Muffins

*C*orn Muffins or corn bread muffins are popular in restaurants because they are convenient to serve. In comparison to the corn bread that institutional chefs bake in large rectangular baking pans, muffins have lots of crust. Use white or yellow cornmeal, whichever you prefer.

DIFFICULTY Moderate. With seven ingredients, this batter is easy to prepare. The recipe makes four cups of batter, the right amount for eighteen medium-size muffin cups.

INGREDIENTS

2 to 3 tablespoons
 stone-ground cornmeal
2 cups self-rising yellow
 cornmeal mix
2 tablespoons sugar
1 teaspoon salt
2 eggs
1/4 cup melted bacon
 grease or lard
2 cups buttermilk

YIELD 18 medium-size muffins

STEPS Preheat the oven to 400°F. Grease 18 (2 1/2-inch or 1/3 cup) muffin cups with nonstick cooking spray. Use your fingertips to sprinkle the muffin cups with half of the stone-ground cornmeal and place the pans in the oven to heat.

In a large mixing bowl, whisk together the self-rising cornmeal, sugar, and salt. Make a well in the center, add the eggs, and stir. Whisk in the melted bacon grease and buttermilk. When the batter is well-mixed, pour it into the hot muffin cups, filling each cup three-quarters full. Sprinkle the top of each muffin with the remaining stone-ground cornmeal.

Bake 20 to 25 minutes. Remove the muffins from the oven and turn them out of the pans onto a wire rack. Serve fresh from the oven.

HEALTHY CHOICE ALTERNATIVE Omit the salt—the self-rising cornmeal contains salt. Replace the bacon grease with oil. If you omit the oil and sugar, you'll be back to making Buttermilk Corn Bread. It also works well for muffins.

Serve in a basket with Angel Biscuits or Cushaw Bread.

HEARTY
Cooking
COUNTRY

Broccoli Corn Bread

*E*ver since former President George Bush said he disliked broccoli, this vegetable has had a little less status. In some country kitchens, however, cooks bristled at the comments and re-emphasized their broccoli recipes. This recipe, a healthful and moist corn bread, is a treat that mountain cooks made long before George Bush lived in the White House.

DIFFICULTY Moderate. With eight ingredients and one step, this recipe is moderate in difficulty.

STEPS Preheat the oven to 425°F. Grease a 13x9x2-inch baking pan.

In a large mixing bowl, combine the cornmeal mix and the salt. Make a well in the center of the cornmeal and whisk in the eggs, melted butter, and buttermilk. Stir in the cheese, broccoli, and onion. Pour the batter into the greased pan, and bake for 50 minutes, or until a toothpick inserted into the center comes out clean. Broil for 1 minute to brown the top.

HEALTHY CHOICE ALTERNATIVE Replace the butter or lard with an additional 1/2 cup nonfat buttermilk. Use nonfat cottage cheese. This broccoli corn bread is less rich, but it will bake nicely.

Serve this corn bread with any dinner or as a light side dish. Serve directly from the baking pan, or slice and serve in a bread basket.

INGREDIENTS
3 cups self-rising cornmeal mix
2 teaspoons seasoned salt
2 eggs
1/4 cup melted butter or lard
3 cups nonfat cultured buttermilk
1 cup cottage cheese
1 bunch (3 cups) fresh broccoli, chopped
1 medium (1 1/2 cups) onion, diced

YIELD 24 servings

Mexican Corn Bread
(Jalapeño Corn Bread)

I can remember eating this Mexican Corn Bread at the Happy Days Diner on Division Street in Pikeville, Kentucky. That was when Ken Damron ran the restaurant. Ken still works on Division Street, but now he is a shoe doctor. He calls his new store Ken's Shoe Clinic. When I walked into the Clinic and asked Ken for his corn bread recipe, he stopped working and started talking. I could see that our conversation made him want to go home and make corn bread for lunch.

This is my adaptation of Ken's formula. Almost a meal in itself, this corn bread is moist, heavy, and full of goodies. When you chop the jalapeño pepper, I suggest that you wear rubber gloves—they keep the heat from the pepper juices off your fingers and out of your mouth. Don't be scared away by the peppers. Once they are cooked, they lose some of their fire.

DIFFICULTY Moderate. With seven ingredients. You'll have to dice the onions and peppers, and then grate the cheese.

STEPS Preheat the oven to 400°F. Spray a 10-inch cast-iron skillet with non-

INGREDIENTS

1 cup plus 2 table-spoons self-rising cornmeal mix
1 egg
1 cup buttermilk
1/2 cup chopped onion
1/2 cup chopped green pepper
3 tablespoons finely chopped fresh jalapeño peppers, plus one whole pepper
4 ounces (1 cup) grated sharp Cheddar cheese

YIELD 8 SERVINGS

stick cooking spray, sprinkle with 2 tablespoons of the cornmeal, and place the pan into the oven to heat.

In a large mixing bowl and using a hand beater or wire whisk, whisk the corn-meal to fluff it up. Form a well in the center and mix in the egg. Stir in the but-termilk, and then add the onion, green pepper, chopped jalapeño pepper, and grated cheese. The batter should be stiff, but it will shake down.

Pour the batter into the hot skillet. Shake the pan and spread the batter flat. For garnish, cut the whole jalapeño pepper into 8 slices and arrange them in a circle on the batter. Bake for 30 to 35 minutes. The top should be brown; broil if necessary. Remove the corn bread from the oven, turn onto a cooling rack, and cool 5 minutes before cutting into wedges.

HEALTHY CHOICE ALTERNATIVE Omit the egg and reduce the cheese to two ounces, or use low-fat cheese.

Serve in the winter with a bowl of Pinto Bean Chili or Winter Vegetable Soup. Ken says, "I like it with fried potatoes, cold tomatoes, and crisp bacon," but he also says he could eat an entire recipe for one meal—"It's dangerous good!"

Hush Puppies

DIFFICULTY Moderate. With six ingredients and one cooking step, this recipe is moderate in dif-ficulty, but remember, all you do is stir up the bat-ter and deep fry.

INGREDIENTS

Oil for deep-frying
1 cup self-rising corn-meal mix
1/4 cup chopped green onions
1 egg
1 tablespoon melted butter or bacon drip-pings
2 to 4 tablespoons but-termilk

YIELD 10 hush puppies or 5 servings

*H*ush puppies are small, round, deep fried, cornmeal biscuits. When you drop the batter in hot oil, you hear loud popping; when the hush puppies are quiet (hush, little one!), they are cooked. I then lift them from the oil, place them on paper towels to drain, and start frying battered catfish—once I have it hot, I like to use the oil a second time.

STEPS In a deep fryer or heavy cast-iron pot, preheat a generous amount of vegetable oil to 375°F. The oil should be 2 inches deep.

In a mixing bowl, combine the cornmeal mix and the chopped onion. Form a well in the center and add the egg and melted butter. From the center out, stir until mixed. Add the buttermilk and stir. The dough should be stiff enough to hold its shape.

Using soup spoons, slip egg-size pieces of the dough into the hot oil. Cook hush puppies at a time, turning after 3 minutes. Cook another 2 minutes, or until golden brown. Drain on paper towels. Serve fresh. Do not store or reheat.

HEALTHY CHOICE ALTERNATIVE Omit the butter or drippings. Drop the dough onto a lightly greased cookie sheet and bake for 12 minutes at 400°F.

Serve these with any fried fish and always with Fried Catfish.

HEARTY
Cooking
COUNTRY

Dumplings:
From the Stew Pot

DUMPLINGS ARE A sweet or savory bread. Some are heavy like pasta; others are light like biscuits. We cook them in the steamy, bubbly broth of a chicken or beef stew. We drop them into blackberry sauce. We boil and steam them with pinto beans, garden greens, rhubarb, sauerkraut, or tomatoes. Dumplings thicken sauces, and sauces moisten dumplings. It's a cozy relationship.

Dumplings are made with wheat flour or cornmeal, to which we may add potatoes, cheese, farina, eggs, butter, bread crumbs, cracklings, and crackers. We usually associate our savory dumplings with chicken, and we flavor them with pepper, celery, onion, caraway, nutmeg, or sage. We associate our sweet dumplings with fresh fruit, and we flavor them with sugar and blackberries!

Dumplings balance our diet and add contrasting flavor to our foods. Some say that the ultimate dumpling is airy and tender, but often in the mountains we prefer them firm and flat.

If you argue with your in-laws about dumplings, you are experiencing a conflict of cultures. Raised dumplings, slick dumplings, gnocchi, damfnudeln, and spaetzle are dumplings—different kinds from different cultures. While you drop some dumplings from a spoon, our slick dumplings are well-kneaded and rolled. Think of slick dumplings as large noodles that you cook in a pot of broth. They are firm, flat, bumpy, and unleavened. They either sink into the broth or swim on top. Dumplings should hold together, but if they are too rich or cooked too long (oh, where is my mother?), they will fall apart. For these dumplings we use the broth from boiled chicken, pinto beans, tomatoes, greens, rhubarb, or blackberries.

Cissy Gregg, writing in the *Louisville Courier-Journal* in 1946, said that the debate between flat strips or round-raised dumplings is not a matter of geography. The preference "is a family affair and we'll hold on to our type, come what may." One can only wonder if Cissy Gregg knew that she was grouping people by their cultural origins: "Those who call fat bits of fluff-duff with stewed chicken by the name of dumplings are one kind of people, while those who make slick dumplings to go with their chicken are another kind."

The history of the slick dumplings served in Appalachian valleys from the Blue Ridge to the Smokies supports the notion of an English-Scottish-Irish connection to Appalachian culture. From cookbooks and food histories, I have traced Appalachian slick dumplings back to their roots in the British Isles. Andre Simon, writing in *A Concise Encyclopedia of Gastronomy*, describes dumplings as "one of the most characteristically English contributions to cookery." He goes on to discuss the English Norfolk raised dumpling and the "hard dumpling" from Sussex (southern England). Sussex hard dumplings are akin to the slick dumplings held dear to some mountain families.

Slick Dumplings
Crackling Dumplings

*T*he recipe that follows is a foundation recipe for Chicken and Dumplings, Bean Dumplings, Tomato Dumplings, Greens and Dumplings, and Ramps and Slick Dumplings. I have adapted it from Olga Latta's 100-year-old recipe in *What's Cooking in Kentucky*. After you cook the dumplings, thicken the broth to make a gravy, likker, or gruel.

"Different though they may be, slick dumplings, like close families everywhere, nestle down in loving companionship with pieces of chicken," says Cissy Gregg. "These dumplings," continues Gregg, "are nothing like that other kind of dumpling, the baking powder dumpling, those fluffy, spongy dumplings."

DIFFICULTY Easy. This recipe calls for five ingredients and two steps.

INGREDIENTS
2 cups all-purpose flour
1 teaspoon salt
1/4 cup melted shortening or chicken fat
1/2 cup chicken stock, pot likker, or water
Instant flour

YIELD 6 to 8 servings

STEPS In a large mixing bowl, combine the all-purpose flour and the salt. With a whisk, stir in the melted shortening. Add the stock and mix until you have a stiff dough. Knead for 30 strokes or until stiff.

On a floured surface, roll the dough with a rolling pin to a thickness of 1/8 to 1/4 inch, as if you were making a pie crust. Use a pizza cutter to cut 1- by 2-inch strips. Dry the surface of the dumplings by sprinkling them with instant flour.

Drop the dumplings, one at a time, into a large pot of simmering broth. To keep the dumplings separated, stir them from the bottom. Cover, reduce the heat, and simmer for 15 minutes.

Remove from the heat, again cover the pan, and cool 30 to 60 minutes—this helps to thicken the gravy and tenderize the dumplings.

TIP The longer these dumplings sit after cooking, the more tender they will be. With my recipe, the dumplings soften in 30 to 60 minutes, they will be more tender the second day, and they store for several days. They do not fall apart.

If you make the recipe richer (with more shortening), the dumplings will become tender more quickly. However, if the recipe is too rich (too much fat), the dumplings will fall apart as they cook.

The goal is to balance dumpling richness with soaking time. For example, I once made the above recipe with 2 tablespoons of shortening, bread flour, no standing time, and 1/3 cup of broth, which resulted in gummy, chewy, and quite awful dumplings. After the dumplings soaked twenty-four hours and I reheated them, they were tender.

HEALTHY CHOICE ALTERNATIVE Replace the chicken fat or shortening with canola oil. Use bean, tomato, or turnip green broth, which are low in fat. Reduce the salt to 1/2 teaspoon. Skim the fat from chicken gruel before serving.

Serve with chicken, beans, greens, and tomatoes.

Crackling Dumplings As you mix the stock into the dough, add ¹/₂ cup cracklings.

Chicken and Dumplings

*A*ccording to Claire Fish, a five-year-old neighbor of mine, chicken and dumplings are the best part of Sunday dinner. On the buffet table there may be thirty choices, but Claire says, "I go straight for those chicken and dumplings." Claire is not alone. Chicken and dumplings are a mountain favorite. We make them with both raised or slick dumplings, though I suggest using slick.

STEPS To make chicken and dumplings, you may stew and debone a whole chicken, or simplify this by using chicken parts. Traditionally, Highlanders went to their henhouse and selected a mature stewing hen to use for chicken and dumplings. Sometimes, in place of the whole chicken, I like to use thighs and breasts. Rather than cooling and deboning these chicken parts, I prepare the dish in one step, serving the chicken parts with the bones.

Alternatively, several hours or the day before cooking the dumplings, bring the water to a boil in a large pot. Add the chicken, butter, bouillon, salt, and pepper, and simmer for 50 minutes, or until the chicken is cooked. Refrigerate until cool. Remove the fat.

Remove the chicken from the gruel, and separate the meat from the bones and skin. Discard the bones and skin. Cover the chicken and refrigerate.

Prepare one recipe of Slick Dumplings. In the large pot, return the gruel to a low boil, and use it to cook the dumplings.

After the dumplings have started to cook, thicken the gruel. Prepare a cold roux: Place the flour in a bowl and slowly whisk in the water. Add this roux gradually, to thicken the gravy. Return the chicken to the pot, and serve hot.

TIP When the chicken is half-cooked, I like to add a pound of prepared raw carrots. You might also add poultry seasoning, fresh onion, garlic powder, and yellow food coloring to the gruel. Why the yellow food coloring? Because the gruel is supposed to be yellow from butter. The use of yellow food coloring is perhaps a habit left from World War II, when people added yellow food coloring to white margarine to make it look like butter, which was unavailable.

HEALTHY CHOICE ALTERNATIVE Omit the butter or lard. Boiled chicken is

DIFFICULTY Difficult. This recipe calls for seven ingredients plus one recipe of Slick Dumplings. To make the complete dish, follow three steps: First, cook, cool, and debone the chicken. Second, prepare and cook the dumplings. Finally, thicken the gruel. In the process you'll dirty a stew pot, two mixing bowls, and a flat surface.

INGREDIENTS

FOR THE CHICKEN AND GRUEL
7 cups water
1 chicken (3 to 4 pounds) cut into pieces
¹/₂ cup lard or butter
1 tablespoon chicken bouillon grains
1 teaspoon salt
¹/₂ teaspoon ground pepper

FOR THE DUMPLINGS
1 recipe Slick Dumplings (page 26)

TO THICKEN THE GRUEL
¹/₂ cup all-purpose flour
¹/₂ cup water

YIELD 6 servings

healthy. When you boil it ahead and chill the chicken in the refrigerator, you can lift the fat off the top. Discard the fat and the skin.

I like to serve this with green beans, mashed potatoes, Macaroni and Cheese, Scalloped Turnips, or Sweet Potato Casserole.

Tomato Dumplings
(Stewed Tomatoes)

DIFFICULTY Difficult. With tomatoes to peel, sausage to fry, eight ingredients, and a recipe for Slick Dumplings, this dish is difficult to prepare.

*W*hen the tomato vines are heavy with fruit, and the farmers are selling their tomatoes by the bushel, I like to make these dumplings. Some mountain families crave cooked tomatoes to such an extent that a lady once told me that tomato pot likker is a source of sin. She said it is a sin to consume too much pot likker at one meal —and the same is true for dumplings and buttermilk.

If you have some vine-ripened tomatoes, let this tomato dish be your source of sin. The tomato sauce is thin, the dumplings few, and the flavor zippy. If, rather than just sauce, you want some chunks of tomato, add half the tomato wedges 1 minute before the cooking time is up.

INGREDIENTS
2 pounds fresh tomatoes
1/2 pound pork sausage
1 1/2 cups tomato juice
1 cup diced celery
1 teaspoon sugar
1/2 teaspoon salt
1/2 teaspoon pepper
1/2 recipe Slick Dumplings (page 26)

YIELD 5 servings

STEPS First, remove the hard stem spot from each tomato. Then, peel the tomatoes by lowering them one at a time for 12 to 14 seconds into fast-boiling water. Allow to cool until you can handle them and easily pull off the skins. Alternatively, instead of boiling in water, slowly turn the tomato over a gas flame, and when the skin breaks, pull it off. Quarter or cube the tomatoes.

In the bottom of a large saucepan, fry the sausage, breaking it into small pieces as it cooks. Drain the grease and reserve it for the dumplings. Add the tomatoes, tomato juice, celery, sugar, salt, and pepper, and bring the mixture to a boil. Simmer for 5 minutes.

Prepare the half-recipe of Slick Dumplings. Add the dumplings to the tomato mixture and simmer for 15 minutes. Let stand for 30 to 60 minutes, and reheat.

HEALTHY CHOICE ALTERNATIVE Omit the pork sausage.

Serve in large soup bowls with a glass of buttermilk and a slice of white onion. Ladle over split Buttermilk Biscuits. Because this dish has just a few dumplings, I like it served over rice, with buttered toast on the side. This reminds me of Spanish rice or the curried lamb I serve over rice.

Bean Bread

The Cherokee Indians were the first mountain country cooks and the original Highlanders. In 1951, the Museum of the Cherokee Indian in North Carolina published a 72-page book titled *Cherokee Cooklore, To Make Bread.* The book is still in print. From this book about the foods of the Cherokee, you can see that they prepared many of "our" native mountain dishes. For example, they cooked mush, corn bread, gritted bread, cornmeal gravy, flat dumplings, succotash, butterbeans, leather breeches, potato soup, pumpkin, ramps, creases, watercress, and squirrel.

They also adapted European foods such as the apple, but by far the majority of their foods were indigenous to the mountains. Consider the list of wild fruits included in this book and used at the Cherokee Indian Feast held on December 4, 1949: blackberries, huckleberries, strawberries, raspberries, elderberries, wild plums, wild cherries, crab apples, ground cherries, persimmons, field apricots, fall grapes, fox grapes, opossum grapes, dewberries, and gooseberries.

The focus of *Cherokee Cooklore* is bean bread, the Cherokee name for bean balls, bean dumplings, or corn dodgers with beans. When I followed the book's modern bean bread recipe, the dumplings absorbed the water and fell apart. I have modified the recipe to include eggs and self-rising cornmeal mix. My recipe holds together.

DIFFICULTY Easy. If you have a pot of beans cooking or if you use canned beans, making this recipe is easy.

STEPS In a large pot, bring water, bean broth, or chicken broth to a boil. Reduce the heat so that it simmers slowly. If using canned beans, rinse, drain, and allow to dry a bit on a paper towel.

In a mixing bowl, stir together the cornmeal, beans, flour, eggs, and salt. The dough should be stiff but moist. Form balls the size of a walnut, roll them tightly between your palms until they are round, and ease them into the simmering pot. Cook for 8 minutes.

HEALTHY CHOICE ALTERNATIVE In place of the two whole eggs, use three egg whites. Omit the salt, and offer it at the table.

Serve these dumplings with Soup Beans, use them to garnish a platter of Chicken Stew or Barbecued Baby Back Ribs, or serve with Squirrel Gravy or buffalo steaks.

INGREDIENTS
1 cup self-rising corn-
   meal mix
1 cup cooked beans,
   white, navy, or pinto
1/4 cup all-purpose flour
2 eggs
1 teaspoon salt

YIELD 10 dumplings or
5 servings

Biscuits, Angel Biscuits, and Yeast Rolls

LONG BEFORE THE arrival of loaf bread, we baked biscuits. Out in the country where there were few bakeries, Highlanders baked at home. Breakfast biscuits, buttermilk biscuits, biscuits and gravy, biscuits with honey, ham biscuits, fried chicken and biscuits, sausage biscuits, biscuits and hot sorghum—we connect biscuits with so many favorite foods that it sometimes seems that no food, no meal, no day would be complete without them. We make them at home and eat them on the road. Our fast-food restaurants—Biscuit World, Hardee's, KFC, Lee's Famous Recipes, Dairy Cheer, and Happy Mart—have capitalized on our weakness for biscuits. Biscuits balance the meal, fill the box, and warm the soul.

When discussing biscuits, the ocean divides and the mountains have no basic claim. Long ago biscuits were twice-baked. Roman legions, medieval crusaders, and the armies of Louis XIV ate the old-style, keep-forever, twice-baked, hard-as-rock bis-cuits, then called stone bread or army biscuits. But today, even east of the Atlantic, few biscuits are twice-baked, and Italian biscotti are the only twice-baked tea cakes I know. Here in the mountains our only twice-cooked biscuits are monkey biscuits—day-old biscuits fried in a mixture of sorghum and butter. Beaten biscuits resemble twice-baked biscuits, but they are more like a cracker and are baked only once.

We roll, cut, bake, and adore our biscuits. But except for their popularity, our biscuits are not really different from ones found in other parts of this country.

As I think through the transition from yeast rolls to raised yeast biscuits, to drop biscuits, to rolled and cut biscuits, to Irish scones, to beaten biscuits, to benne seed biscuits, to crackers, and to cookies, I am confused by the overlapping names. Cookies are crackers, crackers are biscuits, and biscuits are rolls. In this mental transition, this kitchen mélange, we have moved from hard crusts to soft breads, to crackers, to cookies, and we have added sugar to crackers and salt to cookies.

In the southern mountains you hear talk about biscuits the size of a cat's head. No surprise, then, that we call them cat-head biscuits. They are uneven and uncut. To shape these biscuits, we roll the dough into a log and use our fingers to "choke off" the biscuits. Baked in a large pan, the biscuits come from the oven soft, with little crust.

If you are Scottish or Irish, your quick breads are scones, eaten sweet or savory and served for breakfast or tea. Because they may include cream and eggs, scones are often richer than biscuits. Scones are like biscuits in that you can add so many ingredients. Sometimes you want them savory, adding garlic, onions, parsley, dill, ham, or cheese; other times you want them sweet, adding cinnamon, nutmeg, sorghum, sugar, fruit, or nuts.

For me, the ultimate mountain biscuit is salty, light, cooked through, oven-hot, buttermilk-flavored, and crusty brown. While some recommend soft shortening and room temperature ingredients, it seems to me that to achieve a light, flaky biscuit, cold ingredients are preferable. In my recipes, I cut some cold shortening into the flour so that small pieces of shortening remain to be flattened out during kneading. Most mountain country cooks use self-rising flour, which saves mixing the salt and baking powder. If you don't have self-rising flour on your shelf, add 1 teaspoon baking powder and 3/4 teaspoon salt to each cup of all-purpose flour. (To buy honest, mountain-made self-rising flour, see White Lily Foods in the list of Mail-Order Sources.)

Just as you can overmix a flaky pie-crust dough, you can also overmix biscuits. Thin, intact pieces of shortening make the biscuits flaky. With too much mixing, the pieces of shortening will be lost, mixed completely into the flour and unable to form layers in the flour. Don't bother with a rolling pin. Just pat the dough into a flat surface. Reserve 1/4 cup of flour to keep the dough from sticking to the counter surface and your hands. If the dough is too sticky, add extra flour, but do not overwork the dough. Handle it as little as possible.

A sharp-edged, round biscuit cutter (ours measures 2 3/4 inches in diameter by 3/4 inch high) results in a straight-sided biscuit. A sharp, clean cut allows the biscuit to rise high. If your cutter pushes the edges down, your biscuits will be rounded when cooked. Using a knife, you can cut biscuits into any shape, but it seems to me that if you take pride in your cooking, you'll want uniformly round biscuits, and you'll use a biscuit cutter.

While I like to spread my biscuits out on a baking sheet, many mountain cooks bake their biscuits edge to edge in a cast-iron skillet. When you push the edges together, the sides of the biscuits will not form a crust. The biscuits will rise high, and they will be soft-sided and easy to open. If you like the edges crusty, place biscuits about 3/4 inch apart so they can brown all the way around.

To me, really fine biscuits are crisp and crusty on the outside. To make rich and crispy biscuits, melt half a cup of butter in a small dish and dip the top of the biscuits in the butter before placing them on the baking sheet. After baking for 5 minutes, spoon another 3/4 teaspoon of melted butter over each biscuit. For water-crisped crusts, dip the biscuits in water after cutting them out. Then, during baking, use a spray bottle to moisten the surface. Repeat before broiling the tops to a golden brown. (Water crisps the top, but does not brown like butter.)

After baking, I suggest browning the tops by broiling for about 1 minute. Country cooks appreciate a crusty brown top and bottom. Try to plan the baking so that when you take the biscuits from the oven, you are ready to serve them.

Master Recipe: Biscuits
Buttermilk Biscuits, Ham Biscuits, Sausage Biscuits, Ginger Sorghum Biscuits, and Cheese Biscuits

can't guarantee that this recipe for Country Biscuits will yield a biscuit like those you grew up with, but I hope it will get you started down the right path—the path of homemade biscuits. Use this master recipe for your special biscuits and modify it with the variations.

DIFFICULTY Easy. With six ingredients, this recipe is easy. You may be surprised how fast you can make these biscuits.

INGREDIENTS
1 3/4 cups all-purpose flour
1 1/2 teaspoons baking powder
1 teaspoon salt
1 1/2 tablespoons butter or lard, softened
1 1/2 tablespoons butter or lard, chilled
1/2 cup milk

YIELD 8 biscuits or 6 servings

STEPS Place the oven rack in its lowest position, and preheat the oven to 450°F.

In a large bowl, combine 1 1/2 cups of the flour, the baking powder, and salt. Using a pastry blender, cut the chilled butter and the softened butter into the flour until the mixture forms crumbles the size of rice grains. Make a well in the center of the mixture and add the milk. Stir lightly until mixed. Turn out onto a cold, floured surface, and knead five times. Do not overknead.

Sprinkle some of the remaining 1/4 cup flour over the dough, and pat out the dough to a 1/2-inch thickness, using the extra flour to keep the dough from sticking to your hands. Fold the dough in half and pat it out to a 3/4-inch thickness. Fold it in half again and again pat it out to a 3/4-inch thickness.

Using a 2-to-3-inch biscuit cutter, cut the biscuits and place them 1 inch apart on a baking sheet. Press the scraps of dough together, pat out the dough, and cut until all the dough is used.

Bake for 10 minutes. When the biscuits are cooked and the bottoms are brown and crusty, broil the tops to brown them.

HEALTHY CHOICE ALTERNATIVE Years ago most country cooks made their biscuits with hog lard. If cholesterol is a problem, substitute safflower oil for the butter or lard. Your biscuits will not be the same, but they will be free of saturated fat.

Cut the biscuits in half and cover them with Chocolate Gravy or White Sausage Gravy. Serve for breakfast or dinner with real butter, Apple Butter, Sorghum Butter, or Hot Sorghum, or as an accompaniment to Pan-Fried Chicken and Kathy's Coleslaw.

Buttermilk Biscuits
Also called Country Biscuits and Southern-Style Biscuits. In the Master Recipe, replace the milk with 1/2 cup plus 2 tablespoons fat-free cultured buttermilk.

Ham Biscuits Also called Filled Biscuits. Cut 8 slices of country ham or Canadian bacon and put 1 slice inside each biscuit after baking.

Sausage Biscuits Fry 8 patties of pork sausage, and fill each baked biscuit with 1 sausage patty. Serve with Fried Apples, or add several slices of Fried Apples to make a fried apple-and-sausage biscuit sandwich.

Ginger Sorghum Biscuits To the Master Recipe, add 1/2 teaspoon ground ginger and 1/4 cup 100% pure sweet sorghum syrup. Reduce the milk by 3 tablespoons. Baste the biscuits with melted butter. This biscuit does not rise very high, and the top breaks like a sugar cookie. Serve with Sorghum Butter or Hot Sorghum.

Cheese Biscuits In one variation of this biscuit, we roll the dough out as if we were making a cinnamon roll or jelly roll, spread cheese over the dough, roll, cut, and bake. In another variation, we cream butter and cheese, use an equal volume of flour and cheese, and add no liquid. No liquid! This dough melts together, and it comes from the oven rich and cheesy. More often we add cheese to biscuit dough. To the Master Recipe, as you stir in the milk, add 1 cup (4 ounces) coarsely shredded or diced sharp Cheddar cheese or a mixture of Chedder. and Swiss cheese.

Sweet Potato Biscuits
Sweet Potato Casserole

Classic mountain, country to the core—sweet potato biscuits. The biscuit is a show-stopper, a flag-raising treasure, a topic of conversation. I make these biscuits using leftover Sweet Potato Casserole. It provides sweetened, spiced, and pureed sweet potatoes that make the biscuits heavy, moist, and rust colored.

Sweet Potato Casserole Start with 4 cups of fully cooked and mashed sweet potatoes. Purée and combine 1/4 cup orange juice, 1/4 cup brown sugar, 1/4 cup butter, 1/2 teaspoon salt, 1/4 teaspoon mace, and 1/4 teaspoon cinnamon. The flavorings and the potatoes define this bread.

STEPS Preheat the oven to 400°F. Melt 3 tablespoons of the butter and add to an 8x8-inch baking tin.

DIFFICULTY Moderate. Using the five ingredients given here, I rate the recipe moderate in difficulty. Self-rising flour will make it even easier.

INGREDIENTS
1 cup Sweet Potato Casserole
1/4 cup plus 3 tablespoons butter
1 cup all-purpose flour
2 teaspoons baking powder
1 1/2 teaspoons salt

YIELD 8 biscuits

In a bowl, mix the flour, baking powder, and salt. Using a pastry blender, cut the remaining butter and then the sweet potato mixture into the dry ingredients. On a floured surface, mix and knead the dough. Pat out to a 1/2- to 3/4-inch thickness and cut into 2-inch round biscuits. Arrange the biscuits in the tin with the melted butter.

Bake 12 to 15 minutes, or until brown on the edges. To check for doneness, break one open to see that the dough is cooked, not wet and doughy, in the center. Broil to brown the tops.

HEALTHY CHOICE ALTERNATIVE Omit the butter from the pan, and dust the pan or the bottom of the biscuits with flour to keep them from sticking. If you are concerned about saturated fat, replace the 1/4 cup butter with canola oil. Omit the salt.

Serve with butter and linn (basswood) honey or sourwood honey. I like these biscuits for breakfast, lunch, or supper, but they seem to me to be particularly appropriate for Sunday dinner.

■ ■

Linn Honey

Bees make linn honey, also called basswood honey, in July from the flowering American basswood tree. We prize this honey for its light color, runny texture, and mild flavor. I compare eating linn honey to eating a chocolate truffle at room temperature: both release a fast burst of flavor. The "opposite" of linn honey is honey from the locust or honey locust tree. Locust honey is almost black, very thick, and rich, with a sharp and long-lasting flavor. Order linn honey from Mountain State Honey Company in the Mail-Order Sources.

■ ■

Angel Biscuits

*I*n spite of the competition from hundreds of canned, tubed, boxed, or plastic-wrapped breads sold in our markets, angel biscuits remain a popular home-baked mountain classic. If you always thought that opening a plastic bag was the first step to eating bread, now is the time to take the plunge and bake with yeast. Bake angel biscuits. You can't buy them, and they don't come in plastic.

Angel biscuits, which combine baking powder, baking soda, and yeast, are a rich bread made with sugar, butter, buttermilk, and self-rising flour. Traditionally, mountain cooks made angel biscuits ahead of time and refrigerated or froze them until baking. These biscuits have many names, some of which tell something about the biscuit: angel flake biscuits, risen biscuits, yeast biscuits, high biscuits, layered biscuits, cream biscuits, refrigerator biscuits, and freezer biscuits. Yes, with these biscuits, you can make them ahead and freeze and then bake or, as I prefer, bake and then freeze.

Why do I call them angel biscuits? Because they are heavenly. They are close to God, and almost as perfect.

DIFFICULTY Moderate. With five ingredients and two steps, I rate this recipe moderate in difficulty. As compared to Yeast Dinner Rolls, these biscuits are a snap.

STEPS Preheat the oven to 400°F. Grease a 17x12-inch jelly roll pan.

In a small bowl, combine 3/4 cup of the melted butter and the buttermilk. Bring the mixture to 115°F, which should be quite warm to the touch.

In a large mixing bowl, combine 5 3/4 cups of the flour, the sugar, and the yeast. Stir in the warm buttermilk mixture until fully mixed. Knead the dough 5 to 7 times, then let it rest 5 minutes.

Using the remaining flour, lightly flour a work surface, and roll the dough to a 1/2-inch to 3/4-inch thickness. Cut the biscuits with a 2-inch round biscuit cutter, place them edge to edge on the jelly roll pan, and brush with the remaining 3/4 cup melted butter. The biscuits fit nicely in this pan, and the butter will not run off. Cover with plastic wrap, and allow to rise in a warm place for 1 hour, or until double in height.

Bake for 15 minutes or until the tops are golden brown.

INGREDIENTS
1 1/2 cups butter, melted
2 cups buttermilk
1 (2-pound) bag (6 cups) self-rising flour
1/4 cup sugar
1 envelope fast-rising yeast

YIELD 30 large biscuits

TIP If using all-purpose flour, add 1 tablespoon baking powder, 1 tablespoon salt, and 1 teaspoon soda.

HEALTHY CHOICE ALTERNATIVE Reduce the butter to 1/2 cup. Do not brush the biscuits with butter. For my family, I have parted with the old lots-of-butter way and use this alternative recipe.

Serve for breakfast, lunch, or dinner, filled with a slice of country ham, jelly or hot sorghum, or with lightly salted butter.

Highlander Rolls
(No-Knead Hot Rolls, Yeast Dinner Rolls, and Parker House Rolls)

DIFFICULTY Difficult. While I rate this difficult, for yeast bakers this roll is easy. With little kneading, some rapid-rise yeast, nine ingredients, and three risings, you can make these rolls in 3 hours.

*E*liza "Bill" Newsom of Robinson Creek, Kentucky, jokes as she bakes. "There are two times you are not supposed to talk: when your mouth is full or your head is empty."

Several years ago I spent an afternoon baking Highlander Rolls with Bill, and when they were about to come out of the oven, she said, "There were two fellows on an airplane. One bragged about being a Christian. Later, the plane was going to crash and the non-Christian looked at the Christian and said, 'Do something, Christian.' He took up an offering."

Highlander rolls are a fancy dinner roll. You may know them as no-knead hot rolls, yeast dinner rolls, or Parker house rolls. While the amount of butter and sugar varies from cook to cook, this recipe yields a standard soft dinner roll. When you compare this Highlander roll to a hard roll or French bread, this boasts large quantities of fat, sugar, and eggs, which, with the evaporated milk, make the roll rich.

In the late 1930s, Bill Newsom adapted this, her original yeast roll recipe, from a Betty Crocker cookbook. She and many other country cooks have been making rolls like these ever since. When you make them, work in a hot kitchen—summer temperatures are great for yeast.

INGREDIENTS
7 cups hard wheat or bread flour, measured and sifted
1/2 cup sugar
5 teaspoons (2 packs) fast-acting yeast
2 teaspoons salt
1 1/2 cups warm (125°F) water
3/4 cup evaporated milk
1/2 cup butter
2 eggs, at room temperature
2 tablespoons shortening, melted

FOR THE EGG WASH
1 egg
1 tablespoon milk

YIELD 48 rolls

STEPS In a large mixing bowl, combine 6 cups of the flour, the sugar, yeast, and salt. Heat the water, milk, and butter to 125°F. Stir the hot liquids into the dry mixture. Beat the eggs well, and add to the bowl. Stir. Add enough of the remaining flour so that the dough pulls away from the sides of the bowl.

Use 1/2 cup or less of the reserved flour to dust a clean work surface. Knead the dough for 2 minutes and form it into a ball. In a clean mixing bowl, add the melted shortening, and roll the dough to fully coat it. Cover the bowl with plastic wrap, and let the dough rise in a warm place (86°F is ideal) until it has doubled in bulk, about 45 minutes. Press it down with a spoon, and let it rise a second time, about 30 minutes. The surface of the dough will be oily and shiny.

Generously grease two 10x15x1-inch baking pans. Preheat the oven to 350°F. After the dough doubles in size a second time, punch it down and spoon out balls of dough. They should be larger than a walnut and smaller than a large egg, or 2 to 3 tablespoons in size. These make a small roll. Form the rolls so the tops are smooth. Let the rolls rise, uncovered, about 30 minutes, until they double in size.

I like to coat the tops of the rolls with an egg wash, which adds color. Whisk together the egg and milk to make an egg wash. Using a pastry brush, coat the top of each roll. Bake for 25 to 30 minutes. When they are a deep brown, remove from the oven and turn them out on a cloth to cool.

If I am having company, I like to bake these rolls ahead and freeze them. They freeze for a month. To serve them after freezing, place them in a preheated 350°F oven for 10 minutes. Serve directly from the oven.

■ ■

Enjoy the rolls, and consider another mountain joke: A boy sitting in the lap of his grandfather said, "Grandpa, please make noise like a frog." And Grandpa said, "Why?" "Because Daddy said, when you croak, we'll be rich."
One last joke: A little boy's grandparents were coming to visit. The boy ran to meet them and said, "Now Dad will do a trick." When they asked why, the boy replied, "Dad said if you came back again, he'd climb the wall."

■ ■

Three

Salads and Vegetables

Beans, Cushaw, Turnips, and Poke

LP CALDWELL

■ ■

Wilted Lettuce *Wilted Lettuce with Hot Vinaigrette*
(Wilted Greens, Scalded Lettuce, and Smothered Lettuce)

Corn Bread Salad *(Bread Salad)*

Midland Trail Deviled Eggs

Cucumber Salad with Sour Cream

Cucumber Salad with Vinegar

Mom's Potato Salad

Appalachian Potato Salad

Seven-Layer Salad *(Next-Day Salad, Layered Salad, and
Eight-Layer Salad)*

Potherb Salad *(Wild Greens Salad)*

Hot Vinaigrette *Black Walnut Hot Vinaigrette*

Dry-Land Fish and Spring Onions
(Fried Morels with Onions)

Fried Ramps

Ramps and Slick Dumplings

Greenbrier Fiddlehead Salad *Green Bean Salad*

Prepared Poke

Boiled Poke

Poke Sallet *(Poke Frittata)*

Steamed Green Beans

Boiled Green Beans

Cumberland Plateau Green Beans with Bacon

Green Beans and New Potatoes *(Creamed Beans)*

Green Beans, Potatoes, and Onions

Dilled Green Beans with Black Walnuts
(Green Beans with Hot Vinaigrette)

Shuck Beans

Pickled Beans *Dilly Beans*

■ ■

Baked Cushaw

Baked Cushaw with Sorghum

Baked Cushaw with Cinnamon-Sorghum Sauce

Squash and Potato Soup *(Cushaw Soup)*

Cushaw Pie

Savory Cushaw Pie

Cushaw Bread *Cushaw Cake*

Sweet Boiled Turnips *Savory Boiled Turnips*

Mashed Turnips and Potatoes

Scalloped Turnips

Turnip Greens *Kale, Collards, Mustard Greens, and Greens and Dumplings*

Kathy's Coleslaw *(Slaw)*

Fried Cabbage *Skillet Cabbage*

Cabbage Stew

Sauerkraut *(Kraut and Cooked Sauerkraut)*

Kraut Slaw *(Sauerkraut Coleslaw)*

Allegheny Cabbage Casserole

Green Onion Huey *(Creamed Green Onions)*

Fried Okra

Okra and Tomatoes *(Tomato-Butter and Okra)*

Summer Garden Vegetable Stew

Summer Garden Custard Pie
(Onion Custard Pie and Squash Pie)

Grandfather Mountain Carrots and Peas

Sugared Carrots

Broccoli Casserole

Fried Green Tomatoes

Wilted Lettuce Salads

The use of hot bacon grease to wilt lettuce, spinach, cabbage, or dandelion greens is widely adapted in this country and abroad. In the 1946 edition of *Joy of Cooking*, this salad appears as Wilted Lettuce and Wilted Lettuce with Cream Dressing. To make the cream dressing, Irma S. Rombauer instructs you to add heavy cream to the bacon grease, vinegar, salt, and pepper. In the 1973 *Joy of Cooking*, Marion Rombauer Becker changed the name to Wilted Greens and suggested using head lettuce, dandelions, shredded cabbage, or spinach.

Simone Beck, in her book *Food and Friends*, discusses a similar dressing, a hot vinaigrette. Simone Beck is a friend of and coauthor with Julia Child, and a *grande dame* of French cooking. She grew up in Normandy, France. Beck calls it Lorraine Dressing, and she makes it with hot pork grease. When the dressing is ready, she suggests pouring it over dandelion greens. As some families here in the mountains do, she adds the greens to the pan, stirs them to coat, and then serves warm. The mountain recipe for Hot Vinaigrette that I give below is so similar, I can only wonder if mountain cooks have a direct line to Beck's sources in eastern France.

In nearby Alsace, France, there is another common wilted salad. In this case, according to Richard Olney's *Simple French Food*, the Alsatians wilt cabbage in hot water, and then douse it with hot bacon fat, vinegar, and olive oil.

Wilted Lettuce
Wilted Lettuce with Hot Vinaigrette (Wilted Greens, Scalded Lettuce, and Smothered Lettuce)

*W*e remember our Wilted Lettuce with pride and serve it with joy. Historically, wilted lettuce was popular because mountaineers looked forward with excitement to the first fresh salad of spring. To make the salad, we gather the onions, like the lettuce, by cutting them off at the ground. We then wash the lettuce and green onion blades, and finally cover them with hot bacon grease. Darrel Rose of Pikeville, Kentucky, tells the following story about Wilted Lettuce. "An old fellow once told me that killed lettuce put him to sleep. The old man said, 'When I eat killed lettuce I have to go straight to the couch and go to sleep.' Perhaps," Darrel continued, "the combination of bacon grease and onions has an anesthetizing quality."

Up and down the mountains, from the Savage in the north to the Snowbirds in the south, the lettuce of choice is an early spring leaf lettuce, often black-seeded Simpson, which grows fast. (We call it a "cut and come again" lettuce.) You can use any leaf lettuce, such as red sails or bibb, but please, don't use Romaine or iceberg. While most people I know make this salad with just three ingredients—hot bacon grease, lettuce, and green onions—the list of ingredients can also include vinegar, salt, pepper, garlic, sugar, water, and dry mustard. To the lettuce, try adding radishes, endive, or scallions.

DIFFICULTY Easy. With just three ingredients, this recipe is easy.

STEPS Fry the bacon till crisp. Lift the bacon from the pan, and drain, cool, crumble, and set aside. Reserve the bacon grease in the frying pan.

When you are ready to eat, heat the bacon fat until it smokes, pour it over greens, add the crumbled bacon, stir, and serve. Be sure to use a heat-resistant salad bowl.

Serve on warmed plates with chopped hard-boiled eggs, and offer salt and pepper. For a true mountain meal, serve your Wilted Lettuce with Soup Beans, Buttermilk Corn Bread, and a glass of cold buttermilk.

INGREDIENTS
8 strips ($1/2$ pound) bacon, or $1/2$ pound middling meat
1 large head (2 quarts) leaf lettuce, washed and torn into pieces
2 cups chopped green onion blades

YIELD 6 servings

Wilted Lettuce with Hot Vinaigrette

To the bacon grease in the frying pan, whisk in $1/4$ cup vinegar, 3 tablespoons water, 2 teaspoons sugar, 1 teaspoon salt, and $1/2$ teaspoon pepper. For yet another variation, add $1/2$ cup heavy cream to the vinaigrette.

Corn Bread Salad
(Bread Salad)

DIFFICULTY Difficult. With four steps, this seven-ingredient recipe is difficult.

We use croutons in Caesar salad and bread in bread pudding. Italians from Florence to Rome make *panzanella*, a bread salad with bell peppers, tomatoes, and onion. Here in the mountains, we use corn bread to stuff the turkey and thicken soup beans.

Corn Bread Salad is something that reflects our passion for corn bread. The recipe fits into our style of cooking, our kitchen habits, our mountain heritage, and our need for home-cooked food. It calls for traditional ingredients: corn bread, bacon, cheese, tomatoes, and mayonnaise, and in the Healthy Choice Alternative I have adapted corn bread salad to meet today's dietary needs. Thanks to Pat Barnett of Virgie, Kentucky, for getting me started on this cool and tasty salad.

INGREDIENTS
1/2 pone (5 cups diced) Mountain Country Corn Bread (page 20)
1 pound bacon
3 cups diced tomatoes
2 cups diced green, red, or yellow bell pepper
1 cup diced onion
2 cups mayonnaise
2 cups shredded Cheddar cheese

YIELD 9 servings

STEPS The day before you make the salad, bake the corn bread and fry the bacon. Drain the bacon. Cool the corn bread. Chop and refrigerate the tomatoes, peppers, and onion.

Two hours before serving, prepare the salad: Chop the corn bread and bacon into 1/2- to 3/4-inch pieces. In a large bowl, combine the corn bread, half of the bacon, the tomatoes, peppers, onions, mayonnaise, and cheese. Sprinkle the remaining bacon on top. Refrigerate.

HEALTHY CHOICE ALTERNATIVE Start by making my low-fat Simple Corn Bread (page 19). Use only half a pound of bacon, and spread it on top only. Replace the mayonnaise with 2 cups nonfat sour cream, and replace the Cheddar cheese with 2 cups nonfat small curd cottage cheese. This makes a low-calorie, low-fat dressing. If salt is not a concern, add 1 tablespoon salt or flavored salt such as lemon pepper, garlic, or seasoned salt.

Serve for Sunday dinner with fried chicken and hot biscuits.

■ ■

Midland Trail

Parts of U.S. Route 60 and Interstate 64 follow the Midland Trail, a historic route that connects the Allegheny Mountains with the Atlantic Coast at Newport News, Virginia. In its early history this was a trail for driving hogs to eastern markets and carrying mail by stagecoach. What remains are period hotels, friendly people, and beautiful mountains. For a time warp and unparalleled scenery, poke your way along scenic old Route 60, from Lewisburg to Charleston, West Virginia.

HEARTY
Cooking
COUNTRY

Midland Trail Deviled Eggs

I recently attended a potluck church supper. Alongside about thirty home-prepared dishes, there was one plate of eighteen deviled eggs. As the crowd waited for the blessing, some people talked and others eyed the dishes. Every so often someone edged over toward the deviled eggs. One by one they disappeared and then, when there were only about four deviled eggs left, someone took the platter back to the kitchen, and several men working on the dinner finished them off. Lucky for me, I was one of those men.

Popular? Wildly so. No mountain dinner is complete without them.

To "devil" is to mix with hot seasoning or mustard. Deviled (also spelled devilled) foods are hot and spicy. Deviled ham is an example, but according to *The Boston Cooking-School Cook Book,* 1947, you can also devil almonds, bones, crabs, lobster, oysters, raisins, scallops, and tomatoes. For now I'll stick with our most popular deviled food: deviled eggs—great for holiday gatherings or just to complete a Sunday dinner.

While some add sweet relish and sugar, the recipe that follows appeals to most mountain palates.

STEPS Halve the eggs lengthwise and remove the yolks to a mixing bowl. To the yolks add the mayonnaise, pickle juice, mustard, pepper, and salt. Mash thoroughly—I use the cutting blade of a food processor. With either a spoon or a rosette-equipped pastry tube, press the filling into the egg white cups. Garnish with paprika and half a green olive. Chill and serve cold.

HEALTHY CHOICE ALTERNATIVE The problem with this recipe is not the mayonnaise but the egg yolks. Half an egg—one deviled egg—contains 37 calories, 2.5 grams of fat, and 106 milligrams of cholesterol. Some dieticians recommend a maximum of 300 milligrams of cholesterol per day. That means you can enjoy almost three deviled eggs per day!

Serve cold. Serve for lunch or dinner. Serve at a picnic or holiday gathering. No Thanksgiving, Christmas, or Sunday dinner is complete without deviled eggs.

DIFFICULTY Moderate. With eight ingredients and perhaps a garnish, this recipe is moderate in difficulty.

INGREDIENTS
12 hard-boiled eggs, peeled and chilled
1/4 cup mayonnaise
2 tablespoons pickle juice or green-olive juice
2 tablespoons prepared yellow mustard
1/2 teaspoon ground white pepper
1/2 teaspoon salt
Paprika
6 pitted green olives

YIELD 24 deviled eggs, or 12 servings

Salads
and
Vegetables

Cucumber Salad with Sour Cream

I like to think of my diet as a balancing act: I balance types of food with metabolism and foolishness. I eat heavy. I eat light. I eat junk. I exercise. But over time, I balance fun with fat. Cucumbers help. Members of the gourd family, cucumbers are mostly water. They are refreshing and low in calories—only sixteen per cup.

Some cucumbers are bitter and others give people hiccups. Try one of the new hybrid varieties—the bitterness is gone and so is the gene that caused it. New cucumber varieties are burpless too, including the Green Knight, Burpless, Sweet Slice, and Sweet Success.

INGREDIENTS
8 ounces (1 cup) sour cream
1 tablespoon lemon juice
1/2 teaspoon ground white pepper
1/2 teaspoon salt
1/2 teaspoon dill weed
2 medium (2 1/2 cups sliced and peeled) cucumbers
1 small (1 cup sliced) sweet onion

YIELD 6 servings

STEPS Several hours before serving, spoon the sour cream, the lemon juice, pepper, salt, and dill in a small mixing bowl. Refrigerate. Peel and slice the cucumbers and onion. Refrigerate.

At serving time, mix together the cucumbers and sour cream. Keeping the cucumbers separate from the salty sour cream mixture until serving helps to reduce unwanted water.

HEALTHY CHOICE ALTERNATIVE This recipe contains about 90 calories per serving, but you can replace the sour cream with fat-free sour cream or plain yogurt.

Serve on a large lettuce leaf with light crackers.

■ ■

Salting Cucumbers

To reduce unwanted water in your cucumber salad, salt the cucumbers. In another day and time, every thoughtful cook would salt the cucumbers before making cucumber salads. Salting is still a good idea, but I have developed these two cucumber recipes so that you can make them in a few minutes without going through the lengthy salting process.

In case you want to draw water from the cucumbers, here's how: Generously salt the cucumbers and let them stand for two hours. Pour the cucumbers, water, and salt into a colander, and rinse them under cold water. Taste to be sure all the salt has washed away. Drain and dry the cucumbers. They will be limp.

Cucumber Salad with Vinegar

*C*ucumbers grow well in the mountains. Besides using them to make sweet pickles, dill pickles, and bread-and-butter pickles, mountaineers eat cukes straight from the garden or flavored with vinegar. Try this salad with vinegar alone or with vinegar, lemon juice, and water. Some add oil, others add sugar. Pepper is a constant for everyone—except me. In today's kitchen, where time, short cuts, and flavor count bushels, your choice of vinegar makes the difference. The salad's flavor depends on thickness of the slices, the strength of the vinegar, and amount of time in the marinade mixture. I like to think of the vinegar and water mixture as a marinade and the salad as a light relish.

STEPS Peel and slice the cucumbers and onion. Slice thin—thinner slices absorb more vinegar and are easier to eat. Pour the water and vinegar over the cucumbers and onion, and stir to mix. The water and vinegar should almost cover the cucumbers.

Serve immediately, or refrigerate for several hours or overnight—longer storage gives the cucumbers more flavor. You can also increase flavor by using more vinegar.

HEALTHY CHOICE ALTERNATIVE This salad is fat free and has about 10 calories per serving.

Drain the marinade before serving, or serve with tongs, lifting the onions and cucumbers from the liquid. Save the marinade and use it to make another cucumber salad. Serve on a large lettuce leaf with light crackers.

DIFFICULTY Easy. Made with fresh cucumbers, onion, and vinegar, this recipe is easy.

INGREDIENTS
2 medium (2 1/2 cups sliced and peeled) cucumbers
1 small (1 cup sliced) sweet onion
1 cup water
3/4 cup wine vinegar

YIELD 6 servings

Mom's Potato Salad

DIFFICULTY Moderate. In this two-step process you cook, cool, and cure the potatoes, letting them rest overnight, and then the next day, you mix up the salad, using a total of nine ingredients.

*Y*ou've heard it before and it's true again: Mom's potato salad is the best. But my mom's potato salad has changed. Years ago she made potato salad with raw celery, dill pickles, and boiled eggs. Now the celery is half-cooked, and the pickles and eggs are gone. Mom's potato salad is still the best, whatever she does.

Mom's salad is made with diced, firm, and waxy new potatoes. She cooks the potatoes the night before so they have time to age, covered, in the refrigerator. Refrigeration allows the starch to coagulate and makes the potatoes smooth and waxy so that they do not absorb dressing. Then, the next day she dices the potatoes and mixes the salad.

INGREDIENTS

FOR THE SALAD

4 medium-size new potatoes—5 cups cooked and diced potatoes
1 cup diced celery
2 tablespoons grated onion

FOR THE DRESSING

1/2 cup safflower oil
1/4 cup mayonnaise
2 tablespoons red wine vinegar
2 teaspoons Dijon-style mustard
1 1/2 teaspoons salt
1 teaspoon dried dill weed

YIELD 8 servings

STEPS The day before serving, cut the potatoes in half lengthwise and boil for 30 minutes (or, as I do, place them in a pressure cooker, add 1 cup of water, and cook 15 to 20 minutes after the pressure is up). Your potatoes are cooked when you press a fork to the center and feel no resistance, no solid or hard potato.

While the potatoes are cooking, wash, dice, and boil the celery for 7 minutes, until it is tender but not soft. Pour off the cooking water. Run cold water over the celery and refrigerate.

When the potatoes are ready, drain the cooking water. Run the potatoes under cold water and, while hot, pull off the skins. Remove and discard any spots and blemishes.

Let the potatoes cool uncovered for about an hour. Place the peeled potatoes in a covered container and refrigerate overnight. These two steps help to coagulate the starch, giving the potatoes a waxy texture.

Just prior to serving, prepare the salad. In a large mixing bowl whisk together the oil, mayonnaise, vinegar, mustard, salt, and dill weed. When fully mixed, stir in the cooked celery and onion. Dice the potatoes and stir them in. Refrigerate until ready to serve.

HEALTHY CHOICE ALTERNATIVE Do not use Mom's dressing. Use 1 cup of store-bought thick, light, low-calorie, fat- and cholesterol-free Italian-style dressing. Rather than buying a dressing, I like to stir in one recipe of Light Vegetable Dip (page 312).

Serve with Cucumber Salad and Fried Pork Chops.

Appalachian Potato Salad

*A*ppalachian Potato Salad is smooth, creamy, and partly mashed. For the results most mountaineers know, use mature—not new—Idaho or Kennebec baking potatoes, and mix the salad when the potatoes are hot. Do not allow them to sit after cooking.

STEPS Cut the potatoes in half lengthwise. Boil them 30 minutes, or until soft to the center (or, as I do, place them in a pressure cooker, add 1 cup of water, and cook 15 to 20 minutes after the pressure is up).

While the potatoes are cooking, boil the eggs for 10 minutes. Run them under cold water, and peel the shells. Mash the eggs.

When the potatoes are cooked, run them under cold water, and while they're still hot, pull off the skins. Remove and discard the dark spots and blemishes.

In a large mixing bowl, whisk together the oil, mayonnaise, vinegar, mustard, salt, and dill weed. Stir in the eggs and the pickles. Dice the hot potatoes and stir them in. Refrigerate until ready to serve.

HEALTHY CHOICE ALTERNATIVE Do not use this dressing. Use a generous amount of a store-bought thick, light, low-calorie, fat- and cholesterol-free dressing.

Serve this salad with Coleslaw, Fried Pork Chops, and fresh and steamy hot Buttermilk Biscuits.

DIFFICULTY Moderate. In this two-step process, you cook the potatoes and then mix up the salad, using a total of nine ingredients.

INGREDIENTS
4 medium-size potatoes—5 cups cooked and diced potatoes
4 hard-boiled eggs
1/2 cup safflower oil
3/4 cup mayonnaise
2 tablespoons red wine vinegar
2 teaspoons Dijon-style mustard
1 1/2 teaspoons salt
1 teaspoon dill weed
1/2 cup diced pickles, relish, or pimiento

YIELD 8 servings

■ ■

Appalachian Mountains

From the coastal plain of Alabama 1,600 miles north to the St. Lawrence valley in Quebec, Canada, the Appalachian Mountains form a complex system of smaller ranges. These mountains include the White Mountains, Green Mountains, Taconic Mountains, Catskill Mountains, Allegheny Mountains, Black Mountains, Great Smoky Mountains, the Blue Ridge, and the Cumberland Plateau.

When Hernando DeSoto arrived in the mountains in the 16th century he met a tribe of Native Americans that he called Appalachees. From this tribal name he also derived the name Appalachian Mountains.

Salads
and
Vegetables

Seven-Layer Salad
(Next-Day Salad, Layered Salad, and
Eight-Layer Salad)

DIFFICULTY Moderate.
With eight ingredients
and two steps, this recipe
is moderate in difficulty.

This tossed or layered lettuce, vegetable, cheese, and bacon salad stores well and tastes oh so good. Seven-layer salad is made throughout the Midwest and from there east into the Appalachian Mountains. We call it next-day salad, layered salad, and eight-layer salad.

But is this a twenty-four-hour salad? No. I prefer to reserve that name for a sweet salad that contains miniature marshmallows, pineapple, cherries, grapes, and nuts, held together with a whipped cream dressing.

In this salad, the iceberg lettuce and cauliflower make the texture crisp and crunchy. The bacon, mayonnaise, and cheese make it rich and flavorful. You can also add broccoli, water chestnuts, mushrooms, and cooked carrots. For garnish, use chopped green onions, paprika, and small tomatoes. Among lettuce salads, this is unique: It stays fresh for several days. That is because you don't mix it, thus the lettuce stays dry, and the layer of mayonnaise seals the lettuce in the salad bowl.

INGREDIENTS
1/2 head or 6 cups bite-size pieces iceberg lettuce, torn into pieces
1/2 head or 4 cups cauliflower, chopped
1 small red onion or 1 cup sliced red onion
20 ounces frozen baby peas
2 cups mayonnaise
1 pound bacon, cooked and crumbled
8 ounces or 2 cups shredded sharp Cheddar cheese
14 cherry tomatoes for garnish

YIELD 14 servings

STEPS Using a large, clear, straight-sided glass bowl, layer the ingredients in the order given: lettuce, cauliflower, onion, peas, mayonnaise, bacon, and cheese. Spread the mayonnaise to the edge of the bowl so that the vegetables are sealed below. Garnish with tomatoes. Cover with plastic wrap, and chill until ready to serve.

HEALTHY CHOICE ALTERNATIVES Altering this recipe is tough. If you cut the mayonnaise, bacon, or cheese, you don't have the same salad. Still, I cannot close my eyes to the 2 cups of mayonnaise, with its 652 grams of fat and 3,200 calories.

Try replacing the mayonnaise with 2 cups of nonfat sour cream, saving 652 grams of fat and 2,800 calories. Flavor the sour cream with one envelope of dry onion soup mix. Or, use half a pound of bacon and low-fat Cheddar cheese. And, if you like Miracle Whip, in place of the mayonnaise, use 2 cups Fat-Free Miracle Whip.

Serve with crackers or light sandwiches. Serve at potlucks, homecomings, family picnics, or church suppers. The recipe is large, but the salad is popular.

Potherbs, Poke, Ramps, and Fiddleheads

ONE OF THE pastimes of my young adulthood was outdoor survival. For example, in the early 1970s I spent 29 days living off the land. With students from Ripon College in Ripon, Wisconsin, I fished, foraged, and dug for food. In the northern Minnesota lake country, we fished for northern pike, boiled birch sap into syrup, ground lichens into soup, and cooked curly dock with other greens.

With this background I take quickly to preparing wild greens. The poke, fiddleheads, creases, watercress, chickentoe (tanglegut), and dock that grow around Pikeville, Kentucky, have a place in my kitchen. Mountaineers have taught me how they use them. Some of our best foods grow beside the creek, on a hillside, behind the barn, or along fences. Old abandoned strip mines and mining roads are also excellent sources for poke, blackberries, and many other potherbs. Spring is the best time to gather them.

Wild greens will be fresh when you cook them, if you keep them fresh. In addition, they have not been sprayed with chemicals. When you pick wild greens yourself, you know where you got them and who has handled them. Greens such as chickentoe are more tender and flavorful than anything you can buy. If you are not in the habit of using wild greens, remember that a supermarket mind-set will not put wild greens on your table. It takes a lot of time to pick and clean wild greens. They don't come in plastic. You'll have to wash, peel, cook, and maybe cook some more. Before supermarkets, doctors, and vitamin pills reached the more isolated regions of these mountains, Highlanders spent the winter eating stored foods such as pork, dried beans, and potatoes. When spring came and the hills were colored with light green, shady amber, redbud purple, and patches of white service berry, the mountain folks gathered fresh greens, eating them to cleanse the system and because instinctively they knew that fresh greens are healthy food. Little has changed. Wild greens are still healthy food. As we approach the year 2000, we are lucky to have three sources of fresh produce: the hills, our gardens, and the supermarket. (If these fail, try Donaldson Food Center, New Penny Farm, or W. S. Wells and Son in my Mail-Order Sources.)

On a cool spring or summer evening, a Saturday morning, or a Sunday afternoon, you can go to the hills and collect wild edibles, free for the picking. Do respect private property rights and public land laws regarding picking,

Salads
and
Vegetables

however. For the most part these "weeds" are prolific and not endangered, but before you go collecting, do your best to learn about local laws, customs, and plant conditions.

Potherbs have a place in enlightened kitchens. They'll add pleasure to your weekend and roughage to your diet. Consider these choices:

Creases

This dry-land cress, also called bitter cress, poor man's cabbage, and yellow rocket (*Barbarea verna* and *Barbarea vulgaris*), is a green, and you can prepare it like turnip greens or collard greens. It grows up to two feet tall, and in the southern Appalachians, it can be gathered all winter.

Dandelion Greens

Every book says these (*Taraxacum officinale*) are good, but I find them to have a sour taste, one that you must grow to like. Mountain cooks use dandelion greens with leaf lettuce, onion blades, and other spring greens in salads, or they use them as a cooked side dish to accompany a main course item, such as Soup Beans. W. S. Wells and Son sells canned dandelions, which I find much like other canned greens: heavily cooked, drab olive green in color, soft in texture, and with a flavor reminiscent of fresh dandelions.

Dock

Also called sorrel dock or spinach dock (*Rumex crispa*), cook this member of the buckwheat family like you would spinach. Pick and prepare young leaves in the spring.

Fiddleheads

Fiddleheads are a stage of growth, the first stage of a fern leaf. Fiddleheads resemble the coiled end of a fiddle. They are bright green and have a flavor similar to asparagus and green beans. Texture distinguishes fiddleheads from other vegetables. They are crunchy and at the same time slightly gooey or viscous, or mucilaginous like okra.

From Alabama to Vermont you can gather fiddleheads in the hills and on creek banks. While ostrich ferns are the most popular, near my house in Pikeville, Kentucky, we gather Christmas fern fiddleheads (*polystichum acrostichoides*) during April. This twenty-inch-high evergreen fern covers some hills and will have green ferns from the previous season when the fiddleheads push their heads up through dry leaves. Gather young fiddleheads, and try to avoid any with enlarged leaves or expanding heads.

Lambs Quarters

Lambs quarters (*Chenopodium album*) comes up in my garden with the peas, and it grows as fast as, or faster than, peas. My peas die out in June, but lambs quarters stay healthy most of the summer. Pick this scalloped and frosted-blue leaf when it is small, and cook it like other greens.

Morels

Called dry-land fish, hickory chickens, sponge mushrooms, spring mushrooms, and markels (*Morchella esculenta*), morels are treasured for their rich flavor and firm texture. In the same fungus species as the prized French truffle, these are also popular in traditional French restaurants. Morels come up in the spring after a warm rain, when the blue violets are in bloom. Find them in open fields, old orchards, overgrown pastures, and under apple and hickory trees.

We call these mushrooms dry-land fish because they taste like fish and we cook them like fish. In *More Than Moonshine*, Sidney Farr says that her family calls them hickory chickens because they taste like chicken and grow under hickory trees. Others from eastern Kentucky say they taste like oysters. Farr, who grew up at Stoney Fork, Kentucky, says that morels are easy to identify, but she cautions us about a similar-looking mushroom: "Morels are the easiest and safest mushroom to hunt, but mycologists say they have a dangerous look-alike—the helvella, or beef-steak mushroom. The true morel has a cap and stem in one continuous piece. In most mushrooms, the cap hangs over the stem like an umbrella, but the morel cap is attached to the stem at the rim. It is like a cone-shaped sponge, pitted like a honeycomb. The center is hollow."

In specialty food stores and perhaps some markets, you can find two kinds of morels: small dark ones and larger white ones. Both light and dark morels have excellent flavor, often described as smoky, earthy, and nutty. You can buy fresh morels in April, May, and June; dry morels are available all year.

Poke

Poke has several names: pokeweed, inkberry, and pigeonberry (*Phytolacca americana*). Eat the young shoots and young leaves, which sprout from tubers in May. See my discussion of poke in this chapter.

Purslane

Also called pusley (*Portulaca oleracea*), purslane is a low-growing, succulent, late spring and summer garden weed. The fresh leaves are crisp and greasy. Purslane is widespread, growing both in the heat of direct sun or in the shade of your house, in rich or thin, sandy soils. It likes my garden, and I like it in salads.

Ramps

As well as being a member of the lily family, ramps are wild leeks (*Allium tricoccum*). They grow in our cool, richly wooded hills and ravines. We eat the bulbs and leaves, cooked or raw. If you eat the bulbs raw, the resulting offensive smell is so strong that years ago in the mountains of North Carolina teachers are said to have dismissed school because of the odor on the children! From Georgia to Maryland communities come together in April for community ramp suppers and ramp festivals.

Shepherd's Purse

Also called St. James wort or mother's heart (*Capsella bursapastoris*), you can eat this common annual weed cooked or in salads. For salads, select young tender leaves or grind the seeds into meal and use the leaves for tea.

Spring Beauty

Also called tanglegut, chickentoe, mouse's ear, two-leaf, and fairy spuds, this member of the purslane family is one of the first greens of spring. We eat the leaves and stems with Soup Beans and corn bread. The two common varieties (*Claytonia virginica* and *Claytonia lanceolata*) are widely distributed in the mountains, and you can find them in low, moist areas on the edge of the woods or old roads. At high elevations they seem to come up out of the snow.

Watercress

Watercress (*Nasturtium officinale*), a member of the mustard family, grows in or near our streams. Its distinct peppery flavor and crisp texture sets it apart as a green or garnish. We use watercress raw in salads and on sandwiches with mayonnaise.

Potherb Salad
(Wild Greens Salad)

*W*ild greens please primitive mountaineers as well as sophisticated city folk. The problem is that in the city, it is almost impossible to find food gatherers who sell these greens, and in the country, few people take the time to gather them. In this salad, there is a real opportunity for enterprising young chefs or sophisticated rural cooks to distinguish their kitchen. Sorry, mail-order sources are not available for fresh greens.

STEPS After picking fine potherbs, as I suggest in the list of ingredients, wash them until every speck of dirt is gone. Dry them with a lettuce spinner. Mix and chill.

At serving time, dress the salad with Hot Vinaigrette. Serve this salad with Appalachian Potato Salad, Deviled Eggs, saltine crackers, or Buttermilk Corn Bread.

DIFFICULTY Difficult. With five greens to gather and a dressing to prepare, this recipe is difficult.

INGREDIENTS

SELECT ANY FOUR OF THE FOLLOWING
1 cup watercress
1 cup chickentoe
1 cup young dock leaves, cut into thin strips
1 cup small tender lambs quarters, leaves only
1 cup dandelion greens
1 cup purslane
1 cup shepherd's purse

SELECT ONE OF THE FOLLOWING
1/2 cup blue violets
1/2 cup pepper grass
1/4 cup wild onion, minced
1/4 cup ramps, chopped fine
1 recipe Hot Vinaigrette (see below)

YIELD 4 servings

Hot Vinaigrette
Black Walnut Hot Vinaigrette

*W*hile I also use this dressing to make Wilted Lettuce and Green Beans with Hot Vinaigrette, it brings out the best of the Potherb Salad.

STEPS In a skillet, fry the bacon, remove it from the pan, and set aside. To the bacon grease in the pan, whisk in the vinegar, water, sugar, salt, and pepper. Bring to a boil. Crumble the bacon back into the mixture. Stir and serve.

Black Walnut Hot Vinaigrette To the above recipe, add 1/2 cup black walnut pieces.

DIFFICULTY Moderate. With six ingredients, this recipe is moderate in difficulty.

INGREDIENTS
8 strips (1/2 pound) bacon
1/4 cup vinegar
3 tablespoons water
2 teaspoons sugar
1 teaspoon salt
1/2 teaspoon pepper

YIELD 4 servings

Salads and Vegetables

Using Dry-Land Fish

We call our morels dry-land fish. In the kitchen, many of us split our dry-land fish lengthwise, dip them in buttermilk, roll them in cornmeal, and fry them, just like catfish. Others in the southern Highlands fry morels after soaking them 15 minutes in salt water. Some roll halves in flour or meal, dip them in beaten egg, and then fry them in lard.

French chefs prize their morels. The *Larousse Gastronomique,* a fairly complete source on French cooking, recommends that you fry morels and then deglaze the pan with cream. It also suggests serving them au gratin, as garnish for omelettes, as an accompaniment to chicken or sweetbreads, and as seasoning for soups and sauces. *The Escoffier Cookbook,* a guide to French cuisine published in 1903, lists six recipes for morels: essence of morel consommé, creamed morels, morels and chicken, sautéed morels, stuffed morels, and torte of morels.

For creamed morels, *Escoffier* suggests the following: Boil halves or quarters ten minutes with a touch of diced onion, butter, salt, and pepper, being sure to use liquid in the final preparation. Remove the mushrooms, reduce the broth, add instant flour, and thicken. Thin with heavy cream and serve over fresh biscuits or in a puff pastry. I don't know why, but there must be a lot of mountain cooks with a direct line to *Escoffier.* We've long served creamed morels over buttermilk biscuits.

Dry-Land Fish and Spring Onions
(Fried Morels with Onions)

*O*nions grow in the garden, and morels in the orchard. They are ready at the same time, and they often end up in the same skillet with a little lard, which lends flavor and crispness to this recipe. We make fried green onions with mature onion tops. I use tender onion flower stems. A single flower stem, almost an inch in diameter and two feet tall, yields enough onion for this recipe. Cut the onion stem and the morels into one-inch pieces. Bread the onions with the morels like you would bread green tomatoes for fried green tomatoes. Savor your crispy green onions and morels hot from the skillet.

If I make this with dried morels, I soak them for an hour and then press out the water.

STEPS In a large cast-iron skillet, heat half of the lard over medium-high heat until it starts to smoke, or until it reaches 325°F to 350°F. If you are smoking up the kitchen, the lard is too hot. Reduce the heat.

In a mixing bowl, combine the self-rising cornmeal and salt. Add the morels and onions, and stir to coat. Lift the onions and morels into the skillet, and fry about 3 minutes on each side, adding the remaining lard as needed. Fry until golden brown. The onions will blacken in spots, but other parts remain green. Drain on paper towels and serve immediately, or they will get soggy.

HEALTHY CHOICE ALTERNATIVE The results are not the same, but you can substitute safflower oil for the lard or shortening. Adding the safflower oil 1 tablespoon at a time, you may find that you can fry the entire recipe with 1, 2, or 3 tablespoons of oil.

As an appetizer, serve this with Chow Chow, Pickled Beats, and Angel Biscuits, or serve as a side dish with Boiled New Potatoes, Country-Fried Steak, or scrambled eggs. Serve for breakfast with bacon, eggs, and corn bread.

DIFFICULTY Easy. With five ingredients and one cooking step, this recipe is easy.

INGREDIENTS
1/4 cup lard or shortening
1/2 cup self-rising cornmeal mix
1 1/4 teaspoons salt
1 1/2 cups morels
1 1/2 cups sliced green onion

YIELD 4 servings

■ ■

Our Favorite Wild Green

In April 1984, Oliver and Anne Walston traveled from their farm in Cambridge, England, to a small town in West Virginia to eat fresh fried ramps. I know why: It was the flavor—tangy, whole, and hot, a mixture of onion, garlic, and leek.

We eat ramps raw, fried, boiled, stewed, and scrambled with eggs. We usually boil and then fry ramps. We fry them with bacon, sausage, ham, and potatoes. We serve fried ramps with corn bread, biscuits and gravy, soup beans, and sassafras tea. In addition, we make ramp pie, ramp chili, and ramp meat loaf. Glen Facemire (see Ramps in the Mail-Order Sources) sells ramps dried and in jelly and candy.

The strong smell and unique flavor of ramps are the driving force behind our ramp celebrations, festivals, and community dinners. Ramp celebrations I know of include the Chamber of Commerce Ramp Dinner in Richwood, West Virginia, the Mount Rogers Volunteer Fire Department Ramp Festival in western Virginia, and the Ramp Supper at Helvetia, West Virginia.

In this book you'll find many typical ramp supper dishes: Fried Ramps, Soup Beans, Kraut Slaw, Fried Potatoes, Mashed Potatoes, Country Ham with Red-Eye Gravy, Southern Fried Chicken, Buttermilk Corn Bread, Dilly Beans, and Sassafras Tea. In addition to these main dishes ramp suppers may include Potato Candy, peanut butter fudge, and chocolate fudge.

■ ■

Fried Ramps

To extend the ramp season, boil and then freeze your fresh ramps. When parboiled and then frozen, ramps keep their flavor, and you can use them to make these Fried Ramps.

STEPS In a skillet, fry the bacon and, when it is crisp, add the ramps. Fry on low heat, covered, for 6 minutes. Uncover and fry an additional 2 minutes. Sprinkle with the salt, and serve.

HEALTHY CHOICE ALTERNATIVE Boil the ramps until tender, and then fry with 1 tablespoon safflower oil.

Serve these with Southern Fried Chicken, Fried Potatoes, fried chicken livers, scrambled eggs, Buttermilk Biscuits, or Fried Green Tomatoes.

DIFFICULTY Easy. Once the ramps are prepared, this recipe is easy.

INGREDIENTS
4 pieces (3 ounces) bacon, cut in tiny strips
2 cups diced ramps (roots removed)
1/2 teaspoon salt

YIELD 4 servings

Ramps and Slick Dumplings

You can make this soup with leeks, scallions, or onions, but ramps have a distinct—and stronger—flavor for which there is no substitute. In March and April, you can order fresh ramps from Donaldson Food Center; see my list of Mail-Order Sources.

STEPS Prepare the Slick Dumplings according to the recipe instructions. When you have rolled out the dumplings and cut them, dust them with flour; they need to be dry, not damp or sticky. If the surface is dry before you slip them into the broth, they will not stick together.

In a large saucepan, bring the water to a boil. Add 1 cup of the ramps, the potato, butter, and salt or bouillon, and stir. One at a time, slip the dumplings into the water. Return to a boil. Reduce the heat, and simmer for 20 minutes. As the dumplings cook, separate them as needed. After boiling, let the mixture stand for one to twenty-four hours. Reheat and serve.

HEALTHY CHOICE ALTERNATIVE Omit the butter and use canola oil in the dumplings.

Serve in soup plates. Large flat soup plates allow the dumplings to spread out and be fully visible. Garnish each plate with a few of the reserved (2 tablespoons) fresh ramps. Serve with crackers and buttermilk.

DIFFICULTY Moderate. With six ingredients and one cooking step, this recipe is moderate in difficulty.

INGREDIENTS
1/2 recipe Slick Dumplings (page 26)
5 cups water
1 cup plus 2 tablespoons chopped fresh ramps or leeks
1 1/4 cups grated potato
2 tablespoons butter or lard
1 teaspoon salt or 1 tablespoon chicken bouillon grains

YIELD 5 servings

Salads
and
Vegetables

Greenbrier Fiddlehead Salad
Green Bean Salad

DIFFICULTY Moderate. With eight ingredients, and considering the fact that you have to cook the fiddleheads ahead, this salad is moderate in difficulty.

For more than 200 years, Southerners and statesmen have come to The Greenbrier at White Sulphur Springs, West Virginia, to walk, socialize, vacation, and bathe in the water. Today The Greenbrier is a resort, retreat, spa, health clinic, conference center, tennis club, and golf haven. Long before white settlers arrived, Native Americans were here, enjoying the hot springs, hunting, and making their way up the Greenbrier River into the Allegheny Mountains to the west.

If you don't have fiddleheads but like the sound of this sumptuous salad, make it, as I suggest in the variation, with cooked and chilled green beans.

INGREDIENTS

THE FIDDLEHEADS
2 1/2 cups cooked and cooled fiddleheads

FOR THE SALAD AND DRESSING
1/2 cup diced onion
3/4 cup shredded sharp Cheddar cheese
3/4 cup mayonnaise
1/4 cup heavy cream
1/4 cup crumbled Roquefort cheese
1 10-ounce package frozen baby peas
1/2 cup diced tomato

FOR THE GARNISH
tomato slices
fiddleheads

YIELD 5 servings

STEPS In a large pot, steam or boil the fiddleheads for 10 minutes, or until almost tender. Then measure 2 1/2 cups. Cool.

In a large bowl, combine the onion, Cheddar cheese, mayonnaise, cream, and Roquefort cheese. Stir in the fiddleheads, peas, and tomato, reserving a few tomatoes and fiddleheads for garnish.

HEALTHY CHOICE ALTERNATIVE Replace the mayonnaise and heavy cream with 1 cup Light Vegetable Dip (page 312).

Serve as part of a salad plate. Start with a bed of lettuce or spinach and arrange as a trio with Kathy's Cole Slaw and Cucumber Salad or rolled banana-nut salad, accompanied by hot fresh Simple Corn Bread.

Green Bean Salad In place of the fiddleheads, substitute cooked and chilled green beans.

HEARTY
Cooking
COUNTRY

Poke

POKE IS UNDOUBTEDLY our most popular, most available, and most eaten wild potherb. It is also strange. During most of the growing season poke is poisonous, but in the spring it puts up edible, tender shoots and leaves. Poke is special. In comparison to asparagus, for example, I find poke more tender, more succulent, and sweeter. In addition, poke does not have the strong flavor of asparagus.

From a grand tuber the size of your arm or as big as your leg, poke sends shoots up from the soil. Shoots emerge from March through May, depending on your climate. We cut the shoots above the ground.

We then boil, fry, can, and pickle poke. We make it into wine, and according to my favorite source on the subject of poke, Euell Gibbons's *Stalking the Wild Asparagus*, some use a diluted poke-berry tea as tonic or medicine to protect children from boils and pimples. Gibbons also recalls that in his childhood his parents put pieces of poke root in the chickens' water to "protect them from disease." While it is against the law to sell dried poke root for human consumption, I've seen health food stores that sell it for the preparation of tea, and they label dried poke root "not for human consumption."

A Poisonous Plant

In spite of its historical use as a medicine, mature poke leaves, stems, berries, and roots are poisonous, and we cannot eat them. Poke is like rhubarb in that with rhubarb we eat the stems and discard the leaves. Rhubarb leaves are poisonous. Poke is also like apples. Apple seeds are poisonous. We don't eat apple seeds because large quantities (several cups) of them might be fatal.

Rodale's *Illustrated Encyclopedia of Herbs* supports the conventional wisdom on the subject of poke by saying that "children who've eaten the inky poke berries have died." But Rodale's *Encyclopedia* is vague in that it does not say whether the children ate three berries or three cups of berries.

So what part of the poke plant do we eat? We eat the young and tender shoots, three to thirty-six inches tall, and we eat the leaves before they get old. When the stems are filled with pith, we eat them. When the stems thicken and get hollow, they are too old.

POKE IS ALSO called pokeweed, poke sallet, pigeonberry (eaten by pigeons and mockingbirds), inkberry (a common source of ink), garget (inflammation of the udder of a cow), and cancer jalap (suggesting the dried root cures cancer), and is *Phytolacca americana* to the botanists. It grows in

Salads
and
Vegetables

disturbed acidic soil, fence rows, road cuts, and around barns from Maine to Florida and west to the Great Plains. It will also grow in your basement.

In the fall after the first big frost, you can dig up the roots and plant them in a large tub. Three large wash tubs, or about fifteen roots, will feed a family for three months. Leave the tubs outside until they have taken some heavy frosts. Then, anytime from December through February, when you are ready to start eating poke shoots, bring the tubs to a cool dark closet or something like a wine cellar. About once a week you'll be able to cut shoots, and then more will appear.

Euell Gibbons advises you to look for the tall dead many-forked stems in the spring so that you can find the new shoots coming up from the soil. You will find small poke shoots when the fire pinks and winter cress are in bloom. In a good patch, I have cut six pounds of poke in twenty minutes. Gibbons laments the fact that every spring "thousands of tons" of tender poke shoots go to waste.

When poke is in season, you'll find it sold in some Southern markets. If you can't buy it fresh, you'll have to cut it yourself or order some canned, which is available from Oakwood Market, listed in the Mail-Order Sources. Cutting poke is easy. We cut the shoots with a sharp knife, a little above the ground. If the stem is tough or hollow, it is too old, even if it is only a foot tall. If the leaves are pointed upward, like those at the top of a growing corn stalk, and if the stem is tender, they are good to eat, even if the plant is thirty-six inches tall or taller. Healthy, fast-growing poke plants will send up shoots that are one and a half inches across. These thick, solid shoots grow quickly, but I prefer using the thinner stems, those that are about three-quarters of an inch across.

■ ■

A Year with Poke

Poke is a beautiful plant. More than many other plants, it changes with the seasons. I have a poke plant growing in my front yard, just about three feet from the window at which I type. Unfortunately—and the thought is a pity—most of my neighbors and my dear wife, Kathy, think of poke as a weed and appreciate neither its beauty nor its value.

In the spring we eat the shoots, and in the fall the birds come for

the berries. Still, some of my neighbors have the gall to say that I should remove the plant. How can they be so rigid about front-yard landscaping?

Around April 20, as many as eight shoots push up from my poke tuber. Every year the plant gets bigger. Through the early spring the shoots stretch and grow up and out until around June 10, when the first white flowers start to appear. By July 1 the eight-foot-tall plant is a mass of green leaves decorated with long stems of tiny white flowers. The flower's five white petals cluster around a green center, and the bees arrive to pollinate.

Then, in mid-summer, these tiny green centers grow into bright shiny green berries. They stay green until the first of August, and then as the lower leaves die, the berries and plant stalks turn purple. With each passing week in August the plant gets heavier with fruit, and I have to tie up the stalks and prune the branches that break under the weight. The white flowers continue to form, and green berries emerge from their centers. In the late summer, purple dominates.

A freeze of about 28°F will kill the leaves, but the woody stems have plenty of strength to support the fruit. After this frost and during light rains, the many thin stems of purple berries drip purple. With each rain and throughout the winter, purple stain flows from berry stems, turning the soil below purple.

Then, the birds come. Continuing through February, large gray mockingbirds visit the plant and eat the berries. Mockingbirds, with their twelve-inch wingspan tipped in white, dash in, eat from odd positions, and dart away. If the poisonous berries have any negative effect on the mockingbirds, you could never tell from their enthusiasm.

By March and April, all that is left is the gray mass of woody stems and a few dried-up, shriveled berries. Still the birds come. When the new shoots begin to emerge in May, I cut down the old woody stems, and the slow drama begins again.

Prepared Poke

*A*fter you gather a big bunch of poke, pick off the dead grass or dry leaves. If you pulled the poke and have pieces of the tuber on the bottom of the stem, cut off the tuber. It is poisonous.

Fill a large pan with enough water to cover the poke, and bring it to a boil. Add the poke with the leaves, and boil for 3 minutes. Pour off the water and repeat, boiling the poke twice. This twice-boiled and drained poke is what I call prepared poke in the following recipes.

Boiled Poke

DIFFICULTY Easy. With three ingredients and two cooking steps, this recipe is easy.

INGREDIENTS
2 cups (1 pound) pre-
   pared poke stems and
   young leaves
2 tablespoons bacon
   grease or meat fat
1/2 teaspoon salt

YIELD 4 servings

*I*f you have never worked with poke, try it boiled first and then try Poke Sallet. Boiled Poke is the foundation poke recipe.

STEPS Weigh the pound of poke after you have boiled it twice. Chop or slice the poke into 1/2-inch pieces. In a skillet over medium heat, melt the bacon grease and add the poke and salt. Simmer for 10 to 15 minutes, or until the poke is "fried down" and tender.

HEALTHY CHOICE ALTERNATIVE Omit the bacon grease and steam the poke. Serve with a light sauce.

Serve with slices of hard-boiled egg, allowing about one egg per serving, or with Deviled Eggs, Tomato Gravy, Cornmeal Gravy, or the cheese sauce I use on Saucy Macaroni and Cheese (page 157).

Poke Sallet
(Poke Frittata)

DIFFICULTY Moderate. With seven ingredients, this recipe is moderate in difficulty.

I may be the only mountain cook who calls this a frittata, but it reminds me of one. The poke is more flavorful and less watery than zucchini. The mixture of poke, eggs, salt, and pepper is pleasing with or without the optional cheese.

When we talk about poke sallet or poke salad we are not talking about a cold salad. We do not eat raw poke, and we don't serve it cold. We serve poke hot after parboiling it two or three times in fresh water, and then cooking it until tender.

STEPS Select a 10-inch skillet with a cover. Measure the poke after you have boiled it twice as I direct above under Prepared Poke. Chop or slice the poke into ½-inch pieces. In a skillet over medium heat, melt the bacon grease and add the poke. Simmer for 6 minutes.

As the poke simmers, prepare the egg mixture: Break the eggs into a bowl and whisk them together with the milk, salt, and pepper. Stir in the cheese, if using.

Pour the egg mixture over the poke. Cook 15 minutes, covered, over low heat, as you would an omelet.

Serve this with dry toast, a thick slice of country ham, or a baked sweet potato and a fried pork chop.

I hope you enjoy wild poke like so many of us do, and remember that poke is an edible poisonous plant. Do not eat the roots or berries. Do not eat the mature leaves or stems. Eat only the young stems and young leaves.

INGREDIENTS
2 cups (1 pound) pre-
    pared poke stems with
    young leaves
2 tablespoons bacon
    grease
6 eggs
½ cup milk
1 teaspoon salt
½ teaspoon pepper
1 cup (4 ounces) grated
    sharp Cheddar cheese
    (optional)

YIELD 6 servings

Green Beans: Fresh, Dried, and Pickled

IF YOU HAVE ever been to a potluck dinner and eaten slow-cooked white half-runners or shuck beans, I am sure you remember them with pleasure. Our slow-cooked, drab, olive-green beans have flavor and character. They are vastly different from the bright-green, just-blanched, almost-raw, restaurant-style green beans. I hope that when you have some beans to fix, you'll prepare one of these Highland traditions. Remember, the first step to a delectable bean dish is to start with a fresh, robust bean.

Green beans are a cornerstone of mountain cooking. In this chapter I barely scratch the surface of mountain green bean cookery, but through the recipes I present, I suggest the variety of our choices.

Some of the early history of humanity records the fact that Mesopotamians cultivated beans in the Fertile Crescent. According to Reay Tannahill's book, *Food in History*, Sumerian records show that people have been eating beans, lentils, chickpeas, millet, and barley for seven thousand years.

The method of growing beans up corn stalks was a practice of Native

Americans. On this continent dried beans were familiar to the earliest English colonists. In Boston they made Boston baked beans, and in the South they made succotash. Colonists learned to make these beans, baked or boiled with corn, from Native Americans.

After a short time in North America, the Colonists took bean seed back to Europe where the French started eating them young and green. They called them *haricots verts*. After green beans had gone back and forth across the oceans, been carried from the cradle of civilization to high culture, mountaineers ate them in abundance.

WE EAT BEANS in different stages: immature pods, mature but green, mature seeds, or dry seed. All bean plants produce various stages, which depend on the bean's age. For French-style beans, *les haricots verts*, pick the beans when they are small and before they mature. These beans are less than 1/4 inch in diameter. Here in the mountains we let our beans get thick. When the pod matures and thickens and the seed is well formed, we have our common green beans. We use green beans and mature green beans for shuck beans, our term for dried beans (which include the pod and the seed). We often let beans mature so the seed is significant and the pod is still edible. We call these shelled beans, a mixture of pods and seeds. For dried beans, we use the seed only. For these shelled beans we wait until the seed gets mature and dry, and the pod turns hard and brown. Our favorite dry beans are pinto beans.

Most beans sold today are uniform, tender, and stringless. What distinguishes our green bean cookery is the robust character of our string beans—thick, full-seeded, mottled, and meaty. Several bean varieties give the heartiness we treasure. Our most popular summer bean is the white half-runner. In addition you'll find mountain cooks treasure pink half-runners (peanut beans), white McCaslans, Kentucky wonders, white greasies, colored greasies, and other large robust string beans. Pole and wonder beans are favorites. We also like contender, Roma II, and Romano—the pole version of Roma II. In the fall join us for popular fall beans: October shellies, October reds, greasies, greasy cut shorts, or fall white half-runners.

If you are raising a garden, see Green Beans in the Mail-Order Sources. If you want to buy these beans fresh, you may have to drive to the mountains to find them. However, if you watch for them, most supermarkets occasionally sell a Kentucky wonder, white half-runner, or Tennessee pole bean.

Up and down the east coast from South Carolina to New York, gardeners and home cooks snap and string beans. Here in the mountains, more often than not, we break beans. Sure, some argue that we snap, but I'm on the side of breaking. Our traditional beans don't snap, and for some mountaineers, talking about snapping beans sounds odd.

Years ago, as well as today, mountaineers picked beans by the bushel. Then on the porch—sitting on padded rockers, a swing, bench, or hickory bark chair—they talk and break the beans. Everyone helps. When the wash tubs are full, we carry the beans to the stove. Soon hot cauldrons start to bubble. This goes on for hours, day and night, day after day. In the end, when the cooking and canning is done, we take delight in announcing to anyone that will listen the number of quart-size cans: fifty, one hundred, three hundred, or even five hundred. (Two hundred quart jars is common.) Whether the beans were broken or snapped, the jars are ready for the can house.

THE FAMILY OF a friend of mine cans about five hundred quart-size jars of beans in a good year, along with large quantities of tomatoes, tomato juice, and corn. This large family—there were twenty-one children—works together, and when the work is done, the children, some are now sixty years old with grandchildren of their own, carry off the results. These grown children may live in Michigan, Ohio, or Florida, but when there is canning to be done, they come home to the mountains. Days later they leave with cases of cans, carrying a taste of mountain cookery to their homes all over the country. What they don't carry off fills the can house, itself the size of four bedrooms. The supply of canned vegetables lasts all year and maybe part of the next. If you don't have a can house or a big family that will work all day, you can break a pound or two of beans and cook them for supper.

Mountain cooks may boil beans for two hours. Remember that the plant geneticists have not bred all the robust qualities out of our beans. After cooking beans for hours, we serve them "fresh." We also pack these beans into jars for processing—in a pressure canner for an additional twenty to forty minutes.

At serving time, if the beans were canned, we drain them and add salt pork or bacon drippings for flavor. We then cook the beans another twenty minutes or so. Do you get the picture? We cook beans for hours. The end result is an olive-brown color, a burst of flavor, a rich smoky quality, and a tender bite. In my updated recipes, I don't cook the beans quite so long. But I don't go to the other extreme and undercook them either.

You can serve beans sautéed. Sautéing green beans is a gourmet, cooking-school-trained, big-city chef's idea of good. But sautéed beans are not country cooking. Sautéed beans are almost raw, their edges tinged with high heat and a drop of flavored oil. The color is bright but the flavor is harsh. The texture is crunchy. I hope this "fad" will pass. Half-cooked, bright green beans don't cut it on my plate.

Salads
and
Vegetables

Steamed Green Beans

DIFFICULTY Easy.
Take time to break and
string some fresh beans.
Steam them and they are
ready.

*G*reen beans are a first choice, a common choice, a home-choice—a simple goodness. I recall a dinner at my sister-in-law's house in West Virginia that consisted of meat loaf, mashed potatoes, and green beans. To me, the dinner was top of the line, an example of honest comfort food. A week later while walking in an Appalachian section of Cincinnati, I noticed a storefront chalkboard advertising lunch at a small café: "Meat loaf, mashed potatoes, and green beans, $2.99." I didn't eat at the café but recalled my sister-in-law's dinner, complete with hot dinner rolls and a dessert of lemon pound cake.

INGREDIENTS
2 pounds robust green
  beans
Water

YIELD 8 servings

STEPS Wash the beans. Remove the stems and tips. Pull the strings from both spines, and break the beans into 2-inch lengths. Wash the beans again.

Dump the beans in a steamer, and add water as needed. Bring to a boil, steaming 8 to 12 minutes, or until the beans are tender, not crunchy.

HEALTHY CHOICE ALTERNATIVE One-half cup of steamed green beans has about 25 calories and 2 grams of dietary fiber.

The next time your family comes home, treat them to tradition and prepare green beans, mashed potatoes, brown gravy, and meat loaf—common food that we call home cooking.

Green Bean Finishing Touches

When I cook for guests or take beans to a community supper, I am inclined to add a few finishing touches and a few calories. Toasted, slivered hickory nuts, pecans, beechnuts, or black walnuts are a first choice. So too are chopped hard salami, ham, or crushed cooked bacon. I like to add grated cheese, flavored sour cream, or a mornay sauce.

With these garnishes I am careful to add enough salt and pepper, and to toss the beans with a choice of butter or lemon juice, mint, basil, caraway, parsley, dill, garlic, onion, savory, and thyme. These additions distinguish your cooking!

Boiled Green Beans

*B*eing the lazy and health-conscious mountain gourmet that I am, I may simply boil green beans in water for 7 to 10 minutes and serve them, adding nothing. I hope you'll agree that fresh-picked, old-variety, garden-fresh beans are substantial and flavorful. Remember, more robust, mature beans need longer cooking. I suggest a relatively short cooking time, far less than the two to three hours often allowed. In ten or twelve minutes most beans will get tender, and less cooking preserves nutrients and vitamins.

STEPS Wash the beans, removing the stems and tips. Pull the strings from both spines, and break the beans into 2-inch lengths.

In a large pot, bring the water to a boil, and add the salt and beans. The water should cover the beans. Return to a boil, reduce the heat, and simmer for 7 to 12 minutes, or until the beans are tender, not crunchy. Drain and serve hot.

HEALTHY CHOICE ALTERNATIVE Boil without the salt and offer salt at the table. Even when you serve beans from a canning jar with a little bacon grease, they are a healthy vegetable.

Serve for lunch or dinner with Country-Fried Steak and Mashed Potatoes, or Oven-Fried Chicken, Baked Potatoes, and Angel Biscuits.

DIFFICULTY Easy. Take the time to sit down, relax, and break, string, and remove the ends from your fresh beans. Talk. Listen to music. Watch the news. Even though breaking the beans takes time, preparing this dish—boiling beans in salted water—is easy.

INGREDIENTS
2 pounds fresh robust
   green beans
8 cups water
2 teaspoons salt

YIELD 8 servings

Cumberland Plateau Green Beans with Bacon

*T*he Cumberland Plateau forms the southwestern part of the Appalachian Mountains, and it includes mountains in West Virginia, Virginia, Kentucky, and Tennessee. The Cumberland Gap cuts the plateau through the center. Sometimes called the Cumberland Mountains, the term *plateau* is much more descriptive of this region. In some places the plateau breaks like a wall into the Appalachian Valley.

The first Kentucky cookbook, *The Kentucky Housewife*, by Lettice Bryan and dated 1839, offers many recipes for green beans. The cookbook includes stewed green beans, French beans, and common snap or bunch beans. The directions I give below are quite similar to directions given by Bryan for common

DIFFICULTY Moderate. With six ingredients and two cooking steps, this recipe is moderate in difficulty.

beans: ". . . gather in the morning; pick young and tender; draw off the strings; soak in fresh water; add bacon and salt; and boil until tender."

With this recipe I go a bit further. To the bacon and salt I add pepper and onion. This combination is a common Cumberland Plateau favorite. In the tradition of Lettice Bryan, try making this recipe with our favorite summer bean, the white half-runner.

INGREDIENTS
2 pounds white half-runner beans or pole beans, fresh or frozen
2 ounces bacon, chopped into 1/4-inch pieces
1 cup sliced onion
1/2 cup water
1 teaspoon salt
1/4 teaspoon ground pepper

YIELD 8 servings

STEPS If using fresh beans, break, string, and remove the ends from the beans.

Select a large covered saucepan. In the bottom of the pan, fry the bacon. Pour off most of the fat, and add the beans, onion, water, salt, and pepper. Bring to a boil and reduce the heat so that the beans braise. Cover and simmer for 25 minutes, or until the beans are tender and have split open. Add water as needed, but when the beans are ready, almost all the water should have evaporated. Stir and serve.

HEALTHY CHOICE ALTERNATIVE Without the bacon, you won't have Green Beans with Bacon, and you'll miss out on that touch of pork that distinguishes our cooking. This recipe is too good to change!

Served for dinner or supper, the following is a complete meal. Cut fresh sweet white onions and garden-grown red tomatoes into your bowl of beans. Stir them up, add some extra hot pot likker and a wedge of Buttermilk Corn Bread. Eat until you are happy, and then serve another bowl of beans and a glass of buttermilk.

Green Beans and New Potatoes
(Creamed Beans)

DIFFICULTY Moderate. With seven ingredients and two steps, this dish is moderate in difficulty.

INGREDIENTS

FOR THE BRAISED VEGETABLES
4 ounces salt pork
3 medium (1 1/2 pounds) new potatoes
(cont.)

or her stewed beans—we would call these creamed—Lettice Bryan in *The Kentucky Housewife* says, "cover the beans with water; add salt and bacon; cook until they are nearly dry; add butter, flour, pepper, and rich sweet cream; cook again until thick; serve warm."

The cream sauce makes this a glorious combination of beans and potatoes. The sauce should be runny, like pancake batter.

STEPS Cut the salt pork into strips. Clean and peel the potatoes and dice them into pieces the same thickness as the green beans. Wash and trim the ends from the beans, and break them into 1-inch pieces.

In a large saucepan, sauté the salt pork for about 5 minutes. Add enough water to measure 3/4 inch deep. Add the potatoes and beans, and simmer, covered, for 15 minutes. Lift the cooked vegetables into a serving bowl and discard the salt pork. Reserve the cooking liquid.

To the water left in the saucepan, add enough milk to make 2 cups. Whisk in the instant flour, salt, and pepper, and boil 1 minute. Return the vegetables to the saucepan and stir.

HEALTHY CHOICE ALTERNATIVE Cut the salt pork and rely on the sauce for flavor. To add flavor to the sauce, stir in parsley, garlic, or chives.

Serve these with Roast Pork and Stuffed Apples or Barbecued Pork Chops.

1 1/2 pounds green beans

FOR THE SAUCE

2 cups milk, or as needed
1/4 cup instant flour
1 1/2 teaspoons salt
1/2 teaspoon pepper

YIELD 6 servings

Green Beans, Potatoes, and Onions

What a meal: green beans, potatoes, onions, and cured pork. Old recipes call for the use of fried meat grease, bacon grease, lard, or Canadian bacon. I suggest salt pork, but you could also use smoked ham hocks or pork tips.

STEPS Cut the salt pork into thin strips. Wash the potatoes—no need to peel them—and cut each into 6 wedges. Wash and trim the ends from the beans, leaving them whole. Peel and slice the onion.

In a large saucepan, sauté the salt pork for about 5 minutes. Add enough of the water to measure 3/4-inch deep. Add the potatoes and beans, and simmer, covered, for 20 minutes. Add the onions and simmer an additional 10 minutes.

Arrange the cooked vegetables on a platter with the beans in the center, the potatoes around the edge, and the onions on top. Discard the salt pork (or serve the dish with the ham hocks or Canadian bacon, if using). Cover the cooked vegetables with plastic wrap and warm in the microwave oven as needed.

Measure 1 cup of reserved liquid, and whisk in the flour, salt, and pepper. Boil for 1 minute. To serve, spoon the sauce over the vegetables. This topping will be as thick as applesauce.

HEALTHY CHOICE ALTERNATIVE Cut the salt pork, and rely on the sauce for flavor. To add flavor, stir in parsley, garlic, or chives.

Serve for Sunday dinner with roast chicken, duck, or goose.

DIFFICULTY Moderate. With eight ingredients and two steps, this dish is moderate in difficulty.

INGREDIENTS

FOR THE BRAISED VEGETABLES

4 ounces salt pork
2 cups water
3 medium (1 1/2 pounds) potatoes
1 1/2 pounds green beans
1 medium (3/4 pound) sweet onion

FOR THE TOPPING

1 cup vegetable broth, reserved from above
1/4 cup instant flour
1 teaspoon salt
1/4 teaspoon pepper

YIELD 6 servings

DIFFICULTY Moderate. It takes me about 25 minutes to break and string the white half-runners. Then you fry the bacon, steam the beans, and prepare the dressing. You can prepare the beans and dressing ahead and then reheat them.

Dilled Green Beans with Black Walnuts
(Green Beans with Hot Vinaigrette)

*M*ountaineers cook with grease. For example, we usually cook white half-runners, our favorite garden green bean, with water and bacon grease, fat back, or salt pork. In the recipe that follows, I have combined fat-free steamed beans with bacon, bacon grease, dill, and a nutty vinaigrette.

INGREDIENTS

1 1/2 pounds white half-
  runners, fall greasies,
  or any fresh green
  bean
8 strips (1/2 pound)
  bacon
1/4 cup vinegar
3 tablespoons water
2 teaspoons sugar
1 teaspoon salt
1/2 teaspoon ground
  pepper
1/2 cup chopped black
  walnuts, beechnuts, or
  hickory nuts
1/4 cup chopped fresh
  dill

YIELD 6 servings

STEPS Wash, break, and string the green beans. Remove the tips and ends.

In a large pot, steam the green beans for 8 to 12 minutes, depending on size. As the beans steam, fry the bacon in a large skillet. Lift the bacon from the pan and drain on paper towels, reserving the bacon grease. To the grease in the skillet, add the vinegar, water, sugar, salt, and pepper. Bring to a boil and stir. Mince half of the bacon and return it to the skillet.

Grind about 1/4 cup of the nuts, and add them to the skillet. Add the dill, and stir. Add the green beans, bring the mixture to a boil, and stir. Pour into a serving bowl and toss. Garnish with the remaining bacon and nuts.

HEALTHY CHOICE ALTERNATIVES Replace the bacon grease with 2 tablespoons of canola oil. Use the bacon. Second, pour most of the bacon grease out of the skillet, and make the dressing in the bacon grease and drippings that remain.

Serve these beans with roast turkey, pork, or beef, or with Sautéed Trout.

DIFFICULTY Easy. With five ingredients and one cooking step, this recipe is easy.

INGREDIENTS

3 ounces salt pork
3 to 4 cups dried shuck
  beans
1/2 teaspoon salt
(cont.)

Shuck Beans

*W*hile beans used to be dried for winter as an essential food, today we crave the intense flavor present in Shuck Beans, the cooked dried bean. Order shuck beans from Floyd Skean's Happy Mart, listed in the Mail-Order Sources.

STEPS Wash the beans, and discard any that are black or look bad. Cover with water and soak overnight.

Remove the rind and dice the salt pork into 1/4-inch pieces. In a saucepan, sauté the salt pork until it has browned. Add the beans, salt, and pepper. Cover with water and simmer 2 to 6 hours, adding water as needed. Cooking time depends on the size, maturity, and variety of the beans. Use low heat and cover the pot.

When the beans are tender (mash a bean seed to check), remove the lid, increase the heat to medium, and continue to cook until the water has thickened. The remaining pot likker is a full-flavored sauce that you serve with the beans.

HEALTHY CHOICE ALTERNATIVE In this recipe I have cut the salt pork and salt to a minimum, but you can cut them out altogether.

For a healthy meal, serve these beans and pot likker with Country Corn Bread, sliced raw onions, and buttermilk.

¹/₈ teaspoon pepper
Water, as needed

YIELD 4 to 6 servings

■ ■

Shuck Beans for Intense Flavor

In *Shuck Beans, Stack Cakes, and Honest Fried Chicken* by Ronni Lundy, country star Dwight Yoakam recalls those childhood memories. "My granny (Earlene Tibbs) would come to the back porch with a big laundry basket full of beans. We would sit down and we would snap 'em, and string 'em and crack 'em and throw 'em in the pan. We would sit there snapping and stringing for the whole afternoon."

On other occasions Dwight and his mother, Ruth Ann Rankey, would remove the bean strings and then string the beans on a thread for drying. In the winter, they used the beans to make shuck beans.

Whether you know it from a song or learned it from conversations in your garden, this dried bean preparation has many names: shuck beans, shucky beans, leather breeches, or leather britches. When the seed is large but the green pod is still good to eat, mountaineers preserve beans by drying them. Like apples, you can dry beans in a food dryer, on screens in the sun, in a warm smokehouse, a kiln, or in the attic hanging from long strings. Drying is the healthy and old-fashioned method of preserving without chemicals.

While you can string beans of any maturity, we prefer to use well filled, mature beans. After cleaning the beans, break off the ends and pull the strings from both spines of the bean. With the strings removed, you are ready to dry the beans.

The traditional method is to thread the beans on a string and hang them up, sort of like stringing popcorn to decorate a Christmas tree. To string beans, thread a large needle with heavy string and run the needle and thread through the center of the beans. When you have filled a string—anywhere from two to five feet long—tie a loop at one end of the string and hang it from a nail to dry.

Some hang their beans in the sun on the side of an outbuilding. Others say sun-drying changes the flavor, and use an upstairs hallway, rafters in the attic, or planks in the barn.

When the beans are dry enough to "crimp or rattle," store them in paper bags or jars. You may freeze them or let them hang on the string, but as any old timer will tell you, they should not be allowed to get damp with rain or fog, and they must be protected from insects and mice.

While it takes a long time to grow, string, and dry beans, preparing a pot of cooked shuck beans is simple.

■ ■

Pickled Beans
Dilly Beans

DIFFICULTY Easy. With four ingredients, this recipe is easy. You can prepare the beans several days in advance.

INGREDIENTS
1 pound green beans
2 cups water, plus more as needed
2 tablespoons pickling salt
2 tablespoons white vinegar

YIELD 8 servings

*L*ike my Corn Relish, my goal for this recipe is not to store bushels of beans or to make a year's supply, but rather to prepare enough for one gathering.

STEPS Remove the ends, strings, and brown spots from the beans. (You can break the beans, but as a pickle or garnish, I like to serve the beans whole.) Wash the beans thoroughly.

In a saucepan, add the beans and enough water to cover. Boil for 10 minutes, or until tender. Drain and cool. Place the beans in a crock or glass bowl.

Bring 2 cups of water, the pickling salt, and vinegar to a boil. Pour this pickling solution, this brine, over the beans. Store, covered, in glass or china for an hour, a day, or more, and serve. These beans with the brine will store, covered, in a cool area for several months.

Serve these beans chilled, as appetizers or garnish, as an accompaniment to

HEARTY
Cooking
COUNTRY

Jellied Pig's Feet, or with hot foods such as Southern Fried Chicken and Potato Cakes.

Dilly Beans To the above recipe, when you bring the water to a boil, add ½ cup minced fresh dill, 3 cloves minced garlic, ½ teaspoon red pepper flakes, and ¼ teaspoon dry mustard.

Cushaw Squash: Soups, Pies, and More

IN EARLY JULY we see cushaw vines. On small farms, the long vines with high-growing leaves seem to cover everything in sight. Then, starting in mid-September you can see pickup trucks loaded with green-striped squash—farmers moving their cushaws to market. A month later, at the foot of fodder shocks (gathered corn stalks) and mixed with pumpkins and gourds, this squash appears as an ornament.

Cushaw squash is a large, smooth, and hard-skinned winter squash. Here in the mountains we have two kinds of cushaw: green cushaw and white cushaw.

Native Americans have cultivated cushaw squash, along with about twenty-five other squashes, for 9,000 years. In addition to being used for food, cushaw squash has other applications. The squash grows to a length of thirty inches and, when it dries out, after about three years of storage in a dry area, it has a strong and thick skin. When the Spanish explorer Hernando DeSoto visited our mountains in 1540, he found the Native Americans using the dried shells of large squash to carry water and hold dried beans. They used small winter squash as dippers.

Cushaw is not very different from other winter squashes, but its size—and the fact that it grows prolifically in our hot, humid climate—have made it our dominant squash. We make all kinds of dishes with these squash, and when you cut into a twenty-pound cushaw, you'll want to have a number of recipes ready. An open cushaw will store for a week or so in a cool cellar or several weeks in the refrigerator—if you have room. Based on the size of the recipes in this chapter, one large cushaw will yield five to ten different dishes.

Cushaw is a very large, mild-flavored, hearty winter squash. When baked, the flesh is meaty and tender, not as dense as a turban or butternut squash, but not as loose as spaghetti squash.

Green cushaw squashes—actually green-and-white striped—are shaped like yellow crook-neck squash, and they range in weight from ten to twenty-five pounds and in length from twelve to thirty inches. One twenty-pound squash could easily yield enough for sixty servings of baked squash. White cushaw is larger, growing to weigh twenty to thirty pounds. White cushaw is shaped like a pumpkin except more squat. Both green and white cushaw have hard shells. They may have some bumps or ridges near the stem, but most are completely smooth. To purchase seed or squash see Floyd Skean's Happy Mart in the list of Mail-Order Sources.

Consider serving a complete cushaw dinner: For a first course serve Cushaw Soup along with Cushaw Bread and cream cheese with Pear Honey. Follow this with a main course of Savory Cushaw Pie and a cushaw cavity filled with goulash. For dessert serve Cushaw Cake topped with a scoop of vanilla ice cream and Hot Sorghum.

Baked Cushaw

I offer three baked cushaw recipes. Each is a bit more complicated than the one before it. The first recipe emphasizes the natural sweet nutty nature of cushaw, the second adds butter and sorghum, and finally I sweeten the squash with a pear sauce.

I enjoy making this Baked Cushaw because the recipe is easy to prepare, serve, and eat. It allows you to taste the hearty flavor and texture of the squash. Serve this as you would any side dish or vegetable.

DIFFICULTY Very Easy. Once you have cut the squash into pieces, baking with these four ingredients is very easy.

INGREDIENTS
1/4 of a cushaw, or about 5 pounds squash
1 teaspoon salt
1/2 teaspoon paprika
1/4 teaspoon pepper

YIELD 12 servings

STEPS Preheat the oven to 450°F. Wash the squash. Cut about 4 inches off the large end of the cushaw, and remove the seeds. Cover the squash with aluminum foil, place on a large, oven-proof dinner plate, and bake 20 minutes. Reduce the heat to 350°F, and bake an additional 50 minutes. Scoop the squash into a serving bowl, and discard the skin. Sprinkle with the salt, paprika, and pepper.

Baked Cushaw with Sorghum

𝒯he butter and sorghum I use in this recipe make the squash rich and sweet. The squash will absorb much of the sorghum and butter, but what remains in the dish you can spoon over the top.

STEPS Preheat the oven to 450°F. Wash the squash. Cut the cushaw into large serving-size pieces, 2 to 3 inches in size. You do not need to remove the peel. In a 13x9x2-inch casserole dish, arrange the squash pieces with the peeling to the side, not down. Pour the sorghum over the top, and dot with the butter.

Cover with aluminum foil and bake 20 minutes. Reduce the heat to 350°F, and bake an additional 50 minutes. Serve directly from the oven, spooning the sorghum liquid over the squash.

HEALTHY CHOICE ALTERNATIVE Omit the butter.

Spoon the sorghum over the squash. Serve as you would any side dish or vegetable.

DIFFICULTY Easy. Once you have cut the squash into pieces, baking these three ingredients is easy.

INGREDIENTS
$1/5$ of a cushaw, or about 4 pounds squash
$1/3$ cup 100% pure sweet sorghum
$1/3$ cup butter

YIELD 12 servings

Baked Cushaw with Cinnamon-Sorghum Sauce

𝒯he butter, sorghum, cinnamon, and salt I use in this recipe give the squash some extra flavor and richness.

STEPS Preheat the oven to 450°F. Wash the squash, and cut the cushaw into large pieces, 2 to 3 inches in size. You do not need to remove the peel. In a 13x9x2-inch casserole dish, arrange the squash and pear. Place the squash peeling to the side, not down. Combine and then spread the water, sorghum, butter, cinnamon sugar, and salt over the squash and pear.

Cover with aluminum foil, and bake 20 minutes. Reduce the heat to 350°F, and bake an additional 50 minutes.

Now thicken the sauce. Remove the squash from the oven, and pour the liquid into a saucepan. For each cup of liquid, use two tablespoons of instant flour. Sprinkle the flour over the liquid, and whisk it in. Boil for 1 minute. If the sauce is not thick enough, add more flour, and whisk again.

HEALTHY CHOICE ALTERNATIVE Omit the butter.

Spoon the sauce over the squash. Serve as you would any side dish or vegetable.

DIFFICULTY Moderate. Once you have cut the squash into pieces, baking these eight ingredients is easy, but it requires more than an hour. The addition of cooked sauce makes the recipe moderate in difficulty.

INGREDIENTS
$1/5$ of a cushaw, or about 4 pounds squash
1 cup peeled and diced pear
$1/3$ cup water
$1/3$ cup 100% sweet sorghum
$1/3$ cup butter
2 teaspoons cinnamon sugar
$1/2$ teaspoon salt
2 tablespoons instant flour, or more as needed

YIELD 12 servings

Salads
and
Vegetables

Squash and Potato Soup
(Cushaw Soup)

DIFFICULTY Moderate.
With six ingredients and
using a food processor,
this recipe is moderate in
difficulty.

*O*f the cushaw recipes I made during the early 1990s, when my children were teenagers, this one was most popular. I make this soup with any squash—cushaw, acorn, or butternut. Because of its large size, cushaw is the easiest to work with. Because of its flavor, butternut tastes the best. If using butternut or acorn squash, cook them before removing the hard peeling.

Like other cooks, I have made squash soup with pumpkin seasonings—cinnamon, nutmeg, and allspice—but I prefer the more gentle flavors of squash, chicken, salt, and cream.

INGREDIENTS
5 cups or 1 1/2 pounds peeled fresh winter squash
1 medium (8 ounce) potato
1 1/2 cups water
1 1/2 cups chicken broth
1 teaspoon salt
1/3 cup heavy cream

YIELD 6 servings

STEPS Peel and cube the squash and potato. Combine the water and broth. In a medium saucepan, combine half the broth mixture, the salt, squash, and potato. Cover, and simmer/braise for 45 minutes.

Lift the squash and potatoes into a food processor. Add 1 cup of the broth to the food processor. Process until smooth. Return the puree to the saucepan over medium heat. Adjust the thickness of the soup with the remaining broth mixture, adding enough to give the thickness you like—I like it thicker than cream but not as thick as pancake batter. Stir in the cream before serving.

HEALTHY CHOICE ALTERNATIVE Omit the cream and increase the amount of potato to 12 ounces. To reduce salt, make your own chicken broth.

For a light lunch, serve this soup with buttered French bread or Highlander Rolls. Serve with crackers as a first course for dinner, garnished with ribbons of sour cream and cubes of plain flan.

Cushaw Pie

DIFFICULTY Moderate.
With ten ingredients, this
recipe is moderate in difficulty. To simplify, use 2
teaspoons of pumpkin pie
spice in place of the salt
and other spices. Serve
the pie with or without
the garnish.

*M*ake these two cushaw pies in October and November, when cushaw squash are in season and when you can buy candy corn or mallow pumpkins. Because cushaw is soft and light, this pie is delicate. You won't be knocked over by spices or sweetness.

STEPS Bake or boil the cushaw. You can follow my directions for Baked Cushaw, omitting the salt and spices, or you can boil the cushaw 25 minutes until tender.

HEARTY
Cooking
COUNTRY

Prepare the pie: Preheat the oven to 350°F. Place the cushaw, cream, brown sugar, eggs, salt, cinnamon, ginger, nutmeg, and allspice in a food processor, and blend until smooth. Pour into the pie shell and bake for 45 minutes, or until a toothpick inserted into the center comes out clean. Cool and chill.

For the garnish: Garnish with one recipe of Country Whipped Cream: Scoop the whipped cream into a pastry bag equipped with a star tip, and pipe the cream onto the pie, forming eight large stars or swirls. Top each star with a mallow pumpkin or two pieces of candy corn.

HEALTHY CHOICE ALTERNATIVE Replace the cream with 2% milk or evaporated skim milk. Omit 1 egg yolk.

Serve this pie for dessert with coffee or tea.

Savory Cushaw Pie

*T*he Cushaw Pie above is a sweet dessert. This savory pie is light, but not sweet. I serve it as a dinner vegetable or as the centerpiece of a light luncheon, but every so often one of my guests will say, "This pie is like dessert." If you like the idea of eating a light squash pie for dessert, try this. Top with a dollop of Country Whipped Cream (page 316) made without the sugar.

STEPS Place the oven rack at its lowest level, and preheat the oven to 450°F.

In a food processor, combine the cushaw, milk, eggs, sugar, salt, cinnamon, ginger, and allspice, and blend for two 3-second bursts, or until fully mixed. The pieces of squash should be the size of raisins. Pour into the pie shell, and bake for 20 minutes. Reduce the heat to 350°F and bake an additional 30 minutes, or until a toothpick inserted into the center comes out clean.

HEALTHY CHOICE ALTERNATIVE Replace the milk with skim milk. Omit 1 egg.

Serve warm, as you would a quiche. Serve as a side-dish vegetable. Serve with a green salad for lunch.

INGREDIENTS

FOR THE PIE
2 cups cooked cushaw
1 cup cream
1 cup brown sugar
3 eggs
1/2 teaspoon salt
1/2 teaspoon cinnamon
1/4 teaspoon ginger
1/4 teaspoon nutmeg
1/8 teaspoon allspice
1 9-inch Pie Pastry
  Shell (page 275)

FOR THE GARNISH
1 recipe Country
  Whipped Cream
  (page 316)
8 mallow pumpkins or
  16 pieces of candy
  corn

YIELD 8 servings

DIFFICULTY Moderate. With nine ingredients, this pie is moderate in difficulty. To simplify, use 1 1/2 teaspoons of pumpkin pie spice in place of the salt and spices. Serve the pie with or without the garnish.

INGREDIENTS
2 1/4 cups cooked cushaw
  or pumpkin
3/4 cup milk
3 eggs
1/4 cup sugar
1/2 teaspoon salt
1/2 teaspoon cinnamon
1/4 teaspoon ginger
1/8 teaspoon allspice
1 9-inch Pie Pastry
  Shell (page 275)

YIELD 8 servings

Salads
and
Vegetables

Cushaw Bread
Cushaw Cake

DIFFICULTY Moderate. With eight ingredients and an hour of baking, this recipe is moderate in difficulty.

INGREDIENTS
4 cups all-purpose flour
1 tablespoon baking powder
1 tablespoon cinnamon
1½ teaspoons salt
4 eggs
2⅔ cups sugar
1⅓ cups vegetable oil
3 cups grated raw cushaw

YIELD 2 loaves, or 15 servings

*M*ake this moist, melt-in-your-mouth, sweet, cake-like quick bread with green cushaw, white cushaw, zucchini, pumpkin, or any other squash.

STEPS Preheat the oven to 350°F. Grease two 9x4x2-inch loaf pans.

In a large mixing bowl, whisk together the flour, baking powder, cinnamon, and salt. In a second bowl, beat the eggs and then beat in the sugar and oil. Stir in the squash and then the dry ingredients. Mix the batter until barely moistened.

Pour and scrape into the prepared pans. Bake for 1 hour, or until a toothpick inserted into the center comes out clean. The bread should crack in the center and be well-browned on top. Cool for 15 minutes in the pan, and then turn onto a cooling rack. Cool completely, about 2 hours, and then slice or store.

HEALTHY CHOICE ALTERNATIVE Omit the egg yolks and reduce the oil to 1 cup. The squash gives this recipe plenty of moisture.

Serve with cream cheese and blackberry preserves.

Cushaw Cake From the above recipe, omit the salt. Bake for 35 to 40 minutes in three 9-inch round cake pans. Cool completely. Spread the layers with Apple Butter (page 312) and the top and sides with Cream Cheese Frosting (page 271). Or, instead of frosting, serve with a dollop of Country Whipped Cream (page 316). Serve at room temperature.

Turnips, Greens, and Cabbage

Turnips

During November, if you drive into the hollows or out on the mountain ridges where country people live, you'll see bright green patches of turnips. With the sun low in the sky, the turnip leaves glisten against fading brown gardens, catching your eye. If you live north of the Smoky Mountains, they are common; south of the Smoky Mountains you'll more likely see the blue hew of collards. You can use collard and turnip greens interchangeably, but Highlanders who use one don't use the other.

Below the two-foot-tall green tops of turnips, you'll find masses of thick, fleshy turnip roots. We grow varieties such as purple top and Tokyo cross. While we often eat just the greens, we also eat the fleshy root. When selecting turnips from your garden or your produce market, remember that young turnips are sweet and tender, and old turnips are woody and sharp. If mid-January arrives and you still have turnips tucked away in a cellar or back closet, you'd better check on them. They may be growing leaves and stems, and you will need to start cooking them.

If you pull turnips from the ground when they are young and tender, you do not need to peel them. If the skin is thick and has a hard subsurface, however, the turnips must be peeled thickly. The cooking times I give are for mature turnips. Consider the classic choices: raw turnips and baked turnips.

If you serve them peeled, young, and fresh, raw turnips taste sweet and juicy. I like to serve them on a vegetable tray with raw celery, broccoli, carrots, green peppers, and mushrooms. If you are baking a beef or pork roast or a whole turkey, chicken, or duck, drop peeled turnips into the pan an hour before you finish the roasting.

Sweet Boiled Turnips
Savory Boiled Turnips

*B*oiled turnips are a simple pleasure. When I ask my mountain friends about turnips, they talk of boiling them and flavoring them two ways: with fresh butter and sugar or with salt, pepper, and bacon grease.

I offer two easy-to-prepare boiled turnip recipes because this vegetable is a significant part of our food culture. The sweet turnips are quite sweet, and the savory turnips are salty and well peppered.

STEPS Wash and peel the turnips. Slice enough 1/4-inch slices to equal 2 1/2 cups of turnips.

In a large pot, add the turnips with enough water to cover. Bring to a boil, reduce the heat, and simmer 8 to 10 minutes. Drain. Dot with butter and sprinkle with sugar.

HEALTHY CHOICE ALTERNATIVE Omit the butter.

Serve these with a Baked Potato and Pork Barbecue, or with a standing rib roast or baked goose.

Savory Boiled Turnips
In place of the butter and sugar, season the turnips with 1 tablespoon bacon grease, 1/2 teaspoon salt, and 1/4 teaspoon pepper.

DIFFICULTY Easy. With four ingredients, and one step, this recipe is easy.

INGREDIENTS
1 pound fresh young turnips
Water as needed
1 tablespoon unsalted butter
2 teaspoons sugar

YIELD 4 servings

Salads and Vegetables

Mashed Turnips and Potatoes

DIFFICULTY Moderate.
With seven ingredients
and two steps, this recipe
is moderate in difficulty.

INGREDIENTS
3 cups (1 pound)
   turnips
2 cups (2/3 pound)
   potatoes
Water as needed
1/3 cup milk
1/3 cup heavy cream
1 teaspoon salt
1/2 teaspoon pepper

YIELD 6 servings

*C*ook your turnip greens in one pot and your turnip roots in another. The potatoes and cream I add to this dish give a fullness that almost overpowers the turnips, making this an ideal combination. Serve it as a means of introducing turnips to the uninitiated.

STEPS Wash, peel, and slice the turnips and potatoes.

In a large pot, cover the turnips and potatoes with water, as needed, and bring to a boil. Reduce the heat and simmer 10 minutes, or until the potatoes and turnips are tender. (If you slice them the same thickness, they will cook in the same amount of time.) Drain.

In the bowl of a food processor, combine the turnips, potatoes, milk, cream, salt, and pepper. Process about 30 seconds, or until the mixture resembles applesauce.

HEALTHY CHOICE ALTERNATIVE Replace the heavy cream with an equal amount of milk or water.

Serve with a pat of butter in the center of each serving.

Scalloped Turnips

DIFFICULTY Difficult.
With ten ingredients, two
cooking steps, and 30
minutes of baking, this
recipe is difficult.

INGREDIENTS
1 1/2 pounds fresh young
   turnips
1 medium (6 ounce)
   potato
8 cups water
(*cont.*)

*F*or this recipe, I was inspired by *The Illustrated Encyclopedia of American Cooking* and Richard Olney's *Simple French Food*. You'll be drawn to this turnip dish—this *aux gratin de navets*, as the French might call it—because of the white sauce and the aroma of Parmesan cheese. You'll find that the turnips take on the flavor of the cheese and the texture of the potatoes. Broiled so that the top is a spread of gold dotted with brown spots, it appeals to the eye as well as the nose. And, when you taste these, the turnips are a mild counterpoint to the full and flavorful sauce.

STEPS Wash and peel the turnips. Slicing them in 1/4- to 1/8-inch slices should yield about 5 cups. Peel, slice, and dice the potato.

Preheat the oven to 350°F. In a large pot, bring the water to a boil, add the turnips and potatoes, and return to a boil. Reduce the heat, and simmer 3 minutes. Drain and set the vegetables aside.

In a large saucepan over medium heat, melt the butter and stir in the flour. Boil for 1 minute. Whisk in the salt, paprika, pepper, and milk. Boil again for 1 minute. Stir in $^1/_2$ cup Parmesan cheese.

In a 9-inch round casserole dish, arrange the turnips and potato, and pour the cheese sauce over them, smoothing the sauce with the back of a spoon.

Crush the saltine crackers, and mix them with the 3 tablespoons of Parmesan cheese. Spread over the mixture in the casserole. Bake for 30 minutes, or until the casserole bubbles in the center. Broil briefly to brown the top.

HEALTHY CHOICE ALTERNATIVES First, try omitting all or half of the Parmesan cheese and adding 1 teaspoon of salt. Second, omit the butter and make the white sauce with instant flour.

Serve these turnips with Highlander Rolls and Fried Pork Chops.

FOR THE CHEESE SAUCE
$^1/_4$ cup butter
$^1/_4$ cup all-purpose flour
$^3/_4$ teaspoon salt
$^1/_2$ teaspoon paprika
$^1/_2$ teaspoon pepper
2 cups milk
$^1/_2$ cup Parmesan cheese

FOR THE TOPPING
4 saltine crackers
3 tablespoons Parmesan cheese

YIELD 8 servings

Turnip Greens
Kale, Collards, Mustard Greens, and Greens and Dumplings

I can't understand why so many chefs serve undercooked, almost raw vegetables. Yes, the vegetables are bright in color, but they are also tough to chew, hard to digest, and low in flavor. When it comes to greens, mountain cooks appreciate the importance of long cooking. We take the time to cook our less tender greens for an hour or more. The result is a muddy-green, drab olive or almost brown color, full taste, easy chewing, and complete digestion. Slow-cooked greens are an example of simple mountain cooking that takes a little patience.

Greens common to the Appalachian Mountains include turnips, collards, and mustard. Old-timers often yearn for poke, spinach, kale, dock, rape, beet, watercress, and chickentoe greens. You can prepare any of these greens as follows, except that the tender greens—poke, spinach, beet, watercress, and chickentoe—require less cooking.

When are your greens cooked? Cook them until the thickest veins or stems are tender, the mass cuts with the side of a fork, the leaves are mush, and the pot likker (the broth) is full of flavor. To me, the best greens cook for more than an hour, and longer cooking thickens the broth. Because the greens give off water, don't start with more water than I recommend.

Properly cut salt pork adds flavor to greens and other vegetables. When you cut the strips of salt pork, do not cut through the rind. Leave the slices attached.

DIFFICULTY Moderate. With five ingredients and $1^1/_2$ hours of simmering, this vegetable recipe is moderate in difficulty. For me, the tedious part of fixing greens is washing and stripping the leaves, which takes about 12 minutes.

Salads and Vegetables

Start at the top and cut to the skin. Then cut another strip, and continue this across the block. If you want more exposed surface, turn the pork and cut across the strips to dice it, leaving you with slices or dice attached to the rind and easy to lift from the pan.

For heightened flavor and sweetness, pick turnip greens after the first frost.

INGREDIENTS

1 1/2 pounds fresh turnip
    greens
2 cups water
1 ounce salt pork
1/2 teaspoon salt
1/2 teaspoon pepper

YIELD 4 servings

STEPS Wash the greens leaf by leaf, and remove the thick stems. Wash again in a pot of water. With the stems removed, you'll have about 1 1/4 pounds of greens. Gather the leaves into small bunches and, using a chef's knife, slice them into 1/2-inch-wide strips.

In a saucepan, place the greens, water, salt pork, salt, and pepper. Bring to a boil, reduce the heat, and simmer, covered, for 1 1/2 hours.

Lift the greens from the pot with a pair of tongs. Let the pot likker run off, and serve the greens with vinegar. For a smoother texture and easier eating, I like to drop most of the greens into a food processor and process until the pieces are the size of a grain of corn.

HEALTHY CHOICE ALTERNATIVE Omit the pork, and flavor with a little more salt.

Follow tradition and serve these greens in cream soup bowls with a ladleful of the pot likker. Corn Sticks or Heartbeat Corn Bread, dipped or crumbled in the likker, make this a complete meal. Serve with Boiled Turnips, Mashed Turnips and Potatoes, or Scalloped Turnips.

Kale Replace the turnip greens with kale.

Collards Replace the turnip greens with collards. For heightened flavor and sweetness, pick collard greens after the first frost.

Mustard Greens Replace the turnip greens with mustard greens.

Greens and Dumplings When your greens are ready, add enough water to make 2 1/2 cups of pot likker. To this, add half a recipe of Slick Dumplings (page 26) and simmer until the dumplings are tender.

Coleslaw

THE ORIGINAL DUTCH word *koolsla* was introduced into English in about 1785, and meant "cold cabbage salad." Breaking *koolsla* into parts, *kool* meant "cabbage" and *sla* meant "salad." Today coleslaw is a hot or cold cabbage dish. When served cold, coleslaw is prepared by grating raw cabbage and mixing it with a salad dressing. James Beard's *American Cookery* points out that whatever you call it—slaw, coleslaw, *kohlslau*, or coldslaw—this dish is one of the more popular ways to use cabbage.

When I moved to the mountains twenty years ago, I ordered a hot dog with the works—it came with coleslaw, not next to it as I expected, but rather on the hot dog. Cold and oozing with mayonnaise, the coleslaw was spread over the chili, which was also part of the "works."

Making Kathy's Coleslaw is a family tradition. Kathy, my wife, started making it years ago. Our son, Brian, liked Kathy's recipe so much that when, at age thirteen, he started cooking, he debuted with coleslaw. Under Brian's hand, it did not always come out like Kathy's. I remember the time when the bowl of our food processor was in the freezer. So what did he do? He got out a chef's knife and used it to "grate" the cabbage. Even then, with thin-sliced cabbage, we liked the results, and we called it Brian's coarse coleslaw.

Here in the mountains, coleslaw is a daily food, a near-necessity, an almost-staple. To the basic recipe of grated cabbage and salad dressing, you can add stuffed olives, cut apple, celery, or grated carrots. For flavor add caraway or celery seeds, minced onion, and green pepper. If you must, add salt and sugar, but always start with a firm head of cabbage.

Some cookbooks, like some country cooks, are truly slaw-oriented. The *American Home All-Purpose Cookbook* by the staff of *American Home* lists old-fashioned cabbage slaw (made with boiled dressing), green and red cabbage slaw, harlequin slaw (made with carrots, green pepper, and radishes), ham coleslaw, blue cheese coleslaw, hot curried slaw, sauerkraut slaw, California slaw (it includes ginger and mandarin oranges), sweet-and-sour red cabbage slaw (made with bacon, brown sugar, and cornstarch), and, finally, spicy apple slaw (including apples, cinnamon, and cloves).

Salads
and
Vegetables

Kathy's Coleslaw
(Slaw)

*W*hen Kathy takes this coleslaw to a social event, people seem to buzz and talk. Later, they ask for the recipe. It is a simple, modern version of coleslaw. Cold, light, and crunchy, the salad is almost neutral in flavor—not creamy, not salty, and not sweet.

DIFFICULTY Easy. With four ingredients (two of them are prepared salad dressings) this salad is easy.

INGREDIENTS
4 to 5 cups shredded cabbage
1/4 cup mayonnaise
1/4 cup Italian-style dressing
1/2 teaspoon dried dill weed

YIELD 6 servings. For a crowd double the recipe.

STEPS In a large mixing bowl, combine the cabbage, mayonnaise, Italian dressing, and dill weed. If you are inclined to add more flavor, add 1 tablespoon of sugar and 1 teaspoon of salt. Pour and scrape into a serving bowl, and garnish with fresh dill weed and green olives. Refrigerate until ready to serve.

HEALTHY CHOICE ALTERNATIVE In place of the two salad dressings, you may substitute an equal amount of your favorite low-fat or fat-free salad dressing.

Coleslaws are picnic, barbecue, and buffet food. We serve them primarily as salads and also as you would a relish for hot dogs or hamburgers. Serve as a side dish for fried fish and chicken.

Fried Cabbage
Skillet Cabbage

*M*oving from Fried Cabbage to Skillet Cabbage to Cabbage Stew (page 87), I offer a progression of recipes from simple to more complex. Each dish represents traditional mountain cookery, but as you add ingredients, the flavor becomes fuller and more balanced. The stew draws its special flavor from the bacon.

DIFFICULTY Moderate. With six ingredients and about 20 minutes of cooking time, this recipe is moderate in difficulty.

INGREDIENTS
2 ounces bacon or salt pork, diced
1 cup diced onion
6 cups (about 1 pound) thin-sliced cabbage
1/4 cup water
1 teaspoon salt
1/4 teaspoon pepper

YIELD 6 servings

Depending on where you live and whether you grow your own vegetables, cabbage is an early-summer vegetable, a summer vegetable, a fall vegetable, or all three. Along with corn and potatoes, cabbage is a staple in these mountains and around the world.

There is some dispute among mountain cooks over whether the cabbage should be boiled before you fry it or fried fresh. I fry it raw and do not detect a difference.

STEPS In a large skillet, fry the bacon or salt pork. Add the onion and sauté it for 3 minutes. Add the cabbage, water, salt, and pepper. Cover, bring to a boil, and simmer for 12 minutes. Uncover, stir, and fry another 2 minutes, or until the water is almost gone.

If you like the cabbage tender, cook it a little more, about 16 minutes.

HEALTHY CHOICE ALTERNATIVE Rich in vitamin C, cabbage contains significant amounts of indoles (nitrogen compounds) and fiber, both of which may lower the risk of cancer.

For a light meal, serve this with Baked Cushaw, Baked Potatoes, and Sautéed Trout.

Skillet Cabbage To the above recipe, add 1 cup diced green pepper and 2 cups tomato or spaghetti sauce when you remove the lid. Bring to a boil, reduce the heat, and simmer for 2 minutes.

Cabbage Stew

*I*n the rolling hills that lie just below the tops of the Blue Ridge Mountains of North Carolina, farmers grow cabbages in vast fields. This dish combines an old-time Blue Ridge Mountain farmhouse tradition with a little pepper that reminds me of Texas.

STEPS In a large cast-iron skillet, fry the bacon until most of the fat is rendered away and the bacon has darkened in color. Remove the bacon, chop, and set aside. Pour off half the bacon grease, and fry the onion in the remaining grease. Add the tomatoes, bouillon, sugar, salt, and jalapeño pepper or salsa. As the tomato mixture comes to a boil, chop the cabbage. Mix it in and simmer, covered, for 20 minutes. Stir in the flour, bring to a boil, and simmer for 1 minute. Place in a serving bowl and garnish with the chopped bacon.

HEALTHY CHOICE ALTERNATIVE You can cut the salt and bacon entirely, but for flavor, I recommend at least ½ teaspoon of salt and 2 ounces of bacon. Remember that a mountain farmer may have used almost a pound of bacon.

Serve this with Baked Whole Sweet Potatoes, Sweet Potato Biscuits, and Baked Country Ham or Southern Fried Chicken.

DIFFICULTY Moderate. With nine ingredients but only one pan, this recipe is moderate in difficulty.

INGREDIENTS
4 ounces bacon
³/₄ cup chopped onion
8 ounces peeled canned or fresh tomatoes
2 teaspoons beef bouillon grains
1 teaspoon sugar
½ teaspoon salt
½ chopped jalapeño pepper or 1/4 cup hot salsa
4½ cups (³/₄ pound) cabbage
1 tablespoon instant flour

YIELD 6 servings

Salads and Vegetables

Sauerkraut

(Kraut and Cooked Sauerkraut)

*H*ighlanders from the Savage River in western Maryland to the Sautee-Nacoochee Valley in northeast Georgia know that homemade sauerkraut is superior to any they can buy. Besides being crisp and not overly salty, sauerkraut is easy to make.

We grow an abundance of cabbage. It thrives in our high mountains and grows well through the long fall season. Highlanders use much of their cabbage for sauerkraut, storing it in canning jars. Years ago, when quart-size canning jars were not readily available, we made and stored sauerkraut in large stone crocks.

To achieve the optimum level of lactic acid in the finished sauerkraut, use 2¼ to 2½ percent of the cabbage's weight in salt. According to *Food Microbiology* by William Frazier and Dennis Westhoff, if you use too much or too little salt, different bacteria will form, and the cabbage will not have the desired flavor.

I have updated the old recipes for today's kitchen, using pickling salt because it does not contain iodide, which softens the kraut. Pickling salt may also come with a packet of calcium chloride, which makes the sauerkraut even more crisp.

INGREDIENTS

1 large cabbage, a bit over 5 pounds
¼ cup (2 ounces) pickling salt
1 cup water
6 tablespoons bacon drippings

YIELD 12 cups, or 24 servings

STEPS If you have not used your food processor for a while, go now and pull it from the back cabinet. Dust it off. Get out the grater blade, and wash the parts. Shake off the excess water and assemble the appliance. Place it on a sturdy surface, and you are ready to grate the cabbage.

Remove any soft or wilted outer cabbage leaves, quarter the cabbage, and remove the stem. Grate the cabbage.

Dump the grated cabbage into a large glass bowl or crock. Stir in the salt and water. Let stand 30 to 40 minutes or until the brine—cabbage, water, and salt—has covered the cabbage. If the cabbage is not covered, add additional water. Place a clean dinner plate on top of the cabbage, cover with plastic wrap, and press the dinner plate down with four or five additional dinner plates. Or fill a gallon-size plastic milk jug with water, secure the lid, and set it on the dinner plate. The purpose of the weighted plate is to keep a layer of expressed, brined juice on the surface. Covering the brine with plastic wrap protects it from contamination.

Store at room temperature or a bit cooler for 2 to 3 weeks, skimming the foam as needed. When it stops bubbling, it is ready. The sauerkraut should be light in color, crisp, and about 1.7 percent lactic acid. Store in the refrigerator for several months. If at any point the kraut gets soft and slimy, it has gone bad and must be discarded.

Drain the sauerkraut. If it tastes too salty, rinse away the salt. Using a lettuce spinner, remove any remaining liquid. In two large skillets over low heat, fry the kraut in the bacon grease for 10 minutes. Serve.

HEALTHY CHOICE ALTERNATIVE Rinse the salt from the sauerkraut. Reheat in a microwave oven, omitting the bacon grease.

Serve this with baked pork ribs and applesauce, or with frankfurters, sausage, pork chops, or boiled pork knuckles.

Kraut Slaw
(Sauerkraut Coleslaw)

*I*n the late winter, when cabbage is out of season, we make this pickled coleslaw, this sauerkraut coleslaw. It is a joy to serve, and when we gather at heritage festivals kraut slaw is often the talk of the table. Traditionally, mountain cooks make it with vinegar, sugar, salt, and pepper; I omit the vinegar. I also use very little dressing. I don't like coleslaw with lots of mayonnaise, and I find that the onion, green pepper, and sugar here provide adequate flavoring.

STEPS Wash and drain the sauerkraut, and dry it in a lettuce spinner. In a large mixing bowl, combine the sauerkraut with the green pepper, onion, mayonnaise, sugar, and pepper. Cover and refrigerate until ready to serve.

HEALTHY CHOICE ALTERNATIVE With just 4 tablespoons of mayonnaise for 3 cups of sauerkraut, this slaw is low in fat and calories. You can further reduce fat by substituting a fat-free mayonnaise or salad dressing.

Serve this in place of coleslaw, at lunch or any picnic, or with Fried Catfish and Hush Puppies, Sautéed Trout, or shrimp stir-fry.

DIFFICULTY Easy. Stir up six cold ingredients and serve. Use raw, uncooked sauerkraut.

INGREDIENTS
3 cups raw sauerkraut
1/2 cup diced green pepper
1/2 cup chopped onion
1/4 cup mayonnaise
2 teaspoons sugar
1/4 teaspoon pepper

YIELD 6 servings

Salads
and
Vegetables

Allegheny Cabbage Casserole

*F*ormed by the folding of sedimentary rocks, the Allegheny Mountains—located in parts of Pennsylvania, Maryland, West Virginia, Ohio, and Kentucky—are rich in coal, gas, and timber. The highest point in these mountains is 4,800 feet at Spruce Knob, West Virginia. The eastern portion of the Allegheny Mountains is rugged, with an impressive escarpment or wall that faces the Appalachian Valley. I associate the recipe with these mountains.

This recipe is almost the same as that for Broccoli Casserole (page 99), but I like this cheese sauce with cabbage even more than with broccoli. Because we usually serve this casserole at a family or church gathering, the recipe is rather large.

STEPS Grease a 10x6x2-inch casserole dish. Preheat the oven to 350°F. In a medium-size saucepan over medium heat, melt the butter and stir in the flour. Whisk in the milk, bring to a boil, and cook for 1 minute. Remove from the heat, and stir in the Parmesan cheese, Cheddar cheese, salt, and pepper.

In the casserole dish, layer 1 cup of crushed crackers, the cabbage, the sauce, and then the remaining 1 cup of crushed crackers. The crackers on the bottom will absorb water from the cabbage. Bake for 40 minutes, or until it bubbles in the center. Serve.

TIP Because some cheeses are salty, you may want to add the salt after you melt the cheese and taste the sauce.

HEALTHY CHOICE ALTERNATIVE The above recipe is a healthy casserole. Make it even healthier by adding 2 cups boiled and fat-free pinto beans and replacing the cheeses with 1 cup of low-fat cottage cheese. If you add the beans, you'll need to use a 13x9x2-inch pan.

Serve this with Boiled New Potatoes and Green Beans.

INGREDIENTS
3 tablespoons butter
1/4 cup all-purpose flour
2 cups milk
1/3 cup grated Parmesan
  cheese
1/3 cup grated sharp
  Cheddar cheese
1/2 teaspoon salt
1/4 teaspoon white
  pepper
2 cups (1 pack) crushed
  saltine crackers
8 cups (1 1/4 pounds)
  thinly sliced and
  chopped cabbage

YIELD 10 servings

Cooked Vegetables:
Onions, Okra, and Tomatoes

■ ■

Vegetable Plates

Up and down the Blue Ridge Mountains and west to the Appalachians you can find diners, cafes, and restaurants that serve vegetable plates. To order, select three or four vegetables from the list provided. Why is this so common? What do you get on a vegetable plate?

Even our smallest cafes may offer ten vegetables. Keep in mind, however, that the term "vegetables" includes salads, starches, pasta, and traditional vegetables. Order simple dishes such as sliced tomatoes, French fries, and Jell-O, or order house specialties, like those I list here. If you are thinking about vegetable-plate dinners, keep in mind that we always serve this specialty with hot rolls and corn bread.

Using recipes from this book, I suggest the following menu combinations on page 92.

Plate One
Dried Apple Applesauce, Pickled Beans, Fried Potatoes,
Soup Beans, and Macaroni and Cheese

Plate Two
Dilled Green Beans with Black Walnuts, Fried Okra,
Sugared Carrots, and Scalloped Potatoes

Plate Three
Custard Corn Pudding, Sweet Potatoes and Apples,
Kathy's Coleslaw, and Turnip Greens

Plate Four
Pickled Beets, cottage cheese, Cucumber Salad,
and Fried Green Tomatoes

Plate Five
Steamed Green Beans,
Baked Cushaw with Cinnamon-Sorghum Sauce,
Fried Apples, and Appalachian Potato Salad

Plate Six
Fried Mush, Skillet Cabbage, Green Onion Huey,
Mashed Turnips and Potatoes, and Savory Cushaw Pie

■ ■

HEARTY Cooking COUNTRY ■

Green Onion Huey
(Creamed Green Onions)

*M*ountain people refer to green onions as onion blades or spring onions. They are a common garden vegetable. When the blades are twelve inches tall, we cut them in the garden, clean them on the back porch, and eat them fresh out of hand. We also eat green onions with Wilted Lettuce, Soup Beans, Fried Potatoes, and Buttermilk Corn Bread, holding the onions in our hand like a slice of bread.

Years ago, when making this recipe, our cooks first braised the onions on the stove and then baked them. This process, however, adds a step and tends to overcook the onions, robbing them of flavor. To further preserve the delicate onion flavor, Highlanders generally do not add the nutmeg, cheese, pecans, pepper, or sherry that were often used in Southern cities such as Atlanta, Georgia, or Charlotte, North Carolina.

DIFFICULTY Moderate. With six ingredients and one step, this recipe is moderate in difficulty.

STEPS In a large skillet over medium heat, melt the lard or butter. Peel and dice the onions and the green onions into 1-inch or smaller pieces. Reserve 1 tablespoon green onions for garnish. Add the remaining onions to the butter and simmer over low heat, covered, for 7 minutes. The onions should be almost but not fully tender—they will continue to cook as the sauce is prepared.

Push the onions to the side of the pan, and in the center of the pan, stir in the flour and salt. When the flour is moist through and fully mixed with the butter (add more butter if needed), stir in the milk, mixing slowly from the center out. Bring to a boil, and boil for 1 minute. Pour into a serving dish, and garnish with the reserved green onions. Serve hot.

HEALTHY CHOICE ALTERNATIVE Traditionally, Highlanders made this recipe with light or even heavy cream. However, I find the dish very satisfying when made with 2% milk and butter, and you can go a step further by replacing half of the butter and all of the milk with 3/4 cup skim milk. If you are watching salt, omit it and offer it at the table.

Serve this as a side dish to accompany Fried Chicken Livers Baked with Rice. For a special occasion, serve in baked puff pastry shells with whole green onions as garnish.

INGREDIENTS
2 tablespoons lard or butter
1 pound onions
1 1/2 bunches (1 1/2 cups) small green onions
2 tablespoons all-purpose flour
1/2 teaspoon salt
3/4 cup milk

YIELD 5 servings

Fried Okra

*O*kra is a late summer vegetable and a large tall plant that is related to cotton and hibiscus. The pointed, finger-shaped fruit is hairy and a bit slimy. Three- to four-inch yellow flowers with red centers make a showy ornament, and the pods, which develop to ten inches in length, make beautiful additions to dried flower arrangements.

Okra, a native of Africa, is known by various names, including gumbo, bamya, bâmiya, or ladies' fingers. We use okra pods when they are young, tender, and pulpy—before they ripen. Pods should be 1½ to 3 inches long, but I have used larger ones quite successfully. I like to steam or boil okra and serve it as a side dish, but it is also good as part of a boiled mixture with tomatoes. We make okra salad with cooked okra pods and fresh tomato wedges. Finally, we fry okra in batter to make fritters, croquettes, or patties.

Even my children, who don't like okra, like this slow-fried, slime-free recipe—the cooked okra is more like cheese crackers than okra. Fried Okra is different from its close cousin, the traditional egg-battered, soft-centered, and quick-fried okra. In the recipe I present here, you thin-slice the okra and fry it slowly with a light dusting of cornmeal. When cooked, the fried okra is crunchy and dry through to the center—it does not have a soft center. My Fried Okra is as crisp, crunchy, and dainty as potato chips, but it is set apart from potato chips by okra flavor.

INGREDIENTS
½ pound fresh or a pint of okra
4 ounces bacon
2 tablespoons self-rising cornmeal mix
¼ teaspoon salt
⅛ teaspoon pepper

YIELD 4 servings

STEPS Slice the okra into ¼-inch slices. In a large, heavy skillet, fry the bacon until it is crisp. Remove the bacon and drain it on paper towels. Lower the heat.

Combine 1 tablespoon of the cornmeal with the salt and pepper. Sprinkle this over the okra, and stir. Add as much of the remaining cornmeal as will stick to the okra.

Add the okra to the bacon grease, and fry it over medium heat for about 20 minutes, or until the okra starts to brown on both sides. While you might cook this from beginning to end at low-medium, I use medium or high-medium heat first, and then when the okra starts to brown, I reduce the heat—okra burns easily. Add more oil, if necessary.

The goal is to cook the okra until it is brown, crunchy to the center, and about half its original size.

If the grease has not been absorbed, drain the okra on paper towels, and serve with the bacon, either crumbled or in strips.

HEALTHY CHOICE ALTERNATIVE Replace the bacon with canola oil.

Serve as a snack or vegetable.

Okra and Tomatoes
(Tomato-Butter and Okra)

From the time Africans brought okra to this continent, we have used it to thicken vegetables, soups, and stews. In this recipe the okra thickens the tomatoes, and when served the tomatoes, onion, butter, salt, and pepper are sauce for the okra. The salty sauce—I call it tomato-butter—is a wonderful complement to the okra.

STEPS Cut the stem spot from the tomatoes. To peel the tomatoes, place them one at a time in boiling water for 15 seconds, and then pull off the peel.

Slice the peeled tomatoes. Trim the stem from the okra, and cut into bite-size pieces. In a saucepan over medium heat, combine the tomatoes, okra, onion, butter, salt, and pepper. Bring to a boil, reduce the heat, and simmer, uncovered, for 30 to 40 minutes, or until some of the liquid has evaporated, leaving a thickened sauce. Serve.

HEALTHY CHOICE ALTERNATIVE I add the butter and salt for flavor, but they can be omitted. Offer salt at the table.

Serve over rice or as you would any side-dish vegetable, or with Barbecued Chicken, fresh corn on the cob, and sliced fresh tomatoes.

DIFFICULTY Moderate. Because this recipe has six ingredients and the tomatoes need to be peeled, it is moderate in difficulty.

INGREDIENTS
1 1/4 pounds tomatoes
1 pound okra
1 cup diced onion
1/4 cup butter
1 teaspoon salt
1/4 teaspoon pepper

YIELD 6 servings

Summer Garden Vegetable Stew

If you want to give this stew a good Old South name, call it Creole Vegetable Gumbo. In Provence, France, except for our addition of okra, the stew is ratatouille. Here in the mountains, we call it Summer Garden Vegetable Stew. Gumbo is what Southerners call okra or an okra-thickened soup. Ratatouille is a mixed-vegetable dish of eggplant, tomatoes, onions, and bell peppers simmered in olive oil. To modernize the recipe, call it a stir-fry, prepare it in a wok and cook it briefly.

Mountaineers simmer the stew slowly in a saucepan, making it in August, when our garden produce is at its peak. Then, with thoughts of damp winter evenings, we can or freeze it. Making this stew is fun, because you can use any vegetables you have on hand, and you can personalize it to suit your tastes.

DIFFICULTY Moderate. With ten ingredients and one cooking step, this recipe is moderate in difficulty.

Salads
and
Vegetables

INGREDIENTS

2 cups peeled and
    chopped tomatoes
2 cups chopped egg-
    plant
1 cup sliced okra
1 cup diced green bell
    pepper
1 cup diced red onion
2 tablespoons bacon
    grease or olive oil
1 teaspoon sugar
1 teaspoon salt
1/4 teaspoon nutmeg
1/8 teaspoon cayenne
    pepper

YIELD 6 servings

STEPS Wash, chop, slice, and dice the vegetables. In a large saucepan over medium heat, combine the tomatoes, eggplant, okra, bell pepper, onion, oil, sugar, salt, nutmeg, and pepper. Cover, simmer 5 minutes, and stir to mix. Simmer, covered, an additional 15 minutes. Remove the lid and simmer an additional 15 to 30 minutes, or until most of the liquid has boiled away and the vegetables thicken like a stew. Serve.

HEALTHY CHOICE ALTERNATIVE This dish is a simple mixture of boiled vegetables, and with the exception of the oil and salt, it is a healthy choice. If necessary, omit the olive oil. Serve the stew over rice for a healthy, low-fat vegetarian main dish.

Serve this over Buttermilk Corn Bread, or with strips of bacon, a cheese omelet, or Angel Biscuits.

Summer Garden Custard Pie
(Onion Custard Pie and Squash Pie)

The savory custard is a binder for the steamed vegetables. The custard, a mixture of milk and eggs, is so different from other binders, such as white sauce, cheese sauce, or cornstarch glaze. Make the pie with a single vegetable—I like onions—or several vegetables mixed together.

DIFFICULTY Moderate. With six ingredients and two steps, this recipe is moderate in difficulty.

INGREDIENTS

4 cups washed, peeled,
    and diced vegetables,
    such as eggplant, sum-
    mer squash, onions,
    cabbage, red bell pep-
    per, green beans
2 eggs
1 teaspoon salt
1/4 teaspoon ground
    white pepper
1 cup milk
1 9-inch Pie Pastry
    Shell (page 275)

YIELD One 9-inch pie,
or 8 servings

STEPS Place the baking rack on the center shelf of the oven. Preheat the oven to 450°F.

Clean, peel, chop, and steam the vegetables. Steam the vegetables until they are soft but still hold their shape. Beans, of course, take longer than summer squash. Using a single vegetable such as onions simplifies the steaming. Diced onions steam in about 3 minutes, while beans take 10 minutes.

Prepare the custard. While the vegetables steam, combine the eggs, salt, and pepper in a mixing bowl, and whisk until well mixed. Whisk in the milk.

Spread the steamed vegetables in the prepared pie crust. Pour in the custard, and bake for 15 minutes. Reduce the heat to 350°F, and bake an additional 20 to 30 minutes, or until the custard is almost set. Remove from the oven, as it will continue to cook. A knife inserted into the center should come out clean. Garnish each slice with a wedge of yellow squash.

HEALTHY CHOICE ALTERNATIVE Bake in a casserole dish, omitting the pie crust.

Serve hot from the oven. Serve as a side dish or vegetable.

HEARTY
Cooking
COUNTRY

Grandfather Mountain

While we look up to the old man for inspiration, the image we see is lying down. As he lies there, year after year, we celebrate his presence with walks across the swinging bridge, an animal zoo, and the Scotch-Irish festival, a festival held in late June at Linville.

Grandfather Mountain Carrots and Peas

Do you call them carrots and peas or peas and carrots? Perhaps it depends on your preference for one over the other. In any case, carrots and peas are cool-weather crops. Here in eastern Kentucky, as in most of the Highlands, they grow well in the spring, but in some high elevations like areas around Grandfather Mountain—a craggy-looking stone profile of an old man with a beard, a mile-high splendor in western North Carolina—they thrive all summer.

Carrots and peas came together in this dish because gardeners harvest them together. At the market you can buy them canned, but I don't think you'll find this salty mixture any substitute for fresh. Look for small, young, fresh peas—such as snap peas, snow peas, or garden peas—and firm carrots. With your careful selection, this common vegetable dish carries uncommon goodness.

After talking with friends about carrots and peas, I read about them in James Beard's *American Cookery*. He describes the recipe: "This is to be feared. It can be delicious only if the carrots are young, well drained, and nicely buttered, and the peas are fresh and perfectly cooked." Feared? Why should you fear this simple dish? And Beard continues ". . . perfectly cooked." Beard is right, of course, and I hope my directions help you to prepare this simple vegetable "perfectly cooked" and without "fear." As you prepare this vegetable, think of the high hills and the cool valleys around Grandfather Mountain.

STEPS Steam or boil the carrots and peas. If they are 3/8-to 1/4-inch in thickness, they will cook in about 4 minutes. Drain. Combine with the butter, sugar, salt, and pepper, and serve.

TIP If you cut the carrots to the thickness of the peas, you can cook them

DIFFICULTY Easy. With six ingredients and one step, this recipe is easy to prepare.

INGREDIENTS
1 cup diced fresh carrots
1 cup fresh snap, snow, or garden peas
1 1/2 tablespoons butter
1/2 teaspoon sugar
1/4 teaspoon salt
1/8 teaspoon pepper

YIELD 4 servings

Salads
and
Vegetables

together for the same length of time. Otherwise, do as James Beard says and "Cook the peas and carrots separately. Drain and combine. . . ."

HEALTHY CHOICE ALTERNATIVE Omit the butter, sugar, salt, and pepper, and serve with a salt-free spice. In your market, look for seasoned pepper or orange-garlic salt-free spice mixtures.

Serve this dish with Morels Sautéed with Onions, Barbecued Pork Chops, and Simple Corn Bread.

Sugared Carrots

DIFFICULTY Very Easy. Just steam the carrots and sprinkle with sugar.

INGREDIENTS
1 pound carrots
2 tablespoons sugar

YIELD 4 servings

*C*arrots are among the sweetest vegetables, and the added sugar in this dish only complements that natural sweetness. I like to purchase the small peeled and fully prepared carrots, making this dish easy to prepare.

STEPS Wash and peel the carrots. Cut them into 2-inch lengths. If the carrots are more than 3/4 inch in diameter, slice them.

In a saucepan equipped with a steamer insert, add the carrots and enough water for steaming. Steam for 9 minutes, or until the carrots are tender to the center. Pour the carrots into a serving bowl, sprinkle with sugar, and stir to mix. Serve.

HEALTHY CHOICE ALTERNATIVE Carrots are the leading source of carotene or beta carotene in the American diet. The body converts carotene to vitamin A, and a four-ounce serving provides about six times the Recommended Daily Allowance of vitamin A.

Along with sweet potatoes, carrots add color to any main meal.

■ ■

Casserole Binders

When you stir eggs, cheese, milk, cream, or flour into a hot liquid, the liquid thickens and forms a binder. Common binders include white sauce, cheese sauce, canned cream soup, eggs, cheese, and cornstarch. Binders hold casseroles together, and frequently the binders add calories, fat, salt, and cholesterol. Casserole binders contain the many sins of home cooking. This problem is particularly true of casseroles that you "enhance" with boiled eggs, mayonnaise, Velveeta cheese, and heavy cream. Less binder usually means fewer calories.

Broccoli Casserole

have made broccoli casseroles with commercially prepared cream of mushroom soup. I have used canned cream of chicken, canned Cheddar cheese, or canned celery soup. Of course I have. But I can make better broccoli casseroles without help from salt-filled tin cans. You, too, can do without the quick fix—the 11-ounce can. Sometimes you don't want the sodium or the preservatives.

When I omit the manufactured can of soup, I increase my options to determine flavor and nutritional value. I can be creative. I can choose to bind my casserole with crackers, white sauce, cheese, or cornstarch. I can choose skim milk, low-fat milk, whole milk, cream, or eggs. If I want a rich casserole, I use real cream, butter, eggs, bacon, crushed potato chips, mayonnaise, salad dressing, Kraft Cheez Whiz, French fried onions, or buttered Ritz Crackers. If I want a light casserole, I use skim milk, cottage cheese, and dry bread crumbs. I frequently use a white sauce without cheese.

Why start with healthy fresh broccoli and end up with a heavy casserole? Save your sodium for pretzels. Save your calories for pecan pie. Save your fat for real butter. A little cheese, no commercial soup, and fresh broccoli make the following recipe a better broccoli casserole.

STEPS Grease a 2 quart (10x6x2-inch) casserole dish. Preheat the oven to 350°F.

In a saucepan over medium heat, melt the butter and stir in the flour. Whisk in the milk, bring to a boil, and cook for 1 minute. Remove from the heat and stir in the Parmesan cheese, Cheddar cheese, salt, and pepper. Mix the sauce with the broccoli and pour into the casserole dish. Spread the cracker crumbs over the top. Bake 50 minutes or until it bubbles in the center and the water (in comparison to frozen broccoli, fresh broccoli yields some water during baking) is gone. (If you use frozen broccoli, bake 40 minutes.)

TIP Because some cheeses are salty, you may want to add the salt after you melt the cheese and taste the sauce.

HEALTHY CHOICE ALTERNATIVE Make this recipe even healthier by adding 2 cups boiled and fat-free pinto beans and replacing the cheeses with 1 cup of bread crumbs and 1 cup of low-fat cottage cheese. If you add 2 cups of beans, you'll need to use a 13x9x2-inch pan.

Serve this dish with Boiled New Potatoes, Pickled Beets, and Southern Fried Chicken.

DIFFICULTY Moderate. With nine ingredients and one step, this recipe is moderate in difficulty.

INGREDIENTS
3 tablespoons butter
1/4 cup all-purpose flour
2 cups milk
1/3 cup grated Parmesan cheese
1/3 cup grated sharp Cheddar cheese
1/2 teaspoon salt
1/4 teaspoon ground white pepper
2 large bunches (8 cups) fresh broccoli, chopped
1 cup (1/2 pack) crushed saltine crackers

YIELD 10 servings

Fried Green Tomatoes

*F*ried green tomatoes are prepared in three steps: slice the tomatoes, coat them with cornmeal, and fry. But if you have never seen fried green tomatoes, you'll have many questions: What kind of shortening do you use? Do the tomatoes need to be peeled? Do you coat the tomatoes with a batter, flour, or cornmeal? Do you flavor the batter with sugar, black pepper, cayenne, or hot sauce? Be sure to select firm tomatoes that do not show any signs of ripening.

INGREDIENTS
3/4 cup lard
5 medium-size (2 1/2 pounds) green tomatoes
3/4 cup self-rising cornmeal mix
1/2 teaspoon salt
1/2 teaspoon pepper

YIELD 6 servings

STEPS In a 10-inch cast-iron skillet over medium heat, melt the lard until it starts to smoke, or until it reaches 325°F to 350°F. If you are smoking up the kitchen, the lard is too hot. Reduce the heat.

Cut the tomatoes into 3/8-inch slices. If you want batter to stick to the edge of the slices, peel the tomatoes. (I skip that step.)

In a mixing bowl, combine the self-rising cornmeal mix, salt, and pepper, and coat the tomato slices with the mixture. Fry about 2 minutes on each side, or until golden brown. The tomatoes will be cooked through, but not overly crusty on the outside.

Drain on a wire rack and serve. If you let the fried tomatoes sit, what was crisp will be soggy.

HEALTHY CHOICE ALTERNATIVE In this recipe the light coating of cornmeal does not absorb a lot of lard. For a light oven-fried tomato, after dipping the tomatoes in the cornmeal, place them on a cooling rack over a cookie sheet, and bake 20 minutes at 400°F. Broil to brown.

In the movie *Fried Green Tomatoes*, the characters eat fried tomatoes for breakfast, a birthday celebration, an afternoon snack, and fresh out of the skillet at the Whistle Stop Cafe. I suggest serving fried green tomatoes for breakfast with bacon, eggs, and corn bread, or for dinner as a side-dish vegetable.

Four

Starches

Sweet Potatoes, White Potatoes, Corn, and Beans

Baked Whole Sweet Potatoes

Glazed Sweet Potatoes *(Sweet Potato Glaze)*

Sweet Potato Casserole *Sweet Potato Puffs or Sweet Potato Balls*

Fancy Sweet Potato Casserole

Sweet Potatoes and Apples

Sweet Potato Pie

Baked Potatoes

Simple Scalloped Potatoes
Creamy Scalloped Potatoes

Scalloped Potatoes

Fancy Potato Casserole *(Potatoes au Gratin)*

Mashed Kennebec Potatoes *(Mashed Potatoes)*

Potato Cakes
(Mashed Potato Patties and Fried Potato Cakes)

Boiled New Potatoes

Twice-Baked Potatoes
Fancy Twice-Baked Potatoes (Stuffed Potatoes)

Fried Raw Potatoes
Allegheny Home Fries (Country-Fried Potatoes)

Corn on the Cob

Buttered Sweet Corn with Black Pepper
(Baked Fresh Corn)

Succotash

Mush
Fried Mush (Polenta, Cornmeal Mush, and Porridge)

Fried Liver Mush
Fried Sausage Mush

Custard Corn Pudding

Corn Relish

Soup Beans *(Pinto Beans)*

Bean Dumplings
(Soup Beans and Dumplings)

U.S. Senate Bean Soup

Pinto Bean Chili *(Vegetarian Chili)*

Baked Pinto Beans

Pinto Bean Cakes
(Bean Patties and Fried Bean Cakes)

Pinto Bean Pie

Sweet Potatoes

I WILL NEVER forget when I first saw a bushel basket full of sweet potatoes sitting beside a small road near Feds Creek of the Levisa Fork. I was a few miles from the Kentucky-Virginia state line. It was September 1977 and the potatoes were for sale. Can you imagine? Sweet potatoes by the bushel! This was not a produce stand. There was no corn, squash, or white potatoes for sale. From this sight—one that has repeated itself many times—I know that sweet potatoes form a special part of mountain cooking.

The Cherokee Indians were expert farmers, and they grew sweet potatoes here long before white settlers arrived. The settlers carried on the sweet potato tradition, but only in a small way. Today, people in Third World countries consume 98 percent of all sweet potatoes. In India people make poori, a puffed bread, with sweet potatoes, and in China today, sweet potatoes are so popular that big-city vendors sell them roasted from carts like vendors sell pretzels in New York.

We gravitate toward sweet food. Mountaineers seem to have a special gene for sweetness. Our community cookbooks are loaded with desserts, and we often add sugar to vegetables. Sweet potatoes are naturally sweet, but they are not sweet enough. My recipes are typical in that I add sugar. I hope you are ready for a sweet mountain high!

Sweet potatoes are neither potatoes nor yams. Sweet potatoes, like morning glories, belong to the species *Ipomoea batatas*. Yams are members of the genus *Dioscorea*. Unfortunately, some supermarkets mislabel sweet potatoes, calling them yams.

Sweet potatoes are a root vegetable. The flesh ranges from dry (less sweet) to moist (more sweet), and the color of the pulp ranges in color from white to orange to purple. American farmers grow some forty different varieties, and if you look further, you'll find 500 varieties grown around the world, including Georgia jet, Porto Rico, Nemagold, Big Stem, Yellow Jersey, vineless Vardaman, and Golden Maryland. Sweet potatoes are a Native American vegetable, and they do well in our hot, long-season climate. We harvest them in the late fall, or we purchase them fresh, canned, frozen, or dehydrated. Store fresh sweet potatoes in a cool, dark, dry place.

Sweet Potato Menu

This description of a woman serving dinner to a large family is from *The Dollmaker* by Harriette Arnow:

"Gertie, sitting at the foot of the table with a lard bucket of sweet milk on one side of her, buttermilk on the other, a great platter of hot smoking corn bread in front, and other bowls and platters within easy reach, was kept busy filling glasses with milk, buttering bread, and dishing out the new hominy fried in lard and seasoned with sweet milk and black pepper. It was good with the shuck beans, baked sweet potatoes, cucumber pickles, and green tomato ketchup. Gertie served it up with pride, for everything, even the meal in the bread, was a product of her farming."

Baked Whole Sweet Potatoes

Seventy-five years ago, mountaineers baked sweet potatoes in the fireplace, the ashes protecting the potatoes from the hot, glowing coals. More than that, baking sweet potatoes was a Friday night social event. In large households, people would come and go, and friends gathered in front of the hearth, watched the flames, told stories, and waited for their sweet potatoes to cook.

Today, we still serve an occasional plain, baked sweet potato, but in my home, we don't do it often enough. A baked sweet potato is a prize, and it takes no fuss. You don't chop or stir. You don't need gravy. Just bake and serve. I value simple cooking, and, if you start with fresh sweet potatoes, this baked potato is an example of the best.

STEPS Preheat the oven to 350°F. Select fresh, firm, smooth-skinned sweet potatoes. Wash them in cold water, and using a paring knife, remove any blemishes or dark spots. Wrap each potato in foil.

Place the potatoes with the folded side of the foil up in a 13x9x2-inch baking pan and bake for 1 hour. To see if the potatoes are cooked, press the sides. The potatoes should have softened through to the center. I also test with a fork. I press a fork into the side of the potato—it should slide easily to the center.

DIFFICULTY Very easy. With one ingredient, some aluminum foil, and a hot oven, this side dish is very easy to prepare.

INGREDIENTS
Six 8- to 10-ounce sweet potatoes
6 pieces aluminum foil

YIELD 6 servings

TIP I also like to buy sweet potatoes that weigh 1 pound each and cut them in half lengthwise. When baked, the orange centers make a nice presentation around a roast or turkey.

HEALTHY CHOICE ALTERNATIVE A half-cup serving of this dish contains about 100 calories.

Serve baked sweet potatoes as an alternative to baked white potatoes, hot with butter and brown sugar or butter and Hot Sorghum. For a lighter touch, moisten sweet potatoes with chopped pineapple or applesauce. Eat leftovers cold or reheated, use them to make pies, pones, puffs, or casseroles, or offer them with a glaze as in Glazed Sweet Potatoes.

Glazed Sweet Potatoes
(Sweet Potato Glaze)

*T*his combination of butter, brown sugar, sweet potatoes, and pecans is a sensuous mountain specialty. When you lift the soft, moist layers of sweet potato from the casserole, you'll serve a sweetened, spiced, salty delicacy whose smooth texture is broken by the pecan pieces. For today's varied diets, bake the potatoes and offer the Sweet Potato Glaze on the side.

DIFFICULTY Moderate. With eight ingredients and two steps, this recipe is moderate in difficulty.

INGREDIENTS
4 small sweet potatoes, or 2 pounds

FOR THE SWEET POTATO GLAZE
1/2 cup packed brown sugar
1/3 cup chopped pecans
1/4 cup water
1/4 cup butter
1/2 teaspoon cinnamon
1/2 teaspoon salt
1/4 teaspoon ground ginger

YIELD 4 servings

STEPS In a large pot, simmer the potatoes in enough water to cover for about 30 minutes, or until soft through—a fork should slide easily to the center. Drain, cool, and peel the potatoes.

Preheat the oven to 350°F. As the potatoes boil, prepare the glaze In a small bowl, microwave the sugar, pecans, water, butter, cinnamon, salt, and ginger for 2 minutes or until bubbly. Stir and microwave for 1 minute. If using the stovetop, bring to a boil. Stir and simmer 1 minute.

In an 11x7x2-inch baking dish, arrange half the potato slices. Spoon half of the glaze over the potatoes, add the remaining potatoes, and top with the remaining glaze. Bake for 20 minutes. The potatoes will absorb the glaze.

HEALTHY CHOICE ALTERNATIVE For this amount of potatoes, some cooks use twice the amount of glaze. I find that my recipe, with less butter and sugar, saves a few calories and allows the flavor of the sweet potato to stand out. If the recipe still sounds too rich, serve Baked Whole Sweet Potatoes and offer the glaze on the side.

Serve this with baked turkey, Corn Bread Stuffing, Carrots and Peas, and Highlander Rolls, or as a side dish to accompany beef, pork, or chicken.

Sweet Potato Casserole
Sweet Potato Puffs or Sweet Potato Balls

DIFFICULTY Moderate. With seven ingredients and two steps, this recipe is moderate in difficulty.

*S*weet potatoes and casseroles go together like summer and baseball. When you mash or puree cooked sweet potatoes and add other ingredients—persimmon pulp, crushed pineapple, orange juice, sweet milk, or brown sugar—you are making a casserole. Sweet potato casseroles contain many spices: cinnamon, cloves, allspice, mace, and nutmeg. We also add fruit: raisins, apples, lemons, and oranges. From the dairy department, we add cream, butter, milk, yogurt, and sour cream. For sweeteners we use honey, molasses, sorghum, and white or brown sugar. Flavor your casseroles with salt and pepper or add liquor: brandy, sherry, and cognac. Mix and taste to suit your whim. Be a sport with sweet potatoes. Run all the bases, and catch the fly balls. In my opinion, sweet potato casseroles are better than baseball.

Low calorie is a relative term. When compared to the recipe for the Fancy Sweet Potato Casserole that follows, this recipe is low in calories.

STEPS Wash the potatoes and cut away the bad spots. In a large pot with enough water to cover, add the potatoes and simmer for 1 hour. Drain. To peel hot potatoes, hold them on a potholder covered with plastic wrap. The peeling will pull off easily.

Preheat the oven to 350°F. If the potatoes are soft and moist, stir them up. If they seem to be firm and dry, purée them in a food processor.

Measure 4 cups of mashed sweet potato, and add the sugar, butter, salt, mace, and cinnamon. Mix well and pour into a medium-size casserole dish. Bake 25 minutes. Spread the marshmallows over the top and broil about 1 minute, or until the marshmallows puff up and brown.

HEALTHY CHOICE ALTERNATIVE You may want to omit the butter completely, but as directed above, each serving contains only 1½ teaspoons of butter.

INGREDIENTS
3 large (3 pounds) sweet potatoes
¼ cup brown sugar
¼ cup butter
1 teaspoon salt
½ teaspoon mace
½ teaspoon cinnamon
½ cup miniature marshmallows

YIELD 8 servings

Serve this as a substitute for mashed potatoes or with ham or turkey, Buttermilk Biscuits, Shuck Beans, and Baked Cushaw. Garnish with black walnuts and fresh pineapple. Use your leftover casserole to make Sweet Potato Biscuits.

Sweet Potato Puffs or Sweet Potato Balls
Prepare the above recipe, but replace the miniature marshmallows with 6 large marshmallows. Omit the butter. This makes 12 servings.

Using two large spoons, form ⅓-cup-size balls of mashed sweet potato around a center of half a large marshmallow. (If the mashed sweet potato is hard to handle, refrigerate a bit.) Roll the balls in 1 cup of breadcrumbs or cornflake crumbs. Place the balls in a casserole dish, and bake at 350°F for 10 minutes, or until the balls puff up.

Or, deep fry the sweet potato puffs in oil at 375°F for 3 to 4 minutes, or until light brown.

Fancy Sweet Potato Casserole

*T*his casserole is a sweet and rich vegetable, one we serve at homecomings, family reunions, school potlucks, and church suppers. The recipe is big because for us, eating is a social event. If your head says, "No, this recipe is too rich," let your taste buds rule, and at the potluck dinner, kids will say, "This is like candy!"

DIFFICULTY Difficult. With ten ingredients and three steps, this recipe is difficult.

INGREDIENTS

FOR THE CASSEROLE

3 pounds fresh sweet potatoes
1 12-ounce can sweet-ened condensed milk
1/2 cup melted butter
4 eggs
2 cups sugar
1 teaspoon cinnamon
1 teaspoon mace

FOR THE TOPPING

1/2 cup melted butter
3/4 cup brown sugar
1 1/2 cups graham cracker crumbs
1 cup pecans

YIELD 14 servings

STEPS In a large pot with enough water to cover, boil the sweet potatoes until they are cooked through, about 30 minutes. Drain and peel the potatoes. Press them into a large measuring cup until you have 4 cups of potatoes.

Preheat the oven to 400°F. Grease a 13x9x2-inch baking dish.

Using a food processor or electric mixer, mash the potatoes. Add the milk, butter, eggs, sugar, cinnamon, and mace. Mix fully, pour and scrape into the baking dish. Bake for 20 minutes.

While the casserole is baking, prepare the topping. Mix the butter, sugar, graham cracker crumbs, and pecans. When the casserole has baked for 20 minutes, spread the topping on the casserole, and bake an additional 15 minutes.

HEALTHY CHOICE ALTERNATIVE Use my recipe for Sweet Potato Casserole, page 107. When compared to this recipe, the Sweet Potato Casserole is low in calories, sugar, and fat.

Serve this as a vegetable or potato substitute, and be sure to include this casserole as part of your Thanksgiving or Christmas dinner.

Sweet Potatoes and Apples

*Y*ears ago during the summer and fall, many mountaineers lived out of their gardens. This recipe is an example of how they combined fall produce.

Cook this on the stovetop, and serve it in a bowl as you would mashed potatoes. The recipe calls for equal volumes of diced apples and potatoes—at first this seems like a lot of apples, but the apples make the dish sweet and moist, and they shrink a lot during cooking. The sweet potatoes should get almost mushy, and you can serve the apples firm, or cook them until they are soft. It's your choice. The recipe is forgiving.

STEPS Peel and dice the apples and sweet potatoes into $1/2$-inch cubes. In a large covered saucepan bring the sweet potatoes and $1/3$ cup of water to a boil. Reduce the heat and simmer for 15 to 20 minutes, or until the potatoes are soft. Add the apples. Simmer for 3 minutes, or until the apples are tender but not soft. Most of the water should have evaporated.

As the apples simmer, mix the sugar and cornstarch until the lumps disappear. Add the remaining 2 tablespoons of water, 1 teaspoonful at a time, so the sugar/cornstarch mixture first absorbs the water and then dissolves in the water. When the apples are soft, pour the cornstarch mixture into the saucepan, stir, and bring to a boil. Simmer for 1 minute. Serve.

HEALTHY CHOICE ALTERNATIVE Without salt or butter, this recipe is healthy.

Serve this with Pork Barbecue, Fried Pork Chops, or Oven-Fried Bacon-Wrapped Chicken.

DIFFICULTY Moderate. With five ingredients and a sauce, this recipe is moderate in difficulty.

INGREDIENTS
1 large sweet potato, or 2 cups peeled and cubed
2 cooking apples such as Rome Beauty or Granny Smith, 2 cups peeled and cubed
$1/3$ cup water plus 2 tablespoons
$1/4$ cup brown sugar
$1 1/2$ teaspoons cornstarch

YIELD 4 servings

Sweet Potato Pie

*P*repare this pie from October through the winter, when sweet potatoes are in season. In the fall, treat yourself to a packet of candy corn and save eight pieces to garnish this pie.

In comparison to squash pie and pumpkin pie, I prefer this—sweet potato is more substantial, and as a pie ingredient it yields a fuller, more complete, and richer taste.

STEPS In a large pot with enough water to cover, boil the sweet potatoes until cooked through, about 30 minutes. Peel, mash, and measure out 2 cups of potatoes.

In a food processor, combine the sweet potato, brown sugar, cream, eggs, salt, cinnamon, ginger, nutmeg, and allspice, and blend until smooth. Pour into the prepared pie shell, and bake for 45 minutes, or until a toothpick inserted into the center comes out clean. Cool and chill.

Garnish with one recipe of Country Whipped Cream. Using a pastry bag equipped with a star tip, pipe the cream onto the pie, forming eight large stars or swirls. Top each star with a piece of candy corn.

HEALTHY CHOICE ALTERNATIVE Replace the cream with 2% milk.

Serve for dessert with coffee or tea. In place of the whipped cream, offer vanilla ice cream.

White Potatoes

FROM THE ROWS of potatoes I see in gardens, from the polls I have taken, and from the stacks of potato sacks in our supermarkets, I know that white Irish potatoes are basic to the mountain diet. We have an expression that makes the point: "A meal is hardly worth coming home for if potatoes are not on the table."

Long before Columbus discovered America, the Inca people of the Andes Mountains were using potatoes. Historians say their potatoes were small because they ate the big ones and planted the small ones. With this process of selection in use for hundreds of years, their potatoes were perhaps the size of your thumb.

Within about eighty years of Columbus's discovery of America, Europeans were growing—but not eating—potatoes. For a long time they viewed them as a novelty, but by 1610 both the English and Irish were eating potatoes. The Germans were also quick to adopt them, but the French did not use them—they insisted potatoes caused leprosy.

The eventual popularity and abundance of the potato caused the population explosion that occurred in the eighteenth century. Easy to plant and quickly stored, the potatoes grown on two acres could feed nine to ten people for a full year; it would take ten acres of wheat to support the same number. The problem with the potato was that, unlike grains, it could not be stored from year to year. If the potato crop failed, people starved. Thus the infamous Irish potato famine of the 1840s and 1850s.

To distinguish between sweet potatoes and white potatoes, you'll hear mountain people refer to white potatoes as Irish potatoes. I suspect that Irish settlers, forced out of Ireland by the potato famine, brought white potatoes to the mountains. In the minds of Irish emigrants, the potatoes were from Ireland, and they called them Irish potatoes. That is not too surprising considering the fact that the English named a native American bird "turkeys" after the Turks. Why? It was Turks that traded turkeys in English ports.

So while the Irish (and others) grew potatoes in Ireland and brought them to the mountains, white potatoes are not native to Ireland, and Irish is not a potato variety. For the recipes that follow use white potatoes. For some recipes I will specify a potato variety or maturity.

Baked Potatoes

I have to agree with Cissy Gregg, former food editor of Louisville, Kentucky's *Courier-Journal*, who in 1960 wrote, "Anyone can get tired of family, husband, or friends. But who gets tired of a good, luscious baked potato—stuffed, twice-baked, or plain?" I suspect that she was talking about baking a mature Russet, Kennebec, Idaho, or Maine potato—all potatoes with that desirable mealy texture.

Based on my surveys, I know that in the mountains today, baked potatoes are more popular than apple pie or hot dogs. And baked potatoes are easy to prepare—they please the palate and satisfy hunger any time of day.

DIFFICULTY Very Easy. With one ingredient and oven baking, this recipe is very easy.

INGREDIENTS
5 medium potatoes

YIELD 5 servings

STEPS Move the oven rack to the center of the oven. Preheat the oven to 450°F. Scrub the potatoes with a cleaning brush and water. For crisp, hearty skins, do not oil the potatoes and do not wrap them in foil or put them in a pan. Place the potatoes directly on the oven rack.

Bake for 30 minutes. Press a knife into each potato three or four times. (This releases steam, helps the potato cook, and allows you to see how the baking is coming along.) Depending on their size, bake the potatoes up to 30 more minutes.

Test for doneness: When squeezed from the sides, the potatoes should be soft, and a knife should slide easily to the center. For an extra crisp peel, bake an additional 15 minutes.

HEALTHY CHOICE ALTERNATIVE Eat potatoes often, and eat the skins. Remember that potatoes contain complex carbohydrates, protein, vitamins, and minerals. A very large potato may weigh almost a pound. A typical serving is half that size and contains 200 calories. For good health, eat your potatoes baked; an equal amount of French fries contains 700 calories.

Serve these with seasoned salt, margarine, butter, sour cream, or diced onions. Try pouring Chicken Cream Gravy or a cheese sauce over your baked potatoes, or smother with creamed or à la king chicken.

Simple Scalloped Potatoes
Creamy Scalloped Potatoes

DIFFICULTY Easy. With three ingredients and oven baking, this recipe is easy to prepare.

*O*ur mountain scalloped potatoes are no different from those served outside this area, but as with so many of our special foods, mountain cooks like me take great pride in how we prepare this dish. Scalloped potatoes, or potatoes au gratin, are baked in sauce, cream, or broth. We either allow the potatoes to thicken the sauce or we thicken the sauce with flour or cheese. To the potatoes and sauce we might add onions, mushrooms, cheese, or sausage. You can make scalloped potatoes with any white Irish potato, but when possible, I use new potatoes. When cooked, they are firmer, less mushy, and less grainy than mature bakers. For years I made scalloped potatoes with cream, egg yolks, and cheese. As I get older, and as I try to create quicker recipes, I often want a lighter and simpler dish. Consider this recipe, made with broth, flour, and potatoes.

STEPS Prepare the chicken broth: Skim the fat from your leftover and reduced chicken broth, open canned chicken broth, or dissolve chicken bouillon in hot water. Preheat the oven to 350°F, and select an 8-inch round casserole dish. To a small saucepan over medium heat, add the broth and slowly whisk in the instant flour. Bring to a boil for 1 minute, and set aside.

While I remove blemishes, molds, and brown spots, I don't peel new potatoes. Peel old bakers. Slice the potatoes as thin as you can, less than 1/8 inch. Arrange the slices in the casserole dish. Pour the sauce over the potatoes. Bake for 45 minutes, or until the sauce thickens. Baste the potatoes with broth once or twice during cooking. Remove from the oven, and let stand 5 minutes before serving.

HEALTHY CHOICE ALTERNATIVE For those that are purging every gram of fat from their diet, this recipe is fat free. If you make your own broth, it can also be salt free.

I like to use this recipe to balance the menu when I serve a rich dish such as Crackling Corn Bread, Dilled Green Beans with Black Walnuts, Deep Fried Catfish, or Fried Green Tomatoes.

Creamy Scalloped Potatoes Replace the broth with 1³/4 cups half-and-half. To the sauce, add ³/4 teaspoon salt and ¹/4 teaspoon pepper. Top the dish with 2 tablespoons of freshly grated Parmesan cheese. After baking, broil to brown—this will form a tasty au gratin surface.

INGREDIENTS
1³/4 cups double-strength chicken broth
3 tablespoons instant flour
4 cups (1 pound peeled) washed and thinly sliced new potatoes

YIELD 4 servings

■ ■

Milk and Potatoes: Irish Food Ways

Appalachian scholars have documented that the Irish, along with the Scots, Germans, and English, settled the Appalachian Mountains and influenced mountain culture, particularly our food ways. Around the year 1500, the Irish were a pastoral people who kept enough goats, cows, and sheep so they could practically live on the milk (called "white meat") gathered from their flocks. Years later, when the potato arrived and the English forced the Irish to live on smaller plots, the potato replaced much of the white meat.

Still, the Irish cared about milk. They drank fresh milk, sour milk, clotted milk, and buttermilk, and they used milk to make cream, curds, cheese, and butter. They not only drank the milk from cows, but they also drank deer, goat, and sheep milk. In *Simple Cooking, number 38*, John Thorne supports this view by quoting the contemporary writer and traveler John Stevens: "The Irish are the greatest lovers of milk I have ever met. They drink it about twenty different ways, and what is strangest, they love it best when it is sourest."

Thorne goes on to talk about how the Irish boiled potatoes in their skins in a giant cast-iron pot and served them in a basket. To stay warm they sat on the large hearth that fronted a walk-in fireplace, eating potatoes and passing mugs of buttermilk.

This synergy of milk and potatoes has influenced our cooking, from scalloped potatoes to mashed potatoes and many more.

■ ■

Scalloped Potatoes

DIFFICULTY Easy. For this five-ingredient recipe, first prepare a white sauce, and then bake the casserole. Both instant flour and the new potatoes save time.

While the flavor of this dish may be too neutral for some adult palates, many mountain cooks make the dish as I do. The recipe is less rich than the Fancy Potato Casserole that follows. The proportions I use yield extra sauce, which we spread over other food, perhaps trout and broccoli.

STEPS Preheat the oven to 350°F, and select a 13x9x2-inch or 3-quart casserole dish. In a saucepan over medium heat, add the milk and whisk in the instant flour. (If you use all-purpose flour, you must melt the butter, stir in the flour, and then add the milk.) Add the butter and bouillon, and cook until the sauce has boiled for 1 minute.

Arrange the potato slices in the casserole dish. While I remove blemishes, molds, or brown spots, there is no need to peel a new potato. Pour the sauce over the potatoes, and bake for 45 minutes, or about 10 minutes after it bubbles up in the center. Serve.

■ ■

TIP To the above, you might add $^1/_4$ teaspoon of ground black pepper, $^2/_3$ cup of sliced mushrooms, and $^2/_3$ cup of chopped onion. You can also bake sliced ham and pork chops in this dish.

This recipe will not form a crusty au gratin surface unless you sprinkle the top with $^1/_2$ cup cracker crumbs or crumbled dry bread and $^1/_4$ cup grated Parmesan cheese. Do this after 30 minutes of baking.

HEALTHY CHOICE ALTERNATIVE Omit the butter. We usually use butter to moisten flour and make a roux, but in this recipe I use instant flour, which eliminates the need for butter—I add it for flavor and texture.

INGREDIENTS
3 cups milk
$^1/_3$ cup instant flour
6 tablespoons butter
2 tablespoons chicken bouillon grains
5 cups washed and thinly sliced new potatoes

YIELD 9 servings

■ ■

About au Gratin

I think of an au gratin as the browned crust that forms on top of potatoes as they cook. The *Larousse Gastronomique* says that an au gratin is a dish or style of cooking. My mom, the living Larousse in my life, does not agree. She says the French word *gratiné* means grated. Indeed you might grate cheese on top of the potatoes as you cook them.

Traditionally, an au gratin is a baked, heavy, French dish of potatoes, beets, eggplant, or frogs' legs baked in a sauce made with cream, egg yolks, and cheese.

In *American Cookery* James Beard says that our scalloped potatoes resemble the Gratin Dauphinois from the part of France called Dauphine. The simplest American adaptation, he suggests, uses a can of cream of mushroom soup and a can of milk as the sauce. My recipe for Scalloped Potatoes, with just five ingredients, is just as simple and a lot better.

Fancy Potato Casserole
(Potatoes au Gratin)

DIFFICULTY Moderate. This eleven-ingredient, two-step recipe is moderate in difficulty.

INGREDIENTS

FOR THE BÉCHAMEL
SAUCE AND CASSEROLE
6 tablespoons butter
1/3 cup all-purpose flour
3 cups milk
4 ounces Velveeta
    cheese, sliced thin
1/4 cup grated Parmesan
    cheese
2 tablespoons chicken
    bouillon grains
1/2 teaspoon ground
    black pepper
6 cups washed and
    sliced new potatoes
1 1/2 cups sliced fresh
    mushrooms
1 cup diced onions

FOR THE TOPPING
1/2 cup saltine cracker
    crumbs (10 crushed
    saltine crackers)
1/4 cup grated Parmesan
    cheese

YIELD 12 servings

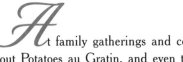t family gatherings and community suppers, all age groups rave about Potatoes au Gratin, and even though the recipe is large, it disappears quickly.

The béchamel sauce reflects our French heritage, and the Velveeta cheese reflects our mountain tastes. I like it with a mixture of Velveeta and Parmesan cheese, but you may prefer, as many mountain cooks do, to use only American or Velveeta cheese. If these are not handy, try using cream cheese.

STEPS Preheat the oven to 350°F, and select a 13x9x2-inch casserole dish. Melt the butter in a medium saucepan. Stir in the flour, add the milk, and cook 1 minute. Remove from the heat and stir in the Velveeta and Parmesan cheese, bouillon, and pepper.

Layer the potatoes, mushrooms, onions, and sauce in the casserole dish. Smooth the top with the back of a spoon. Bake for 30 minutes.

Prepare the topping: Mix the crumbs and cheese. Sprinkle the mixture over the casserole, and return to the oven for another 15 minutes. If the top has not browned, broil for 1 1/2 minutes. Let stand 5 minutes before serving.

Serve this dish with baked ham.

■ ■

Mashed Potatoes

Mashed potatoes are a heavenly food. Boiled, steamed, microwaved, braised, or pressure cooked—what is best? Those who use a microwave claim a dry and full-flavored potato, ideal for mashing. Those who braise (boiling in one half inch of water) also claim a dry potato. Out of habit, I boil the potatoes in water. Because I add potato water or milk back at the end, I have no problem using a soggy boiled potato.

Do you want your mashed potatoes fluffy? There is rather uniform agreement among cooks that old, dry, mealy potatoes—often called Idaho or Maine baking potatoes—result in fluffy mashed potatoes.

Within a single mountain household, a husband and wife or a mother and daughter may make mashed potatoes differently. They have oh so many choices. For example, what do you use to moisten the potatoes: potato water, sweet cream, butter, milk, or skim milk? The old cookbooks recommend sweet cream, but I can't afford the calories. Milk is an excellent compromise, but potato water and butter are also good. Do you like home-style or smooth mashed potatoes? Home-style mashed potatoes contain lumps so those eating them will know they were made with real potatoes. They are popular in big-city bistro-type restaurants, but when I mash potatoes, I press them through a potato ricer, leaving the lumps for city folk.

Mashed Kennebec Potatoes
(Mashed Potatoes)

*I*n 1839 Mrs. Lettice Bryan, writing in *The Kentucky Housewife*, stated, "In the spring, when the potatoes are old and strong, they are much nicer mashed than served whole, though mashed potatoes are fine at any season." I follow her advice and purchase mature Kennebec potatoes for mashing. You can buy Kennebec seed potatoes from Gurney's, listed in the Mail-Order Sources.

STEPS Scrub the potatoes well and cut them in half lengthwise. Remove any dark spots.

Boil the potatoes: Leaving the peeling on the potatoes, boil them in a pot of salted water (1½ teaspoons of salt per quart of water) until tender when pierced with a knife, about 30 minutes. Or you may, as I do, prefer to pressure cook them for 15 minutes. To be sure that they are cooked, cut a piece in half and taste the center. Undercooked potatoes will not mash; overcooked potatoes are difficult to handle. Drain the water and save it for soup.

As the potatoes are cooking, place the milk, butter, and salt in a microwave-safe dish, and microwave on high for about 1½ minutes, or until it bubbles around the edges. Watch it, or it may boil over.

DIFFICULTY Moderate. With four ingredients and two steps, this recipe is moderate in difficulty.

INGREDIENTS
2 pounds potatoes
½ cup milk
¼ cup butter
1 teaspoon salt, plus
  more as needed

YIELD 6 servings

Mash the potatoes: When you have cooked the potatoes, drain them and hold them, one at a time, under cold water so that you can pull or scrape off the peeling. Remove the eyes and blemishes. Then, using a potato ricer, rice the potatoes. With a plastic rubber scraper stir in the milk mixture. Add enough milk and butter to make a soft, smooth puree. When mixed, the potatoes should hold their shape and stand in peaks. While you might mash the potatoes with a light mixer on low speed, I have found that when using a ricer, a rubber scraper is all I need.

Warm the potatoes in a microwave oven as needed.

HEALTHY CHOICE ALTERNATIVE Replace the butter and milk with $3/4$ cup skim milk. Omit the salt, and offer butter and salt at the table.

Serve these potatoes with Steamed Green Beans, Southern Fried Chicken, and Pecan Brown Gravy.

Potato Cakes
(Mashed Potato Patties and Fried Potato Cakes)

DIFFICULTY Moderate. With eight ingredients and one step, this recipe is moderate in difficulty.

*O*ur traditional potato cakes are not cake, biscuit, or bread. Rather, they are fried mashed potatoes, and when served fresh, they are crisp on the outside and soft inside—a heavenly delight. You'll occasionally find a mountain cook who leavens potato cakes with baking powder and bakes them on a cookie sheet like a biscuit, but that's not the way we usually do it. If, however, you are concerned about fat, you can bake, rather than fry, your potato cakes.

For a traditional mountain country dinner, serve these with Soup Beans, a thick slice of sweet onion, and a glass of buttermilk. To please your children or other "unsophisticated" palates, serve these cakes with tomato ketchup or sour cream. For a unique appetizer, make these half the size suggested above and serve with your choice of tomato ragout, Corn Relish, Chow Chow, or Pickled Beets.

STEPS In a large skillet melt half the butter and add half the oil. Mix the potatoes, optional ham and onions, flour, egg, and salt. Mix thoroughly.

At this point the mixture should hold its shape (not be mushy when you touch it). If it does not hold its shape, add one tablespoon of flour at a time until the mixture is firm.

Drop 6 ($1/3$-cup-sized) mounds of potato into the skillet, flatten with the back of the spoon, and fry over low heat for 7 minutes on each side. Add butter and oil as the potatoes absorb it. When ready, the outside surface should be a crusty dark brown, and the cakes should cook to the center. If you used a lot of butter, lift and slide the cooked cakes onto paper towels.

HEALTHY CHOICE ALTERNATIVE Use 2 egg whites in place of 1 egg. To avoid the fat completely: Preheat the oven to 450°F. Dip the bottom surface of the potato cakes in flour so that they will not stick. Place them on a baking sheet, or if you prefer, use a sheet covered with parchment. Flatten the tops with the back of the spoon. Bake for 20 minutes.

Serve hot, directly from the skillet. If you lay these cakes on a dinner plate, the bottoms will steam, and you'll lose the crisp surface.

INGREDIENTS
2 tablespoons butter, bacon grease, or lard
2 tablespoons safflower oil
2 cups mashed potatoes
1/2 cup (3 ounces) minced ham (optional)
1/2 cup diced onions (optional)
1/2 cup flour, plus more as needed
1 egg
1/2 teaspoon garlic salt

YIELD 4 servings

Boiled New Potatoes

*W*hen I slice into a raw new potato it feels thick, moist, and solid against my knife. When I taste a cooked new potato it feels waxy and crunchy. When I slice into an old baker, a mature potato that has been stored, it feels light; it looks dry; it cuts easily. Boiled, steamed, or baked old bakers feel mealy in my mouth. For a delicate side dish, serve new potatoes.

In many parts of the mountains, Highlanders plant potatoes in February, and by May or June they are ready to eat. Picked young, they make a tasty steamed or boiled starch. While the butter and spring onions are a nice addition here, the salt and pepper set this daily fare apart from other foods.

DIFFICULTY Easy. With five ingredients and one cooking step, this recipe is easy.

STEPS Wash, peel, and dice the potatoes into 1-inch pieces. If you are not going to cook them immediately, cover with water and refrigerate.

Put the potatoes into a large saucepan or steamer. Add water and bring to a boil. Reduce the heat, and simmer for 20 minutes, or until the potatoes are tender through to the center. Drain. Pour the potatoes into a serving bowl, and dot with the butter. Sprinkle with the onions, salt, and pepper. Serve.

HEALTHY CHOICE ALTERNATIVE Omit the butter and salt.

Serve with Skillet Cabbage and Country-Fried Steak.

INGREDIENTS
3 pounds new potatoes
1/4 cup butter
2 tablespoons finely chopped spring onions
1 teaspoon salt
1/2 teaspoon pepper

YIELD 5 servings

Twice-Baked Potatoes

A twice-baked potato is baked, mashed, topped, and then baked again. In my mind I picture a steaming hot fresh-from-the-oven, twice-baked potato with a crisp bottom shell, orange-brown cheesy top, and smooth creamy center. I can see it on my dinner plate with a thick slice of prime rib.

Twice-Baked Potatoes will help you to make a Sunday dinner or birthday celebration an occasion. I compare twice-baked potatoes to other special-dinner starches.

When it comes to dinner starches, we have many choices: corn, peas, beans, rice, pasta, and potatoes. They spark hunger pains and focus my senses. I crave starches, but when I start cooking, like so many others, I often reach for potatoes. Potatoes are romantic. Twice-baked potatoes are even more romantic, and I serve them on Valentine's Day.

Whether you call them twice-baked, stuffed baked, or on the half shell, these are mashed potatoes served in potato skins. Those that add blue cheese call them "blue cheese stuffed potatoes," and those that add hot red pepper and diced tomato call them "creole." Add hot-spiced ham and call them "deviled stuffed potatoes." If you make twice-baked potatoes, you have many choices.

In addition to my other suggestions you can make twice-baked potatoes with cooked sausage, ham, or crumbled bacon. You can add heavy cream, honest-to-goodness butter, cholesterol-free margarine, or real sour cream. If you want a quick fix, make them with Campbell's Nacho Cheese Soup or Campbell's Condensed Cream of Mushroom Soup, but don't tell anybody your secret.

One school of twice-baked potato lovers adds onion, chives, and bell peppers. This creole-oriented group might also add chopped fresh tomatoes, hot red peppers, jalapeño peppers, or Tabasco sauce.

Another group seems to stay with dairy products: milk, butter, cream, and sour cream. The fans of dairy products often add grated Parmesan cheese, Cheddar cheese, or gouda.

Some mountaineers add vegetables: fresh peas, chopped green onions, cooked celery, or raw onions. I particularly like diced onions that have been sautéed in butter.

Others add seafood: shrimp, crab meat, anchovies, or sardines. As to flavoring, consider adding salt, white pepper, mixed herbs, garlic, and paprika. You may add chicken or beef bouillon grains, or perhaps a package of dried onion soup mix.

You can make twice-baked potatoes with any mature potato. I prefer an old, dry, mealy potato such as an Idaho or Maine. When I use large potatoes, I cut them in half from end to end. When I use small potatoes, I cut off the top and use a whole potato for each serving.

■ ■

Twice-Baked Potatoes
Fancy Twice-Baked Potatoes (Stuffed Potatoes)

I serve potatoes baked, boiled, and fried. I make potato soup, potato salad, potato pancakes, and potato bread. Some day I'll make tater tots. Mashed potatoes, scalloped potatoes, and fried potatoes have such appeal. But when I need a festive potato, I prepare Twice-Baked Potatoes.

STEPS Preheat the oven to 450°F. Wash and dry the potatoes. For a crisp skin, do not oil the potatoes or wrap them in foil. Place the potatoes in the oven and bake them for 1 hour or more. (Longer baking results in a crisper skin.) The potatoes should be soft when you squeeze them on the sides; a knife should slide easily to the center.

As the potatoes bake, melt the butter in a saucepan and simmer the onions for about 4 minutes, or until they are transparent. Add the milk and salt and heat the milk.

DIFFICULTY Moderate. Making twice-baked potatoes is a three-step process: First, you bake the potatoes; second, you mash the centers; and third, you bake the potatoes a second time. With six ingredients, this recipe is moderate in difficulty. Allow 1 3/4 hours for preparation and baking.

INGREDIENTS
4 medium (3 pounds) baking potatoes
1/4 cup butter
1 cup diced onion
1 cup hot whole milk
1 teaspoon seasoned salt
2 ounces or 1/2 cup grated Cheddar cheese

YIELD 8 servings

■ Starches

Remove the potatoes from the oven and, using a clean potholder to protect your hands, cut the potatoes in half from end to end. Scoop out the center with a soup spoon, leaving a shell about 1/4-inch thick. Work slowly so that you do not break the skin. Reserve the shells.

In a mixing bowl, mash the pulp with a fork or rice it with a potato ricer. Slowly add the hot milk mixture to the mashed potatoes, stirring constantly. Be careful not to add too much milk. The mixture should be thick, not soupy.

Spoon the mixture back into the potato shells, and top with the grated cheese. Place on a baking sheet and bake for 20 minutes. If the tops are not brown, put the potatoes under the broiler for 1 to 2 minutes.

HEALTHY CHOICE ALTERNATIVE For those watching their fat and cholesterol, replace the butter and milk with 1 1/4 cups of home-cooked chicken broth or skim milk. If you are watching salt, omit it. Then, be frivolous and top the potatoes with real grated cheese.

Serve these potatoes with prime rib, pork roast, or barbecued chicken, accompanied by Sugared Carrots and Steamed Green Beans. For a complete meal, add Greenbrier Fiddlehead Salad and Angel Biscuits.

Fancy Twice-Baked Potatoes To the above recipe, add 1/2 cup sour cream and 1 cup grated Cheddar cheese to the cooked onions.

■ ■

Fried Potatoes

These potatoes are an all-American classic, a home-cooked favorite, a lazy-gourmet's side dish, a starchy vegetable, a breakfast tradition. Can you taste them? Can you feel the salt on your tongue, the crisp outside shell, and the soft moist centers? Like mountaineers have known for so long, you know that fried potatoes are fine, fancy, delicate daily fare. Memory food, home food. Get out your skillet!

The controversy surrounding fried potatoes is lively and deserving of attention. Let's enter the fray. The terms fried potatoes, or fried taters, as we use them, include home fries, cottage fries, French fries, potato wedges, and hash browns. Where does one of these styles end and another start?

Fried potatoes are not deep fried; if they are deep fried, call them French fries. If fried strips of potato are thick, they are steak fries; if the strips are thin, they are shoestring potatoes.

From Germans who settled the mountains, we learned to make German fried, home-fried, or cottage-fried potatoes. For German fries we slice and then fry the potatoes, with onion and green pepper. Like fried potatoes, we cook these at medium to low heat in very little oil.

Years ago mountain cooks rolled their potatoes in cornmeal and sprinkled them with flour. They then dropped the battered potatoes into hot frying lard. With both salt and batter, these coated fries are special.

To prepare hashed brown potatoes, we boil potatoes and then grate them into a skillet. We fry them with bacon grease, salt pork, or oil; but in any case we press the grated potatoes into a uniform layer in the pan and fry them as a block. When the potatoes are brown on one side, we either serve them or turn them over and brown the other side too.

For fried potatoes we fry either boiled or raw potatoes. I prefer frying raw potatoes. I make fried potatoes with the skins on or peeled clean, and I fry them sliced, diced, or julienned depending on the look I want.

If you julienne, you'll be making shoestring potatoes. You can also fry grated raw potatoes, and you can "fry" them without oil. In a well-cured heavy skillet potatoes without oil will brown nicely—we call these fried potatoes pan-broiled, as opposed to fried, potatoes.

Fried potatoes are not sautéed. To sauté means to cook quickly over high heat, and we fry potatoes slowly. Fried raw potatoes are not baked, and they are not steamed. On the other hand, my Home Fries, below, are steamed and fried.

Fried Raw Potatoes
Allegheny Home Fries
(Country-Fried Potatoes)

DIFFICULTY Easy. With just four ingredients, this recipe is easy to make.

INGREDIENTS
1 tablespoon butter, olive oil, or bacon grease (just enough to barely cover the bottom of the pan)
3 cups medium-diced firm new potatoes
1 teaspoon seasoned salt
1 cup diced onions (optional)

YIELD 3 servings

*T*o make Fried Raw Potatoes we use peeled and diced potatoes. I like to fry them in little oil over low heat. You can make fried raw potatoes with finely diced (1/4-inch cubes), medium-diced (1/2-inch cubes), or coarsely diced (3/4-inch cubes) potatoes. With larger cubes, more potatoes will fit in a single layer in the skillet, but they will need to cook longer.

Allow 1/3 teaspoon salt and 1/3 cup diced onions for each cup of diced potatoes, but do not crowd the pan—these are not hashed browns.

STEPS Wash the potatoes and remove any brown spots. If you dice the potatoes ahead, store them in the refrigerator in a bowl of water.

In a heavy-bottomed frying pan over low-medium heat, melt the butter and add the potatoes. Cover and fry 10 to 15 minutes. Turn the potatoes, and if they are cooked through to the center, remove the lid, add the onions, and increase the heat to medium. Cook another 10 to 15 minutes, turning them every 5 minutes, or until they have browned on all sides. Serve.

HEALTHY CHOICE ALTERNATIVE You can fry potatoes in little or even no oil. In this recipe I have already reduced the butter to one quarter tablespoon per serving, but you can further reduce it by using nonstick cooking spray. Omit the salt and offer it at the table.

Serve these with green beans, corn bread, and pork chops, or for breakfast with fresh fruit, Buttermilk Biscuits, Country Ham and Red-Eye Gravy, White Sausage Gravy, or Potato Gravy.

Allegheny Home Fries
Home fries are not fried potatoes. To make home fries, double the above recipe. The onions are not optional. Cut the potatoes in half and then slice them. Slice the onions. Layer the sliced potatoes and onions in a frying pan. Cook, covered, over low heat for 30 minutes, turning after 15 minutes. Cook uncovered an additional 15 minutes.

With low heat and so many potatoes in the pan, these fries will be steamed and soft, but tasty. Yield: 6 servings.

Corn:
From Corn on the Cob to Mush and Corn Relish

JESSE STUART, AUTHOR, teacher, and school superintendent, lived from 1906 to 1984 in the hills of northeastern Kentucky. He was the son of tenant farmers and lived most of his life in a farm setting, supplementing his teaching salary with farming and writing.

Writing in 1936 in *Head o' W-Hollow*, Jesse Stuart talks about corn. This chatter is representative of the book, a description of Stuart's hill-country style of living:

> We planted the corn. We plowed it the first time and chopped the weeds out of it. We plowed it the second time and the third time. It was soon over the mule's back. When it got that high we quit plowin it. I'd lay in my bed at night and look at it. I'd look at the moonlight on the cornfield bright as day. I would think: "The night is pretty. The night was made for man and the fox. The night was made for silence. The stars in the sky. The silver-like dew-drops on the corn. The night is pretty, whoever made it and whatever it was made for. I like the night. I love the night." I watched the moonlight flicker on the corn blades. . . .

When Europeans arrived in America, the Native Americans enjoyed a diet that included corn, beans, tomatoes, potatoes, sweet peppers, and pumpkin. They had much to offer a sometimes drab European diet, but over time, it was corn—now grown on this continent for almost 6,000 years—that became dominant. When settlers came to the Appalachian Mountains, they brought this Indian maize with them and planted it in the narrow valleys and up the sides of hills. They found that corn was better adapted than wheat to mountain topography.

Besides feeding corn to chickens and pigs, mountaineers cherished their roasting ears, boiled or roasted and eaten from the cob. When the corn matured and got firm, they made gritted corn for moist bread, and when the corn dried, they ground it into meal or boiled it with lye to make hominy. They ground the hominy to make grits, and with sprouted corn, they made moonshine.

But corn was more than food. Mountaineers used the shucks for animal feed and chair bottoms. They made corn husk mats, hats, and horse collars.

When there was time to spare, they devoted their time to a special craft, the cornshuck doll. Craftspeople make them by moistening dry corn shucks, dying them, cutting them with a scissors, forming doll parts, assembling the parts with thin strips of cornshuck or string, and painting the faces. They use corn silks for hair and small sticks for broom handles or logs. *The Foxfire Book of Toys and Games*, edited by Linda Garland Page and Hilton Smith, lists many other toys made from corn, including corn guns, corncob darts and dolls, and cornstalk airplanes, fiddles, sleds, and slings.

A less-innocent use of this staple crop, corn whisky is such a tradition here that our connections to it seem natural: clear streams, cool mountains, dry corn, pure moonshine, and "revenuers." Moonshine, or as we often call it mountain dew and white lightning, was a cash crop. Aside from the pleasure of drinking our own beverage, perhaps the finest pure whisky anywhere, moonshine was an efficient and profitable way to sell corn, so long as revenue agents did not cause trouble. How profitable was moonshine? Selling a bushel of corn after converting it to moonshine might have been one hundred times as profitable as selling the corn itself.

Making Moonshine

Moonshine is 100-proof whisky made by a special breed of mountain people—moonshiners. How do we make it? We distill moonshine from fermented corn mash. We make the mash from 80 percent ground sprouted corn, and we add some rye, if we have it. Ground corn, rye, water, and sugar are ingredients for mash. The mash is allowed to ferment. If moonshiners have yeast and use it, the fermentation takes four days; if we don't have yeast, fermentation takes about ten days.

The next step in making moonshine is to find a hollow deep in the hills that has cool clean water. Good moonshine water is soft; moonshiners know the water is soft if they see red horsemint growing on the banks. Second, the hollow cannot be discovered by revenue agents. To avoid discovery, careful moonshiners don't let cattle or hogs eat the slop and mess in the creek water, and we don't use wood that makes smoke. Water scented by animals and smoky fires attract agents. Finally, we don't spread gossip, and we don't tell anyone except family about our still.

Then, good moonshiners use fermented mash to "run off" the whisky, distilling it twice with cold running water, not letting the still get too hot or too cold. Lastly, we check the proof. When the drink is ready, we'll look in your eye and say with a slight smile, "This is the best whisky in the world." Making moonshine is an art, and we still have people that practice the trade. Unfortunately, the law does not allow me to give you a mail-order source.

Corn Varieties

Those who grow corn know that the various varieties have different textures, colors, flavors, and keeping qualities.

Not long ago a common mountain corn variety was Hickory King corn, a traditional, open pollinated white corn. It grows tall, up to sixteen feet high, and we use it for hominy and pickles. Hickory King corn, however, lacks the sweetness genes that geneticists developed in the late 1950s. The first hybrids were varieties such as Sunglow and Golden Cross Bantam. A little later agronomists gave us Silver Queen, the standard hybrid for more than thirty years. More recently corn geneticists have developed sugary enhancer hybrids such as Breeder's Choice, Miracle, and Kandy Korn E.H. (Everlasting Heritage). These varieties retain the texture of traditional varieties, but have a higher sugar content and will remain sweet for a week if left on the plant.

Finally, today we have the super-sweet hybrids such as Early Xtra-Sweet, How Sweet It Is, and Honey'N Pearl. These varieties may be twice as sweet as others and you can store them picked without losing flavor.

Highlanders still grow some Hickory King corn. We use it for gritted corn bread, hog feed, and hominy. But most Highlanders now grow sweet corn and you'll find all the new varieties in our gardens.

Corn on the Cob

I can still remember the burned and smoky flavor of the outdoor fire-roasted corn that I ate as a child. Roasting corn over an outdoor fire was exciting. As a child, I liked the smoky flavor, but I ate around the charred kernels. Now as an adult I savor charred kernels. In a large stone and concrete outdoor fireplace-grill, we built a fire of hardwoods—maple, beech, apple, or hickory. As the fire burned, we prepared the corn by pulling back the husks, removing the silks, and then replacing the husks. We soaked the corn in water until we were ready to roast it. When the fire burnt down, we laid the ears on a steel grate. Fifteen minutes later the corn was ready. In the coolness of a summer evening we sat at a picnic table and bit into the charred sweetness.

While corn is available in the market much of the year, July and August offer the pick of the season. Buy freshly picked ears. The husks should be snug and green, and the stalk ends should look fresh, not dried up and chalky in color. The silks should be dark brown. After I look at the ears, I feel them by gripping one at a time as though I was shaking the hand of a good friend. Like a handshake, I am looking for a firm ear, one that does not have soft spots.

If possible, I taste before I buy. Raw sweet corn should be sweet, tender, crunchy, juicy, and delicious before you cook it. Short of tasting, check the kernels to be sure that they look plump and juicy. They should be filled out, but not crowded together or indented. Avoid wormy ears.

INGREDIENTS
Freshly picked corn ears, 1 per serving

YIELD Allow 1 ear per serving

STEPS For fully cleaned corn, remove the husks and silks. A soft scrub brush speeds the removal of silks. Wash. To prepare, choose from boiling, steaming, roasting, or microwaving:

To boil: Bring a large pot of water to a boil. For each three ears, add 1 tablespoon of sugar. Do not add salt, as it toughens the corn. When the water boils, gently slip fully cleaned ears into the pot. Let the water return to a boil, and boil for 3 to 6 minutes, depending on the size and sweetness of the corn. Like pasta, sometimes I like corn al dente. Drain.

To steam: Steam corn on the cob by placing it fully cleaned on a rack over 1 inch of boiling water. Steam 3 to 8 minutes, depending on the size, sweetness, and age of the corn. I also like to steam corn in the husk with the silks (this saves a step) for 4 to 9 minutes. When I take the corn from the pan, I cut off the end of the stalk, insert a skewer, and pull the husks and silks off the ear.

To roast: Roast corn in the oven, over a fire, or on a charcoal grill, either in the husk with the silks or fully cleaned in aluminum foil. When using foil, remove the husks and silks. Wrap in foil, add butter and spices, and twist the ends closed.

If using an oven, bake the corn in the husk with the silks for 25 to 30 minutes at 350°F. On a fire or grill it takes less time, as the temperature will be higher.

When roasting over coals, fire, or gas, prevent burning by placing the corn 10 inches above the heat source and turning the corn every few minutes. If the husks start to burn, spray them with water. The total cooking time may be as little as 6 minutes, again depending on your tastes and the sweetness and tenderness of the corn. On a grill over hot coals, I like to cook fully cleaned ears, quickly caramelizing the natural sugar and charring the hull, as I would when peeling a tomato or roasting bell peppers.

To microwave: This works for up to three ears. Microwave your corn in the husks with the silks, or fully cleaned and wrapped in waxed paper with the ends twisted closed. Arrange the corn in the oven 1 inch apart, and microwave on high for 3 minutes per medium-size ear. Rotate the corn every 3 minutes. When almost cooked, let the ears stand for a few minutes. If you cooked the corn with the husks and silks, add 1 minute per ear to the cooking time. Then, with a heavy chef's knife, cut off the large end. Insert a long skewer into the stalk, and using a potholder hold the husk and pull it and the silks off the ear.

HEALTHY CHOICE ALTERNATIVE Corn is high in carbohydrates, and ounce for ounce it is high in calories. When you serve corn fresh on the cob, corn is a source of fiber, vitamins, and minerals. An average ear of corn has about 100 calories.

Serve corn on the cob hot with butter, salt, and pepper. At our table we hold the corn with corn skewers, handles with points that we press into both ends of the corn. In July or August I'll eat corn on the cob raw, al dente, or fully cooked. I'll eat it hot or cold and without salt, butter, fuss, or guilt. Corn is a sweet vegetable—one of summer's finest joys.

Buttered Sweet Corn with Black Pepper
(Baked Fresh Corn)

*A*fter eating a few batches of corn on the cob in the early summer, I prefer to eat corn cut off the cob. The corn is the same, but corn cut from the cob is less messy. I flavor the corn with butter, salt, and pepper. In our house, cooking and freezing corn is an August chore that pays off all year. We freeze corn either on or off the cob, and we use it in recipes such as this.

DIFFICULTY Easy.
If you start with fresh corn, making this dish has two steps: preparing the corn and mixing the casserole. If you start with prepared corn, the recipe is a snap, calling for just four ingredients.

STEPS Prepare the corn for boiling by removing the husks, silks, and bad spots. In a large pot, bring to a boil enough water to cover. Add the corn. Return to a boil, and boil 3 minutes. Drain and cool.

Starches

INGREDIENTS
3 ears sweet corn, or 2
  cups fresh or frozen
  corn kernels
1 tablespoon butter
$^1\!/_2$ teaspoon salt
$^1\!/_2$ teaspoon pepper

YIELD 4 servings

Cut the corn from the cob using a sharp knife. Don't cut too close to the cob or you'll end up with some of the rough cob mixed with the corn. In a casserole dish, combine the corn, butter, salt, and pepper.

In a microwave, cook for 4 minutes on high; in an oven preheated to 350°F, bake, covered, 20 to 25 minutes. Serve.

HEALTHY CHOICE ALTERNATIVE Replace the butter with butter flavoring and safflower oil. Replace the salt with a salt-free mixture. You can buy salt-free spice mixes composed of sweet bell pepper, dill weed, garlic, ground mustard, lemon peel, oregano, basil, marjoram, thyme, and crushed rosemary, just to name a few.

Serve this corn hot with chilled sliced fresh tomatoes.

Succotash

DIFFICULTY Easy.
With five ingredients and
no real cooking, this
recipe is easy.

*S*uccotash is a starchy vegetable dish that we make with lima beans, corn, and a slight sauce. Ancient, primal, and earthy, succotash is a simple food. Its textures please my palate, and its history intrigues my mind.

When Christopher Columbus arrived in the New World, the so-called Indians were using two thousand different foods derived from plants. Succotash was perhaps their most universal dish. Native Americans grew pole beans in their corn fields, the beans winding their way up and around the cornstalks. At harvest the corn and beans found their way into the same pot, and they called the dish *m'sick-quotash*, *sukquttahash*, and *msakwitash*. To the white settlers, corn was new, and this combination was strange. It took time for Europeans to appreciate succotash; eventually, however, the native food became a favorite.

INGREDIENTS
2$^1\!/_2$ cups cooked cream-
  style corn
1$^3\!/_4$ cups cooked lima
  beans
$^1\!/_4$ cup butter
1 teaspoon salt
1 teaspoon ground white
  pepper

YIELD 8 servings

Because so many mountain cooks have a tradition of making succotash, we have many ways to prepare it. To my recipe many add chopped bacon, cooked tomatoes, butter beans, or onions. Creamed corn, as opposed to kernel corn, makes the dish saucy. Craig Claiborne's *Southern Cooking* presents a succotash made with hominy, fresh corn, lima beans, peas, scallions, and sweet red pepper. Others make succotash as a soup, adding milk or cream and thickening the soup with flour, or as a stew, adding carrots, cabbage, and potatoes.

STEPS Combine corn, beans, butter, salt, and pepper. Heat them in a double boiler or microwave until hot. Serve.

HEALTHY CHOICE ALTERNATIVE Omit the butter.

Serve this dish with Fried Chicken, garden tomatoes, and Hot Rolls, or with Sugared Carrots and Roast Pork with Stuffed Apples.

 Cornmeal

TO MAKE CORNMEAL we grind dry corn between heavy stones or steel rollers. When we use stone wheels, the hull and germ of the corn become part of the mix. Stone-ground cornmeal is more healthy than steel-ground meal, whose product does not contain the hull or germ. The germ contains the fat and minerals, which enhance flavor.

In food specialty stores you can purchase cornmeal in fine, medium, or coarse grinds. I treasure coarse stone-ground cornmeal because it is rough-textured and full-flavored. In addition, it includes the hull and the germ.

Mixing a little coarse stone-ground cornmeal into corn bread gives the pone a more substantial texture. This full kernel, fresh cornmeal represents the best of primitive country cooking, and it is gaining favor among people who are concerned about good health. Stone-ground cornmeal is a natural, rather than highly processed, food.

In the South we are partial to white cornmeal. Northerners use yellow cornmeal—a grain that I associate with pigs, chickens, mules, horses, and cows. Northerners—oh, heaven forbid!—often add sugar to their corn bread, and they add cream and maple syrup to their cornmeal mush. The yellow cornmeal they use—quite likely, it is steel ground and degerminated—may need these ingredients. Better quality cornmeal, such as stone-ground white cornmeal, has a flavor that we Southerners think needs no cream or sugar, we add just a little salt and butter to our white cornmeal mush. Many processors sift cornmeal to remove the hull. We call this sifted meal bolted cornmeal, which is just one processing step away from grits. Corn grits and stone-ground cornmeal are both made with ground corn. Grits, however, are made from hominy. The word *hominy* means that the corn was soaked in an alkali solution, and the hull and germ were removed.

From the Smokies to the Blue Ridge, supermarket managers adjust their shelf space to accommodate the demand for self-rising cornmeal. Stores such as Piggly-Wiggly, Food City, and Winn-Dixie sell up to eight different varieties in bags that range in size from eight ounces to fifty pounds. The twenty-five-pound bag is common.

In addition to the term self-rising, the packages carry one or more of the following labels: enriched, buttermilk, yellow cornmeal, white cornmeal, whole kernel, organic, bolted, tender-rise, and hot-rise. Generally, they contain enriched cornmeal, all-purpose flour, salt, and leavening. Unless labeled whole or whole kernel, they are probably degerminated. These mixes vary in the amount of salt and flour and the coarseness of the cornmeal.

If you buy fresh whole-grain cornmeal, you should store it in a sealed container. If stored too long at room temperature, the fat in the germ will cause it to spoil. It will stay fresh for three months or, if you freeze it, last indefinitely.

SELF-RISING CORNMEAL MIX For consistency, you can also make your own self-rising cornmeal mix. For 1 1/2 cups of self-rising cornmeal, sift together 1 cup cornmeal, 1/2 cup all-purpose flour, 1 1/2 teaspoons baking powder, and 1 teaspoon salt.

■ **Starches**

Mush
Fried Mush (Polenta, Cornmeal Mush, and Porridge)

DIFFICULTY Very Easy. With three ingredients and less than 10 minutes of preparation time, this recipe is very easy to prepare.

*L*ong before Italians made polenta, there was mush. With hand labor and a stone pestle, Native Americans ground corn. Like people around the world today, they made mush with boiled water, salt, and ground corn. The Italians call this combination polenta. The English call it porridge. We call it mush. Cornmeal mush. This side dish, this classic food, is mining camp and farm food. Boiled cornmeal is hearty, healthy, and robust. Mush is stick-to-the-ribs, old-fashioned food. Mountain cooks use mush to make spoon bread, and we fry it to make corn cakes or Fried Mush. For mature eaters, mush is competition for cornflakes, frosted flakes, corn puffs, corn pops, and other crunchy pieces of processed corn that you pour from plastic-lined, highly colored cardboard boxes. For other eaters mush is too hot, too slow, and too soft. It doesn't come in plastic and it is not finger food. Perhaps that explains why I like it.

INGREDIENTS
2½ cups water
1 cup stone-ground cornmeal
1¼ teaspoons salt

YIELD 6 servings

STEPS In a 2-quart microwave-safe container, combine the water, meal, and salt, and whisk until smooth. Microwave on high for 3 minutes. Whisk again, mixing completely, and microwave another 3 minutes on high. Depending on your oven and the cornmeal, this recipe will cook 6 to 9 minutes. When mush is ready, it has absorbed the water and drops off a spoon like mashed potatoes.

HEALTHY CHOICE ALTERNATIVE Eating cornmeal mush is healthy. For a food of ultimate perfection and good health, make mush with fresh whole-grain, stone-ground cornmeal, bottled water, and no salt.

Serve mush sweet or savory—with milk and sugar or butter and salt. For dinner serve mush as a side dish with beef, pork, and greens, in place of potatoes, pasta, beans, or rice. I eat mush for breakfast. For a hearty meal, serve it with Dried Apple Applesauce, eggs, and Biscuits and Gravy.

Fried Mush Fried Mush is dancing-happy breakfast food. When you take it from your skillet or fryer, it should be crunchy and crisp on the outside and soft on the inside. Some cooks dip the slices in a French toast–like batter, others add flour and egg. I do neither.

Prepare one recipe of Mush the night before you plan to fry it. Pour and spread the batter into a 6x3½x2½-inch loaf pan, and refrigerate overnight or until firm. Turn the loaf out of the pan and cut it into ½-inch to ⅓-inch thick slices. Using a skillet, fry the slices over low to medium heat, 10 minutes on each side. Fry in a mixture of safflower oil and butter or pork chop, sausage, or bacon drippings. Alternatively, fry in a deep fryer. Fry the mush slices until they are golden brown on both sides.

Serve with eggs, pork, biscuits, and orange juice. Sprinkle with salt and pepper or douse with butter and a sweet pancake syrup. This Fried Mush has a crunch that may even appeal to corn-flake children.

Fried Liver Mush
Fried Sausage Mush

*L*iver mush or scrapple is popular in the mountains of Georgia and North Carolina. You'll find family-owned restaurants serving it in areas east to Charlotte, North Carolina, and west to the Ozarks. Southern Appalachians make liver mush by boiling shredded pork liver and cornmeal in a spicy pork broth, others make it with sausage, and the Pennsylvania Dutch, as well as butchers around Philadelphia, are famous for their scrapple made with pork scraps and liver. In Cincinnati, established families make scrapple with Irish oats (also called pin or cross-cut oats), and they call it goetta.

Liver mush, scrapple, sausage scrapple, liverell, and liver pudding are related dishes. Some Pennsylvania Germans (and Germans from Palatinate in Bavaria, Germany) call scrapple *pannhâs*, but I also found it spelled as panhoss, panhaus, pawnhaus, or ponhaws. The various scrapples include pieces of chopped pork lean or pork liver, and they are thickened with cornmeal.

The difference between liver sausage and liver mush is the amount of liver. Sausage has more liver than mush. Liver pudding is a pork liver pâté, much like a French liver pâté. It has far more liver than our Fried Liver Mush and we eat it cold on a sandwich or with a salad.

Some liver puddings are more like liverwurst or liver sausage in that they don't have any cornmeal. A well-known liverwurst is braunschweiger. This liver sausage or spread was first made in the town of Braunschweig, Germany, and includes smoked liver, eggs, and milk. Appalachians with a northern European ancestry serve liverwurst with boiled cabbage, mashed potatoes, and creamed turnips.

To my recipe, try adding hot red pepper, ground black pepper, whole pepper corns, chicken bouillon grains, and rubbed sage. When I serve this dish as an appetizer or sandwich meat, I increase the spices; for a main dish or breakfast side dish, I use fewer spices.

DIFFICULTY Moderate. To make this fried mush I boil and stir together five ingredients, chill the mush, and then fry slices.

STEPS Prepare the mush and liver 4 hours ahead or the day before you fry the mush. Wash the livers, cut them in half, and remove the tough connecting membranes. In a saucepan, boil the livers in the water for 3 minutes, or until the liv-

INGREDIENTS
1/2 pound chopped
chicken liver
1 1/2 cups water
3/4 cup coarse stone-
ground cornmeal
1 teaspoon salt
2 tablespoons oil (saf-
flower oil or pork drip-
pings)

YIELD 5 servings

ers are brown through to the center. Lift them from the water and set them aside to cool. Chop into 1/4-inch pieces.

Slowly whisk the cornmeal into the liver broth, add the salt, and return to a boil. Reduce the heat and, stirring frequently, simmer the mush for 5 minutes, or until the corn absorbs all the water and drops off a spoon in globs like mashed potatoes.

Stir the chopped liver into the cooked cornmeal. Pour and smooth the mush into a small 6x3 1/2x2 1/2-inch loaf pan. Cover, cool, and refrigerate at least 4 hours, or until firm.

Turn the loaf of liver mush out of the pan and slice it 1/2-inch thick. In a large skillet, heat 1 tablespoon of the oil. Fry the slices over low heat for 15 minutes. Turn the slices, add the second tablespoon of oil, and fry another 15 minutes, until the mush develops a thick, firm, deep golden brown crust on both sides. Turn off the heat and allow the mush to fry another 5 minutes in the pan. Slow frying allows the crust to develop, but the heat has to be high enough to brown it. Keep warm in a 200°F oven, not a microwave. Serve.

TIP In comparison to other mush recipes, I use less water in this recipe so that when you slice and fry the mush, it will be stiff enough to hold together.

HEALTHY CHOICE ALTERNATIVE Vegetable Scrapple. In 1977 the Culinary Arts Institute published a recipe for vegetable scrapple in *The Fifty States Cookbook*. The Institute attributed the recipe to North Carolina.

Omit the livers. Replace them with 1/2 cup chopped peas, peanuts, or beans and 1/2 cup cooked and diced carrots. Fry in a vegetable oil such as canola or safflower oil. Offer salt and pepper at the table.

Serve Fried Liver Mush for breakfast with eggs, salmon cakes, fried onions, pork, biscuits, cornmeal griddle cakes, orange juice, and coffee. Sprinkle with salt and pepper, or douse with melted butter and pancake syrup. Spread with peanut butter and jelly. Or, place Fried Liver Mush between halves of a biscuit, as you would sausage. Fried Liver Mush can be part of a nutritionally balanced dinner when you serve it with Creamed Spinach, Savory Boiled Turnips, or Puréed Butternut Squash.

In *American Cookery* James Beard suggests using scrapple as a base for quail or partridge. I can imagine slices of turkey or ham laid next to Fried Sausage Mush and topped with gravy or mornay sauce. I can also imagine a low-fat meal of plain tomato sauce spread on a plate and topped with a slice of Fried Liver Mush. For a complete entrée I would garnish the plate with whole steamed fresh vegetables and wild mushrooms.

Fried Sausage Mush Substitute 1/2 pound of any pork sausage for the ¹/₂ pound of liver. Fry, mince, and drain the sausage, patting it with paper towels, before adding it to the mush. Serve as you would Fried Liver Mush, or with ketchup, tomato gravy, or brown gravy.

Custard Corn Pudding

For corn pudding I use cream-style corn, and I'm rather particular about it. If you buy canned cream-style corn, it may be too creamy and too saucy. It may be high in sugar, water, and cornstarch, and it may not contain much corn.

I like to make my own cream-style corn. A handy device called a corn cutter and creamer (sold in the Burpee Gardens seed catalog, listed in the Mail-Order Sources) cuts the kernels vertically through the center and scrapes them, while a horizontal blade cuts them off the cob. I do not add a cream sauce. Rather, by using young milk-stage corn and this tool, the corn forms its own cream. This is an all-natural cream-style corn.

I bake this corn pudding in a water bath—a dish of hot water that surrounds the baking dish—because slow, even heat keeps the egg from curdling.

DIFFICULTY Easy. With four ingredients and one step, this recipe is easy.

STEPS Preheat the oven to 300°F. To prepare a water bath, boil water in a teakettle. Select a 2-quart casserole and a second oven-proof container in which the 2-quart casserole will fit.

In a mixing bowl, beat the eggs and add the milk and salt. Beat until fully mixed. Stir in the corn. Pour the mixture into the 2-quart casserole.

Set this dish in the larger oven-proof container, and add 1¹/₂ inches of the boiling water to the larger container. Bake for 1 hour, or until the center is almost set and a toothpick inserted near the center comes out clean. If at any time the water bath starts to bubble, reduce the oven temperature.

HEALTHY CHOICE ALTERNATIVE Use skim milk and omit the egg yolks. Add 10 minutes to the baking time.

Serve as you would any corn dish. Serve with Fried Catfish and Hush Puppies or Fried Pork Chops and Steamed Green Beans.

INGREDIENTS
2 eggs
1 cup milk
1 teaspoon salt
2 cups cream-style corn

YIELD 8 servings

Corn Relish

*T*alking about corn relish is a pickle of a topic. Some people use the terms pickles and relish interchangeably. While a relish is usually a mixture of chopped preserved vegetables, my corn relish recipe is virtually all corn.

Pickles, relish, chutney, and even ketchup are preserves, meaning that we make them to preserve garden produce for later use. Preserves grew in popularity when glass jars became readily available. With the advent of freezers, convenience foods, and supermarkets, preserving food became less of a necessity and there has been a decline in home pickling.

Despite the decline, Highlanders still make pickles to preserve fresh produce. We do this because pickles are a whole world of texture, flavor, and color, and because our markets cannot possibly offer the variety that we make at home. For a change of pace and an Appalachian tradition, try this Corn Relish.

Some cooks like their corn relish hot, adding red hot peppers or Tabasco sauce. Others use red bell peppers for color, and if we don't have any on hand, we substitute pimiento. Many use celery. Others add flour or cornstarch to thicken the relish, or a bit of sugar to make it sweet.

Old recipes called for a whole head of cabbage and eighteen ears of corn. I offer a small recipe, just enough for a dinner, and I add turmeric to give the relish a bright yellow color. You can make this relish with fresh, canned, or frozen sweet corn.

DIFFICULTY Moderate. With seven ingredients and one cooking step, this recipe is moderate in difficulty. When I use our fresh frozen corn, chop the onions and pepper ahead, and serve the relish hot, this recipe is a snap. It cooks in only 4 minutes.

INGREDIENTS
1/3 cup white vinegar
1/2 cup sugar
1/4 teaspoon dry mustard
1/4 teaspoon turmeric
1 1/4 cups whole kernel yellow corn
1/4 cup diced onion
1/4 cup diced green sweet bell pepper

YIELD 1 1/4 cups or 5 small servings

STEPS In a small saucepan over medium heat, bring the vinegar, sugar, mustard, and turmeric to a boil. Add the corn, onion, and bell pepper, and cook for 4 minutes. Serve hot or cold.

HEALTHY CHOICE ALTERNATIVE Reduce the sugar to 1/4 cup.

Serve as an accompaniment to any festive dinner, or serve with everyday foods such as a ham sandwich, Soup Beans, Shuck Beans, Fried Potatoes, or Southern Fried Chicken.

Pinto Beans and Soup Beans

OUR SUPERMARKETS SELL white beans, red kidneys, and Great Northerns in one-pound bags. In the fall, however, small markets, country stores, and supermarket chains sell pinto beans in three-pound, ten-pound, twenty-five-pound, and even forty-pound bags. What does this tell us? Pinto beans, also called soup beans, may well be our most cooked winter food. They are a lunch food, a dinner food, and a staple. The dominance of the pinto may not be so dramatic north of Kentucky and north of southern West Virginia, but generally the pinto bean is the Southern mountaineer's first choice. In the following recipes, you may use any dry bean.

When you are cooking the larger beans, such as pinto and kidney, these suggestions may help:

1. Cut the cooking time in half by using a pressure cooker.
2. Soak the beans overnight, or boil them for 2 minutes and soak them for 1 hour.
3. The acid of tomatoes slows the cooking time. Add tomatoes at the end.
4. Because a high temperature causes the beans to break, simmer them slowly and for a long time.
5. Soft vegetables such as tomatoes and green peppers add contrast and complementary texture to cooked beans. To maintain the appearance and texture of these vegetables, add them to the beans at the end of the cooking time.

For ten years starting in the mid 1970s, I taught a Pikeville College course called Appalachian Education. In these classes, about five hundred students joined me in the study of local education history, and in the writing of an ethnographic research paper. This work culminated in a jointly written book, *Education in Appalachia's Central Highlands*. As part of the class, students, families, and friends celebrated Appalachian foods with a potluck heritage dinner. I encouraged each student to bring his favorite historical food. One dish I learned to appreciate is soup beans.

Along with corn bread, soup beans are a foundation of Appalachian country cooking. Soup beans are a smooth, pork-flavored pinto bean dish. Our soup beans are a plain food. Free of those bean soup ingredients such as peas, potatoes, tomatoes, carrots, and celery, soup beans are not a complex mixture, like vegetable soup, stew, or chili. In other bean soups you will find red, white, and black beans. Cooks all over the United States make bean soups with limas, lentils, favas, black-eyed peas, and Great Northerns; they may add sausage balls or chorizo. You may know bean soups by names such as Dutch navy or Spanish bean soup. Perhaps you know them as cowpuncher's, cassoulet, and chowder; maybe you call them minestrones or fifteen-bean soups. Soup beans, on the other hand, are plain pork and pintos—a soup and a stew.

Soup Beans
(Pinto Beans)

DIFFICULTY Easy. With three ingredients and overnight soaking, this recipe is easy.

*S*oup beans, either the bean or the prepared dish, are low in cost and are high in fiber, flavor, and protein. Here in the eastern tip of Kentucky I have learned to soak the beans all night and cook them all day, with pork flavoring and pintos. My friend Elvis Hatfield, of Pinson Fork on Pond Creek of Pike County, Kentucky, says his soup bean recipe is made with four ingredients: pinto beans, lard, salt, and pepper. First, he soaks the beans overnight. Then, he puts the ingredients in a saucepan and simmers them all day.

We serve soup beans with other winter foods: corn bread, potatoes, and home-canned relish or pickles.

INGREDIENTS
1 pound dried pinto beans, washed and picked over for pebbles
7 cups of water
8 ounces salt pork or 2 ham hocks (1 pound)

YIELD 10 to 12 servings

STEPS In a glass or ceramic container, soak the beans in the water overnight. Do not drain. Place the beans and water in a saucepan and add the pork. Simmer on medium heat, covered, for 4 to 8 hours. Add water as needed to keep the beans covered. When cooked, the beans hold their shape but are soft throughout. Remove the pork, and serve it as a side dish.

TIP While many serve the broth thin as pot likker to be sopped up with corn bread, I like it thick, like a cream soup. To thicken, boil down the liquid, or use a fork to mash some cooked beans. When I am in a hurry, I take a cup of beans, puree them in a blender, and return them to the soup.

HEALTHY CHOICE ALTERNATIVE Replace the pork with 1/4 cup safflower oil. Add 1 tablespoon salt and 1/2 teaspoon pepper, or offer them at the table.

For a traditional dinner, serve Soup Beans with buttermilk, Simple Corn Bread, and Wilted Lettuce. Another favorite combination is Soup Beans, Fried Potatoes, and Sauerkraut. Common accompaniments include bread and butter pickles, canned hot peppers, sauerkraut and wieners, Corn Relish, dill pickles, green onions, diced onions, Buttermilk Corn Bread, corn muffins, and saltine crackers. Highlanders frequently serve the salt pork or ham hocks as a side dish. We do not waste food. Most mountain families have someone who savors plain boiled salt pork.

Bean Dumplings
(Soup Beans and Dumplings)

*T*his recipe combines our special bean, our Soup Beans, with Slick Dumplings. Like beans and rice or beans and corn bread, this too is a complete meal.

STEPS In a glass or ceramic container, soak the beans in the water overnight. Do not drain.

The next morning, prepare the soup beans: In a saucepan over medium heat, combine the beans, water, and salt pork. Simmer, covered, for 4 to 8 hours. Add water as needed to keep the beans covered. Stir in the salt and pepper. When cooked, the beans hold their shape but are soft throughout. Remove the pork.

Prepare the dumplings: In a mixing bowl, combine the flour with the salt. With a whisk, stir the shortening into the flour. Add the broth or water and mix until you have a stiff dough. Knead for 15 strokes, or until smooth and elastic.

Working on a floured surface and using a rolling pin, roll the dough to 1/8-inch to 1/4-inch thickness, as though you were making a pie crust. Use a pizza cutter or chef's knife to cut 1x2-inch pieces. Dry the surface of the dumplings by sprinkling them with instant flour.

Add water to the pot until you have 3 cups of broth. You need 3 cups of liquid for the dumplings. Drop the dumplings, one at a time, into the pot. To keep the dumplings separated, stir them from the bottom. When the dumplings are in the pot, cover, reduce the heat, and simmer for 15 minutes.

Remove from the heat, cover the pan, and cool 30 to 60 minutes—this helps thicken the bean broth and tenderize the dumplings. Serve.

HEALTHY CHOICE ALTERNATIVE Replace the salt pork with 2 tablespoons safflower oil. Use 1 1/2 teaspoons of salt, or offer it at the table.

Served in soup bowls, these beans and dumplings are a full meal. Serve with milk, buttermilk, or a soft drink.

DIFFICULTY Difficult. Making this dish involves two separate recipes, one for beans and another for dumplings. The two recipes call for nine different ingredients and overnight soaking. You will have to stage the steps over 24 hours, and the recipe is difficult to prepare.

INGREDIENTS

FOR THE SOUP BEANS
1/2 pound dried pinto beans, washed and picked over for pebbles
3 1/2 cups water
4 ounces salt pork
1/2 teaspoon salt
1/2 teaspoon pepper

FOR THE DUMPLINGS
1 cup all-purpose flour
1/2 teaspoon salt
2 tablespoons melted shortening
1/4 cup bean broth or water
Instant flour, as needed

YIELD 6 servings

U.S. Senate Bean Soup

DIFFICULTY Moderate. Because the recipe calls for nine ingredients and overnight soaking, I rate it moderate in difficulty.

INGREDIENTS
1 pound dried pinto beans, washed and picked over for pebbles
8 cups water
2 cups diced onion
2 ham hocks (1 pound)
1 cup grated raw potato
1/4 cup barley
2 teaspoons garlic powder
1 teaspoon salt
1 teaspoon pepper
Sour cream (optional)
Chopped green onion (optional)

YIELD 10 servings

*O*f the many pinto bean recipes that I have made over the last twenty years, this one is my favorite. While I added the barley, the basic recipe is mountain to the bone. Chefs at the Rayburn Senate Office Building in Washington still serve a similar soup.

STEPS In a glass or ceramic container, soak the beans in the water overnight. Do not drain.

In a large saucepan, combine the beans, water, onion, ham hocks, potato, barley, garlic powder, salt, and pepper. Simmer, covered, for 4 hours. Add water as needed to keep the beans covered.

When cooked, the beans hold their shape but are soft throughout. The pork should be tender, almost falling apart. This soup is rather thick, like cream soup or chowder. Serve in soup bowls or plates, and garnish with a dollop of sour cream and a sprinkling of green onion.

HEALTHY CHOICE ALTERNATIVE Replace the pork with 1/4 cup safflower oil. Use 1 tablespoon salt, or add it at the table.

Serve the soup with a raw vegetable plate that includes turnip wedges and sliced sweet white onions, accompanied by Mexican Corn Bread.

Thinking About Chili

I DIVIDE CHILIES into three categories: all-meat, bean and meat, and vegetarian. Most main-dish chili recipes include five major components: meats, beans, vegetables, spices, and thickeners, which I discuss below. While my experience with chili is limited, I hope the following comments will give you ideas for your next pot of pinto beans.

1. *Beans:* Make chili with your favorite cooked beans: pinto beans, white beans, black beans, kidney beans, Great Northern beans, and baby lima beans.
2. *Meats:* Chilies may include top sirloin, London broil, ground chuck, and all types of sausage. For white chili, use chicken breast meat, but chili meats also include venison, turkey, rabbit, lamb, buffalo, ham, or pork.
3. *Vegetables:* Common vegetables we add to chili include tomatoes, onions, and green peppers. Not-so-common additions include olives and celery.
4. *Spices:* Chile peppers, green chiles, red chile pepper, chile powders, salt, ground cumin, and garlic are essential chili spices. Other spices often used in chili include black pepper, ground red pepper, cloves, oregano, marjoram, cumin seeds, onion powder, ground coriander, vinegar, Tabasco sauce, soy sauce, chicken broth, sugar, and cocoa. Cocoa? Yes, cocoa deepens the flavor of chili.
5. *Thickeners:* Chili must be thick. You can thicken it with tomato paste, canned refried beans, mashed beans, grated cheese, cornmeal, masa (corn flour), and flour.

My first impulse for quick-and-easy chili was to mix and heat a 16-ounce can of beans with a 10-ounce can of hot dog chili. Presto! The chili was ready, but I did not write home to my mother about this effort. In our markets you can buy a 2-Alarm Chili Kit that contains seven packets of spices and allows you to make chili as spicy as you wish. The spices include chile pepper, red pepper, paprika, salt, comino/oregano (comino is cumin), onion/garlic, and masa. If you don't want to use cans or packets, consider starting with dry beans.

Pinto Bean Chili
(Vegetarian Chili)

*B*y adding just a few ingredients—chili powder (I use McCormick's Hot Mexican), tomatoes, diced onion, and green pepper—to Soup Beans, you can turn them into chili.

STEPS Pick over the beans for foreign matter, wash them in cold water, rinsing them until the water is clear. Soak overnight in 7 cups of water. Wash and dice the vegetables: onions, green peppers, and tomatoes.

Pour the beans (6 cups soaked beans) and water into a 6-quart saucepan. Stir in the tomato paste, and add 2 cups of the onions, the garlic, chili powder, salt, and cumin. Stir until mixed. Simmer, covered, on low heat for 3 hours, adding water as needed to keep the beans covered.

Stir in the peppers, tomatoes, and remaining 1 cup onions. Simmer an additional 10 minutes. Add 1 pound of browned and drained ground beef, if using.

HEALTHY CHOICE ALTERNATIVE Without beef, this recipe is a fat-free main dish. Omit the salt and offer it at the table.

Spruce up this dish by adding a topping such as sour cream, grated Cheddar cheese, diced onions, chopped green onions, or unsalted cashews. Serve your chili in large bowls with fresh, crispy, steaming hot Buttermilk Corn Bread. Mountain chili also goes nicely with lettuce and spring onions, hot peppers, and a glass of buttermilk.

DIFFICULTY Moderate. With ten ingredients and two easy steps, this recipe is moderate in difficulty.

INGREDIENTS
1 pound (2 cups) dry pinto beans, washed and picked over for pebbles
7 cups water
3/4 cup (6 ounces) tomato paste
3 cups diced onions
4 cloves minced garlic
3 tablespoons chili powder
1 1/2 tablespoons salt
2 teaspoons ground cumin
3 cups diced green bell peppers
3 cups diced fresh tomatoes
1 pound ground beef (optional)

YIELD 14 cups or 9 hearty servings

Baked Pinto Beans

*B*ack in 1961 when Julia Child (with Simone Beck and Louisette Bertholle) wrote her first cookbook, *Mastering the Art of French Cooking*, she called the baked beans French Baked Beans, and she used the word *cassoulet* in small print below. (With the variations and discussion, Child's recipe goes on for six pages, and she recommends two or three days for preparation.) I make the connection between Julia Child's French Baked Beans (well known today as cassoulet) and these Baked Pinto Beans because the names are similar and both recipes use salt pork and slow oven-cooking.

While we often associate baked beans with Boston, these baked pintos are a

DIFFICULTY Moderate. Because the recipe calls for nine ingredients and overnight soaking, I rate it moderate in difficulty.

HEARTY
Cooking ■
COUNTRY

mountain dish. In place of the common ingredient—ground dry mustard—we use ginger, and we add 100% pure sorghum and then we drool over some of the finest baked beans ever. Sometimes we make the dish with kidney beans, white northerns, or a bean mix.

STEPS In a glass or ceramic container, soak the beans in the water overnight. Dice the onion and cut the salt pork into strips.

Preheat the oven to 300°F. Drain the beans and reserve the water. In a 2-quart covered baking dish, combine the beans, onion, salt pork, sorghum, brown sugar, salt, ginger, and red pepper, and stir until mixed. Add 1½ cups of the reserved water, or enough to cover the beans, and mix. Cover, and bake for 6 hours.

Check the beans each hour, adding reserved water as needed to keep the beans covered. During the baking you will need to add water. The liquid should thicken like syrup. If the sauce is not thick, remove the lid and bake another 30 minutes. Serve.

HEALTHY CHOICE ALTERNATIVE Replace the salt pork with 1 tablespoon safflower oil.

Serve with hamburgers or meat loaf, Cucumber Salad with Vinegar, and Appalachian Potato Salad, or with Barbecued Chicken or Barbecued Baby Back Ribs.

INGREDIENTS
½ pound (1 cup) dried pinto beans, washed and picked over for pebbles
4 cups water
1 cup diced onion
2 ounces salt pork
2 tablespoons 100% pure sorghum
2 tablespoons brown sugar
1 teaspoon salt
¼ teaspoon ginger
2 pinches ground red pepper

YIELD 5 servings

Pinto Bean Cakes
(Bean Patties and Fried Bean Cakes)

*B*oiled dry beans are so common in the mountains, you would expect to find cooks using the leftovers for bean cakes. Remember that we make Potato Cakes with leftover mashed potatoes, Fried Mush with leftover boiled cornmeal, and fried dressing with leftover stuffing. Among all these fried cakes gracing our skillets, fried bean cakes may be the most popular. You can find large families that like Pinto Bean Cakes, also called Bean Patties and Fried Bean Cakes, almost as much as they like Soup Beans and even more than they like Potato Cakes. My first experience with bean cakes came when I ordered an appetizer on the Sunset Terrace of the Grove Park Inn Resort in Asheville, North Carolina. The cakes I ate were black-eyed pea cakes, and the chef served them with salsa, sour cream, and chow-chow. Piece by piece I forked away my black-eyed pea cakes. The cakes were dry, but the salsa, chow chow, and sour cream moistened them. In my mind I visualized a mountain cook mashing leftover soup

DIFFICULTY Moderate. With seven ingredients and two steps, this recipe is moderate in difficulty.

beans and adding flour, salt, and pepper. After forming patties and frying them in lard, the cook would serve the patties with dilly bean pickles and hot pepper relish.

Later I talked with mountain cooks about their bean cakes. I found recipes ranging from what I give below to cakes made by adding self-rising flour to mashed beans in a ratio of one part flour to three parts beans. Some cooks prepare these cakes without egg, onion, or batter. Most fry them in lard, and all are careful to cook them through to the center.

INGREDIENTS
3$^{1}/_{3}$ cup cooked or
  canned pinto beans
4 tablespoons vegetable
  oil or bacon drippings
1 cup diced onion
1 teaspoon salt
$^{1}/_{2}$ teaspoon pepper
2 eggs
$^{1}/_{2}$ cup all-purpose flour

YIELD 5 servings

STEPS Prepare one recipe of Soup Beans and reserve 3$^{1}/_{3}$ cups of beans, or purchase 3 (16-ounce) cans of pinto beans. If using canned beans, wash and drain the beans, and lightly pat them dry.

In a large cast-iron skillet, heat 1 tablespoon of the oil and fry the onions until they are clear. Lift out the onions, leaving the oil in the pan.

In a mixing bowl, combine 1$^{1}/_{3}$ cups of the beans, the salt, and pepper. With a potato masher or a fork, mash until smooth. Add the remaining 2 cups beans and the cooked onions, and stir.

Form 10 patties. If they are too soft to hold their shape, add some flour. In a small mixing bowl, beat the eggs. Dip the patties first in the beaten egg and then in the flour. Fry in the skillet over medium heat, adding oil, a tablespoon at a time, as needed. Fry 3 minutes on each side, or until nicely browned. Serve.

HEALTHY CHOICE ALTERNATIVE Cook the onions in water. Fry the patties without egg or flour on a nonstick cooking surface coated with nonstick cooking spray.

Serve as a late-night snack in place of popcorn, or for dinner in place of potatoes or corn. Serve with your choice of sour cream, chow-chow, fried onions, apple chutney, Vidalia onion relish, or green tomato pickles. My daughter, Laura, likes them covered with spicy mustard!

Pinto Bean Pie

DIFFICULTY Moderate. With seven ingredients and one step, this recipe is moderate in difficulty.

*W*hen the first frost nips the poke leaves and the sun is so low in the sky that it barely reaches into our hollows, we turn on our stoves and start cooking pinto beans. Pots of beans simmer on the back of the stove throughout the winter. To make this pie, you start by reaching into your bean pot and with a slotted spoon dip out some tender pintos. Ten minutes later you'll have this bean pie baking in the oven.

HEARTY Cooking COUNTRY

STEPS Preheat the oven to 350°F. In a mixing bowl, mash ¹/₂ cup of the beans with a fork until smooth. Stir in the sugar, coconut, eggs, and butter. Add the vanilla and the remaining ¹/₄ cup whole pinto beans, and stir. Pour into the pie shell, and bake for 1 hour, or until a toothpick inserted into the center comes out clean.

HEALTHY CHOICE ALTERNATIVE Increase the beans to 1 cup (mashing ³/₄ cup) and reduce the sugar and coconut to ¹/₂ cup each. Use ¹/₂ cup safflower oil instead of butter. Serve small pieces with decaffeinated tea and hold the whipped cream.

Keep in mind, if you store this pie more than a day or two, the whole beans in the filling lose moisture and get hard. Serve for dessert with coffee and Country Whipped Cream.

INGREDIENTS
³/₄ cup cooked or
  canned pinto beans
1 cup sugar
1 cup shredded coconut
2 eggs
¹/₂ cup melted butter
1 teaspoon vanilla
1 (9-inch) unbaked Pie
  Pastry Shell (page
  275)

YIELD 8 servings

Topographic Note: Hollows

Southwesterners in states like Arizona and New Mexico talk about box canyons. In our mountains we have hollows, and we call them "hollers." Topography distinguishes the Appalachian region. Mountains have been the yeast of our culture, shaping lives and isolating people.

Because our valleys are so narrow, we don't have backyards. The fronts of many houses face the creek, and the creek runs beside the road. From the creek's edge the hill rises almost straight up. Rock outcroppings are common. Ours is a special beauty. When the gray winter tree barks get covered over with shades of green in the spring, and when the masses of green leaves turn to shades of misty-reddish-brown in the fall, we are surrounded with color. In our mountains we live in the bottom of the hollows and the hollows shoot color to our eyes.

Five

Soups and Casseroles

L P CALDWELL

Winter Vegetable Soup

Bacon-Potato Soup

Corn Chowder

Clear Vegetable and Beef Soup

Summer Garden Vegetable Soup

North Georgia Corn and Tomato Soup
(Cream of Corn and Tomato Soup)

Tomato Celery Soup

Saucy Macaroni and Cheese: White-Sauce Style

(Cheese Sauce)

Custard-Style Macaroni and Cheese

Stuffed Cabbage Rolls

Stuffed Green Peppers

Highlander Corn Bread Pie

(Corn Pone Hamburger Pie)

Fried Chicken Livers Baked with Rice

Old-Time Soups

COMFORT FOODS ARE slow paced, home cooked, and unpackaged. They are foods from the earth, our childhood, and the homeplace. They are part of Sunday dinner and long conversations.

■ ■

Mountain Winter Soups

All through the cold months of December, January, and February, soup pots simmer on the back of the stove. Highlander soups are winter vegetable and beef soups. We make them with tomatoes, potatoes, beans, and corn. They are not the uniform, consistent, tinny-tasting soups that come from a factory-produced can; they are not heavy, and they are not processed.

Winter vegetable soups are healthy. High in fiber and low in fat, they will satisfy your appetite, stick with you, and warm your insides. If you are feeling low or have the flu, they may be the magic, the cure, the secret potion that brings you back.

Homemade winter vegetable soups have a base of stewing beef, cubed beef, hamburger, or corned beef. To this we add vegetables: tomatoes, tomato juice, V-8 vegetable juice, carrots, onions, celery, corn, and potatoes. Some Highlanders add cabbage, green beans, lima beans, northern beans, kidney beans, peas, cauliflower, broccoli, green peppers, and even macaroni. Others use asparagus tops, parsnips, parsley, and salsify. We make these soups in big pots, and when the meal is over, we may send small tubs of leftover soup to the neighbors.

After you serve the soup in individual bowls, your guests will change it: Some fill their bowls with crackers while others add crumbled corn bread. Across the country today, as people yearn for honest healthy food, country soups such as the following are coming back. Let vegetables fill your bowl.

Winter Vegetable Soup

*T*his vegetable soup is fast. If you are on a tight schedule, make vegetable soup on Saturday and serve it the rest of the week. You can make this soup in a giant pot, freeze the leftovers, and serve it on a hurry-up day. With beef, beans, potatoes, and cabbage, a little help from tomato juice, and your favorite bread, this soup is a complete soup supper.

STEPS In a very large pot (8-to10-quart size), fry the beef for about 10 minutes, browning it on all sides. Add the water and simmer the beef for 1 hour. Cool, and skim the fat from the surface.

Add the tomato juice, carrots, celery, potato, and cabbage, and simmer for about 20 minutes. Add the onion and beans. Simmer another 20 minutes. Add the whole tomatoes and their juice, beef bouillon, hot sauce, and corn. Bring to a boil and add the red and green peppers.

HEALTHY CHOICE ALTERNATIVE If you are on a diet, vegetable soup is for you: 1 cup has about 100 calories. Serve a soup bowl full, say 2 cups, and you'll consume 200 calories. Three cups contain 300 calories, 4 cups—400 calories. You can't go wrong with vegetable soup.

Serve at once or store for later use. (This soup tastes better the second day.) Serve with salt and pepper, crackers, Buttermilk Corn Bread, or Highlander Rolls, or with grilled cheese or peanut butter sandwiches. Offer hot chilies and diced sweet onion.

DIFFICULTY Difficult. With fifteen ingredients and two cooking steps, this recipe is difficult. Allow 2½ hours preparation time.

INGREDIENTS
2 pounds stew beef, cut in ¼-inch pieces
4 cups water
4 cups tomato juice
4 carrots (2 cups) sliced ⅛-inch thick
4 stalks celery (2 cups) sliced ¼-inch thick
12 ounces or 1 large potato, diced in ½-inch cubes
½ medium head or 4 cups sliced and chopped cabbage
2 cups diced or 1 large onion
2 cups green beans
1 (28-ounce) can whole tomatoes with the juice
¼ cup beef bouillon grains
1 teaspoon hot red pepper sauce
1½ cups whole kernel corn
1 red bell pepper, seeded and diced
1 green bell pepper, seeded and diced

YIELD 24 cups of soup or 12 servings

Bacon-Potato Soup

INGREDIENTS
2 small (1 pound) pota-
toes
1 ounce or 2 strips
bacon
1 1/2 cups water
3/4 cup diced celery
3/4 cup diced onion
1 tablespoon chicken
bouillon grains
6 ounces cooked and
diced ham
1/2 cup heavy cream
(optional)

YIELD 4 cups or 6
servings

*F*or a rich, full-flavored, bacon-garnished, hearty main-dish potato soup, this one is hard to beat. The puréed vegetables provide the thickening, the cream adds richness, and the result is heavenly—much like a chowder.

STEPS Wash the potatoes and remove spots and blemishes. (No need to peel.) Dice into 3/4-inch pieces to equal about 3 cups. In a large saucepan over medium heat, fry the bacon. Remove the bacon and, when cool, crumble. Set aside. Leave the bacon grease in the saucepan, add the water, and bring to a boil. Add the potatoes and celery, reduce the heat, and simmer for 15 minutes. Add the onion and simmer an additional 5 minutes, or until the potatoes, celery, and onion are tender.

Using a food processor, process three-quarters of the cooked potato, celery, and onion until smooth. If the vegetables get too thick to process, add about 1/3 of the broth, and continue to process until smooth.

Return this puree to the saucepan, and stir. The soup should be thick, like cream soup. If the soup is not thick enough, puree some more vegetables.

Add the bouillon and ham, bring to a boil, and stir. Mix in the cream, and serve, garnished with the crumbled bacon.

HEALTHY CHOICE ALTERNATIVE Replace the cream with low-fat milk. Omit the bacon and ham, and add 1/2 teaspoon salt.

Serve in soup plates with a cold ham and cheese sandwich.

Corn Chowder

*W*hile you might associate this recipe with Iowa or the Heartland, mountaineers also combine corn and potatoes to make this warm winter soup. Here, the chicken bouillon provides both salt and flavor.

STEPS Wash and peel the potato, removing spots and blemishes. Dice into 3/4-inch pieces. In a medium-size saucepan, bring the water to a boil. Add the potatoes and onion, and simmer for 20 to 25 minutes, or until the potatoes are tender.

Using a food processor, process two-thirds of the potatoes and onions until smooth. If needed, add 1/4 cup of the milk to thin the puree. Add the remaining potatoes and process until the largest pieces are the size of a dime or smaller. Return the puree to the saucepan, and stir in the milk. The soup should be thick like cream soup and chunky like chowder. Add the bouillon and the creamed corn, and return to a boil. Stir.

HEALTHY CHOICE ALTERNATIVE   Use skim milk and replace the chicken bouillon grains with low-sodium chicken bouillon grains.

Stir each time you serve as the corn settles. Serve with Highlander Rolls.

INGREDIENTS
1 medium potato
   (3/4 pound)
1 cup water
3/4 cup diced onion
1 cup milk
4 teaspoons chicken
   bouillon grains
1 1/2 cups creamed corn

YIELD 5 servings

Clear Vegetable and Beef Soup

*S*imple and light: Pure broth, clear soup, little beef, and cooked vegetables. Our word for supper comes from soup. The French word *le souper* means supper, and their word *souper* is a verb meaning "to have supper." This clear vegetable soup is an ultimate country supper. Pure and refined, the dish is both French and mountain country.

For the stew meat I buy stir-fry beef, which in our market is strips of sirloin tip steak. Select a robust green bean, a white half-runner, contender, romano, or wonder. If you can't buy these beans, see Henry Fields or Gurney's Seed in the Mail-Order Sources.

This is a large recipe, but it freezes.

STEPS   In a large saucepan over high heat, brown the beef in the oil. Add the water, reduce the heat, and simmer for 25 minutes. Add the potatoes and carrots, and simmer for 15 minutes. Add the beans, onion, bouillon, and pepper, and bring to a boil. Reduce the heat, and simmer for 10 additional minutes. Serve.

HEALTHY CHOICE ALTERNATIVE   No yolks, no cream, one tablespoon of oil, and sixteen ounces of beef for ten servings. This recipe is light: This soup should not bother your heart. Use low-sodium bouillon, and offer salt at the table.

Serve with Buttermilk Biscuits, Sweet Potato Biscuits, or Angel Biscuits.

DIFFICULTY Moderate. With nine ingredients and 50 minutes of simmering, this recipe is moderate in difficulty.

INGREDIENTS
1 pound stew beef, cut
   in 1/3- to 1/2-inch pieces
1 tablespoon safflower
   oil
6 cups water
3 cups peeled and diced
   potatoes
2 cups diced carrots
2 cups (2/3 pound) green
   beans, cut in
   1/2-inch pieces
2 cups diced onion
2 tablespoons beef
   bouillon grains
1/2 teaspoon pepper

YIELD 10 servings

Soups
and
Casseroles

Summer Garden Vegetable Soup

DIFFICULTY Moderate. Once you have gathered the ingredients and chopped the vegetables, this ten-ingredient soup is a snap. I rate the recipe moderate in difficulty.

*B*y mid-July in most parts of the central and southern Appalachian mountains, you'll find tomatoes, beans, corn, squash, and bell peppers ripe in our gardens. A good garden will produce for many months, and the rest of the year you'll find these common vegetables in the market. During the winter, many country cooks have the tomatoes, beans, and corn stored in their can house, and they will use them to make Winter Vegetable Soup.

For this soup, use any summer squash, including yellow, yellow crookneck, zucchini, scallop, or white patty pan. If you pick winter squash such as pumpkin, acorn, or butternut when they are small and tender, you can use them too. By cooking the macaroni separately, you'll keep it from getting soft. Like most mountain vegetable soups, this one will be thick—mostly vegetables and little broth.

INGREDIENTS
2 cups elbow macaroni or small shells
2 pounds fresh tomatoes, cooked, skin removed
1 cup water
2 cups fresh pole beans, cut in 1/2-inch pieces
2 cups fresh kernel corn
1 pound (3 cups) diced summer squash, yellow or zucchini
1 cup diced onion
1 cup green or red bell pepper
2 teaspoons salt
3/4 teaspoon pepper

YIELD 8 servings

STEPS Cook the macaroni according to the directions on the package. Drain, rinse, cover, and keep warm. Boil the tomatoes in the water for 10 minutes. Pull the skins off.

In a large pot over medium heat, bring the tomatoes and water to a boil. Add the beans, and simmer for 8 minutes. Add the corn, squash, and onion. Simmer another 8 minutes. Add the bell pepper, salt, and pepper. Stir well, and remove from the heat.

HEALTHY CHOICE ALTERNATIVE Except for the salt, which you can omit if you have to, this soup is just what the doctor ordered.

Serve hot or cold, and topped with the macaroni. We serve this soup with Skillet Corn Bread or saltine crackers and a slice of raw sweet onion.

Northeast Georgia

From Gainesville on Lake Lanier to Blairsville on Nottley Lake and from Dillard to Toccoa, northeast Georgia is home to numerous state parks as well as the Chattahoochee National Forest. Here, the Blue Ridge Mountains are steep and the roads wind for miles. At each turn it seems that the mountains have a different landmark: church, hotel, courthouse, mill, lake, mound, gorge, bridge, or waterfall. In his cookbook and touring guide, *Somethin's Cookin' in the Mountains*, editor Jay Bucek presents the foods, landmarks, and businesses of northeast Georgia. The book, now in its tenth printing, has been in print since 1982. I associate this soup with north Georgia.

North Georgia Corn and Tomato Soup
(Cream of Corn and Tomato Soup)

This all-vegetable cream soup will warm you up on a gray winter day. We make this soup with Velveeta cheese. It is a wonderful soup thickener, and it makes the soup rich and creamy. Velveeta cheese is a common casserole and soup ingredient, and in the mountains we often use it in place of heavy cream. If you don't have Velveeta cheese, or if you are not in the spirit of traditional mountain cooking, substitute cream cheese or heavy cream.

If your soup, stew, or gravy curdles, you will have globs of milk (curds) floating in water, which looks bad. If you heat milk, buttermilk, or cream too fast, if you get them too hot, if you stir them too fast, or if you lower the pH too much, they will curdle.

To avoid curdling, heat slowly, stir slowly, and keep bases—salt, lemon, tomatoes, and other sources of acid that lower the pH—to a minimum. If you lower the pH from its normal 6.5 to 5.3, your soup will curdle. You can neutralize acids and maintain pH by adding baking soda.

DIFFICULTY Moderate. With nine ingredients and one cooking step, this recipe is moderate in difficulty. If you have the corn and tomatoes ready, you can prepare the soup in 10 minutes.

Soups and Casseroles

In the following recipe, the two cups of tomatoes (not a lot of tomatoes) and the two pinches of baking soda help prevent curdling.

INGREDIENTS

2 cups cooked, peeled, and chopped tomatoes

2 cups cooked creamed corn

1/8 teaspoon baking soda

3 tablespoons butter

1/4 cup all-purpose flour

3 cups 2% milk

1 teaspoon salt

1 teaspoon pepper

4 ounces Velveeta cheese

Croutons (optional)

YIELD 7 servings

STEPS In a large saucepan, combine the tomatoes, corn, and baking soda. Heat through, and set aside. In a second 3-quart saucepan, melt the butter and stir in the flour. Whisk in the milk, and boil for 1 minute. Add the salt, pepper, and Velveeta, and stir until the cheese melts.

When ready to serve, add the hot corn and tomato mixture to the pot. Heat gently, but do not boil. Garnish with croutons, if using.

HEALTHY CHOICE ALTERNATIVE Omit the Velveeta cheese, and use skim milk instead of 2% milk.

Serve this soup with an open-face broiled Velveeta or Cheddar cheese sandwich, or as a first course with Buttermilk Biscuits and Green Pepper Jelly.

Tomato Celery Soup

DIFFICULTY Moderate. With eight ingredients, this recipe is moderate in difficulty.

INGREDIENTS

2 tablespoons lard or butter

3/4 cup diced onion

3/4 cup finely sliced and chopped celery

2 (12-ounce) cans (3 cups) tomato juice

1 teaspoon sugar

1/2 teaspoon salt

1/8 teaspoon ground pepper

2 green onions, diced

YIELD 4 servings

*S*everal years ago on a visit to the Shaker Village at Pleasant Hill, Kentucky, our family stayed at the Trustee House. Established in 1805 as a utopia, Shaker Village currently boasts 27 buildings and 5,000 acres. We sampled the Southern-style home cooking: corn sticks, tomato soup, relish, country ham, pineapple upside-down cake, glazed carrots, hominy grits casserole, oatmeal cookies, and chocolate fudge pie. The relaxing rural atmosphere and the Trustee House's "daily fare" put Pleasant Hill at the top of my list of retreats.

Back at home, I adapted what follows from *We Make You Kindly Welcome*, a Shaker cookbook by Elizabeth C. Kremer. While the Shaker recipe used a can of commercially prepared tomato soup, and while old-style mountain cooks would have used home-canned tomatoes, my recipe cuts the fuss to a minimum by using tomato juice. By starting with tomato juice you do not have to peel, seed, or puree the tomatoes. The result is smooth and tasty.

STEPS In a non-aluminum saucepan over medium to high heat, melt the butter. Add the onions and celery, and sauté until clear and browned on the edges, about 5 minutes. Add the tomato juice, sugar, salt, and pepper, and simmer for 5 minutes. Garnish with the green onion pieces. Let them float on the soup.

HEALTHY CHOICE ALTERNATIVE You can omit the lard or butter and boil the onion and celery, but you'll have to compensate for the loss of flavor.

Replace the lard or butter with 4 teaspoons chicken bouillon grains or $1/3$ cup chopped fresh basil.

For a light lunch, serve this soup with Ham Biscuits, Mexican Corn Bread, or a tuna salad sandwich.

Comforting Casseroles

Saucy Macaroni and Cheese: White-Sauce Style
(Cheese Sauce)

*I*n mountain country kitchens and in most country restaurants, macaroni and cheese is ever-present daily fare. It is an ordinary dish, with a long history. The Italians created macaroni and cheese. The French adapted it quickly, to *macaroni au gratin* and *macaroni à l'Italienne*. This recipe is a combination of both.

While I prefer the chewy robust texture of Custard-Style Macaroni and Cheese (page 158), my family prefers the smooth saucy texture of this White Sauce Macaroni and Cheese. Highlanders prepare it both ways. To make this a hearty main dish, add the diced ham. For a side dish omit it. This is a large recipe intended for a community supper.

STEPS Preheat the oven to 450°F. Grease a 13x9x2-inch casserole dish.

In a large pot, prepare the macaroni: Boil three quarts of water, add the macaroni, and boil for about 10 minutes, or prepare according to the directions on the package. Rinse under hot water.

Prepare the cheese sauce: As the macaroni cooks in one pan, melt the butter and stir in the flour, salt, and pepper in another. When you have fully mixed the butter and flour, add the milk and bring to a boil. Reduce the heat, and boil for 1 minute. Remove from heat and stir in the cheese and cream.

Stir in the ham, if using, and the cooked macaroni. Pour into a baking dish and sprinkle with the Parmesan cheese. Bake 30 minutes. Broil to brown.

TIP If you prepare the recipe with the ham, omit the salt.

DIFFICULTY Difficult. Boil the macaroni, prepare the cheese sauce, and bake the casserole. With ten ingredients, three steps, and 30 minutes of baking, this recipe is difficult.

INGREDIENTS
3 cups macaroni

FOR THE CHEESE SAUCE
6 tablespoons butter
6 tablespoons all-purpose flour
1 teaspoon salt
1 teaspoon pepper
3 cups milk
3 cups (12 ounces) grated Cheddar cheese
$3/4$ cup heavy cream

FOR THE CASSEROLE
1 pound diced cooked ham (optional)
$1/4$ cup grated Parmesan cheese

YIELD 10 servings

Soups and Casseroles

HEALTHY CHOICE ALTERNATIVE Omit the cream. Use low-fat cheese and skim milk. Omit the butter and use instant flour.

Serve this dish with Poke Sallet, Sugared Carrots, or Steamed Green Beans.

Custard-Style Macaroni and Cheese

DIFFICULTY Moderate. With eleven ingredients, three steps, and 1 hour of preparation time, this recipe is moderate in difficulty.

INGREDIENTS

FOR THE MACARONI
2 quarts water
1½ cups macaroni
2 teaspoons salt

FOR THE CUSTARD
AND CHEESE
3 large eggs
1½ cups milk
1 teaspoon salt
½ teaspoon paprika
2 pinches ground red
   (cayenne) pepper
1½ cups (6 ounces)
   grated cheese

FOR THE TOPPING
¼ cup (1 ounce)
   Parmesan cheese
5 saltine crackers
   (¼ cup crumbled)

YIELD 5 servings

*M*y dinner guests are often surprised when I say I am serving macaroni and cheese. But this custard casserole is delicate, sophisticated, and safe— easy to bake and appreciated by both adults and children. With Pierre Franey, the popular *New York Times* food writer, having eaten it as a child in Burgundy, France, and extolling its virtues in his column, and with mountain cooks making it a regular on their tables, its pedigree is pure, and its credentials are high.

To make custard-style macaroni and cheese, bind the cooked macaroni together with a custard of melted cheese, eggs, and milk. Its quality depends on the cheese and the ratio of custard to macaroni. Use any cheese you like, but I suggest Cheddar, Edam, or Gruyere. For a complete main dish, add cubed ham or sausage.

STEPS Up to a day ahead, cook the macaroni in a large pot of salted water as directed on the package. Cook until tender—do not undercook. Rinse thoroughly in cold water and drain. Refrigerate until ready to use.

Preheat the oven to 325°F. Grease a 10x6x2-inch casserole dish.

Prepare the custard: In a mixing bowl, whisk together the eggs, milk, salt, paprika, and ground red pepper. In the casserole dish, layer the cooked macaroni with the cheese, and pour the custard over the top. Bake for 40 minutes, or until set in the center. In a small mixing bowl, combine the Parmesan cheese and crumbled crackers. Spread over the casserole, and broil to brown.

HEALTHY CHOICE ALTERNATIVE To reduce fat, replace the grated cheese with fat-free cottage cheese. Instead of three eggs, use one egg and two egg whites. Use skim milk.

Serve this dish with steamed broccoli and carrots or Red-Eye Gravy and Country Ham.

HEARTY
Cooking
COUNTRY
■ ■

Stuffed Cabbage Rolls
Stuffed Green Peppers

*D*o you remember this old-time Sunday dinner treat? To make them, you roll meat balls into cabbage leaves and bake them in a casserole. In place of the beef, many mountain cooks use ground pork or chopped pork chops.

Mountaineers also make whole stuffed cabbage, leaving the head of cabbage in one piece, opening the leaves like flower petals, spreading the ground meat mixture on each leaf, and then drawing the cabbage back into a ball. Whole stuffed cabbage sounds pretty, but these cabbage rolls are easier to make and serve.

DIFFICULTY Moderate. With ten ingredients and two steps, this recipe is moderate in difficulty.

STEPS Cook the rice with 1 teaspoon of salt according to the package directions.

Select a pot large enough to hold the cabbage, add enough water to cover, and bring the water to a boil. Using a thin paring knife, cut the stem from the bottom of the cabbage. Add the whole cabbage to the water, return to a boil, and boil about 5 minutes to wilt the leaves. Cool, and carefully remove the limp outside leaves. If you don't have 12 limp leaves, return what remains of the cabbage to the boiling water, and repeat. Using a scissors, remove the ribs from the 12 leaves.

Preheat the oven to 350°F. Chop the remaining cabbage and spread the chopped leaves in the bottom of a 13x9x2-inch casserole dish. Cover with tomato sauce.

In a mixing bowl, combine the ground beef, onion, bell pepper, egg, salt, pepper, and cooked rice. Divide the mixture into 12 parts, and form each into a meatball. Place a meatball in the center of a cabbage leaf; fold the sides in and roll to enclose the filling. Repeat for all 12 leaves. Arrange the cabbage rolls, flap side down in the casserole. Cover with foil, and bake for 1 hour and 10 minutes. Serve.

INGREDIENTS
1 cup rice
1 teaspoon salt
1 medium (3-pound) cabbage
4 cups tomato sauce or spaghetti sauce
1 pound lean ground beef
1 cup diced onion
1 cup diced green bell pepper
1 egg
1 teaspoon salt
1 teaspoon pepper

YIELD 12 servings

HEALTHY CHOICE ALTERNATIVE In place of the beef, use ground turkey. Replace the egg with two egg whites. Omit the salt, and add it at the table.

Serve these with a Baked Potato and sour cream, Baked Cushaw, or Sweet Potato Casserole.

Stuffed Green Peppers Follow the recipe above, but use 8 green, red, or yellow sweet bell peppers in place of the cabbage. Remove the stem, seeds, and membranes from the peppers. Boil the peppers 5 minutes, just as you

do the cabbage. If you want the peppers to be bright green and crunchy, there is no need to boil them ahead.

Pour all the tomato sauce into the casserole dish. Fill the peppers with the meat mixture, stand them upright in the dish, and bake, covered with aluminum foil, for 1 hour and 10 minutes. Remove the foil, sprinkle with any type of grated cheese, and serve.

Highlander Corn Bread Pie
(Corn Pone Hamburger Pie)

*R*uth Thomas of Mossy Bottom, Kentucky, raised three children, and like most mothers, she fed them well. One of her favorite dishes was this chili-flavored corn bread pie. I call it a Corn Pone Pie. For a crowd-pleasing summer treat, use fresh tomatoes and corn.

STEPS Preheat the oven to 450°F. Grease the sides of a 2-quart casserole dish.

Prepare the filling: Using a large cast-iron skillet, melt the butter and fry the onions. (This step is worth the effort for the aroma you spread through the house.) Stir in the chili powder and salt. Add and brown the hamburger. Stir in the ketchup, corn, kidney beans, and tomatoes, and simmer for 2 minutes.

Prepare the corn bread: As the hamburger cooks, stir up the corn bread by placing the meal and buttermilk in a bowl and stirring until smooth.

Bake the casserole: Pour the hamburger mixture into the casserole dish and spread it flat. Pour the corn bread batter on top, and bake for 30 minutes. Broil the top of the corn bread to brown, and serve.

HEALTHY CHOICE ALTERNATIVE Replace the butter with olive oil. Use lean beef, or pour off the fat after the beef is cooked. You may omit the salt, but if you use canned corn, beans, and tomatoes, watch the labels, as canned foods may come loaded with sodium.

For a special occasion, serve Corn Bread Pie with Seven-Layer Salad or a green salad. Otherwise, serve as a complete meal.

DIFFICULTY Difficult. Even though you'll find this dish relatively easy to prepare, I rate it difficult because it has two parts, three steps, and eleven ingredients. From start to finish, including baking time, you can prepare it in 1 hour and have time to read the mail or clean the kitchen.

INGREDIENTS

FOR THE FILLING
1 tablespoon butter
1 cup diced onion
   (1 medium onion)
1 tablespoon chili pow-
   der
1/2 teaspoon salt
3/4 pound lean ground
   beef
2 tablespoons ketchup
1 cup fresh whole kernel
   corn
1 cup cooked kidney
   beans
1 cup (8 ounces) peeled
   and quartered toma-
   toes

FOR THE CORN BREAD
1 cup self-rising corn-
   meal mix
7/8 cup buttermilk

YIELD 5 servings

HEARTY
Cooking
COUNTRY

Fried Chicken Livers Baked with Rice

*Y*ears ago, mountain cooks may or may not have known their livers were made with a *meunière*, but they'll quickly tell you that the secret of this recipe is shaking the livers in a brown paper bag so they are coated with flour, salt, and pepper. A *meunière* is a style of cooking where we use flour and spices to coat fish, or in this case liver, and pan-fry quickly over high heat. This process seals in the juices and adds flavor to the dish. You'll be proud to serve this low-cost main dish. Sophisticated palates will savor the moment, compliment the cook, and devour this delicate mixture of liver, bacon, and broth.

STEPS Preheat the oven to 350°F. In a large cast-iron skillet (with a 12-inch skillet, the livers will not crowd the pan), fry the bacon until crisp, and lift it onto a paper towel to drain. Leave the bacon grease in the skillet and use the grease for the next step.

Wash the livers, cut them in half, and remove the tough connecting membranes. Place the flour and livers in a sealed bag and shake until the livers have absorbed the flour.

Arrange the livers evenly in the skillet, and sauté over high heat. Brown them fast—30 seconds on each side and not cooked—and lift and spread them into the casserole dish. Sprinkle the bacon over the livers.

In the same skillet, sauté the onion until it looks clear. Add the rice, and cook until slightly brown. Add the broth, deglaze the pan, and pour the broth over the livers. Spoon the rice evenly over the livers. Cover, and bake for 35 minutes, or until the rice is tender and has absorbed the broth.

HEALTHY CHOICE ALTERNATIVE First, you'll notice that I've not added any salt. There should be enough salt in the bacon and chicken broth. Next, you can use a heart-healthy oil in place of the bacon, but if you really stick with just six ounces of bacon for eight servings, you won't kill anyone, and you'll enjoy some great flavor.

Serve, garnished with parsley, as you would any main dish casserole. Offer salt and pepper.

DIFFICULTY Moderate. With six ingredients and five quick cooking steps —fry bacon, fry livers, fry onions, deglaze, and bake—this recipe is moderate in difficulty.

INGREDIENTS

6 ounces bacon, cut into 1-inch strips
1 pound fresh chicken livers
1/3 cup all-purpose flour
1 cup diced onion
1 cup rice
2 cups chicken broth

YIELD 8 servings

Country Meats

Pork, Chicken, and Beef

Fried Bacon
(Pan-Fried Bacon)

Fried Pork Chops
(Chicken-Fried Pork Chops)

Barbecued Baby Back Ribs
Barbecued Chicken

Texas-Style Barbecue Sauce
Barbecued Country Ham Steak, Barbecued Pork Chops,
and Pork Barbecue

Roast Pork with Stuffed Apples

Hatfield-McCoy Souse
(Head Cheese)

Pig's Feet and Broth
Jellied Pig's Feet Salad and Fried Pig's Feet and Cornmeal Gravy

Pan-Fried Chicken
(Fried Chicken and Floured Fried Chicken)

Southern Fried Chicken
(Buttermilk Batter and Southern Fried Chicken with Cream Gravy)

Chicken Cream Gravy

Oven-Fried Bacon-Wrapped Chicken

Chicken Stew
Chicken Stew Gravy (Gravediggers' Stew)

Cornmeal Gravy and Fried Chicken Livers
(Meal Gravy)

Country-Fried Steak
(Chicken-Fried Steak and Steak and Gravy)

Five-Hour Stew
(Oven Stew)

Daniel Boone Beef Stew
Squirrel Stew (Beef Stew)

Pecan Brown Gravy

Pot Roast
(Lazy Day Pot Roast)

Pork:
Mountain Stock Cured
in the Smokehouse

HOGS ARE WELL adapted to mountain farms, and out here in the country, you'll find that we still raise them. In addition to requiring little space, hogs are efficient converters of kitchen scraps such as potato peelings. When hogs are not eating scraps, they can live in the hills.

Once hogs are fat, we kill, butcher, and store them. "Hog-killing time in the hills is a hard time and a busy time. . . . It means making souse meat and liver mush, turning out sausage, canning backbones and ribs, rendering lard, and salting down hams and bacon," says John Parris in *Mountain Cooking*.

With rural frugality almost an obsession, mountaineers say they eat every part of the pig, from the ears to the lips to the feet. We eat all but the squeal. We salt pork and keep it in a smokehouse. Typically, we do not cure beef. It was not until after World War II that many isolated mountain families received electric service, and with the coming of electricity, they were able to store beef under refrigeration. Prior to that time, pork was the primary source of meat. Today, pork and beef about equal each other in popularity.

Highlanders who know pork know that cracklings are the fibers left after we boil lard from pork fat. I can remember watching Julia Child make a different kind of cracklings, duck cracklings. She trimmed the extra skin from a gigantic Peking duck and dropped it into a frying pan. Over low to moderate heat, she rendered the skin, frying it until the fat melted off the skin. This melting is called rendering. When the skin was golden brown and crisp, she lifted the skins—the duck cracklings—from the fat. She drained them on paper towels, added salt, lifted a piece to her mouth, and munched on the delicacy. She smiled with satisfaction and went on with the duck preparation.

Highlanders follow a similar process when we fry pork rinds, cracklings, and bacon. In the case of pork rinds, we use skin. For cracklings we use fat only, and for bacon we use side meat that has streaks of lean. In each case, we heat the pork over low heat, or render the fat away, and end up with a crunchy delicacy. We use cracklings either as a snack or as an ingredient in corn bread. Both bacon cracklings and plain cracklings turn soft when we bake them inside corn bread. (See the recipe for Skillet Corn Bread.) Pork rinds, cracklings, and bacon give off fat, and when the fat cools we call it lard.

We render lard from pork. When the lard is ready, it is clarified—free of impurities, like clarified butter. The best is leaf lard, from the area around the kidneys. Lard makes fine, flaky pie crusts and helps flavor vegetables and fry mush. I like it for Fried Green Tomatoes, Fried Chicken, Fried Morels, and Fried Potatoes.

Because of its flavor and richness, we prize it in cooking. If you start with a fat pig, you'll end up with lots of lard. If you start with a tiny, skinny pig, you won't get much lard.

I know that being anti-lard is popular these days. For flavor mongers like me, this anti-lard trend is a pity. Tablespoon for tablespoon, lard has $1/3$ the cholesterol and only a few more calories than butter. Using lard is a choice you can make. I only use lard occasionally, but I've used it often enough that my children know what lard is and how it tastes.

Here in the mountains you can buy one-pound bags of Hormel Cracklings for about $1.40. Ask your grocer or look for them displayed with the salt pork or smoked ham hocks. You'll also find that butchers working in open-air markets sell cracklings. Or, order from Poche's Meat Market, listed in the Mail-Order Sources.

Lard is so basic to our cooking that mountain markets sell it in twenty-pound buckets. They also sell 8, 4, 3, 2$1/2$, and 1-pound buckets. Fischer's, Armour, and Field are popular brand names, and they pack lard in white buckets. The print on the buckets is in basic blue, green, and yellow, and the slogans read, "Fine for Pastries," or "No Refrigeration Required."

Bacon is such a treat that I don't think of it as an economical pork cut, which, of course, it is. In comparison to cuts like the leg or loin, bacon is economical because it is cut from the sides of the hog. We call it side meat, streaked lean, or pork flank. Bacon has streaks of lean and fat that your meat packer cures, smokes, and salts. You can buy bacon in slabs, with the rind or sliced without the rind. In our cooking we use medium-thick sliced bacon, usually about sixteen to eighteen slices per pound. Mountain cooks prize bacon fat. We use bacon drippings as a flavoring for vegetables such as green beans, garden greens, and cabbage, and we use bacon grease as a cooking medium for frying many foods.

Fried Bacon
(Pan-Fried Bacon)

DIFFICULTY Very Easy. To prepare bacon, you fry, drain, and serve.

When we fry bacon, we use a cast-iron skillet or other frying pan to render the fat from the strips of side meat or streaked lean. Sometimes we fry the bacon under a bacon button—a thick round piece of wood or plastic that fits into the bottom of a skillet. After laying strips of bacon in the bottom of a cold skillet, place the bacon button on the bacon. Fry as you normally would, and the button keeps it from curling.

INGREDIENTS
12 ounces bacon

YIELD 4 servings

STEPS Let the bacon come to room temperature, or warm it slightly in the microwave oven. (At about 60°F, the strips pull apart easily. If the bacon is cold, the strips may tear when you pull them apart.)

Place the slices in a cold skillet, and fry them over medium or low-medium heat, turning after about 4 minutes. (Use tongs or a sharply pointed fork to turn the bacon.) Fry another 3 minutes. As the bacon cooks, reduce the heat to prevent burning—when bacon is almost ready, it cooks quickly. When the bacon is crisp and brown, place it on paper towels to drain.

Serve with fried eggs, Fried Potatoes, and Tender Corn Bread, or on a sandwich with tomato and lettuce. Bacon is an ingredient in many recipes including Green Beans with Bacon, Wilted Lettuce, Poke Sallet, Corn Bread Salad, and Crackling Corn Bread.

Fried Pork Chops
(Chicken-Fried Pork Chops)

DIFFICULTY Difficult. With twelve ingredients, two bowls, and one frying pan, you'll make some mess doing this.

Pork chops are mountain fare. We bake, fry, and braise them, we flavor them with oranges, apples, and onions, and we cook them in cream, barbecue, wine, or tomato sauce. If you are from the Georgia Highlands, the mountains at the southern tip of our region, you might even cook them in a peanut butter sauce. I prefer a cream gravy.

Since long before the time of the Hatfield-McCoy feud, pork has been a mountain favorite. But pork has changed. Today it is leaner and safer, and you can handle it like other meats, taking no special precautions against disease. The U.S. Food and Drug Administration recommends cooking pork to an internal temperature of 160°F, or until it is a little pink on the inside.

We call these pork chops chicken-fried because we fry them in the same manner as Southern Fried Chicken. After frying the chops with a thick breaded coating, we cover them with a peppery cream gravy.

STEPS Either have the chops cubed in the market or pound them thoroughly with a meat mallet. Trim off the fat and gristle.

Batter and fry the pork: As you prepare the batter, heat half of the oil over medium heat in a large cast-iron skillet. In a small mixing bowl, beat the eggs and add the milk. Whisk in the 1 cup flour and salt. Pour the bread crumbs into a soup plate.

Dip the chops in the egg mixture, and then in the bread crumbs.

In the skillet over low to medium heat, fry the chops 7 minutes on one side, being careful not to burn the batter. Turn the chops, add the remaining oil, and fry 7 minutes on the other side. (If you use a quick-response thermometer, the internal temperature of the pork should read at least 160°F.) Remove the chops from the pan, and keep them warm in the oven.

Prepare the gravy: Using the same skillet, melt the butter and stir in the flour until fully mixed. Whisk in the milk, and use it to deglaze the pan. After the milk boils, cook for 1 minute. Mix in the salt and pepper.

HEALTHY CHOICE ALTERNATIVE Spray a cookie sheet with nonstick cooking spray, and bake the chops at 350°F for 35 minutes. In place of the butter, make the gravy with a cold roux. Omit or reduce the salt, and add it at the table.

After serving the chops, spoon the gravy over the top. Serve these with pear chutney or bread-and-butter pickles, and offer sauerkraut, baked apples, or sweet potatoes. Distinguish the meal with fresh-from-the-oven Skillet Corn Bread or Buttermilk Biscuits.

INGREDIENTS

FOR THE CHOPS
Four 5-ounce center-cut
 pork chops
$^1/_3$ cup vegetable oil
2 eggs
$^2/_3$ cup milk
1 cup all-purpose flour
2 teaspoons salt
1 $^1/_2$ cups bread crumbs

FOR THE GRAVY
$^1/_4$ cup butter
$^1/_4$ cup all-purpose flour
2 cups milk
1 teaspoon salt
1 teaspoon pepper

YIELD 4 servings

Barbecued Baby Back Ribs
Barbecued Chicken

*W*ith this slow-cooker barbecue, you combine opposites: old and new, fast and slow. The combination of slow cooking and fast grilling makes these ribs tender and crisp. When you add a few grilled vegetables, you have another opposite that brings balance: light vegetables and rich pork barbecue.

Slow cooking results in tender ribs, and fast cooking yields flavor. I cook the ribs indoors in a slow-cooker, and outdoors on a grill. The result is a tender, succulent serving, soft meat inside and crisp with burned edges outside.

DIFFICULTY Easy.
With two ingredients, a day of slow cooking, and then a quick grilling, this recipe is easy to prepare. Start the ribs in the morning, and barbecue them just before serving.

Country
Meats

Like glaze on a cake, barbecue sauce completes the dish. Flavored with hickory smoke, honey, and a mix of spices, the sauce adds flavor and moisture. Select one of the many commercial barbecue sauces available, or make your own. I have observed two styles of barbecue sauce: thick Texas style and thin Carolina style. Thick barbecue sauces, like sauces that come out of a Kraft bottle, are Texas style. Hot and spicy, these sauces are almost as thick as ketchup, and I brush them on cooked meat. We make thin barbecue sauces, indigenous to the Carolinas, with spices, vinegar, water, tomato juice, and Worcestershire sauce. These thin sauces are vinegar marinade. These "soppin'" sauces range from thin to thick, depending on the amount of tomato paste or ketchup we add. When using Carolina-style sauces, dip the pieces of meat into the sauce every twenty minutes or so throughout the cooking.

Your butcher cuts baby back, back ribs, or country ribs from a small pig, one that weighs 180 pounds or less. Look for whole racks, eighteen to twenty-four inches long, four to five inches across, and under three pounds.

INGREDIENTS

2 sides baby back ribs (racks weigh 1 3/4 pounds, and are 18 to 24 inches long)

2 cups Texas-Style Barbecue Sauce (page 171) or commercial sauce (such as Kraft Thick 'n Spicy or Mesquite Smoke)

YIELD 6 servings

STEPS Cut each side of ribs so that it will fit into your slow-cooker. Cut the side of ribs into as few pieces as possible. Place the ribs in the slow-cooker and cook at medium for 10 hours. The temperature in the crock pot should stay at about 165°F.

Fifteen minutes before serving time, heat a gas grill. When the grill is hot, move the ribs from the crock pot to the grill. Watch the ribs carefully, or you may burn them. After you grill the ribs for 2 minutes on each side, use a pastry brush to brush the top (tips down, convex side up) side of the ribs with barbecue sauce. To keep the sauce from burning, I don't put it on the bottom. Put the ribs back on the grill, sauce up, and grill for another 1 to 2 minutes. Add more sauce, and grill 1 more minute.

TIP To grill soft vegetables such as eggplant, summer squash, bell peppers, and mushrooms, cut them up, put them on a skewer, and grill for 10 minutes. For hard vegetables such as onions, celery, carrots, and beets, boil until tender and then grill 10 minutes.

While you can serve grilled foods immediately, there is no need to rush your vegetables or ribs to the table. They'll be just as good after they have cooled some. Do not cover them, or they will lose their crispness.

For a complete summer meal, serve with salad, grilled vegetables, a baked potato, and dessert.

Barbecued Chicken
Using chicken quarters, follow the same procedure, reducing the slow-cooking time to 3 hours. For my family, I fix 1 rack of ribs and about 2 pounds of chicken quarters.

HEARTY Cooking COUNTRY

Texas-Style Barbecue Sauce
Barbecued Country Ham Steak, Barbecued Pork Chops, and Pork Barbecue

*U*se this or one of the many commercially available barbecue sauces for the barbecue variations below. When you use a slow-cooker, you can work away from home all day and come home to a hearty and tender supper.

STEPS In a small saucepan, combine the ketchup, water, vinegar, sauce, sugar, flour, salt, and pepper. Stir together and simmer 1 minute.

Barbecued Country Ham Steak
Layer 3 pounds of ham in a slow-cooker with the sauce (2 cups), and cook 5 to 10 hours on medium. Or, bake the ham in a covered roaster at 350°F for 2 to 3 hours. In either case, remove the fat before serving.

Barbecued Pork Chops
In place of the country ham, use 3 pounds center-cut pork chops.

Pork Barbecue
Bake a 3-pound pork loin roast at 500°F for 20 minutes. Reduce the heat to 250°F, and bake an additional 4 to 5 hours. Remove the roast from the pan and chop into small (1/4-inch) pieces. Mix with 2 cups barbecue sauce, and keep warm until serving time. Serve on hamburger buns.

Serve the Country Ham and Pork Barbecue with light side dishes such as fresh-sliced tomatoes, cucumbers, and raw carrots. Offer Succotash, Cabbage Stew, and Sweet Potato Biscuits. Make a barbecue sandwich using biscuits, toast, or a hamburger bun. Serve with garden-fresh, sliced tomatoes, raw carrots, cucumber sticks, Potato Salad, Kathy's Cole Slaw, or Corn Bread Salad.

DIFFICULTY Moderate. With eight ingredients, this recipe is moderate in difficulty.

INGREDIENTS
1 cup tomato ketchup
1/2 cup water
1/4 cup vinegar
1/4 cup Worcestershire sauce
2 tablespoons brown sugar
2 tablespoons instant flour
2 teaspoons charcoal-flavored salt
1/2 teaspoon red pepper flakes

YIELD 6 servings or 2 cups

Roast Pork with Stuffed Apples

DIFFICULTY Moderate. With eight ingredients and two cooking steps, this recipe is moderate in difficulty.

*F*or a beautiful sight and a savory combination, this recipe combines three fall favorites: sweet potatoes, apples, and pork. Pork is a fall food because mountain farmers kill hogs on a cold November or December day. Remember that fifty years ago mountaineers pressed their clothing, spread linens across the dinner table, went to church, and came home to Sunday dinner that might have included this Roast Pork with Stuffed Apples.

The roasting procedure I give here combines high heat to seal in the juices with low heat to tenderize the roast. If you have a little extra Sweet Potato Casserole, you can prepare this main dish with three ingredients: roast, apples, and the casserole. Roasting the apples for an hour at 250°F leaves them firm and not fully cooked—to me, a real treat. The sour and almost crunchy Granny Smith apples contrast nicely with the soft sweet potato puree. When I can't get Granny Smiths, I use Golden Delicious.

INGREDIENTS
1 large (1 1/2 cups mashed) sweet potato
4 large Granny Smith apples
1/4 cup brown sugar
1/4 cup butter
3 tablespoons lemon juice
1/4 teaspoon nutmeg
1/4 teaspoon cinnamon
One 5-pound pork loin roast

YIELD 8 servings

STEPS The day before serving, boil the sweet potato in enough water to cover for 45 minutes, or until tender. As the sweet potato simmers, peel the apples, cut them in half from top to bottom, and remove the core. Use a melon baller to scoop out some more apple, forming a cavity the size of a walnut, or large enough to hold 2 tablespoons. Slice the round surface off the bottom of each apple so that it will sit flat. Place the apples in a bowl, cover with water, stir in 2 tablespoons of the lemon juice, and refrigerate until you are ready to roast them.

To prepare the sweet potato, remove the peeling and measure out 1 1/2 cups of mashed potato. In a food processor, combine the potato, brown sugar, butter, the remaining 1 tablespoon of lemon juice, the nutmeg, and cinnamon. Process until smooth, and set aside.

The next day, preheat the oven to 500°F. Place the pork roast on a rack in a large roasting pan and bake for 15 minutes. Reduce the heat to 250°F and bake for 4 hours.

Mound the sweet potato puree into the apples. Place them in a 13x9x2-inch baking dish. Bake with the pork for 1 hour. Remove the roast from the oven, cool 10 minutes, and slice.

Garnish a large oval platter with fall greens—turnip, kale, or collards—and slices of orange. Place the sliced pork in the center and surround it with the stuffed apples. Sprinkle with your choice of salt, garlic, paprika, pepper, or crushed red pepper. Serve with Pecan Brown Gravy and garnish with pecan halves.

HEARTY Cooking COUNTRY

The Hatfield-McCoy and Souse Feud

I call this Hatfield-McCoy Souse because the infamous feud started after one of the McCoys was killed and a pig was stolen. Pigs, pride, guns, and gardens were all part of survival in the rugged mountains. Today, the feud is history, and the McCoys and the Hatfields blend together like the meat and jelly in souse.

In most rural cultures where farmers butcher livestock, they make a dish such as souse. The preparation renders, preserves, and embellishes the head, cheeks, snouts, underlips, brains, tongue, heart, liver, feet, and even the shoulder of pork, beef, or veal. Souse is either pickled in brine or jellied in aspic.

Here in the mountains, we have a strong tradition of making souse. Like the Germans and Swiss, we serve it on sandwiches. The French serve it as part of an *hors-d'oeuvre* and the Scandinavians as part of a smorgasbord. Our souse has far more aspic than its European counterpart.

Brawn is the French word for head cheese. The French may make brawn with layers of meat and fat, using pork rind as a covering around the outside. *Hure* is another type of French head cheese, shaped like a sausage and made with parts of the head.

You can season head cheese with bay leaf, onions, carrots, celery, ginger, cloves, and nutmeg, but these are not common in the mountains.

In 1839 Lettice Bryan, writing in *The Kentucky Housewife*, gave directions for making souse. "As soon as your hogs are cut up, clean the feet and ears nicely, by scalding and scraping them. Never put them into the fire to loosen the hoofs, as the manner of some indolent cooks. It is apt to scorch the meat, make it dark, and it is then unfit for souse." She goes on to instruct you to soak the meat parts in water and white cornmeal for at least twenty-four hours and then boil until tender. Mary Randolph in her 1824 book, *The Virginia Housewife*, makes this clear when she says, "boil your souse gently, until you can run a straw into the skin with ease."

In our markets today you can buy souse packaged as cold cuts. Even small grocery stores sell two or three different kinds and, interestingly enough, they often have a layer of fat around the outside like the French brawn. Commercially prepared souse includes pimiento, but old-time farmers were trying to save money, so they did not add extra ingredients. Home cooks do not use fat. If you want to re-create a mountain tradition, try making this recipe.

Hatfield-McCoy Souse
(Head Cheese)

Souse is head cheese. Souse is also a coldcut made with pork meat and gelatin. To souse is also to immerse. Here in the mountains we immerse a hog's head, feet, and other parts in brine to clean the parts. Then we cook them in water, remove the meat, and, after adding spices, we chill the mixture to make souse. The cooking creates an aspic which forms a solid jelly. We slice this, serve it on bread, and call it souse.

DIFFICULTY Moderate. Once you have gathered the ingredients, this recipe is moderate in difficulty. If the hog head is clean, skip the first step, but remember that it must be clean.

INGREDIENTS

TO CLEAN THE PORK
1/2 hog head
1 pig's foot
Water
1/2 cup salt

FOR THE SOUSE
2 teaspoons dried sage
1 teaspoon salt
1/2 teaspoon red pepper flakes
1/4 teaspoon ground cloves

YIELD 1 1/2 pounds head cheese or 12 (2-ounce) servings

STEPS If possible, have your butcher quarter the hog head. Remove and discard the fat, eyes, brains, skin, and hair. Place the head and feet in a large bucket, cover with water, and add the salt. Stir until the salt dissolves. Soak 5 hours. Drain and rinse well. Wash and scrub until clean. If you have trouble cleaning the head, soak it again.

Place the cleaned parts in a large pan, cover with water, and boil 3 to 5 hours, or until the meat is tender and loose from the bones. Remove the meat and chop it, measuring out 3 cups. Continue to simmer the broth until you reduce it by half. Strain.

To the 3 cups of meat add 2 cups of the broth (do not add any fat), the sage, 1/2 teaspoon salt, the red pepper flakes, and the cloves. Boil for 10 minutes, and pour into a 9x4x2-inch loaf pan. Cool. Slice.

If you want less jelly or aspic mixed in with the meat, cover the meat with a cheesecloth, weigh it down, and then chill. When you remove the cheesecloth, remove the extra jelly.

HEARTY
Cooking
COUNTRY

HEALTHY CHOICE ALTERNATIVE Souse is light and fat free.

Serve this as an appetizer on lettuce with liver sausage, carrots, celery, and pickles. Slice and use on a sandwich with a slice of sweet onion. Serve for lunch as an open-faced sandwich with Kathy's Cole Slaw and Appalachian Potato Salad.

Pig's Feet and Broth

Jellied Pig's Feet Salad and Fried Pig's Feet and Cornmeal Gravy

*W*hen I was a child my favorite meat was leg of lamb, and from the leg I liked the shank most. It has lots of cartilage. Pig's feet remind me of lamb shank because they have almost no meat, and they are gelatinous, mostly cartilage. Fully cooked, the cartilage is smooth, soft, and tasty. We serve pig's feet pickled, boiled, broiled, or as part of a salad. We serve them cold with a cheesy salad dressing, and to that we add pickled beets and spring greens. We serve them hot with fresh green beans, usually sturdy beans like white half-runners or Tennessee pole beans. We serve them with a pot of Soup Beans and we might add them to U.S. Senate Bean Soup. We also purchase them precooked, and we grill them with fresh summer vegetables. We also freshen them up and crisp the outside by broiling them. Germans living in the mountains will spread them with mustard, sprinkle them with bread crumbs, broil them, and serve with sauerkraut and mashed potatoes. We frequently serve pickled pig's feet with sauerkraut and bread-and-butter pickles. We also use them as a primary ingredient for souse.

Mountain cooks are not the only ones fixing pig's feet. James Beard's *American Cookery* offers five recipes, and the French classic, *The Escoffier Cookbook,* offers truffled pig's feet and breaded pig's feet. If you want to hold the feet together and maintain their shape, you'll have to wrap them in muslin or cheesecloth before you boil them. When they are cool, remove the cloth. Without the cheesecloth the feet will pull together and curve into round irregular masses.

The tradition of eating pig's feet grew out of our need to save everything, including the feet. You'll be surprised at the flavor of this milky, gelatinous broth, and you'll see that the feet have almost no fat.

DIFFICULTY Easy. With five ingredients and stovetop boiling, this soup is easy to prepare.

STEPS In a large saucepan, cover the feet with water, and bring to a boil. Cover, reduce the heat, and simmer for 2½ hours. Add water as needed to keep

INGREDIENTS
2 pig's feet (1 pound)
  cut in half through the
  center
1 1/2 cups chopped cel-
  ery
1 1/2 cups diced onions
1 teaspoon salt
1/4 teaspoon pepper

YIELD 4 servings

the pig's feet covered. Add the celery, and simmer 10 minutes. Add the onion, salt, and pepper and simmer an additional 10 minutes.

HEALTHY CHOICE ALTERNATIVE Pour or ladle off the fat that comes to the top of the broth. A four-ounce serving of pig's feet has about 220 calories and 19 grams of protein. That compares to four ounces of lean beef, with about 290 calories and 28 grams of protein.

Serve a cup of the broth, celery, and onions in a flat soup plate. Add one pig's foot. Eat the pig's foot with a knife and fork, and the soup with a soup spoon. Offer corn bread, hot rolls, or biscuits, with butter and Green Pepper Jelly.

Jellied Pig's Feet Salad

Jellied Pig's Feet Salad Follow the recipe for Pig's Feet and Broth. Cool. Remove the bones and separate the gelatin and skin into small pieces. Dice half a red bell pepper, and add to the mixture. Pour the mixture into a loaf pan or ring mold. Refrigerate 4 hours or until solid. Slice and serve on a bed of wild spring greens or lettuce. Add Pickled Beets, Pickled Green Beans, and rolled banana-nut salad. For a complete meal add to the bed of lettuce a serving of Appalachian Potato Salad, Cucumber Salad with Sour Cream, and Mexican Corn Bread.

Fried Pig's Feet and Cornmeal Gravy

Fried Pig's Feet and Cornmeal Gravy Boil the pig's feet for 2 1/2 hours. Cool, and remove the bones. Dip the meat in well-beaten eggs and then in well-salted and peppered cornmeal. Fry in 1/4 inch of oil for about 20 minutes, or until well browned on all sides.

Remove the pig's feet to a serving platter, hold in a warm oven, and prepare the Cornmeal Gravy, below.

Cornmeal Gravy

Cornmeal Gravy Using about 1/4 cup of the grease left in the skillet, add 1/3 cup cornmeal and 1 1/2 cups milk. Stir and simmer for 1 minute. At serving time, pour the hot gravy over the fried pig's feet. Serve as a main dish with Pickled Beets, Chow Chow, and Skillet Corn Bread.

Chicken:
Baked, Boiled, and Fried

Fried Chicken

Fried chicken is a universally popular Southern dish, but the South is a diverse region, and our cooks prepare fried chicken in many ways. Typically the disputes regarding the proper way to fry chicken center on the source of the chicken, choice of oil, kind of batter, use of spices, selection of frying pan, and appropriate side dishes. Today we argue about fat and how to reduce it.

We prepare fried chicken either coated with batter and covered with cream gravy or dredged in flour. In either case we pan-fry the chicken in a generous amount of oil. Rarely is it deep-fried or sautéed. In many cooking households there is some friendly—or not-so-friendly—discussion about the "right" way to prepare fried chicken. We argue about fixing the chicken with a batter, without a batter, or double coated; we fix the coating with or without cornmeal, cracker crumbs, bread crumbs, Rice Krispies, or Corn Flake Crumbs; we serve the chicken with or without gravy; we cook it covered or uncovered. Those who use Shake 'n Bake, fry in the oven.

There is no doubt in my mind that fresh chickens make succulent fried chicken. To serve the absolute best pan-fried chicken, you'll have to start with a fresh, home-grown chicken. Chickens raised in the open—we call them yard birds, and you may know them as free-range chickens—are free to eat what they want. Yard birds scratch the dirt, eating what they find, and they don't taste like the factory-produced poultry sold in our markets.

Unfortunately, I can only dream about yard birds. If you are like me and have to settle for supermarket poultry, don't give up on chicken. We can still fry some mighty tasty pieces.

The second critical, divisive, and determining issue is your selection of the frying medium, the oil. Do you choose canola, corn, or Crisco? Safflower, olive, or walnut? Butter, clarified butter, or margarine? Fat back, bacon drippings, or lard? Duck fat? Oils are different, and the choice of oil makes a difference in flavor, texture, color, and smell.

Sure spices, gravy, frying pan, and batter count for bushels; but the tippers of the scales, the cornerstone ingredients that make a county fair blue ribbon piece of pan-fried chicken, are the chicken and the oil. Even when I can't find barnyard-raised chickens, I can use the oil I want: duck fat, bacon grease, lard, or Crisco. When I'm thinking about good health, I use safflower oil.

Some cooks prepare their chicken by soaking it several hours in milk or buttermilk. If you skip the soaking, dip the chicken in a milk and egg mixture and then coat it with flour, a process called dredging. After you coat the chicken with flour, you can do as some country cooks do and allow it to air dry for an hour. Chicken purists, I suspect, use only flour. Those who want a heavy coating start with a batter made from a mix of cornmeal, flour, milk, and eggs. After they apply this heavy batter to the chicken, they roll it in crumbs from bread, crackers, corn bread, or cornflakes, giving a thick coating.

Thirty-five years ago, when cooking with oil was not a sin, oven-fried chicken was baked in oil. The chicken pieces would bake for an hour, and every ten minutes or so you would baste the pieces with oil. In the health-conscious nineties, oven-fried means no oil. It may also mean a box of Shake 'n Bake or Oven Fry Coating. For this drop of good health you will pay dearly—these boxes of crumbs are expensive, costing almost as much as the chicken they will cover! But then, time is everything. To save money, reduce salt, and nudge the spices, I prefer to mix my own coating.

You don't want to overcook chicken—it dries the meat, robs it of flavor, and makes it tough. Because the dark meat needs more cooking time than white meat, you should separate the two. If you have a lot of chicken, fry dark and light meats in separate pans. Fry chicken until the red blood near the bone has turned brown. Test by cutting to the bone and looking for streaks of red. The juice should run clear. Few cooks use thermometers, but if you do, fry the chicken until its internal temperature reaches 170°F to 175°F.

Until I bought a chicken fryer, I always fried chicken in my old black cast-iron skillet. I've owned the skillet for 25 years and use it for almost everything, including baking biscuits. Now I like to cover the chicken. I use a Dutch oven or a chicken fryer, a cast-iron pan equipped with a nippled lid—its many little points gather the moisture and cause it to drip back onto the chicken. Other lids have ribs that serve the same purpose. (Lodge Manufacturing Co. in South Pittsburgh, Tennessee, makes a cast-iron chicken skillet equipped with a nippled lid. See Lodge in the list of Mail-Order Sources.) Another good pan is the covered, thermostat-controlled electric skillet. With my stainless steel electric fry pan from Farberware, I sometimes brown chicken uncovered at 365°F and then simmer it covered at 275°F. Other pan options include aluminum, dry frying pans, copper, and nonstick coated pans such as Silverstone. Any sturdy pan will fry chicken, but mountain cooks tend toward cast-iron.

Salt, pepper, paprika, and parsley are the most common fried chicken flavorings, with the occasional use of Tabasco sauce, bourbon, wine, or lemon juice. Parsley, fresh or dried, is without doubt the most common fried chicken garnish. Sprinkle it over the fried chicken, or stick sprigs underneath.

HEARTY
Cooking
COUNTRY

Pan-Fried Chicken
(Fried Chicken and Floured Fried Chicken)

*G*etting succulent fried chicken prepared and served requires special care. My wife's uncle, Frank Rogers, gave me this simple recipe, and it really works. Frank does not cover the chicken with a batter. He uses no milk, no eggs, no cornmeal, no crumbs, and no crushed cornflakes. Frank keeps the cooking and standing times to a minimum so that the chicken does not dry out.

Frank grew up in Kingstree, South Carolina, and learned this procedure from his mother. She was a country girl, and her recipe is easy. You simply coat the chicken with flour, fry it, and serve it—hold the gravy.

Frank's mother never used a quick-response thermometer. Checking the temperature is my adaptation, a crutch for the modern cook who does not raise chickens, who does not work as a full-time homemaker, who does not feed a large family, and who does not fry chicken very often.

DIFFICULTY Easy. With five ingredients and one cooking step, this recipe is easy.

STEPS Wash the chicken and soak it for several hours in enough salted water to cover.

As the chicken soaks, mix the flour, paprika, and salt in the bottom of a soup plate. In a skillet, heat 1/4-inch of oil until it starts to smoke. Dredge (we say, rub) the chicken in the flour mixture, and place it in the skillet. (If you want a little more crust on your chicken, pack the flour on the chicken as if you were a child making mud pies.)

Fry over a high heat until the chicken has browned on all sides. Reduce the heat and cover the pan, simmering for an additional 20 minutes, or until the chicken reads 160°F on a quick-response thermometer. Uncover, and fry for 5 to 10 more minutes, or until the chicken is crisp and the internal temperature reads 170°F to 175°F. Drain on paper towels, and serve.

INGREDIENTS
2 to 3 pounds cut-up
 fryer parts
1/2 cup all-purpose flour
2 teaspoons paprika
2 teaspoons salt
1 to 2 cups safflower oil,
 or as needed

YIELD 4 to 6 servings

HEALTHY CHOICE ALTERNATIVE First, use skinned chicken. For small portions and healthy convenience, ask your butcher for chicken tenders. Bake them at 400°F, flour coated, on a lightly greased cookie sheet until the juices run clear.

Or, after soaking and flouring, arrange the chicken on a greased rack in a baking pan and bake at 400°F for 40 minutes. Cut into the center of one piece to see that the juices run clear, or until the internal temperature reads 170°F to 175°F on a quick-response thermometer.

Serve this chicken with mashed potatoes and gravy, Corn on the Cob, and

Kathy's Coleslaw. Serve with biscuits and honey, biscuits and Chicken Cream Gravy, or chicken biscuits (biscuits that are fried like hush puppies in the chicken oil). Served with peas and watermelon rind pickles, this dish is a touch of the Deep South, something from the mountains of northeast Georgia. Corn oysters and potato pancakes are special to some folks, while others think of this fried chicken as picnic fare and serve it cold with potato salad and fresh, cold watermelon.

Southern Fried Chicken
(Buttermilk Batter and Southern Fried Chicken with Cream Gravy)

*I*f I don't have the Chicken Cream Gravy (page 181) running all over my fried chicken, I don't call it Southern Fried Chicken. It's a symbiotic relationship: One is not complete without the other. Here the bacon grease adds flavor to the chicken. Mixing the egg with buttermilk, rather than milk, makes the coating thicker.

DIFFICULTY Difficult. With nine ingredients, a brown bag, a bowl, a frying pan, and two frying steps, this recipe is difficult to prepare.

INGREDIENTS

FOR THE FRIED CHICKEN
2 pounds chicken pieces
8 ounces bacon
1/2 cup safflower oil

FOR THE BUTTERMILK BATTER
2/3 cup self-rising cornmeal mix
1 tablespoon paprika
1 teaspoon salt
1/2 teaspoon pepper
1/4 cup buttermilk
1 egg

YIELD 4 servings

STEPS In a large cast-iron skillet, fry the bacon and set it aside. Add oil to the pan until you have about 1/4 inch, and heat it to 365°F—the oil will start to smoke, and when a drop of water falls into the oil, the drop will pop back at you.

Wash and dry the chicken. In the bottom of a large brown paper grocery bag, combine the cornmeal mix, paprika, salt, and pepper. In a small mixing bowl, whisk together the buttermilk and egg. Dip the chicken pieces into this mixture. Lay the chicken onto the bottom of the bag, fold the bag closed, and shake until coated.

Slowly ease the chicken into the skillet, and brown it on all sides, cooking, uncovered, for 10 to 15 minutes. Reduce the heat to medium, 275°F, and simmer, uncovered, an additional 20 to 30 minutes, turning after 10 to 15 minutes. Drain the chicken on the brown paper bag. Serve.

HEALTHY CHOICE ALTERNATIVE Do not use saturated fats such as lard, bacon grease, or butter. Use vegetable oil, and omit the bacon.

To further reduce fat, use skinless chicken and bake it on a cookie sheet. Bake the chicken at 400°F for 40 minutes. Cut into the center of one piece to see that the juices run clear. If you are using a thermometer you want the internal temperature to read 170°F to 175°F. Serve with Chicken Cream Gravy, and enjoy low-fat Southern Fried Chicken.

Add salt, pepper, garlic, and parsley later.

Serve this smothered with Chicken Cream Gravy, and round out the meal with Mashed Kennebec Potatoes, Buttermilk Biscuits, and a garden salad of lettuce, cucumbers, and onions. I serve the bacon over the chicken or on a salad with the meal. In the summer, I serve the chicken with a platter of chilled watermelon, cantaloupe, strawberries, and grapes.

Chicken Cream Gravy

We generally do not use cream in cream gravy. Instead, mountain cooks use whole milk or evaporated milk. We call this a cream gravy because, colloquially, we refer to evaporated milk as cream. This gravy should be the thickness of pancake batter, not a heavy blob of goo that sits on top of your fried chicken.

I suspect that our cream gravy has its roots in fricasséed chicken. A hundred years ago, people made fricasséed chicken by browning flour-dredged chicken pieces in lard, covering them with water, and simmering until tender. They removed the chicken from the pot and added flour and perhaps cream, which became cream gravy.

DIFFICULTY Easy. With five ingredients and one step, this recipe is easy.

STEPS As the fried chicken cools on a serving plate, pour all but 2 to 3 tablespoons of the oil from the frying pan. Leave the other drippings in the pan. Stir in the flour, and cook until beige or light brown. Whisk in the milk, bouillon, pepper, and salt. Bring to a boil, reduce the heat, and simmer for 1 minute.

HEALTHY CHOICE ALTERNATIVE Make the gravy in a saucepan without oil. Heat the milk, bouillon, salt, and pepper, then slowly whisk in instant flour, and boil for 1 minute. Use low-sodium chicken bouillon grains.

INGREDIENTS
1/4 cup all-purpose flour
2 cups milk
1 tablespoon chicken bouillon grains
3/4 teaspoon pepper
1/2 teaspoon salt

YIELD 5 servings

Serve this gravy over Southern Fried Chicken, sliced turkey, Mashed Kennebec Potatoes, or Corn Bread Dressing.

Oven-Fried Bacon-Wrapped Chicken

DIFFICULTY Moderate. By the time you wash the chicken, wrap the chicken with bacon, mix the cornmeal coating, and bake for 50 minutes, this recipe with just seven ingredients is moderate in difficulty.

INGREDIENTS

1 strip bacon for each piece of chicken
2 to 4 pounds (approximately 7 pieces) skinless chicken thighs
1 toothpick for each piece of chicken
1 cup self-rising cornmeal mix
2 tablespoons salt
1 teaspoon paprika
1 teaspoon pepper

YIELD Allow 1½ pieces of chicken per serving

*T*he two tablespoons of salt in this recipe are not a misprint. This baked chicken will be less salty than what you buy in a box, at KFC, Chick-Fil-A, or other fast-food stores. I don't use all of the cornmeal coating; some of it is left in the bag.

STEPS Bring the bacon to room temperature or warm it to about 80°F in a microwave oven. (Softened bacon will stretch and stick to the chicken.) Preheat the oven to 350°F. Wash the chicken. Select a roasting pan equipped with an inside rack.

Wrap each piece of chicken with a strip of bacon, and secure it with a toothpick. In a gallon-size zip-sealed plastic bag, combine the cornmeal mix, salt, paprika, and pepper. Add the chicken about 4 pieces at a time, seal the bag, and roll on the table to coat.

Place the chicken on the baking rack, and bake until done! Don't you "love" those directions? The cooking time will depend on the size of the chicken pieces and the starting temperature. If the chicken is cold, it takes longer. Bake 50 to 60 minutes or until the juices run clear, not bloody. To use this "juices run clear" test, insert a knife to the bone, pull it out, and let the juices run for 3 or 4 minutes. If any red comes out, the chicken is not cooked. The internal temperature should reach 175°F. I check it with a quick-response thermometer.

HEALTHY CHOICE ALTERNATIVE Omit the bacon. If you use skinless chicken and omit the bacon, the cornmeal coating will come from the oven dry, but it will still be tasty.

Chicken Stew
Chicken Stew Gravy (Gravediggers' Stew)

*J*bbie Ledford, a homemaker from Linden, Tennessee, often writes about her cooking and family, and in her book, *Hill Country Cookin' and Memoirs*, she offers a chicken stew that she calls gravediggers' stew. In the winter when you drive along state highways or county roads, you can spot private cemeteries every few miles. Mountaineers bury family members on hills above their homes. If the cemetery is on a steep hill, the grave has to be dug by hand. Friends and family often volunteer for the job, using picks and shovels. When the grave is ready, the diggers are hungry, and according to Ledford's book, they may get the chance to eat gravediggers' stew.

Ledford makes her stew with boiled chicken and onions, adding home-canned vegetables such as corn, butter beans, lima beans, and tomatoes. I make boiled chicken stew with fresh potatoes, carrots, celery, and onions, as I suggest here. In both cases we serve the extra broth hot with corn bread or use it to simmer dumplings.

DIFFICULTY Moderate. With seven ingredients, this recipe is moderate in difficulty. Hopefully your family will appreciate the fact that you have deboned the chicken—this step is messy and takes some time.

STEPS Wash the chicken. In a large pot, simmer the chicken and potatoes in the water for 45 minutes. Lift them from the broth, and skim off the fat.

As the chicken cools, lower the carrots and onions into the pot, and simmer for 20 minutes, or until tender. Add the salt and pepper. When the chicken is cool, remove the bones and skin. Return the meat and the potatoes to the pot, and heat through.

HEALTHY CHOICE ALTERNATIVE Because this dinner is boiled, the chicken fat will rise to the top of the broth. Skim the fat, and discard. For more healthy eating, use more vegetables and larger potatoes. Careful, now: Don't add a scoop of sour cream or fat pat of butter to that potato—moisten it with chicken broth or gravy.

Serve this stew with corn bread, or crumble it into the broth. Or, arrange the chicken, potatoes, carrots, and onions on a platter, cover to keep warm, and serve with the gravy.

INGREDIENTS
One 3- to 4-pound whole frying chicken
4 small potatoes, quartered
8 cups water
4 large carrots, peeled, quartered
4 small onions, whole
1 tablespoon salt
1 teaspoon pepper

YIELD 4 servings

Chicken Stew Gravy To thicken the broth for a gravy, make a cold roux: In a medium mixing bowl, whisk together 6 tablespoons of flour and enough cold water to reach the consistency of heavy cream. In a saucepan, combine the roux with 3 cups of the broth, and bring to a boil. Boil 1 minute. Adjust the flavor with salt and pepper. Pour half of this sauce over the platter of chicken and vegetables, and serve the other half on the side.

■ ■

Funeral Menus

When someone dies the family gathers at their home, and neighbors bring an abundance of food. This Gravediggers' Stew would be an appropriate gift for such an occasion. The family suffering the loss will also appreciate other large, casserole-type dishes. For example we often take one of my favorite cakes, a Jam Cake. In the summer I'll take a Blackberry Delight, and in the winter I'll take warm dumplings. At the time of death, this gathering of family and sharing of food suggests the importance we place on relationships and the value we place on life.

Menu Suggestions

Fancy Cheese Grits Casserole, Kraut Slaw, Dilly Beans, Broccoli Corn Bread, Chicken and Dumplings, Greenbrier Fiddlehead Salad, Cabbage Stew, Broccoli Casserole, U.S. Senate Bean Soup, Fancy Sweet Potato Casserole, Custard Corn Pudding, Stuffed Cabbage Rolls, Stuffed Green Peppers, Pork Barbecue, Sorghum Pie, Pecan Fudge-Nuts, or Chocolate Pecan Pie.

■ ■

Cornmeal Gravy and Fried Chicken Livers
(Meal Gravy)

When I prepare this recipe I layer the bacon, onions, livers, and gravy on a platter. By making each layer smaller than the one below it, I expose all four layers, making an attractive presentation.

STEPS   In a large cast-iron skillet, fry the bacon until crisp, and lift it onto a paper towel to drain. Place on a platter, and keep warm in the oven. Leave the bacon grease in the skillet.

Sauté (high heat and fast cooking) the onions. As they cook, place the bacon on an oval serving platter. Slide the platter into a warm oven.

When the onions are clear, remove them from the pan and spread them over the bacon. Wash the livers and cut them in half, removing the tough connecting membranes. Place the flour and livers in a sealed bag and roll the bag on the counter until the livers have absorbed the flour.

Using the same heavy cast-iron skillet, sauté the livers, spreading them evenly over the surface of the pan. It takes about 3 minutes. During this short time you will place the livers in the pan, sauté them, turn them, and complete the cooking. The livers are cooked when they are red in the middle and soft throughout. If your livers are firm, they are overcooked. Lift the livers out of the skillet and spread them over the onions.

Prepare the Meal Gravy: Stir the cornmeal, milk, salt, and pepper into the skillet. Whisk together, bring to a boil, and simmer for 1 minute. Scrape the goodies off the bottom of the pan. Stir well and spread this thick gravy over the livers. Serve. You'll have layers: bacon, onions, liver, and gravy.

HEALTHY CHOICE ALTERNATIVE   Use a heart-healthy oil in place of the bacon, but if you really stick with just three ounces of bacon for four servings, you won't clog a healthy person's arteries, and you'll enjoy some great flavor.

Consider reserving two pieces of bacon and a piece of chicken liver to garnish the top of this thick gravy. Serve for breakfast, lunch, or dinner, spooning the livers and gravy over toast, waffles, rice, or an omelet.

DIFFICULTY Moderate. With eight ingredients and four quick cooking steps, this recipe is moderate in difficulty.

INGREDIENTS
3 ounces bacon, cut into 1-inch strips
1/2 cup diced onion
1/2 pound fresh chicken livers
2 to 3 tablespoons all-purpose flour

FOR THE MEAL GRAVY
3 tablespoons cornmeal
3/4 cup milk
1/4 teaspoon salt
1/4 teaspoon pepper

YIELD 4 servings

Country-Fried Steak
(Chicken-Fried Steak and Steak and Gravy)

I was having lunch at the Moose Cafe at the Western North Carolina Farmers Market in Asheville, North Carolina. I immediately liked the place. The atmosphere was old country mixed with a touch of plastic. The menu was handwritten on a sheet of plain copy paper. The main-dish selections were old-fashioned. I ordered the country-style steak. I could smell it cooking, and my mouth watered in anticipation. As I waited, the waitress brought hot biscuits and corn bread. With these she served boxed margarine, fresh clove-spiced apple butter, and warm bottled sorghum.

My steak was just as good. From that day on, I decided that my Country-Fried Steak would be like theirs. I didn't ask for the recipe; I didn't need to. Their steak started with a tender piece of cube steak, heavily battered, pan braised, and covered with gravy. I could cut it with a fork. I particularly like the cream gravy in this recipe. With my directions below, you double-batter and then fry the steak. The first coating, the egg-flour-milk mixture, should be thick like pancake batter. It covers the steak and then absorbs the second coating, the cracker crumbs. After frying the steak, simmer it in the gravy. This softens the fried batter, tenderizes the steak, and thickens the gravy. The minced onions add texture and flavor.

STEPS In the market select thin twice-cubed steak. Use top, bottom, or eye round steak. If your steaks are not double cubed (that means the butcher runs them through a tenderizing machine twice), take the back of a heavy knife or a meat-tenderizing mallet and pound on the steaks until they almost fall apart. I like them fully chopped before I start cooking them.

Crush crackers to make 1 1/2 cups cracker crumbs.

Batter and fry the steaks: As you prepare the batter, heat 2 tablespoons of the oil in a very large (12-inch) cast-iron skillet. In a medium mixing bowl, beat the eggs and add the milk. Whisk in the 3/4 cup flour and salt. Pour the cracker crumbs into a soup plate. Dip the steaks, first in the egg-milk mixture and then in the crumbs. Press the crumbs into the steaks.

Over low-medium heat, fry the battered steaks for 6 minutes on one side, add the remaining 2 tablespoons of oil, and fry 6 minutes on the other side. Remove the steaks from the pan.

Prepare the gravy: Stir the flour into the pan, and add enough oil to wet the flour. Stir until fully mixed; a bit at a time, whisk in the milk, and deglaze the pan. Add the onions, and after the milk boils, cook 1 minute. Mix in the salt and pepper.

DIFFICULTY Difficult. With nine ingredients, two bowls, and one frying pan, you'll make some mess preparing this recipe.

INGREDIENTS

FOR THE STEAK

Four 5-ounce beef cube steaks (top, bottom, or eye round)
1 1/2 cups saltine cracker crumbs
1/4 cup vegetable oil
2 eggs
2/3 cup milk
3/4 cup all-purpose flour
1 teaspoon salt

FOR THE GRAVY

1/4 cup all-purpose flour
1/4 cup vegetable oil
2 3/4 cups milk
1/4 cup minced onions
1 teaspoon salt
1 teaspoon pepper

YIELD 4 servings

HEARTY
Cooking
COUNTRY

Return the steaks to the pan, and cook another 20 minutes over very low heat. When turning the steaks or moving them to the serving platter, slide a large spatula under the steak so as not to tear off the now-moist batter. Spoon the gravy over the steaks, and serve.

HEALTHY CHOICE ALTERNATIVE For the steaks, replace the whole eggs with egg whites and the milk with skim milk. For the gravy, use a cold roux in place of the oil. Omit the salt.

Complete this meal with Steamed Green Beans and Mashed Kennebec Potatoes, or offer creamed corn, Collard Greens, steamed cabbage, Baked Whole Sweet Potatoes, Sugared Carrots, Skillet Corn Bread, or Buttermilk Biscuits.

■ ■

Four Five-Hour Secrets

To bring this simple, slow, tasty, and healthy mixture to perfection, I suggest four secrets:

1. Low heat. Cook this stew at 300°F, so the beef will be tender and nothing will burn.

2. Tapioca. Extracted from the roots of the cassava plant, tapioca thickens this stew. You do not mix it with butter to make a roux. In the market you'll find tapioca granules sold with the puddings. Grocers often stock Minute Tapioca, and you may have used it as a thickening for pies and puddings.

3. Covered pot. Using a covered roaster keeps the moisture in and prevents a dry film from forming on the stew.

4. Tomato juice. Tomato juice is a full-flavored, low-calorie, nonfat thickener. For a little more zip, substitute V-8 juice, Bloody Mary mix, or Snap-E-Tom Tomato Cocktail. I use plain tomato juice.

Five-Hour Stew
(Oven Stew)

DIFFICULTY Moderate. With nine ingredients and 5 hours of baking, this recipe is moderate in difficulty.

*Y*ou've got company coming, but what will you prepare? This stew feeds a crowd—and even picky eaters ask for seconds.

Five-Hour Stew is a busy-person, I-hate-to-cook, let-me-out-of-the-kitchen stew. Years ago mountain cooks might have called it wash-day stew. For this dish you don't need a routing sheet to display the directions, and you don't shop for twenty ingredients. You don't dredge the beef in flour or brown it in oil. You don't braise, raise or lower the heat, or stir. You don't skim, roast, blanch, or drain. These old stewing "essentials" are out the window, and you are out of the kitchen.

INGREDIENTS
46 ounces tomato juice
3 pounds beef stew meat
5 tablespoons Minute Tapioca
1 tablespoon salt
1 teaspoon pepper
4 cups chopped and sliced potatoes
2 cups peeled and sliced carrots
2 cups diced celery
2 cups sliced onion

YIELD 16 servings

STEPS Select a large, 8-quart, covered roasting pan or Dutch oven.

Preheat the oven to 300°F. Pour the tomato juice into the bottom of the pan. Layer in this order: half the beef, tapioca, salt, pepper, potatoes, carrots, celery, and onion. Repeat in the same order. Cover and bake for 5 hours.

HEALTHY CHOICE ALTERNATIVE With lean beef, this stew is a healthy, low-fat, mostly vegetable main dish. If you prefer chicken, use skinless chicken, and bake for 4 hours.

Serve with a plain bread, such as Highlander Rolls or Buttermilk Biscuits.

Daniel Boone Beef Stew
Squirrel Stew (Beef Stew)

DIFFICULTY Moderate. With nine ingredients and one cooking step, this recipe is moderate in difficulty

*I*n Tennessee and Kentucky we call him D. Boone. He is like a friend, and he explored these hills. Born in 1734, Daniel Boone died in 1820, and he left his mark as an explorer and clever woodsman. While historians will debate his importance, his reputation is legendary. He stands for courage and strength against a brutal wilderness. Even more than a real figure, Daniel Boone is a symbol. He represents ingenuity, survival, independence, and freedom.

A master of the frontier and a leader of American western expansion, Daniel Boone was the first to settle an area just west of the Appalachian Mountains, called Kentucky. His settlement is called Boonesborough. Boone probably did not make this stew with beef, but it is likely that a member of his family made a similar stew using squirrel or venison.

When I was growing up, Mom did not allow me to cook in the kitchen. My first cooking took place over an open fire. On Boy Scout camp-outs, I cooked beef stew: stewing beef, carrots, potatoes, and celery, water, salt and pepper. I thought it was the best stew in the world. When I moved to Appalachia and found mountaineers making a similar stew, I had to try their recipe.

STEPS   Cut the beef into $1/2$-inch cubes. In a large saucepan, blacken the stew meat, cooking over high heat for 10 minutes, turning it only when it sticks to the pan or when it gets good and black on the bottom. If the meat yields a lot of water, pour off the excess, reserving it for the stew. (The meat will not blacken if it boils in its own juices.)

Reduce the heat and add $4^{1/2}$ cups of the water. Cover and simmer for 1 hour, or until the meat gets tender. Remove from the heat, and skim off any fat on top. Add the potatoes, carrots, celery, salt, and pepper. Simmer for 20 minutes, or until the vegetables are tender.

At this point, you should have about 3 cups of broth. If needed, add water to equal 3 cups.. In a small mixing bowl, whisk together the flour and the remaining $1/4$ cup water, adding the water slowly. Mix until smooth. Add this cold roux to the stew, and mix well. Bring to a boil, and simmer for 1 minute. Add the undrained beans, return the pot to a boil, and serve.

TIP   The broth from the stew and the flour should cook together to yield a thick sauce for the stew. The gravy should be as thick as chowder. If it is not thick enough, I add a bit of instant flour.

HEALTHY CHOICE ALTERNATIVE   With about three ounces of meat per serving, this is a healthy, low-fat dish. Try to purchase lean beef. Omit the salt and offer it at the table.

Serve this stew in soup plates with Quick Kernel Corn Bread or Angel Biscuits. Complete the meal with cold buttermilk, Deviled Eggs, and a side dish of Kathy's Coleslaw.

Squirrel Stew   In place of the beef, use 3 pounds fresh squirrel, cut into serving-size pieces.

INGREDIENTS

FOR THE STEW

2 pounds beef stew meat
$4^{3}/4$ cups water
2 pounds potatoes, diced
1 pound carrots, peeled and quartered
2 cups chopped celery
1 tablespoon salt
$1/2$ teaspoon pepper

FOR THE GRAVY

$1/4$ cup all-purpose flour
$1/4$ cup water
One 15-ounce can pinto beans, undrained

YIELD 12 servings

Pecan Brown Gravy

This variation on brown beef gravy is not new. The recipe is not based on my imagination nor the creativity of a slick, culinary school-trained, big-city chef. While it sounds gourmet, the combination of savory sauce and mild pecans is old mountain. In 1928 Mrs. Henrietta Stanley Dull, food editor of the *Atlanta Journal*, published a similar recipe in her book, *Southern Cooking*. This recipe became popular among mountain cooks, and I have adapted it for today's kitchen.

INGREDIENTS
^{1}/4 cup butter
^{1}/4 cup all-purpose flour
2 cups beef stock, or 2
  cups water plus 2
  tablespoons beef bouil-
  lon grains
^{1}/2 cup coarsley chopped
  pecans

YIELD 6 servings
(2^1/4 cups)

STEPS In a medium saucepan over medium heat, melt the butter, and whisk in the flour. Cook slowly until fully mixed. Add the stock, and deglaze the pan. Stir in the pecans, boil for 1 minute, and serve hot.

HEALTHY CHOICE ALTERNATIVE Omit the butter. Pour the stock into a saucepan and then whisk in ^{1}/4 cup instant flour (you can mix it into the hot liquid). Reduce the pecans to ^{1}/4 cup.

Serve this gravy over meats, vegetables, and potatoes, or use it to smother toast, biscuits, or a hot roast beef sandwich and Mashed Kennebec Potatoes.

Pot Roast
(Lazy Day Pot Roast)

*S*ettlers from Germany, France, and England made pot roasts, but in the last sixty years many food writers have identified this one-pot meal with the Midwest, New England, and our eastern mountains. I associate its popularity with the popularity of the large cast-iron pots that we hung over the hearth.

Mountaineers traditionally made pot roasts with chicken and pork. After World War II, beef became popular and the mountain pot roast became more like a Yankee pot roast. Sauerbraten, the German sweet sour beef pot roast, is generally not part of our mountain heritage.

To pot roast is to braise. Using several cups of liquid and a covered pot, I steam a poor cut of beef slowly until it is tender. The moist heat inside the closed pot will draw out every drop of natural juice. I solve the problem of a dry roast by slicing the roast thinly and across the grain and then moistening it with gravy.

In addition to the potatoes, carrots, and onions I use in this recipe, consider adding cabbage, tomatoes, turnips, sweet potatoes, and celery. For flavor, add whole cloves of garlic, ground cinnamon, leftover coffee, green peppers, and hot banana peppers.

DIFFICULTY Easy? Moderate? Difficult? I don't know. It takes a lot of work to prepare ten servings of anything, but I call this a "lazy day" pot roast because you may do half of the work the first day. No doubt, however, I also think this recipe is rather difficult.

STEPS Preheat the oven to 275°F. Place the roast in a very large roasting pot. Add the broth, cover, and bake for 4 to 7 hours. Add the carrots, potatoes, and onions, cover, and bake another 1½ hours. Separate the vegetables, roast, and stock. Cool and refrigerate.

The next day, or when the roast is cold, make the brown gravy. Remove and discard the fat from the stock. Pour the broth into a measuring cup, and if needed, add water to make 3 cups. In a small bowl make a cold roux by moistening the flour with broth, adding 1 tablespoon of broth at a time. Do not add more broth until the flour is smooth. Continue adding cold broth to the flour until it is as thin as tomato juice. Add this back into the broth, and pour into a saucepan. Boil for 1 minute, and remove from the heat. Stir in the sour cream.

Lay the chilled roast on a cutting board, and slice it across the grain, about ¼ inch thick. Cut the potatoes in half and the carrots into thirds. Arrange on a platter, top with half of the gravy, and reheat, covered, in the microwave or a warm oven. Reheat the remaining gravy, and serve.

HEALTHY CHOICE ALTERNATIVE Omit the sour cream.

This is a meal in one pot. Serve on a platter and offer Highlander Rolls, real butter, and a green salad. For a big group, add green beans and Simple Corn Bread.

INGREDIENTS
One 5-pound rolled and tied bottom round or chuck roast
2½ cups beef broth
10 large carrots, peeled
10 medium potatoes, peeled
4 medium onions, peeled
3 tablespoons all-purpose flour
1 cup sour cream

YIELD 10 servings

Seven

Fish and Wild Game

Baked Trout

Sautéed Trout

Scalloped Oysters

Fried Catfish

Deep-Fried Catfish

Fried Turtle Baked with Rice

Turtle Chowder

Fried Rabbit

Fried Squirrel

Rabbit with Sausage Gravy

Squirrel with Sausage Gravy

Squirrel Gravy

Rabbit Gravy

Mount Rogers Venison Chili

Beef Chili

Baked Trout

DIFFICULTY Easy.
With two ingredients and less than 30 minutes of baking, this recipe is easy.

INGREDIENTS
Nonstick woking spray
Five 10-ounce brook or
  rainbow trout, cleaned
  with heads intact

YIELD 5 servings

*B*ecause we raise most of our fresh-water trout in commercial hatcheries, they are available year round. If you are baking a casserole, a sweet potato, or a berry cobbler, or if your oven is hot for any reason, add baked trout to your menu. This fish recipe is a snap, and you can use it for salmon or any whitefish.

STEPS Preheat the oven to 350°F. Spray a large jelly roll pan with nonstick cooking spray.

Arrange the trout on the pan, spray them with nonstick cooking spray, and bake for 20 to 25 minutes, or until the trout flakes from the bone at the thickest point. Also test by pushing a fork into the thickest part of one trout: If it is cooked, there is no resistance and no rubbery fish. Serve.

Serve with your choice of a wedge of lemon, parsley, melted butter, mayonnaise, salt, and pepper, or with my Light Vegetable Dip, Tomato Gravy, or Cornmeal Gravy. Because I associate small trout with spring, I like this dish with Scalloped Potatoes and mixed vegetables of the season, or with Poke Greens and Spinach or Morels Sautéed with Onions.

Sautéed Trout

DIFFICULTY Moderate.
With seven ingredients and one cooking step, this recipe is moderate in difficulty.

INGREDIENTS
3/4 cup flour
1 tablespoon salt
1 tablespoon dried
  parsley
Five 10-ounce brook or
  rainbow trout, cleaned
  with heads intact
2 tablespoons oil
2 tablespoons butter
1 lemon, cut in half

YIELD 5 servings

*T*oday, those of us who live in the mountains are proud of our cold clear streams and the always-fearful trout we can spot in the pools. Bicycling across a bridge or walking on a streamside path, I often stop to look for trout.

STEPS In a large paper bag, mix and shake the flour, salt, and parsley. Add the fish and shake until it is fully coated with flour. Shake the excess flour back into the bag as you remove the fish.

Fry the fish immediately before serving. In a very large skillet over medium heat, heat 1 tablespoon each of the oil and the butter. Add the fish, and fry 4 minutes on each side, adding the remaining oil and butter just before you turn the fish. Fry the trout until it pulls from the bone at the thickest point, usually the mid-section. When the fish are ready to serve, squeeze lemon juice over them. Serve with wedges of lemon. Garnish with parsley or other fresh greens.

HEALTHY CHOICE ALTERNATIVE I consider this a lightly fried fish, nothing like pan-fried or deep-fried. To reduce fat even further, bake the trout.

HEARTY
Cooking
COUNTRY

Serve this with Deviled Eggs or Cucumber Salad, and offer Fried Mush, Boiled New Potatoes, Sweet Potato Biscuits, and Skillet Cabbage as side dishes.

Scalloped Oysters

For thousands of years before the arrival of Europeans, Native Americans had been eating oysters. This was evident when settlers found great mounds of oyster shells along both East and West Coasts. In 1871, Mrs. Porter's *New Southern Cookery* presented the following recipe for scalloped oysters: "Take baker's bread at least three days old. Strain your oysters, put a layer of them on the bottom of your dish, with bits of butter, salt, pepper and a little mace; spread over them a layer of bread-crumbs, and continue till the dish is full, having bread-crumbs on top. Pour in a cup of the liquor of the oysters. Bake an hour. Be careful not to have the layers of bread too thick."

At about the time Mrs. Porter wrote her book, the westward expansion of the railroads made the ever-popular oyster available in the upper South and Midwest. Twenty years later, during the Gay Nineties, oysters were the rage, and young people lined up to eat them at oyster bars and served them at oyster suppers. It would be another twenty to forty years before oysters reached some of the more isolated parts of the mountains, and in spite of this late arrival, their popularity never ebbed.

Scalloped oysters are a breaded casserole. In addition to the ingredients I offer, you'll be on target with tradition if you add pepper, mustard, nutmeg, lemon juice, sherry, chopped celery, or parsley to your casserole.

DIFFICULTY Moderate. With seven ingredients and two steps, this recipe is moderate in difficulty.

STEPS Preheat the oven to 350°F, and select a 13x9x2-inch casserole dish.

Sauté the onions in the butter, and stir in the salt. Spread half of the crackers over the bottom of a casserole dish and spread the sautéed onions on the crackers. Reserving five oysters for garnish, spread the oysters over the onions. Add the remaining cracker crumbs.

Blend the cream and liquor ($\frac{1}{2}$ to $\frac{3}{4}$ cup of liquor plus 1 cup cream) together, and pour the mixture over the crackers. Sprinkle with bread crumbs, garnish with reserved oysters, and bake for 30 minutes or until the casserole bubbles in the center.

HEALTHY CHOICE ALTERNATIVE Replace the cream with milk, steam rather than sauté the onions, and omit the butter.

INGREDIENTS
2 cups diced onions
3 tablespoons butter
2 teaspoons celery salt
2 cups cracker crumbs
1 quart oysters with liquor reserved
1 cup cream
2 cups toasted bread crumbs

YIELD 12 servings

While oysters are available throughout the fall and winter, they are most popular

Fish and Wild Game

during the seven-week holiday period from Thanksgiving to New Year's Day. Serve this recipe as a side dish with roast turkey, baked ham, or standing rib roast, and offer Baked Cushaw or Boiled Turnips.

Fried Catfish
Deep-Fried Catfish

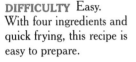n slow-moving creeks and in small rivers with muddy banks, we grovel for catfish. To grovel is to wade along the creek bank in a low position and reach into mud holes, pulling out an occasional channel catfish. Skinned and cleaned, these channel cats yield a golden platter of fried catfish, but your market-purchased fillets will do just as well. For crispy-fried fish so good it is beyond description, I deep fry the catfish. The crisp and crunchy outside cornmeal coating contrasts delicately with the smooth, succulent center.

DIFFICULTY Easy. With four ingredients and quick frying, this recipe is easy to prepare.

INGREDIENTS
1 1/2 pounds catfish fillets
1/2 cup cornmeal
1 teaspoon seasoned salt
2 tablespoons corn oil

YIELD 4 servings

STEPS Wash the fillets in cold water, and cut them into serving-size pieces. Pour the cornmeal and salt into a plastic bag, seal, and shake to mix. Add the catfish, seal again, and roll the bag on the counter until you have coated the fish.

Fry the fish immediately before serving. In a heavy skillet, heat the corn oil to 350°F. Ease the fish into the pan, and fry 3 minutes on each side (1/2-inch-thick fillets). Serve.

HEALTHY CHOICE ALTERNATIVE I've already reduced the oil to a minimum, but you can bake the fish without oil at 450°F for 15 minutes.

Serve this with Midland Trail Deviled Eggs, Kathy's Coleslaw, and Hush Puppies.

Deep-Fried Catfish After I make Hush Puppies, I like to use the same oil to deep fry 1 1/2 pounds of catfish. In place of the cornmeal and salt above, mix 1 egg with 1/4 cup buttermilk. Coat the fish fillets with this mixture, and drop them into a bag with a mixture of 2/3 cup self-rising cornmeal mix, 1 tablespoon paprika, 1 teaspoon salt, and 1/2 teaspoon pepper. Seal the bag, shake to coat the fish, and slip them into the hot oil (365°F). Fry about 2 1/2 minutes on each side, and drain on paper towels. This is the same batter I use on Southern Fried Chicken. I call it Buttermilk Batter.

HEARTY
Cooking
COUNTRY

Fried Turtle Baked with Rice

In our wide and lazy rivers, we have big—I mean big—soft-shell and snapping turtles. These one- to three-foot-wide, thick-legged monsters can move fast. But they cannot outmaneuver the hook and line that fishermen set. The turtles take the hook, baited with chicken livers, and then the fishermen ease the turtles up the river bank.

If you don't pull your turtles from slow-moving rivers, I suggest that you consult Millard's Turtle in my Mail-Order Sources. Good quality snapping turtle meat is light red, and it includes some jelly-like white meat, which is the best part. Millard guarantees that his deboned turtle meat is free of fat. If you are just getting acquainted with turtle meat, it is easy to confuse the fat, which is yellow in color, with the white meat, which is more beige. This recipe, a combination of rice and turtle, is similar to Chicken Livers with Rice.

STEPS Preheat the oven to 350°F. In a large skillet over high heat, heat 2 tablespoons of the safflower oil until just before it smokes. Cut the turtle into bite-size (1/2-inch) pieces. Dump the turtle pieces, flour, and salt into a sealable plastic bag, and shake until the turtle meat has absorbed the flour. Ease the turtle pieces into the hot skillet, and sauté over high heat. Brown the turtle pieces quickly for 2 minutes—and then scrape them around so as to fry the other side. Repeat until completely browned.

Arrange the turtle meat in a 2-quart casserole dish. In the same skillet, add the remaining 1 tablespoon oil, and sauté the onion until clear. Add the rice and broth, bring to a boil, and deglaze the pan. Pour the broth and rice over the turtle, and spread it out until smooth. Cover, and bake for 35 minutes, or until the rice is tender and has absorbed the broth.

HEALTHY CHOICE ALTERNATIVE If you are concerned about salt, use homemade chicken broth and omit the salt. In this recipe I suggest using a heart-healthy oil and not much of it.

Serve this as a main dish casserole, with garden-fresh, peeled and sliced tomato or with a molded salad or tomato aspic. Offer salt and pepper at the table.

DIFFICULTY Moderate. With seven ingredients and four cooking steps, this recipe is moderate in difficulty.

INGREDIENTS
3 tablespoons safflower oil
1 1/2 pounds boneless and trimmed turtle meat
1/3 cup all-purpose flour
1 teaspoon salt
1 cup diced onion
1 cup rice, 20 minute variety
2 cups chicken broth

YIELD 8 servings

Fish
and
Wild Game

Turtle Chowder

DIFFICULTY Moderate. With eight ingredients and 25 minutes of stove-top cooking, this recipe is moderate in difficulty.

INGREDIENTS
2 cups water
1 1/4 cups (1/2 pound) boneless and trimmed turtle meat, cut in 1/2-inch pieces
2 1/2 cups diced pota-toes, 1/3 inch in size
1/2 cup chopped celery
1/2 cup diced onions
2 tablespoons plus 1 teaspoon instant flour
3/4 teaspoon salt
1/2 cup heavy cream

YIELD 4 servings

*T*he flavor blend that delights your taste buds when you sip this chowder is the combination of turtle and cream. Most chowder recipes direct you to start by frying salt pork or bacon and then adding onion. With turtle and cream, you don't need the pork.

STEPS In a heavy saucepan over medium heat, stir together the water and turtle pieces. Bring to a boil, reduce the heat, and simmer for 30 minutes. Add the potatoes and celery and simmer an additional 5 minutes. Add the onions, flour, and salt, and stir. Simmer an additional 5 minutes. Remove from the heat, and add the cream. After adding the cream, do not boil. (If the chowder gets too hot, the cream will curdle.) Serve.

HEALTHY CHOICE ALTERNATIVE If you omit the cream and reduce the flour by 1 tablespoon, you'll have a light chowder.

Serve with saltine crackers. Serve for lunch with a Souse sandwich and molded salad.

■ ■

Rabbit vs. Squirrel

Rabbit and squirrel are different meats. Tasted side by side, rabbit is like chicken, and squirrel is a bit more tender. Squirrel meat is soft, like raccoon or turtle. I present the rabbit and squirrel together because squirrel gravy is a common and treasured mountain specialty and merits a place in this collection. Though I don't hunt, we have many hunters who shoot squirrels and we have cooks that prepare them for family and community suppers.

Unfortunately, I could not find a mail-order source for squirrel, and so I offer the rabbit as an alternative. You can buy rabbit in stores or order it from International Home Cooking, listed in my Mail-Order Sources. With increased interest in native American foods, perhaps squirrel will become available to those who do not hunt.

Fried Rabbit
Fried Squirrel

*W*hen you first read this recipe, you may think that it contains a lot of salt and pepper, but for a coating, believe me it is not too much. The amount of salt I use is less than you'll find in a box of commercially prepared coating. As for the onions, lemon juice, and lemon peel, they add moisture and flavor.

STEPS In a gallon-size plastic zippered bag shake together the flour, salt, and pepper. Add the rabbit parts and shake or roll them until coated.

In a large skillet, heat the lard to 365°F or until just before it smokes. Ease the rabbit parts into the skillet and fry, uncovered, for 4 minutes on each side. Reduce the heat to medium, cover the pan, and simmer for 20 minutes. Remove the lid, and add the onions, lemon juice, and lemon peel. Fry the rabbit another 4 minutes on each side. Serve.

HEALTHY CHOICE ALTERNATIVE Reduce the salt to 1 teaspoon. Omit the oil and onion. Bake the rabbit at 350°F in a 13x9x2-inch pan for 45 minutes, or until the largest piece has no red color left when you cut it to the bone.

When I bake rabbit like this, I prefer to double coat it. I dip it first in a fully mixed and ready-to-use pancake batter, and then in bread or cracker crumbs. It comes from the oven crunchy and lower in fat.

Serve this with Baked Sweet Potatoes and Turnip Greens, and add a garnish of Corn Relish or Pickled Green Beans.

Fried Squirrel Use squirrel meat in place of the rabbit.

DIFFICULTY Moderate. With eight ingredients and one cooking step, this recipe is moderate in difficulty.

INGREDIENTS
1/2 cup all-purpose flour
2 teaspoons salt
1 teaspoon pepper
1 small (2 pounds) rabbit, cut up
3/4 cup lard or safflower oil
1 1/2 cups diced onion
1/4 cup lemon juice
6 slices lemon peel or peeling from half a lemon

YIELD 4 servings

Rabbit with Sausage Gravy
Squirrel with Sausage Gravy

*A*ll the old mountain recipes recommend marinating the rabbit overnight in a solution of water, salt, and vinegar. However, if you buy a young, fresh rabbit, it will be tender enough that you do not have to marinate it. The three cups of water I use in this recipe should not evaporate during the hour of simmering, but if the gravy gets too thick, add a bit of water.

DIFFICULTY Moderate. With seven ingredients and one step, this recipe is moderate in difficulty. Depending on the quality of the rabbit meat, it may take 1 1/2 hours for the rabbit to get tender.

INGREDIENTS
$^1/_2$ pound pork sausage
5 tablespoons all-
   purpose flour
$^1/_2$ teaspoon salt
$^1/_2$ teaspoon pepper
3 cups water
1 (3 to 4 pounds)
   rabbit, cut up
1 cup sour cream

YIELD 5 servings

STEPS In a large skillet, fry the sausage, breaking it into small pieces as it cooks. Stir in the flour, salt, and pepper. Some pork sausage has so little fat that you may have to add oil to moisten the flour.

Stir in the water and add the rabbit. Stir several times in the first 5 minutes of cooking. Simmer, covered, for 1 hour, or until the meat is tender. Then simmer, uncovered, for 30 minutes, or until the gravy is thick. Stir in the sour cream just before serving.

HEALTHY CHOICE ALTERNATIVE When you have fried the sausage, add 1 cup of water to the pan, and bring to a boil. This brings the grease to the top. Pour off the water and the grease. Rather than mixing the flour with the grease, make a cold roux or use instant flour. Now you can enjoy sausage gravy without grease.

Serve for dinner with corn on the cob, biscuits, and green beans.

Squirrel with Sausage Gravy Replace the rabbit with squirrel meat.

Squirrel Gravy
Rabbit Gravy

DIFFICULTY Moderate. With seven ingredients and three steps, this recipe is moderate in difficulty.

*I*n this recipe, we fry the squirrel first and then boil it. Although the frying is an extra step, it makes the gravy tasty. When the meat is cool, carefully remove the bones. Remember that squirrel meat is like crabmeat, in that the bones are hard to remove and some always seem to be left in the gravy.

STEPS Heat the 2 tablespoons lard in a large covered skillet. I use a chicken fryer with a lid. Cut the squirrel into serving-size pieces and wash in cold water.

Pour the flour, salt, and pepper into a sealable bag. Place the squirrel in the bag and roll it around to coat the squirrel with flour. Lift the squirrel from the bag, leaving the excess flour in the bag. At least $^1/_4$ cup flour should remain in the bag. Gently place each piece of squirrel into the hot grease. Fry uncovered over medium heat for 20 minutes, turning the meat several times as it fries.

When the squirrel is cooked and golden brown, pour off any remaining grease, leaving the drippings in the pan. Add water to cover, bring to a boil, cover, and simmer for 1 hour or until the meat pulls easily from the bone. Add water, if it gets low. Lift the squirrel from the pan and set aside to cool.

Prepare the gravy: Remove the meat from the bones, measuring out $1^1/_4$ cups. Pour the cooking liquid from the skillet into a measuring cup, and add water to equal 2 cups. Melt the 3 tablespoons lard in the skillet and stir in the remaining 1/4 cup of the flour mixture from the bag. When the flour and lard are smooth and fully mixed, whisk in the 2 cups of broth, bring to a boil, and boil for 1 minute. Stir in the 1 1/4 cups of squirrel, and if needed, loosen the gravy with the milk.

When is the gravy too thick? The gravy should not be a glob that sits on top of a split biscuit, but rather, it should pour and spread like thick pancake batter. Serve hot.

HEALTHY CHOICE ALTERNATIVE Fry the squirrel in 2 tablespoons safflower oil. Omit the lard from the gravy and use instant flour.

Serve this for breakfast or dinner over biscuits.

Rabbit Gravy Replace the squirrel with rabbit meat.

INGREDIENTS

FOR THE SQUIRREL
2 tablespoons lard, butter, or safflower oil
1 small (1 pound) squirrel
3/4 cup all-purpose flour
1 1/2 teaspoons salt
3/4 teaspoons pepper
2 1/2 cups water

FOR THE GRAVY
Water
3 tablespoons lard, butter, or safflower oil
1/4 cup all-purpose flour, salt, and pepper mixture
3/4 cup milk

YIELD 6 servings

Mount Rogers Venison Chili
Beef Chili

*A*t 5,729 feet, Mount Rogers is the highest point in Virginia. You'll find this heavily wooded, spruce-dotted, round-topped attraction located near the boarders of North Carolina and Tennessee. In the stew pots of caravaners, hikers, fishermen, and equestrians who flock to the Mount Rogers Recreation Area, you'll often find a chili like this, and occasionally these outdoor enthusiasts make it with venison. Using both diced and ground venison gives a full, meaty, and flavorful sauce. Then, rather than adding flour or masa (corn flour), I thicken the chili with tomato paste. In southwestern Virginia, our cooks go easy on the spices. If you like hot chili, add some liquid hot sauce.

STEPS In a large saucepan over medium heat, combine the venison pieces and the tomato juice. Bring to a boil, and add the garlic, chili powder, cumin, salt, and pepper. Simmer, covered, for 1 hour. Stir in the ground venison and tomato paste (this thickens the sauce). Return to a boil, and then simmer 5 minutes. Serve.

Serve in a bowl. Ladle over hamburger buns like barbecue, and offer a green vegetable on the side. Pour over rice. Serve with mashed potatoes and green beans.

Beef Chili Substitute beef for the venison.

DIFFICULTY Moderate. With nine ingredients and 1 hour of stovetop cooking, this recipe is moderate in difficulty.

INGREDIENTS
2 pounds venison, cut in 1/2-inch pieces
2 cups tomato juice
4 cloves garlic, minced
2 tablespoons McCormick's Hot Mexican Chili Powder
2 teaspoons cumin
1 1/2 teaspoons salt
1/2 teaspoon ground black pepper
1 pound ground venison
One 6-ounce can tomato paste

YIELD 10 servings

Fish
and
Wild Game

Eight

Desserts

Delights, Cobblers, Apples, Pawpaws, Sassafras, and Pecans

■■■■■■■■■■■■■■■■■■■■■■■■■■■■■■

Blackberry Delight *Raspberry Delight*

Chocolate Delight

Dirt Pudding Delight

Strawberry Salad
(Strawberry 'n Pretzel Delight and Pretzel Cake)

Mountain Banana Pudding

Lemon Curd

Blackberry Cobbler

Peach Cobbler

Great Smoky Mountains Apple Cobbler
Dutch Apple Pie (Streusel-Topped Apple Cobbler)

Sorghum Pecan Pie Bars

Sorghum Pie

Hot Sorghum *Fried Sorghum*

Sorghum Butter

Gingerbread-Apple Upside-Down Cake
Sorghum Gingerbread

Bread Pudding *Sorghum Bread Pudding*

Dried Apples

Applesauce from Dried Apples
(Dried Apple Applesauce)

Dried Apple Stack Pies

Dried Apple Pie

Dried Apple Stack Cake

■■■■■■■■■■■■■■■■■■■■■■■■■■■■■■

■ ■

Fried Apple Pies

Highlander Double-Crust Apple Pie with Raisins

Fresh Apple Cake with Black Walnuts

Pawpaw Cookies with Black Walnuts

Shenandoah Valley Banana Bread *Pawpaw Bread*

Pawpaw, Cornmeal, and Hickory Nut Muffins

Persimmon Pudding *Pawpaw Pudding*

Persimmon Butterscotch Cookies

Persimmon Pudding-Cake

Blue Ridge Sassafras Tea

Sassafras Custard Pudding

Sassafras Apple Syrup

Sassafras Apple Butter
Sassafras-Caramel Granola Cookie Dessert

Sassafras Hard Rock Candy
Cinnamon Hard Rock Candy

North Carolina Roasted Pecans *Roasted Butternuts*

Pecan Fudge-Nuts *(Chocolate Roasted Pecans)*

Dry-Roasted Pecans
*Sugared Pecans and Spicy Orange-Sugared Pecans
(Pecan Delights and Candied Pecans)*

Pecan Pie
Black Walnut Pie (Homecoming Pecan Pie)

Pecan Shortbread

■ ■

Delights and Cobblers

Delights

Delights are delightful casserole desserts, smooth and sweet. Mountain delights are many-layered puddings with bottom crusts, and I like to serve them well chilled in a decorative casserole dish.

The four delights I offer here represent a mountain treasure. I suggest making them on my Healthy Choice nonfat Baked Meringue Shell. All these recipes are large, yielding twelve or more servings. As easy-to-carry, portable desserts, they usually make their way to community suppers.

Delights, I hypothesize, are descendants of two large groups of French desserts, the charlottes and vacherins. Scholars have documented the French ancestry of some mountaineers, and our tradition of making these desserts supports that position. A French charlotte is a molded pudding-like dessert with a crust made of ladyfinger cookies, such as the strawberry charlotte russe. A vacherin is a meringue shell filled with fruit and whipped cream. In French pâtisseries, you see them shaped like Easter baskets, complete with handles.

Delights are layered cheese custard, whipped cream, or gelatin desserts. Mountain cooks prepare delights with a cream cheese layer, a pudding, cream, or fruit layer, and whipped topping. Irene Hayes in *What's Cooking in Kentucky* includes four delights (Danish, Date, Nut, and Raspberry) among her many desserts, each with a different bottom crust: meringue shell, chocolate sandwich cookie, white cake, or vanilla wafer. Delights may include a gelatin-thickened fruit such as pineapple, fruit cocktail, and cherries. In place of this, some use cherry or blackberry pie filling, or crushed pineapple and apple-mint jelly for a mint delight. Others make a lemon delight with an angel food cake base, or a pineapple-banana delight with a graham cracker crust and pecans and coconut on top. As always, these are topped with whipped cream. Try creating your own many-layered delights!

Blackberry Delight
Raspberry Delight

*B*lackberries grow wild on hillsides, along highways, and around old pastures. During the month of July, and in August in the cooler areas, we pick them and make them into jam, cobblers, and delights.

The Baked Meringue Shell I use for this recipe is a light, nonfat crust, excellent for any delight, especially my Strawberry or Chocolate Delights. Mountaineers with a French heritage might call this a Blackberry Vacherin Chantilly.

STEPS Prepare the Baked Meringue Shell a day in advance. Preheat the oven to 225°F, and lightly grease and flour a 13x9x2-inch pan.

In a mixing bowl and using a balloon whisk, beat the egg whites with the cream of tartar until frothy. Two tablespoons at a time, add the $3/4$ cup confectioners' sugar, beating for 6 to 8 minutes, or until the meringue is very stiff and shiny.

Spread the meringue evenly across the bottom of the pan, and bake for 2 hours. The meringue crust should be dry throughout and close to white in color. Cool. When the crust is fully dried and cool, you should be able to pop it out of the pan, tap it on the bottom, and hear a hollow sound.

As close to serving time as possible, but up to 3 hours ahead, prepare the layered topping. Chill the beaters and mixing bowl.

Spread the jam on the meringue shell. Using the chilled bowl, whip until stiff the heavy cream and $1/2$ cup sugar. Divide the whipped cream in half, and whip one half of it with the cream cheese and 1 cup sugar. When this mixture is smooth, fold in $41/2$ cups blackberries.

Spread the blackberry mixture over the jam in a thin layer. Spread the remaining whipped cream on top. One at a time, place the remaining $11/2$ cups blackberries, top side up, evenly over the whipped cream. When placed, they will be $1/2$ to $3/4$ inch apart.

Refrigerate up to 3 hours. When served, the crust should be crisp. If you leave the crust overnight, it will soften, diminish in thickness, and lose its function.

TIP Pastry Cream: A traditional pastry cream is a cooked filling of milk, sugar, eggs, and flour. Sometimes French chefs lighten the cream by adding whipped cream. In this recipe the mixture of whipped cream, cream cheese, and sugar is a cheese-based pastry cream, and I use it as a filling for cold fruit tarts, cream puffs, and éclairs.

DIFFICULTY Moderate. With eight ingredients and two steps, this recipe is moderate in difficulty. To simplify, replace the Baked Meringue Shell with two commercially prepared graham cracker crumb pie crusts.

INGREDIENTS

FOR THE BAKED MERINGUE SHELL

3 egg whites, at room temperature
$1/4$ teaspoon cream of tartar
$3/4$ cup powdered sugar

FOR THE LAYERED TOPPING

1 (10-ounce) jar blackberry jam
2 cups heavy whipping cream
$11/2$ cups confectioners' sugar, divided
1 (8-ounce) package soft cream cheese, at room temperature
6 cups fresh blackberries

YIELD 12 servings

HEALTHY CHOICE ALTERNATIVE While you could make this dessert with the Pecan Crust presented under the Chocolate Delight, this meringue shell is fat free. The heavy cream and cream cheese, however, make this a rich dessert.

Raspberry Delight Substitute raspberry jam for the blackberry jam and fresh raspberries for the fresh blackberries.

Chocolate Delight

*I*n hushed tones my friend and neighbor, Cathy Lowe, calls this Chocolate Delight "the next best thing to Robert Redford." And then quietly she adds, "Some people call it a Better Than Sex Cake." Cathy goes on to describe it as cool and light. "It is mild-flavored, cool, refreshing, and smooth. When you first see it you think it's heavy, but it isn't." This delight is a four-layer dessert of chocolate pudding and cream cheese, with a nut-based crust and a frozen-dessert topping. As you take your first bite, you may like this dessert as much as Cathy likes Robert Redford.

DIFFICULTY Moderate. While this dessert has four layers, it calls for just ten ingredients, and none of the steps are complicated. Bake the crust ahead.

INGREDIENTS

FOR THE PECAN CRUST
1 cup pecans
1/2 cup butter, softened
1 cup all-purpose flour

FOR THE FIRST LAYER
1 (8-ounce) package cream cheese, at room temperature
1 cup sugar
1/2 of a (12-ounce) carton frozen dessert topping

FOR THE SECOND LAYER
3 cups milk
1 (6-ounce) box instant chocolate pudding
1 (6-ounce) box instant vanilla pudding

FOR THE TOPPING
The remaining frozen dessert topping
1 bar of semi-sweet or milk chocolate

YIELD 12 servings

STEPS Preheat the oven to 350°F. Chop the nuts in a food processor until they are the size of rice grains. Add the butter and flour and process until the mixture starts to form small balls. Spread this on the bottom of an ungreased 13x9x2-inch baking pan. Use your fingers, dipped in flour, to flatten the crust. Bake until the edges are brown, 15 to 20 minutes. Remove from the oven and cool. Defrost the frozen dessert topping in the refrigerator.

When the crust is fully cool, put the cream cheese and sugar into the food processor and process until fully mixed. A small amount at a time, add the dessert topping. Spread this layer on the crust.

Pour the milk into a bowl and add the chocolate and vanilla puddings (do not follow the instructions on the package). Mix thoroughly with a hand beater or wire whisk, and beat until the lumps are gone. Spread this layer over the cheese layer.

Top with the remaining dessert topping, and using the chocolate bar, grate a few specks of chocolate evenly over the top. Refrigerate or freeze, allowing 4 hours to thaw in the refrigerator.

HEALTHY CHOICE ALTERNATIVE Replace the pecan crust with the Baked Meringue Shell (page 209).

Dirt Pudding Delight

A delightful Pikeville College student brought this pudding to an elementary-education class I was teaching.

She used the dirt pudding to demonstrate an art lesson. The pudding was the "dirt" that filled "flower pot" ice cream cones. Straws supported marshmallow "flowers." Each "plant" had a gummy "worm" crawling out of the soil. From the time I first tasted this delight, the smooth, cool, vanilla and chocolate flavor lingered in my mind. Perhaps it stayed with me because of the contrast between the chocolate cookie pieces and the velvety pudding. I asked her for the recipe, and learned that you could make this pudding in a dormitory—no cooking required.

DIFFICULTY Easy. With just four ingredients and no cooking, this recipe is easy to prepare.

STEPS About 6 hours before making the pudding, defrost the dessert topping in the refrigerator. Crumble the cookies, using the palms of your hands and squeezing about four cookies at a time.

In a 13x9x2-inch glass dish, spread two-thirds of the cookie crumbs on the bottom. In a large mixing bowl, combine the milk and the instant pudding, stirring hard with a hand whisk. Whisk and then fold in 6 ounces of the dessert topping. Spread this mixture over the cookie crumbs. Let the pudding mixture thicken 5 minutes in the refrigerator, and then spread the remaining dessert topping over it. Finally, spread the remaining third of the cookie crumbs. To garnish your pudding, let your creativity go wild: plant flowers and raise worms!

HEALTHY CHOICE ALTERNATIVE Traditional sandwich cookies have lots of fat. By substituting a 9-ounce pack of chocolate wafers for the sandwich cookies, you'll cut 64 grams of fat and 1,120 calories from this recipe.

Serve with milk or coffee and cookies. For contrast, serve with fresh fruit such as blueberries, strawberries, or kiwi.

INGREDIENTS
12 ounces frozen dessert topping
One 16-ounce package chocolate sandwich cookies
4 cups cold milk
Two 3.4-ounce boxes instant chocolate or vanilla pudding

YIELD 12 servings

Strawberry Salad
(Strawberry 'n Pretzel Delight and Pretzel Cake)

This dessert is silky, light, dreamy, and creamy. When I first heard its other name, Pretzel Cake, I could only imagine that I would use the crushed pretzels as bread crumbs, like the Germans do in torten. Then when I tasted the salad, I knew it was not a cake or a torte. We call it a pretzel cake, a delight, a strawberry salad, or a sweet dessert. We make it with five distinct layers: a salty butter-and-pretzel crust, a smooth and sweet cream cheese layer, a strawberry gelatin layer, and a silky dessert topping, decorated with fresh strawberries. My problem with the dish is that it takes eleven packages of commercially prepared, boxed food: a bag of pretzels, a box of butter, two cartons of frozen dessert topping, a package of cream cheese, two packages of frozen strawberries, a box or two of Jell-O, and a pint of fresh strawberries. But I include this salad because highly respected country cooks get wildly animated when talking about it, and I find the contrast of the salty pretzel-and-butter crust with the sweet strawberry topping special.

DIFFICULTY Difficult. While even a novice cook can melt and mix the layers for this dessert, I rate it difficult because it has nine ingredients and four steps. It will take about 4 hours to assemble.

INGREDIENTS

FOR THE CRUST

2 1/2 cups (about 6 ounces) coarsely crushed salty pretzels
3/4 cup melted butter or margarine
3 tablespoons sugar

FOR THE CREAM CHEESE LAYER

1 (8-ounce) package soft cream cheese, at room temperature
1 cup sugar
1 (8-ounce) container frozen dessert topping

FOR THE STRAWBERRY LAYER

1 (6-ounce) box strawberry-flavored gelatin
2 cups boiling water
2 (10-ounce) packages frozen sliced strawberries

FOR THE TOP LAYER

1 (8-ounce) container frozen dessert topping
1 pint fresh strawberries, washed and stems removed

YIELD 24 servings

STEPS Defrost the frozen dessert topping in the refrigerator.

Prepare the crust: Preheat the oven to 375°F. Pour the pretzel crumbs into an ungreased 13x9x2-inch baking dish. Combine the melted butter and sugar, and pour over the pretzel crumbs. Stir until mixed, spread evenly across the pan, and bake for 10 minutes. Cool completely.

Prepare the cream cheese layer: In a mixing bowl, beat together the cream cheese and the sugar. A quarter at a time, fold the dessert topping into the cheese mixture. Spread over the crust, and chill thoroughly.

Prepare the strawberry layer: In a mixing bowl, dissolve the gelatin in the boiling water. Add the frozen strawberries, and chill until thick, almost set. Spread over the cream cheese layer. Chill until set. Spread the remaining container of dessert topping on top, and garnish with the fresh strawberries.

HEALTHY CHOICE ALTERNATIVE Replace the pretzel crust with the Baked Meringue Shell (page 209).

Mountain Banana Pudding

I can still remember my first dinner in Pikeville, Kentucky. It was September 19, 1975, we were tired from the drive from Baltimore, and we had not yet fully moved into our new house. Driving my 1969 Dodge Charger, we went to dinner at the Star Light Dining Room, owned by Richard Wells, and located in Pikeville on the South Mayo Trail.

Effie Ratliff was the operator and cook. She was known for her Sunday buffets. Hers was "the" place to be seen after church. As part of that first dinner, now more than twenty years ago, I ordered banana pudding—I still remember it. Effie's banana pudding was mother food, made from scratch and served warm.

You are in for a real treat when you use marshmallow cream as the sugar for a meringue topping. Marshmallow cream is a puffy, air-filled sugar substance. There are no grains of sugar to dissolve, and this meringue will never make tears (drops of sugar water) on the meringue's surface.

DIFFICULTY Moderate. With eight ingredients and two steps, this recipe is moderate in difficulty.

STEPS In a cold saucepan, whisk together the sugar and flour until smooth. Slowly whisk in the milk, and then cook over medium heat until the mixture bubbles for 1 minute.

Separate the eggs. In a small bowl, whisk the yolks until smooth. Whisk about a third of the hot milk mixture into the yolks, and then return this to the saucepan. Whisk and cook again until the yolks thicken or reach 177°F. Do not let the mixture boil, and do not let the yolks cook through. Stir in the vanilla. Remove the custard from the heat and cool for 20 minutes.

Line the bottom of a small (6-cup or 6x10-inch) casserole dish with 12 vanilla wafers, and slice 2 bananas lengthwise over the wafers. Cover with a third of the custard and repeat, adding 12 more vanilla wafers and the remaining 2 bananas. Press 10 wafers into an upright position around the edges, touching the sides of the dish. Top with the remaining third of the custard.

Meringue Topping: Preheat the oven to 450°F. In a mixing bowl, beat the egg whites until almost stiff, and slowly add the marshmallow cream. When fully mixed and stiff, spread the meringue over the pudding, sealing to the standing vanilla wafers. With the back of a spoon, draw the meringue into peaks. Garnish by pressing the remaining 6 vanilla wafers across the center of the pudding. Bake for 3 minutes, or until the peaks of the meringue brown. To cool fully, refrigerate for 4 hours.

INGREDIENTS
1 cup sugar
1/3 cup all-purpose flour
2 1/2 cups whole milk
4 eggs, at room temperature
2 teaspoons vanilla
40 (6 ounces)vanilla wafers
4 (1 1/2 to 2 pounds)ripe bananas
1/2 cup marshmallow cream

YIELD 10 servings

TIP Buy the bananas several days before making the pudding so they have time to ripen. Ideally, they will have black spots. Cooling the custard before you add the bananas and baking the meringue quickly should help keep the bananas looking fresh. Do not store this pudding much more than a day, because eventually the bananas turn brown and the meringue shrinks. When you assemble the pudding, the bananas do not have to be fully covered with pudding. The meringue will cover them.

HEALTHY CHOICE ALTERNATIVE Use 1/2 cup sugar, 2% milk, and 2 of the 4 egg yolks.

Serve warm or cold with coffee or tea. We like banana pudding warm, and we serve it in small dessert bowls.

Lemon Curd

DIFFICULTY Easy. With four ingredients and one cooking step, this recipe is easy.

*L*emon curd is a smooth, highly flavored dessert, filling, or spread. Containing lemon juice, sugar, eggs, and butter, lemon curd is an English–Blue Ridge Mountain specialty. I first used a lemon curd on lemon butter bars, and later I learned to appreciate it as a pudding, filling, or spread. While mountain country cooks have been making lemon curd for generations, I have recently noticed it for sale in gourmet shops, catalogs, and large markets. A recent Crabtree and Evelyn catalog (Woodstock, Connecticut) included an English country lemon curd, and they too made it with eggs, lemon juice, sugar, and butter.

When I cook eggs for a sauce like this, I like to use a heavy copper saucepan, which both distributes the heat and cools quickly. Do not cook this in aluminum.

Because lemon is the essence of this dessert, keep in mind that you can enhance its flavor by using fresh lemons. If you are a real lemon lover, scrape the lemon pulp and add it to the curd. You can also add 2 teaspoons of lemon zest, but as I prefer a smooth, silky curd, I omit the pulp and zest. Start with room temperature lemons—they are easier to squeeze.

INGREDIENTS
1/2 cup fresh-squeezed lemon juice
1 cup sugar
3 whole eggs
6 tablespoons unsalted butter

YIELD Almost 2 cups or 4 servings

STEPS In a medium saucepan over low heat, combine the lemon juice, sugar, and eggs. Add the butter, and continue to heat until the mixture thickens and reaches 174°F. Do not boil or the eggs will curdle. If the eggs curdle, press the mixture through a strainer, leaving the cooked egg behind.

Remove from the heat and pour into a cool container or four individual serving dishes. Cover the curd with plastic wrap. Refrigerate until stiff, 3 hours or more. This dish keeps for two weeks in the refrigerator.

HEALTHY CHOICE ALTERNATIVE Lemon Spread: For a fat-free alternative, mix ¹/₂ cup sugar with 3 tablespoons cornstarch, and combine with 1¹/₂ cups orange juice and ¹/₄ cup lemon juice. Boil for 1 minute, cool, and serve. This "pudding" gets firm in the refrigerator but spreads well. Keep it cool or it will melt.

Spread this with a pat of cold butter on a toasted English muffin, or Sorghum Gingerbread, or sliced Savage Mountain Pound Cake. Use as a filling for sponge cake or a lemon cake roll, or serve as a pudding.

Cobblers

Country cooks are berry pickers, and we know cobblers. If you like to avoid rolling pie crust and forming it into a double-crust pie, consider cobblers, grunts, slumps, and clafoutis. They appeal to our weakness for fruit, sugar, and flour. For these desserts the dough may be sweet or savory, rich or light, thick like biscuit dough, thin like pancake batter, or anything in between. We place the dough over, under, or in the fruit, and we roll it out flat or drop it from a spoon. Some say that a cobbler is supposed to have a rough surface like a cobblestone street, and others suggest that the top crust is pieced together like the work of a cobbler.

Mountain cooks thicken cobblers three ways: first, by reducing the fruit; second, by adding a thickener such as cornstarch, flour, or tapioca; and, finally, with a mixture of sugar, eggs, and butter. When we use this latter option, our filling resembles a transparent, chess, or pecan pie.

Cobbler recipes are so diverse that some absorb a crumb topping, while others completely absorb a fruit filling. Let me explain. In the case of the crumb-topped cobbler, we use enough fruit and liquid so that they absorb the topping. In the end, we have some crust on the top, but basically we have thickened the fruit with a crumbly mixture. At the other extreme, the cobbler absorbs the fruit. The French call this a clafouti, and the dough is a batter. Here, we pour fruit over the batter, and when we take this cobbler-clafouti from the oven, it is a bit cake-like, but the fruit and fruit sauce are spread from top to bottom. Our most pie-like cobbler is a blackberry or peach cobbler, baked in a straight-sided casserole dish. For this cobbler we line the pan with crust, add the fruit filling, and cover the top with a thick lattice crust.

In the recipes that follow I offer baking powder biscuit-type cobblers, a rolled pie pastry cobbler made without baking powder, and a crumb-topped streusel-apple cobbler. I use peaches, rhubarb, blackberries, and apples, but we also use cherries, pie cherries, plums, pears, apricots, raspberries, black caps, huckleberries, and blueberries. You can substitute one crust for another. Let's try some cobblers, shall we?

Blackberry Cobbler

DIFFICULTY Moderate. With five ingredients, a rolled crust, and nearly an hour of baking, this recipe is moderate in difficulty.

I hate to admit it, but I will pay a high price to buy fresh blackberries in the winter so that I can make this cobbler. On the other hand, if you can find frozen or canned berries that are to your liking, use them, and by all means, make this in July and August, when blackberries are in season. This cobbler is an example of one made with a rolled pastry similar to that used for pie crust. As with other cobblers, you do not have to add so much flour to the filling that it cooks stiff enough to cut with a knife. The filling should be runny, like a thick chowder.

INGREDIENTS

FOR THE FILLING

2 cups (16 ounces or 3 one-pint boxes) mashed fresh blackberries

1 cup plus 1 tablespoon sugar

FOR THE TOP CRUST

1 cup plus 3 tablespoons all-purpose flour

1/3 cup cold butter or lard

3 tablespoons ice water

YIELD 6 servings

STEPS Preheat the oven to 450°F. In a mixing bowl, combine the berries with 1 cup of the sugar and 3 tablespoons of the flour. Spread the mixture in an 8x8x2-inch baking pan.

For the crust, mix the remaining 1 cup of flour and 1 tablespoon of sugar, and cut in the butter. Add the ice water, and mix well. Draw the mixture into a ball, knead six times, and then, between sheets of waxed paper, roll the dough into a square that will fit the baking pan. Cut four holes for steam vents; I use an apple corer, cutting out round holes the size of a dime. Flip the dough onto the berries, center it, and cut the edges square or turn them under. Bake for 20 minutes, or until the top crust starts to brown. Reduce the heat to 350°F, and bake an additional 25 minutes, or until the berries bubble up through the steam vents. If the top is not brown, broil for 1 1/2 minutes. Cool 15 to 20 minutes. Serve.

HEALTHY CHOICE ALTERNATIVE Replace this rich pie pastry with 1/3 of a recipe of my oil-and-water Healthy Choice Pie Crust, page 276.

While the cobbler is still warm, spoon it into small serving bowls and top with ice cream, heavy cream, or whipped cream. Serve with a hard sauce or Buttermilk Glaze.

Peach Cobbler

By June 1, our markets carry tree-ripened peaches from Florida or Georgia. From the Alleghenies to the Smokies and from the Blue Ridge west to the Highland Rim, this shortcake-style or biscuit-type cobbler is a favorite. I pre-cook the filling so that when I place the biscuit-type dough on the cobbler, it will start to cook immediately and not get soggy.

STEPS Preheat the oven to 350°F. Arrange the sliced peaches in an 8x8x2-inch baking pan.

In a small mixing bowl, combine the 3/4 cup sugar, cornstarch, and cinnamon. Whisk until the lumps of cornstarch are gone. Pour over the fruit, and place the pan in the oven to warm.

Prepare the crust: In a small mixing bowl, whisk together the flour, 2 table-spoons sugar, and baking powder. Stir in the cream. Pat the crust into a flat 8x8-inch shape, cut it into quarters (for ease of moving it to the pan), and lay it over the peaches. With a knife slash four steam vents. Return the pan to the oven, and bake for 45 minutes, or until the fruit mixture bubbles up through the center.

HEALTHY CHOICE ALTERNATIVE Replace the heavy cream with skim milk, making the crust less tender. Then, without salt, eggs, or fat, this dessert should fit into a variety of diets. To cut calories, reduce the sugar in the filling to 1/2 cup.

Serve warm from the oven, topped with ice cream, heavy cream, or whipped cream. Serve in bowls with a hard sauce or Buttermilk Glaze.

DIFFICULTY Moderate. With seven ingredients, two steps, and 45 minutes of baking, this recipe is moderate in difficulty.

INGREDIENTS

FOR THE FILLING
3 cups sliced fresh peaches
3/4 cup plus 2 table-spoons sugar
1 tablespoon cornstarch
1/4 teaspoon cinnamon

FOR THE CRUST
3/4 cup all-purpose flour
1 teaspoon baking pow-der
1/4 cup heavy cream

YIELD 8 servings

Great Smoky Mountains Apple Cobbler
Dutch Apple Pie (Streusel-Topped Apple Cobbler)

Cut in half by the Tennessee and North Carolina state line, the Great Smoky Mountains National Park attracts visitors from around the world. In fact, the park attracts more visitors per year (9 million) than any other national park. Visitors come to see the mist on the Smoky Mountains, to hike the trails, to fish

DIFFICULTY Moderate. With seven ingredients and 50 minutes of bak-ing, this recipe is moder-ate in difficulty.

for trout, to hear water rushing, and to observe the plant life that changes with the elevations. From the valley floor the Smokies rise to 6,643 feet at the top of Clingmans Dome.

Clingmans Dome is the highest point in Tennessee. The valleys below the mountains, valleys with names such as Pigeon, Walden, and Sweet Water, support lush and productive apple trees. Country cooks and restaurants around the area serve apple cobbler, sometimes with a streusel topping.

This dessert is sweet, sticky, and gooey, and we make it with just seven ingredients. A streusel topping is a crumb topping, and it is easier to make than a pie crust. For my apple desserts, I use half firm Granny Smiths and half soft apples, such as Rome Beauties, resulting in a cobbler that is sweet, not runny, and full of apple-cinnamon flavor.

INGREDIENTS

FOR THE STREUSEL TOPPING

3/4 cup all-purpose flour
1/3 cup brown sugar
1/3 cup sugar
1/2 teaspoon cinnamon
   or apple pie spice
6 tablespoons unsalted
   butter

FOR THE FILLING

3/4 cup sugar
3 tablespoons all-
   purpose flour
1 1/2 teaspoons cinnamon
   or apple pie spice
4 cups peeled, cored,
   and diced apples

YIELD 6 servings

STEPS Preheat the oven to 350°F, and select an 8x8x2-inch baking tin. To prepare the topping, in a mixing bowl and using your fingertips, combine 3/4 cup flour, the brown sugar, 1/3 cup sugar, and 1/2 teaspoon cinnamon. Using a pastry blender, cut in the butter. With your fingertips, work the mixture until fully mixed and crumbly. The size of the pieces should be something between coarse cornmeal and small grains of rice. Set aside and prepare the filling.

In a large bowl, whisk until smooth the dry ingredients: 3/4 cup sugar, 3 tablespoons flour, and 1 1/2 teaspoons cinnamon. Add the apples, and stir. Pour into the baking pan. Cover with the streusel topping, and bake for 50 minutes, or until the cobbler puffs up in the center and browns across the top. Serve.

HEALTHY CHOICE ALTERNATIVE For the topping, use 3 tablespoons butter and 3 tablespoons water. For the filling, reduce the sugar to 1/2 cup.

Hot from the oven this cobbler is stiff enough to serve warm. The next day when you take the cobbler from the refrigerator it is stiff—microwave before serving. Serve the cobbler in dessert bowls and add ice cream, heavy cream, or whipped cream.

Dutch Apple Pie
Bake the cobbler filling and streusel topping in an unbaked pie shell.

Sweet Sorghum:
Bars, Butter, Pie, and Pudding

ON EVEN THE smallest plots, mountain farmers have enough space to plant a patch of sweet sorghum. Half an acre yields fifty to one hundred gallons of sorghum syrup and makes a valuable cash crop. Sorghum, like corn and sugar cane, is a grass, and people the world over cultivate it for food, forage, and syrup. Sweet sorghum is closely related to grain, field, or grass sorghum. While grain sorghum, or milo, is a forage for livestock, our sweet sorghum is intended for the sorghum press. Today, at sorghum festivals scattered throughout the region, we gather to celebrate fall and to make sorghum. At these festivals you'll see stacks of the three- to fifteen-foot-long bright green sorghum cane stalks waiting to be hand fed into a sorghum press and boiled into syrup.

In talking with Danny Townsend of Townsend's Sorghum Mill (see the Mail-Order Sources), I learned something about the quality of sorghum syrup. The big fear among sorghum producers is that syrup labeled sorghum may also contain corn syrup, molasses, and artificial flavorings and colors. If sorghum contains corn syrup or other additives, it should be properly labeled.

I agree with Danny and like to buy pure cane sorghum. The flavor of sorghum syrup depends on the season, the soil, the variety grown, and the plant's maturity at harvest, not to mention the processing and storage. Careful evaporation, using even heat and a low temperature, keeps the syrup from burning.

Molasses and sorghum are both liquid sweeteners made from tall grasses, but that is where the similarities end. We make molasses from cane sugar plants, and we make sorghum from sweet sorghum plants. Sugar cane will not grow in the mountains—our climate is too cold. Sorghum, on the other hand, is an annual grown from seed during the warm months.

I use 100 percent pure sweet sorghum for my recipes. Mountaineers often call this molasses, but the word *molasses* is a colloquial—and incorrect—term for sorghum syrup. If you buy syrup made from sweet sorghum plants, you should call it sorghum syrup or sweet sorghum. If the sugar comes from sugar cane plants, it is molasses.

While molasses is a by-product of sugar production, sorghum is the end product of sorghum production, made by pressing the juice from the plants and boiling it into a concentrate. We remove nothing but impurities and foam. While sorghum has a sweet and full sorghum flavor, molasses is stronger in flavor, less sweet, and bitter. Some say molasses tastes like medicine. Molasses is strong because it contains the impurities that are left after the white sugar has been removed. We don't serve molasses as a syrup.

When processors remove sugar from cane, they make three strengths of molasses: first, second, and blackstrap. Each strength or level is darker and has more impurities than the one before it. Blackstrap is so dark, strong, and caramelized that, while sold in some stores, it is usually eaten by animals.

You can make these sorghum recipes using light corn syrup, dark corn syrup, sweet sorghum, molasses, honey, or maple syrup. Sorghum is sweet and has a slightly burned and distinctive sorghum flavor. Molasses is strong, sharp, bitter, and less sweet. If you want to add a little tangy, earthy, burnt flavor to your cooking, use molasses. For slightly more sweetness and a true mountain flavor, use sweet sorghum. Corn syrup—both light and dark—is the choice for those who want less sweetness and no flavor. We use corn syrup to prevent crystallization in candy. Corn syrup is the least sweet, only one-half to one-third as sweet as sugar. Honey, on the other hand, is quite sweet—about seven-eighths as sweet as sugar. Maple syrup is about three-fourths as sweet as sugar, and sorghum is a little more than half as sweet.

Sorghum is rich in minerals, calcium, iron, and potassium. In comparing sorghum and sugar, sugar lacks both the flavor and minerals of sorghum. Ounce for ounce, sugar and sorghum contain the same number of calories, about 110 per ounce. In comparing sorghum to maple syrup, honey, and molasses, sorghum has the highest mineral count and honey has the lowest. However, even sorghum is no panacea for good health. To get your recommended daily allowance of iron and calcium from sorghum you need about six tablespoonfuls or three hundred thirty calories worth. That's not very healthy. In addition, some of the iron, calcium, and phosphorus contained in sorghum is not assimilable by the body. Sure, sorghum is more nutritious than refined sugar, but if you eat enough of it to meet your daily mineral needs, you'll probably gain weight.

■ ■

Sorghum Feed Menus

At sorghum feeds held in the fall, mountain communities celebrate the new crop. At these suppers you'll find some of our favorite foods, like the following:

Menu One
Corn Relish, Southern Fried Chicken, Sweet Potato Casserole,
Green Beans with Bacon, Buttermilk Biscuits and Hot Sorghum, and
Sorghum Pecan Pie Bars

Menu Two
Fried Pork Chops, Sorghum Gingerbread,
Dilled Green Beans with Black Walnuts, Boiled Turnips
with sorghum syrup, Sorghum Pie, and Sorghum Popcorn
Balls

Menu Three
Green Beans with Bacon, Baked Cushaw with Sorghum,
Soup Beans, Kraut Slaw, Boiled New Potatoes, banana-
pecan bread, Sorghum Bread Pudding, and
Black Walnut Sugar Cookies

■ ■

Sorghum Pecan Pie Bars

*A*lso called honeymoon squares or pecan slices, this pecan pie bar is finger food. Its thick savory crust and sweet pecan topping distinguish it from other bar cookies.

DIFFICULTY Moderate. With eight ingredients and two steps, these bars are moderate in difficulty.

STEPS Place the baking rack in the center position, and preheat the oven to 350°F. Line a 13x9x2-inch baking pan with aluminum foil. Grease the foil with nonstick cooking spray, particularly the sides. Check the pecans for shell and remove any bad pecans.

Prepare the crust: In a mixing bowl, combine the flour and salt. Using a pastry blender, cut in the butter. Add enough ice water to the egg to make ⅓ cup, and sprinkle over the flour. Stir and knead until smooth, about 20 strokes. Press the dough evenly into the foil-lined pan.

Prepare the filling: In a medium mixing bowl, beat the eggs slowly with a hand mixer and add the sorghum, sugar, butter, and flour. Beat slowly, stirring in the pecans. Pour over the crust, and bake for 45 to 55 minutes, or until set in the center.

Cool and then refrigerate. When cold, use the foil to lift the bars from the pan. Invert and remove the foil. Turn right-side up and cut into bars, 5 cuts long and 6 cuts across.

HEALTHY CHOICE ALTERNATIVE To save on calories and fat, eat just one of these bars. It takes four of them to equal a piece of pecan pie.

INGREDIENTS

FOR THE CRUST
3 cups all-purpose flour
1 teaspoon salt
1 cup cold butter
Ice water to equal ⅓ cup
1 egg

FOR THE FILLING
3 eggs
1 cup 100% pure sweet sorghum
1 cup sugar
⅓ cup melted butter
2 tablespoons all-purpose flour
1½ cups pecans

YIELD 30 bars

Served on buffet tables or at covered dish suppers, these bars make pecan pie into snack food. At home serve them as an accompaniment to vanilla ice cream, with Hot Sorghum and coffee.

Sorghum Pie

*T*his pie is neither a Pennsylvania Dutch shoofly pie nor a molasses crumb pie. Some mountain cooks make the shoofly pie, but more often we make a pie like the one I offer here, a type of transparent pie. The Pennsylvania Dutch make their molasses crumb pies with large amounts of flour, sugar, and crumbs layered with a molasses-and-water mixture. Crumb pies are very different from this egg-based Appalachian sorghum pie. I do not add butter and flour to this pie—with all these eggs, the filling cooks stiffly and smoothly without them. The cooled pie cuts and serves without oozing or tearing. A thick crust helps in serving.

Be generous, and take the liberty to enhance the traditional recipe with a real whipped cream topping.

DIFFICULTY Difficult. If you follow my directions, you will prepare three recipes: pie crust, filling, and topping. Combined, the recipes call for nine different ingredients. I suggest that you bake the pie the day before you make the topping and serve the pie.

INGREDIENTS
1/2 recipe Pie Pastry Shell (page 275)
5 eggs
1/3 cup sugar
1 1/4 cups 100% pure sweet sorghum
1 recipe Country Whipped Cream (page 316)

YIELD 8 servings

STEPS Preheat the oven to 350°F. Line a 9-inch pie pan with the Pie Pastry Shell.

In a medium mixing bowl, beat the eggs until they are smooth. Add the sugar and sorghum, and beat again. Pour into the unbaked pie shell, but don't overload—you want to be able to carry it to the oven without spilling. Bake for 40 minutes, or until puffed up in the center and a toothpick inserted into the center comes out clean. Cool. Refrigerate.

Prepare one recipe of Country Whipped Cream. Spread over the pie, or offer it on the side, serve.

HEALTHY CHOICE ALTERNATIVE There is nothing healthy about this. Serve it for a special occasion.

While many years ago people most often ate this pie for breakfast, today we serve it for dessert, a holiday feast, or perhaps an after-school snack.

Hot Sorghum
Fried Sorghum

*W*hen we mix sorghum with baking soda and bring it to a boil, it makes a large amount of foam. Volume may increase six times, and when it settles down, some of the foam remains. The soda and cooking make the sorghum fuller, less sharp, and almost creamy. The foam allows you to incorporate air into the syrup making it milder, and the cooking draws water out and makes the syrup thicker. Spread or pour the foamed syrup across your biscuits or hot cakes like you would a marshmallow frosting. Let the syrup run to the plate. Sop it up. Enjoy the thick foamy sweetness of 100 percent pure sweet sorghum syrup.

STEPS Pour the sorghum into a medium bowl and sprinkle the soda, one pinch at a time, evenly over the top. Stir to mix. Microwave on high for 1½ minutes—the sorghum will foam. Stir, and serve immediately, or let it cool a little. When it cools, microwave again. Stir again.

Store in the refrigerator and reheat in your microwave oven. Like any syrup, foamy sorghum gets stiff when cold.

HEALTHY CHOICE ALTERNATIVE This spread is so sweet that when I use it on breakfast breads, I don't need any butter.

When I serve the syrup cold, the foam is like a frosting; when I serve the syrup hot, it pours like a pancake syrup or sauce. I prefer to use this foamy sweetener hot, and get excited when I pour it over hot Buttermilk Biscuits. For an ultimate treat, split a fresh crusty biscuit in half, add several pats of butter, and then pour foamed syrup over the top. With the biscuit ready to eat, I cut it with a knife and fork, sop up the sorghum, and eat it like a pork chop. It is just as good! Offer Hot Sorghum with pancakes, waffles, muffins, or French toast, or serve over Cushaw Bread or Baked Cushaw.

Fried Sorghum Simmer the sorghum and baking soda in a skillet until foamy and thick.

DIFFICULTY Very Easy. With two ingredients and less than 2 minutes in the microwave oven, this recipe is easy.

INGREDIENTS
½ cup 100% pure
   sweet sorghum
⅛ teaspoon baking soda

YIELD 1½ cups or 6 servings

Sorghum Butter

DIFFICULTY Easy.
With two ingredients, this
recipe is easy.

*L*ots of mountaineers make sorghum butter. Their ratio of butter to sorghum ranges from four parts butter/one part sorghum to one part butter/two parts sorghum. The flavor of your sorghum butter depends on this ratio and the strength of the sorghum.

INGREDIENTS
3 tablespoons unsalted
  butter, at room temper-
  ature
2 tablespoons 100%
  pure sweet sorghum

YIELD 4 servings

STEPS In a mixing bowl, combine the butter and sorghum. Whisk until smooth and light. Refrigerate, and serve.

Spread this sweet butter over a split biscuit and serve with Country-Fried Steak or Southern Fried Chicken. Or, serve for breakfast with biscuits and fried potatoes, country ham, and scrambled eggs, or over waffles, pancakes, or French toast.

Gingerbread-Apple Upside-Down Cake
Sorghum Gingerbread

DIFFICULTY Difficult.
This dessert has three layers, three steps, and fifteen ingredients.

*G*ingerbread comes in many shapes, flavors, and textures. It can be thick or thin, cookie or cake, sharp or mild, sweet or savory, and hard or soft.
    Through the ages gingerbread has reflected various human tastes ranging from robust and masculine to light and feminine.
    Up and down the Appalachian Mountains from New York to Georgia, across the Alleghenies and Shenandoahs, from the Blue Ridge to the Smokies, mountaineers make gingerbread with flour, soda, salt, and molasses or sorghum. Our gingerbread recipes become breads, cookies, and sweet cakes.
    Every culture and region has its special gingerbread. Often, the recipes were born in old Europe. The French add fruits; the Germans sweeten with honey. For the French, gingerbread is *pain d'épice*; for the Germans the bread is *lebkuchen*; and for the Italians it is *panforte*. Each of these is quite different and different again from the ancient ginger-flavored breads: Chinese *mikong* and Roman *panis mellitus*.
    In the town of Hindman, Kentucky, people gather each September to celebrate the tradition of eating gingerbread on election day. At the Gingerbread Festival you can see the world's largest gingerbread man (about eight feet tall),

buy a gingerbread cookbook, and taste many varieties of gingerbread. (For further information contact the Chamber of Commerce at P.O. Box 374, Hindman, KY 41822; 606 785-5544.)

When I baked this upside-down cake on my television show, the mail came for months, and when I served it to my daughter's teenage friends, they could not get enough. At church dinners people snap it up, and if I have it in the house, I eat it for breakfast, lunch, or supper. Gooey and sweet on top, moist and spicy on the bottom, and garnished with whipped cream, small bites fill my mouth with total sensation.

STEPS To prepare the whipped cream (up to two days in advance): Chill beaters and mixing bowl in refrigerator until cold. In the mixing bowl, beat the cream, brown sugar, and vanilla on high until stiff peaks form. Cover and refrigerate.

Preheat the oven to 350°F.

To make the topping: In a 10½-inch cast-iron skillet over medium heat, melt the butter. Add the brown sugar and cinnamon, and stir. Cook until the sugar melts. Remove from the heat, and spread the apples evenly in the skillet over the melted butter and sugar, tapping them down to form a flat surface.

To prepare the Sorghum Gingerbread: In a mixing bowl, combine the dry ingredients: flour, baking powder, ginger, cinnamon, salt, and cloves. Set aside. In a second bowl, cream the sorghum, butter, brown sugar, and egg. Add dry mixture to the sorghum mixture alternately with the milk. Pour the batter slowly over the apples in the skillet. Spread as you pour.

Bake for 35 minutes, or until raised in the center and a toothpick inserted into the center comes out clean. Remove from the oven and run spatula around the side of pan. Cool for 1 minute. Place a serving platter face-down over the pan, and invert the cake onto the platter.

HEALTHY CHOICE ALTERNATIVE Omit the Country Whipped Cream. You may also omit the egg and mix the batter with water or coffee instead of milk. Omit the butter from the apple topping (replace it with an equal amount of water), but don't omit it from the batter.

Serve warm or at room temperature, garnished with a dollop of the Country Whipped Cream.

Sorghum Gingerbread
To make a plain, cake-like gingerbread, bake the above Sorghum Gingerbread recipe at 350°F for 40 minutes in a greased and floured 8x8-inch pan. Omit the apple topping, and serve with applesauce.

INGREDIENTS

FOR THE COUNTRY WHIPPED CREAM
2 cups heavy cream
½ cup brown sugar
2 teaspoons vanilla

FOR THE APPLE TOPPING
⅓ cup butter
1 cup brown sugar
1 teaspoon cinnamon
4 apples, peeled, cored, and sliced thin to equal 5 cups

FOR THE SORGHUM GINGERBREAD
1¼ cups all-purpose flour
1 teaspoon baking powder
1 teaspoon ginger
½ teaspoon cinnamon
½ teaspoon salt
¼ teaspoon ground cloves
½ cup 100% pure sweet sorghum
½ cup butter, at room temperature
¼ cup brown sugar
1 egg
½ cup milk

YIELD 8 servings

Bread Pudding
Sorghum Bread Pudding

DIFFICULTY Moderate. If you have to make the biscuits, this pudding is difficult to prepare. If you have leftover biscuits, this recipe is moderately difficult.

*A*lthough I use a mixture of milk, egg, and sugar over the bread, this is not a custard. Later, when I lift the pudding from the oven, it is puffed up, slightly sweet, and like no other dessert. The mass of biscuits has soaked up the milk and egg mixture, and the pudding is soft, moist, and substantial. What distinguishes our bread pudding from so many others is the bread. Some cooks make bread pudding with what I suspect is soft mushy bread from a plastic bag. Others make it with 2½ cups of bread crumbs, which to me yields a heavy pudding. Here in the mountains, we make bread pudding with biscuits. I use day-old, crusty Buttermilk Biscuits. I use leftover breakfast biscuits or I go out to my favorite fast-food source and buy their rich, salty, and crusty biscuits.

INGREDIENTS
3 eggs
³/4 cup sugar
1 teaspoon vanilla
3 cups milk
6 biscuits (3 inches wide, 1½ inches high)
¼ cup raisins
Cinnamon sugar, as needed

YIELD 6 servings

STEPS Preheat the oven to 325°F. Select a 2-quart casserole dish and a pan large enough to hold it in a water bath. Fill the larger pan with hot water, and place it in the oven.

In a mixing bowl, whisk together the eggs, sugar, and vanilla. Add the milk. Cut the biscuits in thirds across the center (top to bottom) and arrange them in the casserole. Sprinkle the raisins over the biscuits, and pour the milk mixture over the biscuits. Place the dish in the hot water bath in the oven.

Bake for 1 hour, or until the custard is set or when a toothpick inserted into the center comes out clean. Cool, and serve or refrigerate. Smooth any bubbles on top of the custard, and sprinkle with cinnamon sugar. Serve.

HEALTHY CHOICE ALTERNATIVE Start with a low-fat biscuit. Use three egg whites and no yolks.

Serve warm or cold (I prefer it warm, about an hour after I take it from the oven). This pudding is right without a topping, but if you want to sweeten it, to make it moist and luscious, cover it with Boiled Custard. Other possible toppings include Pear Honey, Lemon Glaze, Green Pepper Jelly, Country Whipped Cream, Hot Sorghum, Buttermilk Glaze, or Chocolate Gravy.

Sorghum Bread Pudding To the above recipe, after adding the sugar, add ¼ cup of 100% pure sweet sorghum.

Apple Traditions

FOODS PUT ME a little less in touch with my cultural heritage, inner being, and these mountains. As a food critic, I am quite eclectic, and yet when I get excited about a food, it is often a common dish. I tend to avoid making dishes that are a combination of several recipes. I often find the complexity unnecessary, the time spent a waste. On the other hand, I am overwhelmed by applesauce. I get excited by hot cocoa. I can indulge in custard. I dream of sweet corn and waxy potato salad.

Several years after I came to the mountains, I spent time buying and selling real estate. I traveled in the country and visited with people who advertised property for sale. As we talked about property, I was impressed by how often these owners told me about their apple trees, bragging about quality and variety, and relating the number of trees on their property to a sign of wealth.

In our markets good apples are available all year, but during apple season—July through November—I often find firm, highly flavored local apples, and I use and enjoy them while they last. If local apples are not available, I like to mix Granny Smiths with a soft apple, such as Rome Beauties. If it is early in the season, I'll use small, green June apples.

As a means of preserving the crop for winter, mountain families used to dry bushels of apples. They scrubbed, peeled, cored, and sliced the apples. Then, to dry apples they strung them like beads on strings and hung the strings in a warm, dry place. They also laid them between screens and dried them in the sun.

Many families dried apples in large kilns. The kilns were the size of a queen-size bed, and they placed the apples on sheets of tin inside the kilns. Drying took from twelve hours to a week, depending on the conditions. In place of kilns some mountaineers used junked cars—space begging for a good use. Junked cars usually sit in the sun and absorb heat. The roof of the car protects the apples from the rain, and a broken window or two provides ventilation.

Today we might choose to prepare or buy dried apples, not because we have to preserve the crop to survive the winter, but because dried apples are a tasty and healthy snack with concentrated apple flavor. When I do not have home-dried apples, I buy commercially dried apples in the local market. To buy home-dried apples see Mullins' Orchard in the list of Mail-Order Sources.

Dried Apples

DIFFICULTY Easy.
To make dried apples fol-
low three steps: gather
apples, prepare them for
drying, and dry the
apples.

INGREDIENTS
5 pounds apples
Fruit Fresh fruit
   preservative

YIELD 5 cups
(8 ounces) dried apples

*S*erve these traditional dried apples as a snack or part of a fruit plate or use as an ingredient for Dried Apple Applesauce. Dried apples also make a nice garnish for applesauce or any pie or cake that calls for dried apples.

STEPS Wash, peel, and core the apples. Slice in even thicknesses, for even drying. Sprinkle with Fruit Fresh, to preserve the light color.

Dry the apples with natural evaporation or in a commercial fruit dryer, according to the manufacturer's directions. Lay the apples in a single layer on screen racks or window screens. Depending on the temperature and humidity, dry the apples from 12 hours to 1 week.

The apples are dry when the outside is rough and leathery and the inside is soft. They should be firm but not brittle. Store in sealed plastic bags.

Applesauce from Dried Apples
(Dried Apple Applesauce)

DIFFICULTY Easy.
With four ingredients and one step, this recipe is easy.

*W*ith apples dried and tucked away for winter, our cooks used them to make applesauce. They served it for breakfast or used it to make Dried Apple Stack Cakes, Fried Apple Pies, Dried Apple Pies, and Dried Apple Stack Pies. The favorites were stack cakes and fried pies.

They flavored the apples with butter, lard, cinnamon, allspice, cloves, and slices of unpeeled lemon or orange. I am proud to offer you this simple concept, this common country classic.

INGREDIENTS
8 cups of home dried
   (very dry) apples
6 cups water
1 cup sugar
1/2 teaspoon cinnamon

YIELD 8 cups

STEPS In a large pot, bring the apples, water, and sugar to a boil. Reduce the heat, and simmer for 30 minutes. (Or, as I like to do, cook the ingredients in a pressure cooker for 10 minutes.) Stir in the cinnamon. Using a food mill, high-speed mixer, or food processor, process the apple mixture until it is as smooth as applesauce. Cool, and serve.

TIP If you don't have home-dried apples, use 24 ounces commercial, soft-dried apples and 7 cups of water.

HEARTY
Cooking
COUNTRY ■

HEALTHY CHOICE ALTERNATIVE Omit the sugar. Apples are often sweet enough without added sugar.

Serve this as a vegetable side dish or for lunch with cottage cheese and ginger-bread. Spoon it over waffles and pancakes, or serve as a dessert, heated and topped with a scoop of vanilla ice cream.

Dried Apple Stack Pies

*U*sing light metal pie pans, cooks of fifty years ago often made several of these pies, stacked them in a pie basket, and carried them to a social event. Stack pies were so popular that they made them with cushaw, peach, pear, plum, persimmon, or pumpkin butter. Today you can order these butters from A. M. Braswell or Gallery Crafts, listed in the Mail-Order Sources.

This double-crust pie is thin, about 1/2 an inch thick. Think of this dish as similar to fig or apple newtons, with a firm fruit filling and a crust on the top and bottom.

DIFFICULTY Difficult. With seven ingredients, crusts to roll and form, and two cooking steps, this recipe is difficult.

STEPS Prepare the Dried Apple Applesauce. (I like to do this the day before and refrigerate it overnight.)

Preheat the oven to 450°F. Select two light-weight (9-inch) pie pans. Prepare the Pie Pastry Shell as directed, except divide the dough in two and roll out four pie crusts. Roll the dough smaller than usual, and do not bring it all the way up the side of the pans. Spread 1 cup of the Dried Apple Applesauce on both of the lower crusts and top with the second crusts. Crimp the edges.

Bake for 25 minutes, or until the crust is brown on the edges and baked through. Cool 30 minutes or more.

HEALTHY CHOICE ALTERNATIVE For the crust use my oil-and-water Healthy Choice Alternative Pie Pastry Shell (page 276).

INGREDIENTS
2 cups Dried Apple Applesauce (page 228)
1 recipe Pie Pastry Shell (page 275)
YIELD 2 pies or 16 servings

Serve warm with hot coffee or Sassafras Tea and vanilla ice cream doused with Buttermilk Glaze and a sprinkling of black walnut pieces. Or, serve for breakfast with scrambled eggs and bacon.

Dried Apple Pie

*W*hile my Dried Apple Stack Pie is thin, this pie fills the pan. Because I have added raisins and pecans, this pie is a bit more complex.

DIFFICULTY Difficult. Any double-crust pie made with your scratch crust is difficult to prepare. In this case, you also have to prepare Dried Apple Applesauce. It takes about 1 hour to get this ready for baking.

INGREDIENTS

1³/4 cups Dried-Apple Applesauce (page 228)
1³/4 cups diced fresh apples
¹/2 cup sugar
¹/2 cup pecan pieces
¹/4 cup raisins
1 tablespoon lemon juice
¹/2 teaspoon cinnamon
1 recipe Pie Pastry Shell (page 275)

YIELD 8 servings

STEPS Preheat the oven to 450°F.

In a large bowl, combine the Dried Apple Applesauce, diced apples, sugar, pecans, raisins, lemon juice, and cinnamon. Roll out the Pie Pastry Shell for one 9-inch double-crust pie. Place the bottom crust in a 9-inch deep-dish pie pan, add the apple mixture, and top with the second crust. Crimp the edges.

Bake for 15 minutes. Reduce the oven temperature to 350°F and bake an additional 40 minutes. The pie has to cook through to the center. The Dried Apple Applesauce and raisins should absorb any liquid released by the apples so that the pie filling is stiff and serves easily.

HEALTHY CHOICE ALTERNATIVE Use my oil-and-water Healthy Choice Alternative Pie Pastry Shell (page 276) for the crust. Notice that this pie filling does not have any butter and relies on the Dried Apple Applesauce for thickening.

Serve this pie warm, topped with Country Whipped Cream or vanilla ice cream and garnished with pecan halves and Dried Apple Applesauce or fresh apple wedges.

Dried Apple Stack Cake

*W*e have stack chairs and stack tables. When it comes to pancakes, you can order a short or a long stack. A stack is also a volume of coal that measures four cubic yards. Here in Appalachia, when coal mines are shut off, they are stacked out. For special stacks there are stack poles, stack guards, stack stands, and stack rooms. If you stack the deck, your opponent may blow his or her stack. Highlanders make two stacked desserts: stack pies and stack cakes.

Fifty years ago, before professionals, hobby cooks, and intellectuals started getting a grip on ethnic foods, mountaineers from New Found and Snowbird in North Carolina to the Yew and Cheat of West Virginia made stack cakes. In addition, cooks from most of West Virginia, western North Carolina, eastern Kentucky, and eastern Tennessee made stack cakes—a specialty of the central Appalachian Highlands.

We make a classic stack cake with a stiff, ginger-flavored, cookie-like dough and a sweet, spiced apple filling. When served, the cake is tall, heavy, and moist. The apple filling oozes between each layer. The top layer usually has nothing on it.

A stack cake is spicy, many layered, lowfat, and not sweet. If there were food families, it would be a first cousin to the apple stack pie and a second cousin to gingerbread. Some say that James Harrod, the colonist and farmer and the founder of Harrodsburg, brought the stack cake to Kentucky. Whether or not that was the case, this cake remained popular because, according to author and historian Sidney Saylor Farr, in a 1983 *Courier-Journal* interview, "Mountain people couldn't afford big, layered wedding cakes. As a substitute, women coming to a wedding each donated layers of cake. . . ." The idea of a cooperative stack cake makes sense when you remember that people here also helped one another with corn shelling, bean stringing, sorghum processing, and barn raising.

While I call this a Dried Apple Stack Cake, others call it a stack cake, apple stack cake, old-fashioned stack cake, Confederates old-fashioned stack cake, Appalachian stack cake, Kentucky's pioneer wash day cake, and a stackcake, spelled as one word. Mountain cooks called it a wash day cake because they made it on Monday and served it on Wednesday, the day they did the wash. Recall that in the old days we did the wash with arm muscles and boards rather than Clorox and Tide. Wash day was a busy day. There was little time for cooking.

From my review of more than twenty stack cake recipes, I know that ginger is its essential spice. Other popular spices include pumpkin pie spice, apple pie spice, cinnamon, cloves, nutmeg, allspice, and vanilla. My Stack Cake recipe, which calls for a total of $3^3/_4$ teaspoons of spices, is fully flavored but not sharp.

DIFFICULTY Very Difficult. This cake combines fifteen ingredients in two parts: a filling and eleven baked layers.

■ ■

Ginger

Ginger was among the first spices to reach southeastern Europe. Gingerbread was baked on the island of Rhodes near Greece in 2400 B.C. Can you imagine working in your kitchen, making a stack cake and knowing that you are carrying on one of the oldest sweet food traditions known to the western world?

The Romans, copying Greek tradition, distributed ginger throughout their empire. They served it with meat because it helped digest food and "loosened the belly."

Ginger is a reedlike plant native to the East Indies and the Pacific Islands. We use the rhizome (underground stem) in cooking. Today, we can buy ginger in four forms: fresh whole, fresh shredded, preserved in sugar, and ground. When we harvest it at about six months, ginger is tender, and we use it to make crystallized ginger—a confection, not a spice.

We use mature, year-old ginger in drinks such as ginger beer and ginger ale. We use ground ginger in mincemeat, ginger snaps, gingerbread, and stack cakes. People in India use it not only in curry powder, but also on meat, fish, rice, and vegetables. The Japanese serve ginger fresh and shredded in clear soups.

Jamaican ginger is often considered to be the finest. Jamaican is a light, buff color. In processing the root, commercial enterprises remove the outer cork layer, leaving clean, hard, and fibrous ginger ready for grinding.

■ ■

Stack cake apples are not just any apples. For some the choice is a question of dried or fresh apples; others choose between applesauce, apple butter, or a mixture of the two. Still others discuss fresh apple varieties—Winesap, Rome Beauty, McIntosh—seeking a tart cooking apple. Based on my experimentation, I prefer dried apples.

The number of layers varies from six to sixteen, with many cooks boasting about their many thin layers. Cooks who pride themselves by making a many-layered stack cake either use seven to eight cups of flour and press the layers by hand, or they cut the amount of flour to three to four cups and add more milk, pouring this runny, pancake-like batter into cake pans. The pancake-type stack cake is fast and easy, but it does not absorb as much apple filling and is not as heavy as one that has more flour. Traditionally, mountain cooks use their fingers to hand press the stiff dough into a number-10 iron skillet. The technique of pressing the dough into thin layers has been the focus of many stack cake lessons. Some mountain cooks feel that a hand-pressed cake is better than a poured one. From my perspective, hand-pressing takes extra time and may result in thicker layers. I make thin layers with a rolling pin.

Years ago, about twenty-five of my students sampled this cake. and their comments were generally polite and complimentary. One woman, however, made an important comment: "This stack cake is not like my grandmother's." I am sure it was not.

Stack cakes are not all the same, and they are not all good. I have eaten stack cakes made with pancake batter and others made with graham crackers and apple butter—these are not old-fashioned. But even these cakes tell us something about the importance of stack cakes: People will take any possible short cut to re-create the stack cake, a prized trophy of mountain cooking.

Because the stack cake is widely distributed and has a long history, there is no exact recipe. The flavor, texture, and look of the cake varies from mountain to mountain and from family to family. What follows will not guarantee that you can make a stack cake like your grandmother's, but it provides specific steps and exact quantities that will get you started. My method uses modern kitchen equipment, and I make the cake in a relatively short time.

STEPS Prepare the apple filling ahead so that it will be cool when you bake the layers. In a large pot, combine the apples, water, and sugar, and bring to a boil. Reduce the heat, and simmer for 30 minutes. (I cook them for 10 minutes in a pressure cooker.) Stir in the cinnamon, nutmeg, and cloves. Use a mixer, food processor, or a potato masher to break up the apples so that they are smooth, like applesauce. Measure out 8 cups. Cool.

Preheat the oven to 350°F. Cut eleven 12-inch pieces of waxed paper or parchment. (I prefer parchment because the parchment does not smoke during baking, and the cake does not stick.)

In a large mixing bowl, whisk together 8 cups of the flour, the baking powder, ginger, nutmeg, allspice, and salt. Make a large well or nest in the center of the flour and pour in the milk, eggs, sugar, and sorghum, and beat until well mixed. Add the butter and continue to beat until fully mixed and smooth. Mixing with your hands, slowly incorporate the flour mixture as you would for bread. When the dough is dry enough to handle, stop adding flour—some may remain in the bowl.

Roll the dough into a log and cut it into ten equal-size parts—1 cup each. Roll the pieces into a ball; if they are sticky, roll them in the remaining 1/4 cup flour.

INGREDIENTS

FOR THE APPLE FILLING
8 cups home-dried (very dry) apples
5 1/2 cups water
1 cup sugar
1/2 teaspoon cinnamon
1/2 teaspoon nutmeg
1/4 teaspoon cloves

FOR THE CAKE
8 1/4 cups all-purpose flour, divided
2 teaspoons baking powder
2 teaspoons ground ginger
1/2 teaspoon nutmeg
1/2 teaspoon allspice
1/2 teaspoon salt
1/2 cup milk
2 eggs
1 cup sugar
1 cup 100% pure sweet sorghum
1 cup unsalted butter, melted

YIELD 24 servings

On a sheet of parchment or waxed paper, press each ball into a flat disk. Using a rolling pin, roll it out as you would a pie crust. Using extra flour as needed to keep the dough from sticking to the rolling pin, roll the dough into a flat disk a little larger than a 9-inch round cake pan. Then press the 9-inch pan into the dough so that the rim cuts the dough into a circle. Save the scraps for an eleventh layer. When you have rolled out and trimmed the layer, slide the paper and layer onto a cookie sheet. Bake for 8 minutes, or until the layer is very brown on the edges and browned across the top. Repeat for each layer.

Remove the layers from the oven and place them on cooling racks or towels. When the layers are cool and you have discarded the baking papers, you are ready to stack the cake.

Assemble the cake: Place the first layer on a cake plate and spread about 3/4 cup of the apple filling over the layer. Repeat this with each of the layers. Do not spread apple filling on the top layer.

Let the cake stand 6 to 12 hours at room temperature. This allows the moisture from the apple filling to soak into the layers. Refrigerate for 12 to 36 hours, or freeze the cake for several months.

TIP If home-dried apples aren't available, use 24 ounces of commercial, soft-dried apples and 6½ cups of water. I sometimes enhance the top of the cake by brushing it with egg white before I refrigerate it (to make it shine) or by dusting it with confectioners' sugar just before serving.

HEALTHY CHOICE ALTERNATIVE For this recipe you use 1 cup of butter and 2 eggs for 8 cups of flour. With 24 servings, each one is low in fat and sugar. A piece of my stack cake usually has less sugar than a bowl of cereal!

Martha Hawkins, who lives on Elkhorn Creek below Pine Mountain between Virginia and Kentucky, likes to eat a piece of stack cake any time of year, and she eats it for breakfast! I do too—I bake a piece of stack cake in my toaster oven, and it comes out smelling like ginger-cinnamon toast with apples. With dried apples or good cooking apples available all year, you can make stack cakes for any occasion. However we usually serve stack cakes for special occasions: birthdays, family reunions, music festivals, heritage fairs, Thanksgiving, Christmas, and Sunday dinner. "At fall festivals, people run to get a stack cake. You can't buy them in a store," says Martha.

Apple Turnovers

While the fried apple pie has a strong mountain tradition, when I bake it, I call it a turnover or rollover. Turnovers may be smaller than fried apple pies. They are about three inches across. Turnovers are usually a factory-baked product available anywhere in this country.

We fill homemade turnovers with fruit butters: apple, peach, plum, or berry. Some use preserves or mincemeat. We also fill turnovers with a mixture of raisins, dates, prunes, nuts, and orange juice.

Perhaps the oldest version of the fried apple pie is the sweet rissole. In 1651, François-Pierre de la Varenne, the cook to King Henri IV of France, described the rissole as a short crust filled with minced meat and deep fried. Today the French make sweet and savory rissoles, using puff pastry that they cut to form a crescent. They fill them, as we might expect, with cooked fruit, pastry cream, or jam.

A German variation of the turnover is the kipfel. To make kipfels, German cooks cut pie or cookie dough (*muerbe teig*) into squares and shape it into triangles or crescents. As with turnovers, they fill the kipfels with chopped fruits, nuts, brown sugar, or jam.

In addition to French rissoles and German kipfels, Italians make savory *calzones*, Latin Americans are fond of their sweet or savory *empanadas*, eastern Europeans treasure their *pierogi*, and Indians boast of their *samosas*. The mountain adaptation of this seemingly universal half-pie combines our most abundant fruit, the apple, with a savory crust.

Fried Apple Pies

*F*ried apple pies are a treasured snack, a Sunday dessert, and a county fair money maker. We call them moon pies, apple turnovers, half-moon pies, and crescent pies. A good fried apple pie has a highly spiced, concentrated "appley" center filling, and a crisp rich crust. This recipe yields pies that are not sweet. If you want to sweeten them, drizzle one recipe of White Frosting (page 316) over the pies after they are cool.

Because we do not make this pie with a flaky crust, fried apple pie dough is rich, sweet, and well kneaded. Some recipes call for evaporated milk, and many use an egg or two. In any case, the dough I recommend is smooth and elastic. Cut it into a circle the size of a coffee saucer. Use a saucer or other small plate as a pattern, placing the saucer on the dough and cutting the circle with a sharp knife.

We cook fried apple pies three ways: deep-fried, fried, and baked. We deep fry in oil at 375°F until the crust is golden brown. If you add too many pies to the fryer at one time, the temperature will go down and cause the dough to become grease-soaked.

We usually pan fry the pies in a heavy skillet with vegetable oil, shortening, or lard. Here, too, the temperature must remain high, 375°F. We fry the pies on both sides until the crust is golden brown, and then place them on a paper towel to drain. I also bake these pies—call them turnovers—on a cookie sheet at 450°F.

INGREDIENTS

FOR THE DRIED APPLE FILLING

2 cups home-dried (very dry) apples, or 6 ounces commercial soft-dried apples
1 2/3 cups water
1/4 cup sugar
1/2 teaspoon cinnamon
1/2 teaspoon allspice

FOR THE DOUGH

2 cups all-purpose flour
2/3 cup butter or lard, softened
(cont.)

STEPS To make the apple filling: In a large pot, combine the dried apples, water, sugar, cinnamon, and allspice, and bring to a boil. Reduce the heat and simmer for 30 minutes. Using a food processor, puree the mixture. Set aside.

To make the dough: In a mixing bowl, combine the flour, butter, and sugar. Using a pastry blender, cut the butter into the flour, and mix in the egg. Mix well and, on a floured surface, knead several minutes until the mixture is fully mixed and forms a cohesive ball.

Roll the dough into a long log, and divide it into eight equal parts. Flour the dough and the rolling surface, and using a light rolling pin(with so little dough, a heavy rolling pin gives uneven results), roll each piece of dough into an 8- or 9-inch round. Add flour as needed to keep the dough from sticking.

Dipping your fingertips into a bowl of water, moisten the edge of the dough, and place 1/4 cup of the apple mixture on one side. Fold the free side over the apple mixture to make a half-moon shape. Even the edges with a knife, and seal by crimping with a fork.

HEARTY
Cooking
COUNTRY

In a large skillet, heat ⅛ inch of oil to 375°F. Fry the pies about 6 minutes on each side, or until you have cooked the dough through. Add oil as needed.

3 tablespoons sugar
1 egg
Oil or lard for frying

TIP Sealed storage makes fried apple pies soggy. If you serve the pies within 3 hours of baking, keep them uncovered on cooling racks at room temperature. If you store them more than a few hours, they need to be freshened up in a hot oven. Bake them for 10 minutes at 350°F.

YIELD 8 servings

HEALTHY CHOICE ALTERNATIVE For Baked Apple Turnovers, skip the frying, and place the turnovers on a cookie sheet. Brush them with melted butter—or skip the butter altogether—and bake them at 450°F for 15 minutes. When they are brown or crispy and the dough is baked through, place them under the broiler for a minute to darken the top crust.

While you may serve fried apple pies hot or cold, they are at their best when you eat them fresh from the frying pan, deep fryer, or oven, sprinkled with powdered or granulated sugar. Tempting as a snack or pick-up food, fried apple pies are also served as a dessert. I like to add a topping, such as Buttermilk Glaze, Lemon Glaze, Sugar Syrup, Country Whipped Cream, White Frosting, or vanilla ice cream.

Highlanders

While you may associate Highlanders with the harsh mountains of northern Scotland or perhaps with Scottish soldiers, many scholars refer to people of the high Appalachian plateau as Highlanders. In that context the term is not a reference to those few people living in the small towns of Highland Springs, Virginia; Highland Heights, Ohio; Highland, Maryland; or Highland Mills, Georgia. Being an Appalachian Highlander is not popular. There is no Highland state and no Highland university. I know of nobody living in these mountains that would say, "I am a Highlander." People don't identify with the Highlands. They identify with their states or their university teams. If they root for the University of West Virginia or Appalachian State University in Boone, North Carolina, they are Mountaineers. If they root for East Tennessee State University in Johnson City, they are Buccaneers. In spite of all this, this pie is a Highlander pie, a pie worth cheering for.

Highlander Double-Crust Apple Pie with Raisins

*F*all in the Central and Southern Highlands is the time for a homemade Highlander apple pie. This double-crust apple pie has a sweet raisin-and-sorghum-flavored filling and a rich flaky crust. Treat your family and friends to the best. When you bake this pie, its aroma tantalizes anyone who is in the house. When you serve it, you'll have an inspiring sensation.

STEPS   To prepare the filling: In a mixing bowl, combine the sugar, flour, cornstarch, cinnamon, and nutmeg. Wash, peel, slice, and dice the apples. Measure out 3½ cups, and add to the dry ingredients. Stir. Set aside.

To prepare the crust: Preheat the oven to 450°F.

In a mixing bowl, whisk together the egg yolk and water. Prepare one recipe of Pie Pastry Shell, and roll the dough as you would for a double-crust pie. Line a 9-inch deep-dish pie pan with one of the rolled crusts. Pour the filling into the pie shell. Spread the raisins and pour the sorghum over the apples. Dot with the butter, and add the top crust. Brush the egg yolk and water mixture on the top crust, and sprinkle with the cinnamon sugar.

Bake the pie at 450°F for 20 minutes. Reduce the heat to 350°F, and bake an additional 40 minutes. Remove the pie from the oven when it bubbles through to the center. Cool for 1 hour.

TIP   If the apples are dry, add 2 tablespoons of milk or cream.

HEALTHY CHOICE ALTERNATIVE   Reduce the sugar to ½ cup. Use my Healthy Choice Pie Crust (page 276).

Serve with vanilla ice cream and a hot drink.

DIFFICULTY Difficult. This common pie is among the most difficult desserts I make—it takes experience to make a flaky top crust and a bottom crust that is flaky and does not leak. It takes practice to get the fruit soft but not runny. Rolling the crusts, transferring them to the baking pan, and joining the two edges—these also present a challenge. For a quick alternative use two Pillsbury Ready Crusts. Using fresh apples and thirteen ingredients, it will take 1 hour to prepare this for baking. It then bakes for 1 hour and needs to cool for another hour.

INGREDIENTS

FOR THE FILLING
1 cup sugar
2 tablespoons all-
  purpose flour
1 tablespoon cornstarch
1 teaspoon cinnamon
¼ teaspoon nutmeg
3 large cooking apples
⅓ cup raisins
⅓ cup sweet sorghum
1 tablespoon butter

FOR THE CRUST
1 egg yolk
1 tablespoon water
1 recipe Pie Pastry
  Shell (page 275)
Cinnamon sugar
YIELD 8 servings

Mountain Nuts

A ready supply of wild nuts has influenced our cooking. Our nut pies, cakes, and cookies are as much a part of our culture as are the walks we take when the leaves change colors in the fall. We preserve our wild nut traditions with fall gatherings and festivals. We use nuts that are available free for the time it takes to pick them up.

Beechnuts

The American Beech tree produces the beechnut used in cooking. The tree is also called the "lovers' tree" because young people carve their initials on the smooth gray bark. Beechnut trees are part of the beech family, a family with about 100 species native to North America, including chestnuts, oaks, chinkapins, and tanoaks. We eat beechnuts raw or cooked, and we use them in any recipe that calls for pecans. They are especially good when substituted for pecans in pecan pie.

Black Walnuts

Black walnut trees grow from New England across the northern states to Minnesota and south from Texas to Florida. In the mountains, they prefer cool damp valleys, but they also grow in the open. The fruit is almost round and has a green husk and a strong, corrugated shell. Black walnut trees produce a sharp, strong-flavored, oily nut. Highlanders who like black walnuts either have a mature palate or they acquired the taste early in life. In this book you'll find them used in the Fresh Apple Cake, Black Walnut Cake, and Black Walnut Sugar Cookies.

Butternuts

Closely related to black walnuts, butternuts—also called oilnuts and white walnuts—do not grow far south of Tennessee. During the fall and early winter we use this rich and oily nut in cakes and cookies, but because of the high oil content it does not store well.

Hickory Nuts

Hickory nuts, most of which are edible, grow on large deciduous trees. Hickories are part of the walnut family and include twenty or more varieties. Many of them grow in the Appalachian Mountains. Hickory nuts—also called yellow walnuts—are prized by Southern cooks as they include pecans, mockernuts, shagbarks, pignuts, and black hickory nuts.

Peanuts

Peanuts are a legume, not a nut. They flower above the ground on a plant similar to peas, but then the flowers bend over and the seeds grow in the ground. Peanuts are also called earth nuts, groundnuts, and goober peas.

Pecans

Pecan trees are pecan hickories, a tree within the walnut family. For a discussion of pecans, see page 254.

Walnuts

The walnut family includes walnuts and hickories. English walnuts, also called Persian, are not native to the Appalachian region.

■ ■

Fresh Apple Cake with Black Walnuts

*S*ummer or winter, this cake is time-tested and popular—delicious, filling, unencumbered, sweet, and nutty, with a texture like a brownie—crunchy on the outside, moist on the inside. Go for it. As we do with prune, carrot, or pumpkin cakes, we make fresh apple cakes with either oil or margarine. Some add cinnamon, allspice, raisins, coconut, and butterscotch chips. You may also vary the cake by reducing the flour by 1 cup and adding 1 cup of rolled oats.

DIFFICULTY Moderate. With ten ingredients and one step, this recipe is moderate in difficulty. The time-consuming parts of making this cake are getting the butter soft and preparing the apples.

■ Desserts

INGREDIENTS

1 cup Country Crock margarine, at room temperature
2 cups sugar
3 eggs
1 teaspoon vanilla
2½ cups all-purpose flour
1 teaspoon baking powder
1 teaspoon baking soda
½ teaspoon salt
2½ cups peeled, cored, and chopped apples
1 cup (½ inch size) black walnut pieces

YIELD 12 servings

STEPS Preheat the oven to 350°F. Grease and flour a 13x9x2-inch baking pan. In a mixing bowl, cream together the margarine and sugar. Add the eggs, one at a time, and stir in the vanilla. Sift together the flour, baking powder, baking soda, and salt, and stir into the butter mixture. The batter will be thick.

Using a rubber spatula, stir in the apples and walnuts. Spread the cake batter into the prepared pan, and bake 45 minutes or until it has browned across the top and a toothpick inserted into the center comes out clean. Cool 30 minutes.

HEALTHY CHOICE ALTERNATIVE Replace the margarine with canola oil. If that is not enough, replace half of the oil with ½ cup applesauce. If salt is a problem, omit it.

My first choice is to serve this cake like I would serve a brownie, without glaze, topping, or ice cream. You can serve it with a generous topping of vanilla ice cream, Hot Sorghum, and black walnuts. Try it with Country Whipped Cream or Buttermilk Glaze.

Pawpaw Cookies with Black Walnuts

DIFFICULTY Moderate. With seven ingredients and one step, this drop cookie is moderate in difficulty.

*P*awpaws are a wild fruit and a member of the custard apple family, *Annonaceae*. Much like a tropical fruit, pawpaws are shaped like overgrown peanuts or bananas, and they taste a bit like mangos. Pawpaws grow on our cool, moist creek banks, and they are widespread, growing throughout the South and in most of the states that touch the Ohio River. Pawpaws grow on a small understory tree, and they ripen in September. They are most flavorful after they soften and the skin turns yellow and has brown spots. Pawpaws are two to five inches in length, and their flavor varies from fruit to fruit—if you taste a pawpaw you don't like, try another one. Pawpaws are like pears in that they do not all taste the same.

Pawpaws have lots of seeds, as many as twenty per fruit. The skin tastes sharp or bitter. The easiest way to remove the peeling is to cut the fruit in half and press the pulpy center through a food mill, leaving the skin and seeds behind.

In developing pawpaw recipes almost thirty years ago, Marilyn Kluger in *The Wild Flavor* offered three rules: Use pawpaws in desserts with a custard base and in recipes that call for bananas. Kluger's third rule is to eat pawpaws raw, as a treat when she gathers them in the woods. With these rules in mind, Kluger goes on to offer recipes for pawpaw chiffon pie, pawpaw cream pie, pawpaw custard ice cream, pawpaw cake, and pawpaw bread. I have a fourth rule: Prepare these dishes in the fall, when the pawpaws are ripe.

Mountain markets that are either yuppie-modern or old-style and tradition-bound sell pawpaws in the fall—native foods are back in style.

STEPS Preheat the oven to 350°F and grease one large cookie sheet.

Peel and seed fresh pawpaws and process in a food processor until fine. Sift together the flour and baking powder, and set aside. In a mixing bowl, cream together the butter and sugar, and add the egg. Stir in the flour mixture, and then add the pawpaw pulp. Chop half the nuts (reserve 16 pieces) and blend them in.

Drop the dough by teaspoonfuls onto the prepared cookie sheet, and press a piece of black walnut onto the top of each cookie. Bake for 12 minutes or until brown across the top.

HEALTHY CHOICE ALTERNATIVE Replace the butter with canola oil, reduce the sugar to 1/4 cup, and omit the chopped black walnuts, using 16 pieces for garnish.

Serve with coffee or milk and softened ice cream.

INGREDIENTS
3/4 cup pawpaw pulp
1 cup all-purpose flour
1/2 teaspoon baking powder
1/4 cup butter
1/2 cup brown sugar
1 egg
1/2 cup black walnuts

YIELD 16 cookies

Shenandoah Valley Banana Bread
Pawpaw Bread

*R*unning northeast between the Allegheny and Blue Ridge Mountains, the Shenandoah River empties into the Potomac River at Harpers Ferry, West Virginia. The river, with its north and south forks, forms the Shenandoah Valley. Farmhouse cooks living in the valley have made a banana bread like this for generations, and cooks living farther south and in the damp valleys of the Ohio River make the bread with pawpaws.

This banana loaf is a quick bread with lots of nuts. Mountain cooks make many breads like this one, adding fresh or dried apples, apricots, blackberries, cranberries, pumpkin, coconut, oatmeal, raisins, and grated zucchini or carrots. We also add spices such as ginger, cinnamon, and nutmeg. I sometimes mix and match the various ingredients, but I prefer pawpaws over anything else. A large recipe, this bread was a coveted prize at basket suppers about fifty years ago. In

DIFFICULTY Moderate. With eight ingredients and two steps, this bread is moderate in difficulty.

place of basket suppers, I put the second loaf in the freezer, or I'll take both loaves to a community affair.

INGREDIENTS

1 cup melted butter
2 cups sugar
4 eggs
2 cups mashed banana
1 tablespoon lemon juice
4 cups sifted all-purpose flour
2 teaspoons baking powder
3 cups pecan pieces plus 16 pecan halves

YIELD 2 loaves or 24 servings

STEPS Preheat the oven to 375°F. Grease two 9x4x2-inch loaf pans.

In a mixing bowl, beat together the butter, sugar, and eggs. Add the mashed bananas and lemon juice, and stir. Sift together the flour and baking powder, and stir them into the batter. Mix in the pecans, and scrape the batter into the prepared pans. Garnish each loaf with 8 pecan halves.

Bake for 1 hour and 15 minutes. The top corners of the loaf will burn, but that adds flavor and character, giving the bread an earthy look. Serve warm.

HEALTHY CHOICE ALTERNATIVE While you will not have the same full-tasting banana bread, you may prefer to make the following: Omit the pecans, or use just 1 cup. Replace the butter with safflower oil. Add 1/2 teaspoon of salt. Replace the egg yolks with an extra 1/2 cup mashed banana. Reduce the sugar to 1 1/2 cups.

Like other quick breads, this banana bread peaks in flavor and texture when we eat it fresh from the oven or when we toast it. I like to spread it with cream cheese and Green Pepper Jelly. I also offer it with Boiled Custard or vanilla ice cream and Hot Sorghum.

Pawpaw Bread In place of the banana, use 2 cups pawpaw pulp.

Pawpaw, Cornmeal, and Hickory Nut Muffins

After a warm rain in the fall of the year, when the creeks rush out of the hollows, I have walked in the woods and gathered pawpaws and hickory nuts. They thrive on the cool north-facing creek banks throughout our region. For this recipe I sometimes substitute bananas for pawpaws, and I may use pecans in place of hickory nuts. Like so many muffin recipes, this goes together quickly, and by modern standards, the ingredients are healthy.

STEPS Wash and peel the pawpaws, and press them through a food mill. Measure out 1 cup of pulp. Assemble and measure your ingredients so you can mix the batter quickly.

Preheat the oven to 400°F. Using nonstick vegetable spray, grease 18 medium (2½-inch or ⅓ cup) muffin cups. (If cornmeal is handy, I sprinkle a little into the bottom of each muffin cup.)

In a large bowl, whisk together the flour, cornmeal, and baking powder. Form a well in the center of the dry ingredients, add the egg, and whisk until well mixed. Whisk in the sorghum, oil, and milk, stirring until they are almost mixed.

Using a rubber spatula, stir in the nuts and raisins. Do not overmix. Pour the batter into the muffin cups, filling each about two-thirds full. Bake for 17 minutes, or until a toothpick inserted into the center comes out clean. The muffins should be crusty on top and brown on the bottom. Cool for 3 minutes on a wire rack, and then lift the muffins from the pan onto a wire rack to cool for another 10 minutes.

HEALTHY CHOICE ALTERNATIVE Replace the milk with nonfat yogurt or evaporated skim milk. Reduce the oil to 2 tablespoons, and use 2 egg whites in place of the whole egg. Omit the nuts.

Enjoy these muffins for a morning snack or a quick lunch. Serve with butter, Pear Honey, and hot tea. I like them with peanut butter, blackberry jam, and cold milk.

DIFFICULTY Moderate. I rate this moderate because the recipe calls for eleven ingredients. Once you have pawpaws and nuts together, mixing and baking are fast.

INGREDIENTS
1 pound ripe pawpaws or ¾ pound ripe bananas
Non-stick vegetable spray
1½ cups all-purpose flour
½ cup white cornmeal
1 tablespoon baking powder
1 egg
⅓ cup 100% pure sweet sorghum
¼ cup oil
1 cup 2% milk
½ cup hickory nuts or pecan pieces
½ cup raisins

YIELD 18 muffins

245

Desserts

Persimmons

PERSIMMONS GROW WILD in dry woodlands, open fields, and fence rows from the Gulf Coast to Connecticut. Unlike the foreign imports, our persimmons have seeds, perhaps ten or twelve pumpkin-size seeds in each small fruit.

Persimmons load the trees throughout the fall and start falling after the first frost. About three weeks later they are at their prime, covering the ground and changing from bitter to sweet and from green to orange. Eat persimmons after a hard frost, about 25°F. When the persimmons have frozen, they are sweet—I like to stand under the tree and enjoy them just like the possums do. Possums around my house jump on the fruit, so if I don't eat it, the possums will.

Like dates, persimmons are sweet. Native Americans dried persimmons, ground the fruit into flour, and baked it in a primitive bread. To separate the pulp from the skin and seeds, cook the fruit and work it through a food mill. I sometimes purchase sweetened canned persimmon pulp from Dymple's Delight, listed in the Mail-Order Sources.

Persimmon Pudding
Pawpaw Pudding

DIFFICULTY Moderate. With eight ingredients, this recipe is moderate in difficulty.

*P*ersimmon pudding is a bit like a brownie, but heavier, more moist, and much sweeter. When I bake this pudding-cake, it rises up, and when it cools, it falls back down. I find persimmon pudding sticky, chewy, and smooth. It reminds me of a heavy date or plum pudding.

To this pudding, we may add the common Christmas spices: cloves, ginger, nutmeg, and allspice. If you have never made persimmon pudding, I suggest that you try it without the spices to get a feel for the flavor of the persimmons and the texture of the pudding. Once you have experimented, add raisins, dates, soft nuts, vanilla, and other spices. If you are adding ingredients, add up to two teaspoons of spices and up to two cups of nuts, raisins, and dates. If you use Dymple's Delight persimmon pulp (see Mail-Order Sources), use two cups and omit the sugar.

HEARTY
Cooking ■
COUNTRY

STEPS Preheat the oven to 350°F. Grease a 13x9x2-inch glass baking dish. In a large mixing bowl, whisk together the sugar, bread flour, baking powder, and cinnamon. Form a well in the center of the dry ingredients, and add the eggs, whisking until fully mixed. Mix in the persimmon pulp, milk, and butter. Pour the batter into the baking dish. Bake for 50 minutes, or until a toothpick inserted into the center of the pudding comes out clean. If you jiggle the pan, the center should be set.

HEALTHY CHOICE ALTERNATIVE Use 2 cups skim milk, omit the butter and use only 1 egg.

Serve this pudding in the late fall, winter, or through the Thanksgiving and Christmas holidays. Cut the pudding into squares, and serve it with vanilla ice cream, Country Whipped Cream, hard sauce, or crème anglaise, to break the sweetness. Sip some hot coffee or drink an espresso coffee after you eat the pudding.

Pawpaw Pudding Replace the persimmon pulp with 2 cups pawpaw pulp.

INGREDIENTS
2 cups sugar
1 1/2 cups bread flour
1 teaspoon baking powder
1/2 teaspoon cinnamon
3 eggs
2 cups fresh persimmon pulp
1 1/2 cups milk
1/2 cup melted butter

YIELD 12 servings

Persimmon Butterscotch Cookies

*T*o make real butterscotch, you cook butter and brown sugar together. This cookie, true to its name, tastes of brown sugar and butter—and persimmons, of course. Not sweet, the cookie needs a little White Frosting.

I adapted this recipe from several persimmon cookie recipes in *Persimmon Recipes* by Dymple Green. While I like to use fresh persimmons, sometimes I use canned pulp from Dymple's (see the Mail-Order Sources). When using Dymple's Delight Persimmon Pulp, I use one cup and omit the sugar.

STEPS In a large pot in enough water to cover, cook 1 pound of fresh persimmons until tender, about 15 minutes. Press the cooked persimmons through a food mill to remove the skin and seeds. Measure out 1 cup pulp.

Preheat the oven to 350°F. Grease three cookie sheets.

In a mixing bowl, cream together the butter and sugar. Beat in the egg and persimmon pulp. In a second bowl, whisk together the flour, baking powder, and cinnamon, and stir them into the wet ingredients. Stir in the butterscotch pieces.

DIFFICULTY Moderate. With eight ingredients and two steps, this drop cookie is moderate in difficulty.

INGREDIENTS
1 pound fresh persimmons
1/2 cup softened butter
1 cup brown sugar
1 egg
2 cups all-purpose flour
1 teaspoon baking powder
1/2 teaspoon cinnamon
1 cup butterscotch pieces

YIELD 24 (3-inch) cookies

Drop the dough by soup-spoonfuls onto the cookie sheets. Bake for 12 minutes, or until brown across the top. Cool. Drizzle with the White Frosting.

HEALTHY CHOICE ALTERNATIVE As cookies go, most are a lot richer and sweeter than these. Treat yourself!

Persimmon Pudding-Cake

DIFFICULTY Moderate. With nine ingredients, I rate this no-topping-needed cake moderate in difficulty.

INGREDIENTS
1 cup all-purpose flour
1 teaspoon baking powder
1/2 teaspoon cinnamon
1/2 teaspoon ground nutmeg
1 cup milk
1 cup persimmon pulp
1 cup sugar
3 eggs
1/2 cup melted butter

YIELD 9 squares or 9 servings

This dessert—neither a cake nor a pudding, but rather a bit of both—has a wonderful persimmon flavor. Select persimmons that have been sweetened by a hard frost.

STEPS Place the rack in the center of the oven. Preheat the oven to 350°F. Grease and flour an 8x8x2-inch baking pan.

In a mixing bowl, combine the flour and baking powder. Add the cinnamon and nutmeg, and stir. Set aside.

In a second bowl, combine the milk, persimmon pulp, sugar, eggs, and butter. Stir into the dry ingredients until fully mixed. Pour into the prepared pan. Bake for 40 minutes, or until a toothpick inserted into the center comes out clean. Cut into 9 squares, and serve.

HEALTHY CHOICE ALTERNATIVE Use skim milk and omit 1 egg yolk. To reduce cholesterol even further, replace the butter with safflower or canola oil.

Serve this dessert warm with a dollop of cold Country Whipped Cream.

HEARTY
Cooking
COUNTRY

Sassafras

NOT LONG AGO we had a bad winter storm, and a heavy snow uprooted a sassafras tree. I was in luck—I cut the exposed roots for sassafras tea. When I don't have such a storm, I have to dig and cut the roots or I buy sassafras tea concentrate. Sassafras roots are most potent when you dig and cut them during the winter, after the sap has gone down in the fall and before it comes up in the spring.

Years ago when I first started cooking mountain foods, two good friends came to our house to play bridge. They brought us a gift: sassafras roots. The three large sassafras roots were fresh, partly debarked, and tied with a red ribbon. We removed the ribbon, popped the roots into a pot of boiling water, boiled them for ten minutes, and spent the evening playing bridge and drinking tea.

Years later, after drinking sassafras tea all my life, I researched the topic. I read that sassafras was poisonous. At first I could not believe what I read. Then in disbelief, I laughed out loud. As a boy I had sucked on the roots. I have used filé powder—ground sassafras leaves—in gumbo. How could I account for the conflict between my experience and what I had just read? Is sassafras some kind of carcinogen?

I called the U.S. Food and Drug Administration (FDA). I put my feet back on the ground and stopped laughing. From several sources I learned that large amounts of the safrole, contained in sassafras oil (the oil is found in sassafras bark), caused liver cancer in rodents, and was banned by the FDA, as per the *Federal Register*, December 3, 1960 (Vol. 25, page 12,412).

Safrole is no longer contained in root beer or Pappy's Sassafras Concentrate Instant Tea. Because of the FDA ruling, I cannot recommend that you make sassafras tea, candy, jelly, or cake using wild sassafras root bark. However, my experience and the talk of many mountaineers suggest otherwise.

Don Nordhaus, owner of H & K Products and the manufacturer of Pappy's Sassafras Concentrate Instant Tea, says that his company makes their tea from select heavy outside bark and the cambrian layer of sassafras roots. They process the concentrate to remove the safrole, following FDA guidelines.

Mountaineers have used sassafras in cakes, syrups, candies, and puddings, and you can continue the tradition. To make sassafras syrup, cook pectin and sugar with strong tea. As to candy, add strong tea to sugar, and boil it until it reaches the hard crack stage. Then break it up and enjoy the flavor

For a Mail-Order Source, see H & K Products..

Blue Ridge Sassafras Tea

DIFFICULTY Very Easy. Boil sassafras roots in water.

As I drive down the Skyline Drive and then the Blue Ridge Parkway, from Front Royal, Virginia, to Asheville, North Carolina, I find small communities and individual mountaineers who still treasure their sassafras tea. I delight in these drives as they twist their way up, down, and through the heart of the Blue Ridge.

The Blue Ridge Mountains with their damp and rugged valleys have been a major force in shaping the culture of the region, isolating mountaineers, creating small farms, and supporting lush growth, often much like a tropical rain forest.

Mountaineers have used sassafras, maple, spicebush, and sweet birch teas as beverages and tonics. In the early history of this country colonists exported sassafras wood, bark, and roots to England where the English used them to make tonics. Colonists believed that strong sassafras tea or tonic cured fevers, stomach ulcers, skin rashes, rheumatism, syphilis, dysentery, and gout. Sassafras tonic was popular as an antispasmodic, stimulant, and blood thinner. According to the book *Foxfire 2*, some mountaineers of northeast Georgia had a saying: "Drink sassafras during the month of March and you won't need a doctor all year."

Delicate and pinkish-brown in color, this tea tastes a little like root beer. To make sassafras tea today you can risk the FDA ruling and gather roots from the mountains, or play it safe and buy Pappy's Sassafras Concentrate Instant Tea (see H & K Products in the Mail-Order Sources).

INGREDIENTS
5 cups water
2 sassafras roots
(4 to 5 inches long
and 3/4 inch in
diameter) without the
bark

YIELD 5 cups

STEPS   In a large pot or teapot, boil the water and add the roots. Simmer for 10 minutes. Remove the roots and save them for another batch of tea. Flavor with sugar, sorghum, or lemon. Serve hot or cold.

HEALTHY CHOICE ALTERNATIVE   While Native Americans, white settlers, and mountaineers drank sassafras tea that contained safrole for hundreds and thousands of years, and while they believed that it led to good health, I have no basis on which to disagree with the FDA ruling on safrole. For your safety use Pappy's Sassafras Concentrate Instant Tea. This tea is safrole- and caffeine-free, and has just 1 calorie per cup.

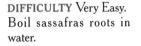

Sassafras Custard Pudding

*T*his pudding is a custard with a touch of sassafras. The quarter cup added to this custard gives more smell than taste. Order Pappy's Sassafras Instant Tea from H & K Products (listed in the Mail-Order Sources).

STEPS Select five 4-ounce custard cups. Preheat the oven to 325°F. Prepare a water bath large enough to hold the custard cups, boil 2 quarts of water, and cover the bottom of the pan with a dishcloth.

In a medium bowl, combine the milk, eggs, sugar, and tea until smooth and fully blended. Divide the mixture among the custard cups. Place the cups on the cloth and pour the hot water in the pan, bringing the water two-thirds up the side of the custard cups.

Bake for 50 minutes, or until a knife inserted near the center comes out clean. Do not allow the water bath to boil during baking. Remove from the oven just before the custard is set in the center. The custard will continue to cook as it cools. Refrigerate, and serve cold.

HEALTHY CHOICE ALTERNATIVE Use 2% or skim milk and 4 egg whites in place of the 3 eggs. Add 1/2 teaspoon vanilla. Bake for 1 hour 10 minutes. This fat-free custard has the same smoothness, but is softer and more jiggly.

DIFFICULTY Easy. With four ingredients and slow baking, this recipe is easy to prepare.

INGREDIENTS
2 cups milk
3 eggs
1/3 cup sugar
1/4 Pappy's Sassafras
 Instant Tea

YIELD 5 servings

Sassafras Apple Syrup

*W*hile the old cookbooks use sugar or honey and long cooking times to thicken this syrup, I have opted for pectin, which is fast. I usually avoid commercial pectins because they result in a product that is less concentrated, but when you are using tea concentrate, you can increase or decrease the apple juice to tea ratio to get the flavor you want. For this recipe I am generous with the tea, and still you'll find this syrup to be mild in flavor, soft rather than stiff, and with just a touch of apple.

STEPS In a large saucepan, heat the tea and apple juice, and stir in the sugar. Stirring occasionally, bring the mixture to a full rolling boil. Stir in the pectin, and boil for 1 minute.

Remove from the heat. With a large spoon, skim the foam, lifting off the bubbles. Pour into a serving dish. Cool.

DIFFICULTY Easy. With four ingredients and 10 minutes of cooking, this recipe is moderate in difficulty.

INGREDIENTS
1/2 cup Pappy's
 Sassafras Instant Tea
 Concentrate
1/2 cup apple juice
1 3/4 cups sugar
1 1/2 ounces Certo Fruit
 Pectin

YIELD 2 cups

HEALTHY CHOICE ALTERNATIVE If you pour this syrup on pancakes in place of butter or peanut butter, you save both fat grams and calories.

Served in a clear glass pitcher, the syrup is a beautiful amber color. Use as you would any syrup over biscuits, pancakes, or waffles.

Sassafras Apple Butter
Sassafras-Caramel Granola Cookie Dessert

*H*ere I combine sassafras tea and dried apples to make a sweet sassafras topping.

DIFFICULTY Easy. With four ingredients and one cooking step, this recipe is easy to prepare.

INGREDIENTS
2 cups dried apples
1 cup Pappy's Sassafras
   Tea Concentrate
3/4 cup water
3/4 cup sugar

YIELD 2 cups

STEPS In a large saucepan, boil the dried apples, tea, and water for 25 minutes (or pressure cook for 8 minutes). In a food processor, process the apples and about a third of the liquid until the apples are broken up. (You want some pieces of apple to be coarse like grains of rice.) Stir in the remaining liquid and the sugar, cool, and serve.

HEALTHY CHOICE ALTERNATIVE This apple butter is a healthy sweetener.

Serve this as a garnish for Potato Cakes, Bean Cakes, Country-Fried Steak, or Pork Barbecue. Use as a dip for graham crackers or potato chips. Spread the butter on bread or biscuits over cream cheese or peanut butter.

Sassafras-Caramel Granola Cookie Dessert Place a Chocolate Chip Granola Cookie (page 289) in a small fruit bowl. Put a heaping tablespoonful of Sassafras Apple Butter on one side and cream caramels on the other side. Microwave each serving on high for 45 seconds. Top with a dollop of Country Whipped Cream (page 316) or vanilla ice cream.

HEARTY
Cooking
COUNTRY

Sassafras Hard Rock Candy
Cinnamon Hard Rock Candy

*T*he fact that mountaineers have long made hard rock candy with sassafras was documented in the book *Foxfire 2*. The directions are brief, but editor Eliot Wigginton and his students instruct us to "grate sassafras bark, boil, strain, and pour into boiling sugar; then let harden and break into small pieces."

DIFFICULTY Easy. With three ingredients and one cooking step, this brittle is easy to prepare.

STEPS Lightly grease an 11x7x2-inch baking tin or a large cookie sheet.

Pour and stir the sugar, tea, and syrup into a very large microwave-safe container. Stir until fully mixed. Microwave the mixture on high for 7 minutes (or cook on the stovetop until it reaches 295°F). It should begin to get darker in color. Cooking takes 7 minutes in a 1.2 cubic foot, 900-watt microwave oven.

Spread the candy onto the prepared pan. The mixture is hot, so be careful.

Cool on a rack for 30 minutes. Remove from pan and break into irregular 1- to 2-inch pieces. Store in an airtight container.

This candy is heritage dinner, family reunion, or country fair food. Serve it in a clear, covered candy dish on a coffee table.

INGREDIENTS
1 cup sugar
3 tablespoons Pappy's Sassafras Instant Tea Concentrate
3 tablespoons corn syrup

YIELD $^1/_2$ pound or 24 pieces

Cinnamon Hard Rock Candy Replace the sassafras with 1 bottle (0.8 fluid ounce) of cinnamon oil and add 3 drops red food coloring. Dust with confectioners' sugar.

Pecans

WE EAT PECANS out of hand—plain, salted, spiced, sweetened, and covered with chocolate. Cooked in candy, cakes, pies, puddings, breads, buns, salads and stuffing, pecans are the premier, native Southern nut, one that European visitors often take home after a visit in the South.

The name pecan is derived from *pakan*, a word used by Native Americans. Prior to cultivation, pecan trees, a member of the hickory family, grew west of the Mississippi and south into Mexico. Two hundred years ago Thomas Jefferson, farming at Monticello, Virginia, was among the first to cultivate pecans, and he allegedly helped George Washington get them started at Mount Vernon. Today, Dougherty County, Georgia, boasts the cultivation of 250,000 pecan trees, more than any other county in the United States.

While pecan trees grow in open fields and on fence lines as far north as Kentucky and West Virginia, they prefer the slightly warmer climate of the southern Appalachian Mountains and the coastal plains. The trees thrive in shady, low, damp areas. In the upper reaches of the mountains and in my hometown of Pikeville, Kentucky, pecans do not come off the trees until December, and it takes a strong January wind to bring the last ones down.

Because of their high fat content, pecans have a short shelf life, lasting as little as two months if kept shelled on a kitchen shelf. In the shell they will keep for months, and in the freezer they will be good for years. Fresh pecans smell and taste good, and when they spoil, they turn rancid and smell or taste sharp and strong.

North Carolina Roasted Pecans
Roasted Butternuts

*B*rittle, crunchy, tender, salty, complex—all these describe North Carolina Roasted Pecans. They are a little like potato chips, but better. As fall progresses slowly through September and October, I cannot wait for fresh pecans to appear in our markets. But wait I must. I buy new-season pecans in November, and then, back from the market, I'll turn on the oven, get out the skillet, and roast these temptations. The low roasting temperature in this recipe crisps the pecans through to the center.

STEPS Preheat the oven to 225°F. In a large cast-iron skillet over medium heat, melt the butter. Add and blend in the Worcestershire sauce, lemon pepper, and garlic salt. Add the pecans, and stir until coated. Place the skillet in the oven, and bake for 1 hour or longer. Bake until the nuts are brown and crisp through to the center. Baking time depends on the size of the pecans.

HEALTHY CHOICE ALTERNATIVE If your pecans measure 60 per cup, ten pecans contain 120 calories and 12.5 grams of fat. With a glass of carbonated water, five to ten of these pecans are not a high-calorie or high-fat snack.

Serve these as an appetizer or party snack with a glass of ice-cold carbonated water, or for a hog-wild rich event, serve with a glass of Boiled Custard.

Roasted Butternuts Substitute butternuts for the pecans, but reduce the baking time to 30 minutes.

DIFFICULTY Easy. With five ingredients and one step, this recipe is easy.

INGREDIENTS
2 tablespoons butter
2 teaspoons Worcestershire sauce
1 teaspoon lemon pepper
1 teaspoon garlic salt
2 cups pecan halves

YIELD 2 cups or 18 servings

Pecan Fudge-Nuts
(Chocolate Roasted Pecans)

I suggest making this snack—this confection I call Chocolate Roasted Pecans—in the late fall and winter months when the weather is dry and the pecans are fresh.

STEPS In a bowl, cover the pecans with hot tap water. In a mixing bowl, combine the chocolate powder, confectioners' sugar, and cocoa. Drain the pecans

DIFFICULTY Easy. With five ingredients and one step, this recipe is easy.

INGREDIENTS
1 3/4 cups pecan halves
Water
1/4 cup instant chocolate
  milk powder
2 tablespoons confec-
  tioners' sugar
1/2 teaspoon cocoa

YIELD 1 3/4 cups or
12 snack servings

and stir them into the dry ingredients. When the nuts are fully coated, pour them on a cookie sheet with sides. Bake at 225°F for 1 hour, or until the nuts are brown through the center. Cool and serve. Store in an airtight container.

Dry-Roasted Pecans
Sugared Pecans and Spicy Orange-Sugared Pecans
(Pecan Delights and Candied Pecans)

*I*n this recipe I first make the Dry-Roasted Pecans. I then coat the nuts with sugar, cinnamon, and orange, keeping the flavors mild and allowing the toasted pecans to dominate. Roasting pecans enhances their flavor and texture and serving the two recipes together is complementary.

DIFFICULTY Easy.
With four ingredients and a sugar syrup that is not sensitive to cooking temperature, this candy is easy to make.

STEPS Prepare Dry-Roasted Pecans: Spread the pecans on a jelly roll pan and bake at 225°F for 1 to 1 1/2 hours, depending on the size of the pecans. Bake until the pecans are crisp through to the center. The center will turn from white to amber and the outside will darken. You don't need to preheat the oven.

INGREDIENTS
1 1/4 cups pecan halves
1 cup sugar
1/4 cup orange juice
1/4 teaspoon cinnamon

Sugared Pecans In a saucepan, combine the sugar, orange juice, and cinnamon. Bring to a boil, stir again, and simmer for 5 minutes, or until the syrup forms a soft ball when dripped into cold water. (We call this the soft ball stage—240°F on a candy thermometer.)

YIELD 30 pieces, 1/2 pound, or about 2 1/2 cups of candy

Remove from the heat, and stir in the pecans. Let the mixture cool for about 4 minutes or place it in a bath of ice or in cold water. Stir this as much as you want, but when the candy gets cool, it will start to crystallize or sugar. Continue stirring, perhaps another 4 minutes, until the candy is dry and forms a mass. Turn the mass back onto the jelly roll pan, and use two forks to separate the pecans into pieces of candy. I like pieces with 2 or 3 pecans and measuring about 1 inch across.

Store in an airtight container. If your candy softens or absorbs humidity, bake it in a cool oven, about 200°F, for 1 hour.

HEALTHY CHOICE ALTERNATIVE The whole recipe contains 1,701 calories and 191 grams of fat. At 30 pieces per batch, 1 piece contains about 57 calories and 3 grams of fat.

Serve these as candy or a snack. Serve after a candlelight dinner with Hot Tea or Mulled Cider. I associate Sugared Pecans with the holiday season from Thanksgiving to New Year's.

Spicy Orange-Sugared Pecans Add spices to the above recipe, increasing the cinnamon to ³/₄ teaspoon and adding ¹/₄ teaspoon ground ginger and 1 tablespoon grated orange zest.

■ ■

Sugared Pecans

I started out calling these orange-glazed pecans, but after thinking it over, I knew that using the word glazed was wrong. When you glaze nuts, flowers, or fruits, you coat them with a thin layer of clear sugar that you have cooked to the hard crack stage, about 300°F. For sugared pecans you don't cook the sugar that much, only to the soft ball stage, about 240°F, and when the candy is ready, the sugar is opaque, not clear. I changed the name to Sugared Pecans.

Sugared pecans are a candy or confection made by coating pecans with a thick layer of sugar. The Pennsylvania Dutch make sugared almonds and in Georgia you can buy sugared peanuts, but here in the mountains we make sugared pecans.

Sugared pecans are soft and tender. Unlike hard candy, they are easy to chew.

The key to making sugared pecans is to stir the hot cooked sugar syrup so that it crystallizes—it forms an opaque, sugary-looking mass, with white dry crystal-like surfaces. The timing of this stirring is so different from fudge. Fudge, as you know, is a smooth, soft candy we also cook to the soft ball stage. But for fudge if you stir it at the wrong time, you'll get crystals—grainy fudge. For these Sugared Pecans you want the crystals, and you can stir whenever you want: at the beginning, in the middle, and at the end.

You can make sugared pecans with water or other liquid such as orange juice, or you can wet the sugar with dairy products such as milk, cream, buttermilk, or sour cream. I find that the richness of the dairy products in this candy detracts from the pecan flavor I like to emphasize.

The simplest sugared pecan recipe calls for 2 cups sugar, $\frac{1}{2}$ cup water, and 2 cups pecans. Other recipes emphasize spices and include flavorings such as salt, nutmeg, cloves, and vanilla.

■ ■

Pecan Pie
Black Walnut Pie (Homecoming Pecan Pie)

DIFFICULTY Difficult. With ten ingredients and two crusts to roll, this recipe is difficult to prepare. If you buy the pie crusts, you'll cut the steps in half.

I dream about this pie. The combination of savory crust, sweet filling, and crunchy nuts has excited Southerners for sixty years. I make this pie when I want some sweet, down-home, old-fashioned mountain goodness. Pecan pies are not an old Southern dish. In spite of their relatively recent appearance on the scene, people from other parts of the United States consider pecan pie to be a most Southern dessert. What follows is a mountain variation. Thanks, Yvonne Lockhart, of Winn's Branch at Meta, Kentucky, for sharing this recipe.

This recipe yields two pies. For a homecoming I make four. Pecan pie is so popular I hate to make just one. Two pies disappear quickly, and if they don't get eaten, I freeze what is leftover. My instructions are a bit detailed, but they guide you to use your food processor to make a light and flaky pie crust—one you'll be proud to serve. If you want other directions, use my Pie Pastry Shell recipe or any other pie shell.

Why a food processor? The food processor's cutting blade cuts and mixes the dough quickly, keeping your hands clean, the shortening cold, and the crust flaky.

STEPS Select two 9-inch pie tins and chill them in the refrigerator. Preheat the oven to 350°F. Get out your waxed paper, rolling pin, pastry cloth, or crust mold—whatever you use to roll the dough.

Place $\frac{1}{2}$ cup of water in $\frac{1}{2}$ cup of ice and set aside. In a food processor fitted

HEARTY
Cooking
COUNTRY

■ ■

with a cutting blade, combine the flour and salt, and pulse on and off to mix. In tablespoon-size pieces, add the Crisco. Process in 3-second pulses until the flour and shortening are barely combined. Add the ice water, and process again for 2 or 3 seconds until you can form the dough into a cohesive mass. If the dough does not hold together, add water and process briefly. Remove the dough, and form it into two flat cakes.

Roll out two crusts using waxed paper and a rolling pin. Place the crusts in the cold pie tins, and flute the edges. Spray the crusts with a thin layer of non-stick cooking spray. Cover and refrigerate as you prepare the filling.

To prepare the filling: In a large bowl, beat the eggs and add the sugar, corn syrup, butter, and vanilla. Stir until fully mixed, and add the pecans. Pour the mixture into the pie shells. Bake for 55 minutes, or until raised in the center, brown across the top, and firm when jiggled.

TIP This pie freezes for six months. To defrost, remove from the freezer and let the pie stand on a cooling rack for 5 hours. An hour before serving time, bake at 350°F for 20 minutes.

HEALTHY CHOICE ALTERNATIVE This pie is rich and high in calories. If you are watching calories, eat a tiny piece. In addition, I think the pies are still very special when I make them with 3 cups of pecans.

Serve this pie after a meal of Mustard Greens and Roast Chicken, or offer it as part of a celebration dinner. Serve fresh and warm from the oven with vanilla ice cream and coffee.

Black Walnut Pie
In place of the 4 cups pecan pieces, use 2 cups black walnut pieces.

INGREDIENTS

FOR THE PIE CRUST

$2^2/_3$ cups all-purpose flour
1 teaspoon salt
1 cup cold—frozen is better—Crisco shortening
6 tablespoons ice water

FOR THE FILLING

6 eggs
2 cups sugar
2 cups light corn syrup
$^1/_2$ cup melted butter
1 tablespoon vanilla
4 cups pecan pieces

YIELD 2 pies and 20 servings

Pecan Shortbread

INGREDIENTS
1 cup pecan pieces
2 cups unsalted butter,
  softened
1 cup sugar
$^1/_2$ teaspoon salt
$4^1/_4$ cups all-purpose
  flour

YIELD 70 cookies

ay it with tulips, say it with chocolates, say it with poetry—the words "I love you" are in style. For your valentine, or for your love any day of the year, take a moment to bake this shortbread. When the pan of bars is fully baked and still warm, cut hearts instead of rectangles. At Easter cut rabbits, and at Christmas cut stars.

STEPS Preheat the oven to 325°F. Using a food processor, process the nuts until they resemble coarse sand. Set aside.

Using a mixer, cream the butter, sugar, and salt until they turn white, light, and fluffy. Scrape the sides of the bowl as needed. Stir in the nuts, and sift in the flour, stirring it in with a plastic scraper. Mix as little as possible.

Spoon the dough into an ungreased $10^1/_2$x$15^1/_2$-inch baking pan. Spread and smooth out the dough. It will not change shape when it bakes, so after covering the dough with waxed paper, level it with a spatula or roll it level with a can of cold soda. Remove the paper.

Bake for 40 to 45 minutes or until lightly brown. Cool for 10 minutes. Slice it into 70 pieces: Make fourteen long cuts (these cuts are $15^1/_2$ inches long) down the pan and five across (these cuts are $10^1/_2$ inches long). Cool in the pan another 30 minutes.

HEALTHY CHOICE ALTERNATIVE If I changed this cookie, I would not have the same unique flavor. Very special, each cookie has 96 calories and 6.4 grams of fat.

Serve these with coffee and vanilla ice cream, or as a snack with North Carolina Roasted Pecans or Pecan Fudge-Nuts.

Homecomings

When mountain families gather, we may call the event a homecoming. The house may be old or new, big or small, in a city or on a small creek, but the kitchen fills up with food, and the house fills up with family. Each family brings something special, and Homecoming Pecan Pie is sometimes the most special of all.

A family homecoming includes distant relatives. A church homecoming includes people from many states. We gather for funerals, Thanksgiving, and community festivals. Always we have homecomings, and when the tables are loaded with food, songs sung, basketball played, cards dealt, tales told, and blessings said, the children start through the line. Surely they look for a pecan pie.

We come home to the family church or the family homeplace. In either case we line up long folding tables, cover them with white tablecloths, and arrange the food, starting with meats and ending with desserts. We appreciate any home-prepared dish, but we have some traditional favorites:

Fall

Corn Relish, Pickled Beets, Chicken and Dumplings,
Southern Fried Chicken, Soup Beans, Cabbage Stew,
Sweet Potato Casserole, Buttermilk Corn Bread, Pumpkin Roll,
Pecan Pie, Dried Apple Stack Cake, Popcorn Balls

Winter

Pig's Feet and Broth, Buttermilk Biscuits and Country Ham,
Squirrel Gravy and Biscuits, Venison Chili, Broccoli Casserole,
Shuck Beans, Scalloped Potatoes, Sorghum Pie,
Dirt Pudding Delight, Scotch Shortbread, Coffee, and Hot Cocoa

Spring

Rabbit with Sausage Gravy, Pork Roast with Stuffed Apples,
Poke Greens with Spinach, Fried Morels, Wilted Lettuce,
Highlander Rolls, Angel Food Cake with Strawberry Cream,
Forgotten Kisses, Persimmon Pudding or Persimmon Pudding-
Cake, Bourbon Balls

Summer

Corn Pone Hamburger Pie,
Barbecued Baby Back Ribs, Tomato Dumplings, Broccoli
Casserole, Corn on the Cob, Scalloped Turnips, Twice-Baked
Potatoes, Skillet Corn Bread, Sorghum Pecan Pie Bars,
Jam Cake, Forgotten Kisses

Nine

More Desserts

Cakes, Pies, Cookies, and Candy

Black Walnut Cake *(Coal Camp Cake)*

Holiday Pumpkin Roll

Prune Cake

Angel Food Cake

Pumpkin Layer Cake

Jam Cake *(John L. Lewis Jam Cake)*

Savage Mountain Pound Cake

Pie Pastry Shell
Double-Crust Pie Shell and Healthy Choice Pie Crust

Peanut Butter Pie *Vanilla Cream Pie, Banana Cream Pie, Coconut Cream Pie, Chocolate Cream Pie, and Chocolate Peanut Butter Cream Pie*

Peach Pie

Buttermilk Pie

Chocolate Pecan Pie

Hawksbill Chess Pie

Black Walnut Sugar Cookies

Forgotten Kisses

Scotch Shortbread

Apricot Unbeatables

Dried-Apple Chocolate Chip Cookies

Christmas Rocks *(Fruitcake Cookies)*

Chocolate Chip Granola Cookies
Chocolate Chip Granola Bars (Appalachian Trail Cookies)

Cream Pull Candy *(Marble Top Candy)*

Potato Candy

Peanut Butter Divinity Pinwheel Candy
(Peanut Butter Rolls)

Chocolate Coating

Buck-Eyes *Peanut Butter Log*

Bourbon Balls

Mount Mitchell Popcorn Balls *Sorghum Popcorn Balls*

Peanut Popcorn Candy

Black Walnut Cake

(Coal Camp Cake)

*B*lack walnut trees grow wild throughout the East. When they produce, we have an abundance of nuts. Most go to the squirrels, but those who know this nut gather them up. English walnuts, on the other hand, are not a native nut, and they taste different from black walnuts, which are sharper, more flavorful, softer, and less crunchy. If you are replacing English walnuts with black walnuts, use about half the amount.

Cracking black walnuts is difficult. First, the hull gives off a dark stain, and then the shells are as hard as stone. You can buy a special nut cracker, or knock them with a hammer against a concrete slab.

Thanks to some sensitive homemakers living in the Southern Highlands, we have preserved this buttermilk and butter cake for seventy-five years. I got the recipe from a good friend, Margie Dixon Adkins, who grew up in a camp house at Wheelwright, Kentucky. Margie and her family have made this cake using a similar recipe for more than fifty years, and yes, they use a lot of raisins and black walnuts.

DIFFICULTY Moderate. With nine ingredients and one baking step, this cake is moderate in difficulty.

INGREDIENTS
6 ounces (³/4 cup) raisins
6 ounces(1 ¹/4 cups) black walnuts
1 cup plus 3 tablespoons all-purpose flour
¹/2 teaspoon baking soda
¹/3 cup melted butter
³/4 cup sugar
2 eggs
¹/3 cup buttermilk
1 teaspoon vanilla

YIELD 10 servings

STEPS Preheat the oven to 325°F. Grease and flour a 9x4x2-inch loaf pan. In a bowl, dredge the raisins and nuts in the flour and baking soda.

In a second bowl, whisk together the butter and sugar. Add the eggs one at a time. Whisk in the flour mixture, buttermilk, and vanilla. Pour into the loaf pan, and bake for 1 hour and 5 minutes, or until a toothpick inserted into the center comes out clean.

The cake keeps well and may be wrapped in a brandy- or grape juice-soaked cheesecloth.

HEALTHY CHOICE ALTERNATIVE Use canola oil in place of the butter, and omit 1 egg yolk.

Fresh from the oven, the outside crust is crusty—the way I like it. Offer this on a Christmas holiday buffet as an alternative to fruitcake, and top each slice with vanilla ice cream or Buttermilk Glaze. This cake is an excellent choice for a Christmas bazaar or bake sale.

HEARTY Cooking COUNTRY ■

Fall Menu

When the family drives up the hollow to the old home place for the last warm-season gathering of fall, we serve pumpkin rolls, black walnut cakes, sugar cookies, and persimmon puddings. We make cream pies, vegetable soups, chicken casseroles, sorghum biscuits, mashed potatoes, and loaf breads. We serve caramel apples, fried apples, and popcorn balls. A favorite dessert is this Pumpkin Roll.

Holiday Pumpkin Roll

*W*ith this dessert we celebrate fall, Halloween, and Thanksgiving. The cake's colors reflect the colors on our hills. Enjoying the long fall season, mountaineers decorate their front yards with ghosts, pumpkins, cornstalks, and witches. They pull pranks, play spooky music, and create haunted houses.

I make a pumpkin roll, like a jelly roll or an ice cream roll, with a sponge cake recipe. When the cake is cool, I roll it with a white filling and it looks like potato candy or pinwheel cookies. The completed pumpkin roll will be an orange-brownish color, dotted with nuts, and shaped like a long cylinder.

STEPS Allow the cream cheese and butter to come to room temperature. Place the oven rack in the bottom quarter of the oven. Preheat the oven to 375°F. Grease a 17x12-inch jelly roll pan, line the pan with parchment or waxed paper, and grease and flour the paper.

To prepare the cake: Mix the flour and baking powder and set aside. In a medium mixing bowl, whisk the eggs and add the sugar. Add the pumpkin and cinnamon and whisk them in. Add the flour mixture, whisking until fully mixed.

Using a rubber scraper, pour and spread this mixture into the jelly roll pan. Sprinkle the pecan pieces evenly across the top, and bake for 15 minutes, or until the edges are slightly browned. Remove from the oven and cool on a wire rack for 10 minutes.

As the cake is cooling, use a strainer to spread a thin layer of confectioners' sugar on a clean dishcloth. The area covered by the confectioners' sugar should be a little larger than the jelly roll pan. Turn the cake onto the dishcloth, and tug

DIFFICULTY Difficult. With twelve ingredients and two steps, this cake is difficult. Start making it early in the day, or make it a day ahead.

INGREDIENTS

FOR THE CAKE
3/4 cup self-rising flour
1 teaspoon baking
  powder
3 eggs
1 cup sugar
3/4 cup canned pumpkin
2 teaspoons cinnamon
1 cup pecan pieces
1/2 cup confectioners'
  sugar
(cont.)

**More
Desserts**

FOR THE CREAM CHEESE
FILLING
1 cup (8 ounces) cream
cheese
1/2 cup butter
1 teaspoon vanilla or
butternut flavoring
1 cup confectioners'
sugar
15 pieces corn candy or
mallow pumpkins

YIELD 15 small servings

at the waxed paper to loosen the cake from the pan. Remove the waxed paper and, starting on the long edge of the cake, roll up the cake with the dishcloth inside it. Return the rolled cake to the wire rack and allow it to cool fully, 1 hour or more.

When the cake is cool, prepare the filling. In a small mixing bowl, combine the cream cheese, butter, and vanilla, and stir in the sugar until smooth. Unroll the cake and spread the filling, reserving about 3 tablespoons. Roll the cake again, and use 1½ tablespoons of the reserved filling to fill in the ends of the cake. With the remaining 1½ tablespoons filling, dab 15 spots in a line across the top of the pumpkin roll. Place a mallow pumpkin candy in the center of each.

Refrigerate the roll for several hours or up to two days before serving. Because the mallow pumpkins absorb moisture and then leak, do not add them until a few hours before serving.

HEALTHY CHOICE ALTERNATIVE In comparison to butter cakes, this sponge cake is quite light. You can lighten it even more by replacing the 3 whole eggs with 5 egg whites. Use half the frosting. Cut the cake into fifteen pieces and eat only one piece.

For a festive fall dessert, serve this cake with coffee or tea and chocolate mints.

Prune Cake

DIFFICULTY Very Difficult. As presented here, this cake has fourteen ingredients and two cooking steps. The three recipes (including the Country Whipped Cream) call for fifteen different ingredients and merit a rating of very difficult.

*D*uring the winter months, this cake, glaze, and cream topping make an extravagant ending to a dinner of Winter Vegetable Soup and Buttermilk Corn Bread. This Prune Cake is a lightly spiced, moist, fruit and nut cake. It compares well to an applesauce cake, jam cake, or fresh apple cake.

While I have revised and improved the common prune cake recipes, I am not the first to write about prune cakes. I have ten or more regional cookbooks with prune cake recipes, and they include the buttermilk glaze.

We eat prunes baked, boiled, whipped, or as a filling for cakes or cookies. We make them into butter, bars, betty, compote, soufflé, pie, or turnovers. We pickle them, mold them, or stuff them with dressings.

The French soak them in liqueur or brandy, and then flame them; the Germans fry them with bacon; Algerians serve them with lamb and cinnamon;

Danes serve them with roast pork; and the Irish serve them with roast duck and baked apples. Like others who live in the mountains, I like them baked in a cake.

STEPS Reserve 6 whole prunes for garnish. Cut the remaining prunes in quarters. In a saucepan with enough water to cover, simmer for 10 minutes. Let the prunes cool in the water. While prunes absorb most of the water, drain what is left (now it is prune juice) and reserve the prunes.

Prepare the cake: Preheat the oven to 350°F. Grease a tube or bundt pan or use a 13x9x2-inch baking pan.

In a mixing bowl, sift together the flour, baking powder, cinnamon, nutmeg, and allspice. Set aside. In a second mixing bowl, mix the oil, sugar, eggs, and vanilla. Blend in the flour mixture and the buttermilk. Stir in the prunes and nuts. Pour and scrape the batter into the prepared baking pan. Bake for 1 hour, or until a toothpick inserted in the center comes out clean.

Prepare the Buttermilk Glaze: Five minutes before you remove the cake from the oven, prepare the Buttermilk Glaze. In a small saucepan, combine the sugar, buttermilk, butter, syrup, and vanilla. Bring to a boil, and boil for 1 minute. Slowly, when you remove the cake from the oven, pour the hot Buttermilk Glaze over the cake. Using a skewer or fork, poke holes in the cake so the sauce soaks in. When the cake has absorbed the glaze, invert the cake and unmold it onto a cake plate. Garnish with the reserved prunes.

TIP For this recipe, I plump the prunes. I purchase a 12-ounce package of Del Monte seedless prunes—they are medium in size, soft and moist, and of excellent quality. To plump a prune, soak or boil it. Cover the prunes with water, orange juice, tea, or port wine, and soak them for 24 hours, or simmer for 10 minutes. (I simmer them and then let them cool in the liquid.)

HEALTHY CHOICE ALTERNATIVE Use nonfat buttermilk, and omit 1 egg yolk. When making the Buttermilk Glaze, replace the butter with buttermilk.

Slice and serve warm with tea or coffee and add a dollop of Country Whipped Cream to each serving.

INGREDIENTS

FOR THE CAKE
12 ounces pitted prunes
2 cups all-purpose flour
1 teaspoon baking powder
1 teaspoon cinnamon
1/2 teaspoon ground nutmeg
1/4 teaspoon allspice
1 cup safflower or canola oil
1 1/2 cups sugar
3 eggs
1 teaspoon vanilla
1 cup buttermilk
1 cup chopped pecans

FOR THE BUTTERMILK GLAZE
1 cup sugar
1/2 cup buttermilk
1/4 cup butter
2 tablespoons light corn syrup
1 teaspoon vanilla

YIELD 18 servings

Angel Food Cake

I know some pretty good cooks who say the only box cake they use is for an angel food cake. I, however, prefer this from-scratch, almost-off-the Swans Down box recipe. When I make angel food cake from scratch, I am sure that it is free of fat, preservatives, and baking powder. I then transform the cake into a most desirable temptation with Strawberry Cream.

DIFFICULTY Difficult. With nine ingredients, this one-bowl cake and whipped cream are difficult to prepare. Allow time to beat the egg whites, bake for 40 minutes and cool for 1 1/2 hours.

INGREDIENTS

FOR THE CAKE
1 cup cake flour
1 1/2 cups sugar
12 egg whites (1 1/2 cups) at room temperature
1 1/4 teaspoons cream of tartar
1 teaspoon vanilla extract
1/4 teaspoon salt
1/4 teaspoon almond extract

FOR THE STRAWBERRY CREAM
2 (1-pint) boxes strawberries
2 cups heavy cream
1/2 cup sugar
2 teaspoons vanilla extract

YIELD 12 servings

STEPS Preheat the oven to 375°F. Select a 10-inch loose-bottom tube pan. Do not grease.

In a mixing bowl, sift together five times the flour and 3/4 cup of the sugar. (This repeated sifting separates the grains of flour and adds lightness to the cake.) Set aside.

In a second bowl, beat the egg whites, cream of tartar, vanilla, salt, and almond extract until soft peaks form. Add the remaining 3/4 cup sugar, 2 tablespoons at a time. Beat until the sugar dissolves. Test it between your fingers—if you feel grains of sugar, keep beating.

Sift a quarter of the flour mixture over the egg whites and, using a rubber spatula, gently fold it in with a circular down, up, and over motion. Add the remaining flour a quarter at a time, folding just enough for the flour to disappear. Pour and spread the batter into the pan. Bake for 40 minutes, or until the cake springs back when you touch it or a toothpick inserted into the center of the cake comes out clean. Invert the pan by placing the cone onto the neck of a large, pointed bottle. Cool for 1 1/2 hours. Pressing against the sides of the pan, cut the cake from the sides of the pan, and lift out the pan bottom. Cut the cake from the cone and bottom of the pan.

To prepare the Strawberry Cream, wash, dry, and slice the strawberries. In a chilled bowl and using a chilled beater, whip the cream with the sugar and vanilla. When the cream is stiff, fold the berries into the cream. Refrigerate.

SIFTING TIP I use all kinds of kitchen tools, and I own hundreds of them. However, I have several flour sifters and don't like any of them. Instead, I use a strainer. I move the flour through the strainer with some quick side-to-side action of my wrist, tapping the strainer, or by shaking up and down to roll the flour.

HEALTHY CHOICE ALTERNATIVE This cake, without any modification and without the Strawberry Cream, is fat free. It always has been.

Serve this cake topped with a large dollop of Strawberry Cream on each piece. Use another pint of strawberries for garnish. I also like to use the cake for fondue, dipping it into chocolate sauce or Chocolate Gravy.

HEARTY
Cooking
COUNTRY

Pumpkin Layer Cake

*U*sing canned pumpkin, I make this cake at any time of year, but especially in the fall. The cake is moist and sweet. The feeling of smooth moisture on your tongue is from the oil—hence the term oil cake. I have found that in spite of the fat and calories, people really like this cake with the Cream Cheese Frosting. The frosting recipe is a double and yields about six cups. Sometimes I use less frosting, but with this amount, even an amateur cake decorator like me can cover a less than perfect cake. If the layers are round on top, I use the frosting to flatten them; if the sides slope in, I use the frosting to straighten them.

STEPS Preheat the oven to 350°F. Grease and flour two 9-inch round cake pans.

In a large mixing bowl, whisk together the flour, sugar, baking powder, salt, cinnamon, cloves, and nutmeg. Form a well in the center of the dry ingredients, and add the oil and the eggs. Thoroughly whisk together the oil and eggs, and then incorporate the flour and pumpkin. Stir until well mixed. Pour into the cake pans.

Bake for 30 minutes, or until a toothpick inserted into the center comes out clean. Cool on racks for 10 minutes. With a spatula, cut around the edges, invert, and remove the cakes from the pans. Cool 1 hour.

Prepare the frosting: If your cream cheese and butter are not soft enough to beat with a mixer, warm them in your microwave oven. Careful now, don't let them get too warm, or the frosting will be too soft to spread. Using a high-powered mixer, beat together the cream cheese, butter, and vanilla. Slowly sift and stir in the sugar until smooth. Frost the cake one layer at a time, stacking the layers as you go. Then, frost the top and sides of the cake. Garnish the sides of the cake with black walnuts, sticking them on one nut at a time. Refrigerate.

HEALTHY CHOICE ALTERNATIVE Omit the frosting, and serve the cake without stacking the layers. This cake is moist and rich, and I enjoy it without frosting. You can offer Applesauce, Apple Butter, Country Whipped Cream, Sugar Syrup, Buttermilk Glaze, or Hot Sorghum on the side. If you choose to splurge and go all the way, cool the cake and you'll be able to slice it into 24 thin pieces, cutting calories per piece in half.

You may serve this cake at any temperature, but I like to slice it cold and then warm each piece in the microwave. If you can afford the calories, top the warm cake and the frosting-turned-to-glaze with a scoop of vanilla ice cream.

DIFFICULTY Difficult. With fifteen ingredients, this three-layer, frosted cake is difficult to prepare.

INGREDIENTS

FOR THE CAKE
2 cups all-purpose flour
2 cups sugar
2 teaspoons baking powder
1 teaspoon salt
1 teaspoon cinnamon
1 teaspoon ground cloves
1/2 teaspoon nutmeg
1 cup canola oil
4 eggs
2 cups pumpkin (*not* pumpkin pie filling)

FOR THE CREAM CHEESE FROSTING
Two 8-ounce packages cream cheese
1 cup unsalted butter
2 teaspoons vanilla
2 pounds confectioners' sugar
1/2 cup black walnuts

YIELD 12 servings

More Desserts

Jam Cake
(John L. Lewis Jam Cake)

DIFFICULTY Very Difficult. With sixteen ingredients and two steps, this cake is very difficult to prepare.

INGREDIENTS

FOR THE CAKE
1 teaspoon baking soda
1 cup nonfat cultured buttermilk
1 cup butter, at room temperature
2 cups firmly packed light brown sugar
3 cups all-purpose flour
2 teaspoons cocoa
1 teaspoon cinnamon
1/2 teaspoon nutmeg
4 eggs
1 1/2 cups seedless blackberry jam
1 cup chopped nuts, such as pecans, black walnuts, or English walnuts

FOR THE CARAMEL FROSTING
1 1/2 cups firmly packed brown sugar
5 tablespoons shortening
3 tablespoons butter
1/2 cup milk
3 cups confectioners' sugar
2 teaspoons vanilla
2 cups seedless blackberry jam

YIELD 16 servings and 2 2/3 cups frosting

*I*t has been said that the jam cake was John L. Lewis's favorite cake. For more than fifty years, starting in 1906, Lewis was a mine union leader, and as he worked with the miners in the coal fields of Appalachia, he occasionally got a piece of this cake. As President of the United Mine Workers of America, he has been credited with much of the progress achieved by miners.

While I think a jam cake should taste like the jam that goes into it, I have found that the flavor depends more on the spices, nuts, and fruits. Jam cakes are generally firm and dry. They keep and travel well, making them good for Christmas dinners, potlucks, or reunions. To moisten the cake, I serve it with a blackberry sauce and vanilla ice cream.

STEPS Preheat the oven to 350°F. Grease and flour three 9-inch cake pans. Stir the baking soda into the buttermilk and set aside.

In a large mixing bowl, cream together the butter and brown sugar, scraping the sides of the bowl as needed. In a second bowl, combine the flour, cocoa, cinnamon, and nutmeg. Add the eggs to the butter mixture one at a time, beating well after each addition. When well mixed, add the flour alternately with the buttermilk, scraping the sides of the bowl as you mix. Stir in the blackberry jam and nuts until well combined.

Pour the batter evenly into the cake pans. Bake for 30 minutes, or until a toothpick inserted into the center comes out clean. Cool in the pans for 10 minutes. Then remove the cake from the pans, and cool completely on wire racks.

Do not prepare the frosting until the cake layers are cool. In a small saucepan, combine the brown sugar, shortening, butter, and milk, and heat to boiling over medium heat, stirring frequently. Reduce the heat, and simmer for 3 minutes. Remove from the heat, and cool completely. In a mixing bowl, combine the brown sugar mixture, the confectioners' sugar, and vanilla, beating on high until thick enough to spread.

Place the first cake layer on a serving platter, and spread with 1 cup of the blackberry jam. Add the second layer, and repeat with the remaining 1 cup jam. Top with the third layer, and frost the top and sides with the Caramel Frosting.

Store, covered, for up to 1 week. This cake improves with age.

HEALTHY CHOICE ALTERNATIVE While this cake has lots of sugar and calories, it is low in fat, containing only 1 1/2 tablespoons of butter or shortening and 1/4 of an egg yolk per serving.

Serve this cake with ice cream, hard sauce, hot applesauce, or blackberry sauce.

HEARTY
Cooking
COUNTRY

The cake is brought to full glory when I serve it with fresh fruit, such as blackberries, raspberries, strawberries, or bananas, and Country Whipped Cream.

Savage Mountain Pound Cake

*I*n the far reaches of western Maryland, about thirty miles west of Cumberland, you can visit Savage Mountain and hike the Big Savage Trail. While you are there you might, but probably won't, come across this cake—the area is wild and sparsely populated. While the Savage Mountain Wildlands are primitive, the cake is fine-textured, soft, and has a New England nutmeg accent. The Bourbon Honey Sauce is my creation, and it reminds me of our backwoods.

STEPS Place the oven rack in the center of the oven. Preheat the oven to 375°F. Grease two 9x4x2-inch loaf pans. Cut two pieces of parchment or waxed paper to measure 8x15 inches. (Three inches of parchment will stick up above the sides of the pan.) Line the pans, and grease and flour the paper.

Sift the flour and baking powder into a bowl, and set aside. In a second bowl, cream the butter and sugar until light. Beat on high for several minutes, and use a rubber scraper to help get it mixed. Add the vanilla, nutmeg, and cinnamon, and stir. Add the eggs one at a time, mixing thoroughly after each addition. Mix in the milk and the flour mixture alternately, starting and ending with dry ingredients.

Pour and scrape the batter into the pans and level it. Bake for 1 hour and 10 minutes. After 1 hour, check for doneness—if a toothpick inserted into the center comes out clean, remove the cakes from the oven. Cool on a wire rack for 15 minutes.

With a spatula, cut the ends of the cake from the pan. Use the parchment to pull the cake from the pans. Cool for 2 hours.

To make the sauce, combine the bourbon, honey, raisins, and water in a bowl and warm in the microwave. Stir and serve.

HEALTHY CHOICE ALTERNATIVE This alternative is not a traditional pound cake, but if you are concerned about saturated fats, I offer a reasonable substitute: Replace the butter with 1 cup vegetable oil, reduce the eggs to 4, and increase the milk to 1½ cups.

Some say that pound cakes are better after you store them at room temperature for a day; I like them warm from the oven and a day later. Serve this cake with a scoop of vanilla ice cream and pass the Bourbon Honey Sauce.

DIFFICULTY Moderate. While the cake has nine ingredients and the sauce has four, both are easy to prepare.

INGREDIENTS

FOR THE POUND CAKE
4 cups all-purpose flour
1 tablespoon baking powder
2 cups butter at room temperature
4 cups confectioners' sugar
1 tablespoon vanilla
½ teaspoon nutmeg
½ teaspoon cinnamon
8 eggs
1⅓ cups milk

FOR THE BOURBON SAUCE
½ cup bourbon
½ cup honey
⅓ cup raisins
1 tablespoon water

YIELD 20 servings (The sauce makes 10 servings.)

Mountain Pies

WE THE COOKS of the Blue Ridge, Appalachian, and Smoky Mountains make twice as many pies as cakes. Some of our pies—lemon slice, sweet potato, pawpaw, and pumpkin—announce their contents with their name, and others—shoofly, derby, million dollar, affinity, chess, mince, transparent, and impossible—test the imagination. As you might think, our turtle and grasshopper, poor man's and mother's, Betty's and Rose's pies contain neither turtles, nor poor men, nor roses.

We identify our light pies with names such as angel, elegant, heavenly, luscious, and chiffon. For light pie toppings, nothing is lighter than a mile-high meringue. For places that sound curious we have Hawaiian, Parisienne, and California pies. Closer to home we know Mississippi mud and Tar Heel pies. We remember our politicians with Washington, Tyler, and Jeff Davis pies. Brand names that make their way into pie vocabulary include Ritz, Milky Way, and Toll House. We serve our pies sweet or savory, hot or cold, thick or thin, light or heavy, single- or double-crusted. Stack pies are thin, turnovers are small, and upside-down pies have fruit on top.

Fifty years ago, when large numbers of our people grew what they ate, cut timber with axes, crossed rivers in boats, and mined coal by hand, we ate pies for breakfast and supper. Rather than being a passport to marriage, as they were years ago, today pies are a standard for celebration, an occasional treat, and a cook's glory.

Pastry Blender

A pastry blender is a hand tool with five blades. Its five U-shaped blades cut the shortening, without warming it, when you press them through the shortening against the bottom of a round bowl. This results in evenly distributed tiny pieces of fat and a flakier pastry. The metal blades, as opposed to your fingers, do not warm the fat. Some chefs cut the shortening into the flour with a food processor, but I wash my own dishes, and a food processor is a lot to clean up.

Pie Pastry Shell
Double-Crust Pie Shell and Healthy Choice Pie Crust

*F*or an old-fashioned mountain treat, I suggest that on one occasion, to experiment with what some say is the ultimate in pie crusts, you try this: Replace the butter and solid shortening in this recipe with lard. Ask your butcher for rendered lard. You may end up with the most tender and flaky pie crust you have ever eaten.

I use this savory, flaky, traditional pastry for any nine-inch pie. The recipe makes two single-crust pies or one double-crust pie.

STEPS If possible, work in a cool area and on a cool surface. Use cold ingredients, and handle the dough as little as possible. The goal is to keep the shortenings from melting into the flour. Using waxed paper makes handling and cleanup easy.

In a mixing bowl, sift together the flour and sugar. Using a pastry blender, cut the solid shortening into the flour. Slice the butter 1/8-inch thick, add to the flour, and cut it in until the pieces are the size of a large grain of rice or a bit larger. Fluff the mixture with a fork.

Dribble the water over the flour mixture, stirring with a fork as you dribble. Mix but do not knead. Separate the dough to make two crusts, allowing slightly more dough for the bottom crust of a double-crust pie. Draw the dough into a ball.

The amount of water needed is a judgment call: The degree to which you incorporate the shortening and the age and moisture of the flour are the determining factors. If the dough is too wet, it will stick to the waxed paper. If it is too dry, it will not hold together.

To roll out the crust, tear two sheets of waxed paper and flour your hands. If the dough is moist, sprinkle a little flour on top. Press the dough into a round, flat disc. Flip the dough over and sprinkle some flour on the other side.

With a piece of waxed paper both over and under the dough, roll the crust to a diameter of 10 inches using a rolling pin. The dough should be 3/16-inch thick. Transfer the dough to the pie pan, and repeat for the other crust.

There are two ways to transfer the dough: Method One: Pull one sheet of the waxed paper off the crust. Lay the paper back on the crust, and grabbing the upper corners of both pieces of waxed paper, flip the crust over. Pull off the other piece of paper and discard. Grasping the center of both sides of the remaining sheet of waxed paper, lift the crust (it will fold in half) onto the pie pan. Fold the top half open and remove the waxed paper. Try not to break the dough. If it does break, moisten your fingers, pull it together, and patch it.

DIFFICULTY Moderate. After cutting five ingredients together, you roll the crust and transfer it to a pie pan. Allow 20 minutes to get this crust ready for baking.

INGREDIENTS
3 cups all-purpose flour
3 tablespoons sugar
1/2 cup solid shortening
1/2 cup cold butter
6 tablespoons ice water

YIELD 1 double-crust pie or 2 pie shells

■ More Desserts

Or, Method Two: Loosen both sheets of waxed paper from the dough. Remove the top piece of paper. Slide a cookie sheet under the lower piece and the dough. Center your pie pan upside down on top of the dough. Flip it over so the dough falls into the pan. Remove the cookie sheet and the paper. Lift the crust edges down into the pan. Do not stretch the dough.

Inevitably, the crust and the edge of the crust are uneven or broken, and you need to fix them. Use a knife to trim the edges of the crust even with the pie pan. Then use the trimmings to patch the crust and reinforce the top edges or bottom where needed.

Cover the crust with a piece of 14-inch-wide plastic wrap, and smooth the dough by rubbing your fingers over the plastic. The plastic wrap helps me form and shape the crust. When I want a decorative edge pattern I remove the plastic wrap and mark the edge of the crust with the tines of a fork. (For freezing or storage, leave the plastic wrap on the crust.)

Bake at 350°F for 15 minutes. Or, cover with plastic wrap and refrigerate for three days or freeze for three months. If time allows, use the prepared crust cold, directly from the refrigerator or freezer.

HEALTHY CHOICE ALTERNATIVE Reduce the recipe by one-third to save one-third of the fat and calories: Use 2 cups all-purpose flour, 2 tablespoons sugar, $1/3$ cup solid shortening, $1/3$ cup butter, and $1/4$ cup water.

Double-Crust Pie Shell Roll the top crust, and cut several air vents. In addition to a center, dime-shaped air vent, I make four other vents in the shape of leaves. Use a paring knife to cut and lift the vents from the dough. Where the two crusts will be joined, use your fingertips and water to moisten the top of the bottom crust. Dip your fingertips in water and work the water over the seam. Add the filling and top crust. Join and crimp the two crusts together. Form the edges, fluting them into a zigzag pattern.

Healthy Choice Pie Crust Replace the solid shortening, butter, and ice water with $1/2$ cup plus 1 tablespoon vegetable oil and $1/2$ cup plus 1 tablespoon water. Replace the all-purpose flour with self-rising flour. It makes the crust brittle and adds salt. Don't forget the 3 tablespoons of sugar. Stir the ingredients until smooth, and roll out the dough. This dough is elastic, and when you take it from the oven, the crust is light, tender, substantial, and crunchy like a thick cracker. The dough is not sensitive to over-mixing or variations in temperature.

Comparing Cream Pies, Custard Pies, and Pastry Cream

All of these sweet fillings are made by thickening milk. Cream, custard, and pastry cream fillings are thickened with eggs, flour, or cornstarch and flavored with our favorite dessert flavorings, from butterscotch to chocolate.

Cream pies are thickened with cornstarch so that when the filling is cold they slice straight and hold their shape. Custard pies also hold their shape, but they are thickened with whole eggs, not cornstarch. Finally, pastry creams are thickened with flour and used as fillings for fruit tarts or éclairs. If only these categories were this distinct, our understanding of these recipes would be simple. In practice, there is overlap among the three categories, with some cream pies containing whole eggs and some custards containing flour.

Peanut Butter Pie
Vanilla Cream Pie, Banana Cream Pie, Coconut Cream Pie, Chocolate Cream Pie, and Chocolate Peanut Butter Cream Pie

I like peanut butter pie with a thick, homemade, savory, flaky pie crust, a cooked vanilla cream filling, and peanut butter crumbles. This pie has not been around very long—perhaps twenty-five years. In spite of this short history, the pie has spread like a wildfire, and many variations are popular.

Each of these variations is a different pie. First, to make pudding peanut butter pie, we mix cream cheese, dessert topping, peanut butter, sugar, and perhaps milk; pour it into a pie shell, chill, and serve.

For a peanut butter cream pie, we cook peanut butter with a cream pie filling, making the pie much like a chocolate cream pie. In a third variation, a simple cream pie, we bake evaporated milk and egg yolks with sugar and peanut butter.

Finally, we make the supreme, my favorite, the fourth variation, a vanilla cream

DIFFICULTY Difficult. With eleven ingredients and four time-consuming but not difficult steps, this pie is difficult to make.

pie with peanut butter crumbles. To make the crumbles, we combine peanut butter and confectioners' sugar, and then spread them in a single layer on the bottom of the pie. We top these pies with dessert topping, whipped cream, or meringue, —the most popular choice. I hope you find mine to be the easiest, no-fail meringue ever. I guarantee its success.

INGREDIENTS

FOR THE PIE CRUST
1 fully baked Pie Pastry Shell (page 275), or a commercially prepared pie crust

FOR THE PEANUT BUTTER CRUMBLES
3/4 cup confectioners' sugar
1/3 cup peanut butter

FOR THE CREAM FILLING
2/3 cup sugar
1/4 cup cornstarch
3 egg yolks
1/4 cup heavy whipping cream
2 cups milk
2 tablespoons butter
2 teaspoons vanilla extract

FOR THE NEVER-FAIL MERINGUE TOPPING
5 large egg whites, at room temperature
5 ounces Kraft Marshmallow Cream

YIELD 8 servings

STEPS Prepare the pie about 6 hours ahead of serving time to allow for proper chilling.

To make the crumbles, combine the sugar and peanut butter, using a pastry blender to cut and mix the sugar until it forms small granules, like coarse-ground coffee. Reserving 2 teaspoons for garnish, spread the peanut butter crumbles into the bottom of the baked pie crust.

To prepare the filling, in a medium saucepan, combine the sugar and cornstarch until smooth. In a bowl, mix the yolks, cream, and milk. Stir the milk mixture into the sugar mixture, and cook over medium heat for 15 minutes, or until it has boiled for 1 minute. Stir with a whisk to keep it smooth. Remove from the heat, and stir in the butter and vanilla. Allow to cool for 10 minutes. Pour into the pie shell, and cool for about 1 hour.

Preheat the oven to 350°F. To prepare the meringue, using a high-speed electric mixer (and a copper insert if you have one), beat the egg whites until soft peaks form. Add the marshmallow cream a heaping tablespoonful at a time, beating well between additions. When fully mixed and stiff, spread the meringue over the cool pie. Using a large rubber spatula, mound the meringue onto the center of the custard and spread it out over the crust edges. Use the back of a spoon to draw the meringue into peaks.

Spread the reserved peanut butter crumbles over the meringue. Bake for 10 minutes, or until the peaks are golden brown. Cool on a wire rack. Refrigerate for several hours or until cold through to the center.

Serve cold from the refrigerator.

Vanilla Cream Pie
Omit the Peanut Butter Crumbles, and increase the vanilla to 1 tablespoon.

Banana Cream Pie
In place of the Peanut Butter Crumbles, cover the pie crust with sliced bananas. Use 2 to 3 bananas or 2 cups sliced.

Coconut Cream Pie
In place of the Peanut Butter Crumbles, stir in 1 1/2 cups (3.5 ounces) of sweetened flaked coconut after you stir in the butter and vanilla. Sprinkle 1 tablespoon coconut over the meringue before baking.

HEARTY
Cooking
COUNTRY

Chocolate Cream Pie Omit the Peanut Butter Crumbles. Stir ¹/₃ cup of cocoa powder into the sugar and cornstarch. Increase the sugar to 1 cup plus 2 tablespoons. More sugar makes the filling runny. Whisk the sugar, cocoa, and cornstarch until fully incorporated and the lumps are gone.

Chocolate Peanut Butter Cream Pie Use the Peanut Butter Crumbles with the Chocolate Cream Pie above, spreading them below the chocolate filling.

Peach Pie

From mid-June through August our fresh peaches are a roadside standard. Try to buy free-stone tree-ripened specimens. If nectarines look better, use them in place of peaches. What to look for in a good peach? Flavor, texture, juiciness. Good peaches are soft, juicy, and succulent. I want ripe, delicate, easily bruised peaches. A poor peach is hard, crunchy, or mealy, and lacks flavor. When I bite into one, juice does not run down my face and hands, as it should.

STEPS Preheat the oven to 350°F.

In a mixing bowl, combine the sugar, cornstarch, and nutmeg, and whisk until blended. Set aside.

Prepare the peaches: To peel, lower the peaches one at a time into boiling water for 10 to 15 seconds, and then pull off the peeling. If the peeling is not loose, boil longer. Slice the peeled peaches into wedges to make 4¹/₂ cups.

Pour the sugar mixture over the peaches, and stir. Pour into the pie shell, and bake for 50 minutes, or until it bubbles in the center. Let the pie cool, and then refrigerate.

To prepare the topping, using a chilled bowl and beaters, combine cold cream and sugar, and beat until double in bulk and stiff. When the pie is cold, spread the whipped cream on top.

Cut the remaining unpeeled peach in eight sections, sprinkle with Fruit Fresh, and place 1 wedge, peel-side up, in the center of each piece of pie.

HEALTHY CHOICE ALTERNATIVE This pie, like other traditional pies, is rich. While this pie crust will not be full until you add the topping, we often eat the pie without the whipped cream. Or, we may serve it with a commercially prepared low-fat dairy topping, and then add the garnish.

DIFFICULTY Difficult. This pie is difficult partly because I find it hard to buy good peaches. In addition, you have to prepare or buy a crust, peel and slice the peaches, mix, bake, and cool the pie, whip and spread the cream, and garnish. The cool taste is worth the effort, and the pie is a simple beauty.

INGREDIENTS

FOR THE PIE
1 cup sugar
6 tablespoons cornstarch
¹/₄ teaspoon nutmeg
5 large peaches
1 unbaked 9-inch Pie Pastry Shell (page 275)

FOR THE TOPPING
1 cup heavy cream, chilled
¹/₄ cup sugar
1 teaspoon vanilla
1 peach for garnish
Fruit Fresh fruit preservative

YIELD 8 servings

More Desserts

Buttermilk

In the South, buttermilk is a drink and an ingredient of great importance. Like cream, buttermilk is thick and full bodied, and like wine it fills my mouth with a lasting tart flavor. But in spite of that richness and full flavor, most buttermilk has neither fat nor alcohol.

As a drink, nonfat buttermilk is tangy and nutritious. Here in the mountains we drink buttermilk straight from the carton, and we also drink it sweetened, or we mix it with tomato juice, yogurt, or pureed fruit.

As an ingredient, buttermilk adds flavor and leavening to cakes, pancakes, biscuits, and corn bread. We use buttermilk to make pies, to coat fish and chicken, to enrich cold soups, and to flavor sugar and cream for buttermilk fudge.

Years ago, when mountaineers made their own butter, buttermilk was a by-product of this process. Today buttermilk is a cultured milk product. Nonfat buttermilk is common in our markets and is made from skim milk. In comparison to skim milk, nonfat buttermilk will have about the same amount of calories, calcium, protein, and carbohydrates. Buttermilk may, however, have two to four times the amount of sodium as milk.

When we use buttermilk in baking it enhances flavor and texture and acts as a leavening agent. One-half cup of buttermilk and $\frac{1}{4}$ teaspoon of baking powder equals about 1 teaspoon of baking powder. Because of its acidity, we use buttermilk to activate baking soda.

Buttermilk curdles easily. If you add too much heat, stir too vigorously, or salt too heavily, buttermilk will curdle. In breads or cakes this curdling does not affect flavor or baking quality. In soups, gravies, or stews, however, curdled buttermilk looks unappetizing. Particles of protein—curds—float around, so that rather than a thick, flavorful gravy, you have liquid and curds. To avoid curdling, heat slowly, stir slowly, and do not add salt.

Buttermilk Pie

*F*or more than one hundred years, cooks in the South have been using buttermilk to make this custard-like or chess-style pie. Also called transparent pies, this type of pie includes pecan pie and chess pie. According to Susan G. Purdy in *As Easy as Pie*, these pies are a unique Southern specialty, developed to use an abundant supply of eggs, butter, and sugar.

STEPS Preheat the oven to 400°F.

Because the crust must hold the filling without leaking, bake the crust using pie weights or dry beans, and do not prick holes in the crust. Fill the crust with the weights or beans, and bake for 15 minutes. Allow to cool for 10 minutes, and then remove the weights.

Reduce the oven temperature to 300°F. In a mixing bowl, beat together the butter, sugar, and eggs, and then add the flour. Stir in the buttermilk and vanilla. Pour the filling into the pie shell, allowing enough space to carry it easily to the oven without spilling.

Bake for 45 minutes, or until raised in the center. If the top of the baked pie is too light in color, broil for 1 minute or less, or sprinkle with grated nutmeg. Cool and refrigerate for 2 hours.

HEALTHY CHOICE ALTERNATIVE From the traditional formula for this pie, I have cut 1 egg and reduced the butter by about 1/4 cup. I specify nonfat buttermilk and use far less sugar than some recipes. Remember, however, pie is pie, and with a traditional crust, it has lots of fat and calories. To save time and calories, bake this filling in custard dishes, omitting the crust. Serve with vanilla wafers.

Serve this pie chilled, topped with Country Whipped Cream.

DIFFICULTY Moderate. With seven ingredients and two baking steps, this pie is moderate in difficulty.

INGREDIENTS
One 9-inch Pie Pastry
  Shell (page 275)
1/3 cup melted butter
1 cup sugar
2 eggs
2 tablespoons all-
  purpose flour
1 cup nonfat buttermilk
1 teaspoon vanilla

YIELD 8 servings

Chocolate Pecan Pie

DIFFICULTY Moderate. With eight ingredients, this recipe is moderate in difficulty.

INGREDIENTS
1 unbaked 9-inch Pie Pastry Shell (page 275)
2 large eggs
1 cup sugar
1 cup light corn syrup
1/4 cup melted butter
2 teaspoons vanilla
3/4 cup chocolate chips
1 1/2 cups pecan pieces

YIELD 8 good-size servings

*I*f pecan pie alone is not sweet and rich enough, try this, the epitome of sweetness and one of the highest-calorie desserts I know. It always pleases my guests.

STEPS Preheat the oven to 450°F.

In a large mixing bowl, beat the eggs and add the sugar, corn syrup, butter, and vanilla, stirring until fully mixed. Add the chocolate chips and pecans, and stir. Pour this mixture into the Pie Pastry Shell.

Bake for 20 minutes. Reduce the heat to 350°F, and bake for 25 to 35 minutes, or until raised in the center. Remove from the oven, and cool on a wire rack.

TIP This pie freezes for up to four months. To defrost, remove from the freezer and let the pie stand on a cooling rack for 5 hours. One hour before serving time, bake at 350°F for 20 minutes.

HEALTHY CHOICE ALTERNATIVE This delicacy is not for the light-hearted or heart-troubled. Each piece, it seems, has almost enough calories to support a teenager or marathoner for a day!

Serve this pie after a light meal of Savory Boiled Turnips and Roast Chicken or as part of a celebration dinner. Serve fresh and warm from the oven, with vanilla ice cream.

Hawksbill Chess Pie

DIFFICULTY Moderate. If I have one of my Pie Pastry Shells in the freezer, making this pie with six other ingredients is moderate in difficulty.

*A*t 4,049 feet above sea level, Hawksbill Summit is the highest point in Shenandoah National Park. The area is most popular in October when leaves show their colors. I named this pie after Hawksbill Summit because of its popularity with cooks both east and west of the Blue Ridge. In an occasional restaurant outside the Shenandoah National Park you'll find pies like this, and long before I started cooking, this sugar, egg, and milk pie was popular. Southern cooks called it chess pie. How did it get its name? Making the pie is so simple that people would say, "It's jes' pie," and that phrase, if you listen carefully and drop the "it is," sounds like "chess pie."

Chess pie is like a custard pie, but the added flour and butter give it a fuller taste and texture. This pie tastes of butter and caramel, and its texture is solid and thick.

STEPS Preheat the oven to 350°F. In a mixing bowl, beat together the milk, eggs, butter, and vanilla. Blend the sugar with the flour, and beat into the milk mixture. Pour the mixture into the pastry shell.

Bake for 45 minutes, or until the center puffs up and a knife inserted near the center comes out clean.

HEALTHY CHOICE ALTERNATIVE You can reduce the eggs to 2 and cut the butter to ¼ cup, but I prefer using the old recipe and eating a small piece.

Serve this pie cold with Country Whipped Cream, Pear Honey, or Lemon Glaze.

INGREDIENTS
1 unbaked 9-inch Pie Pastry Shell (page 275)
1 cup evaporated milk
3 eggs
½ cup melted butter (do not use margarine)
1 teaspoon vanilla
1½ cups sugar
2 tablespoons all-purpose flour

YIELD 8 servings

Black Walnut Sugar Cookies

For a slight black walnut aroma and flavor, try this rich old-fashioned sugar cookie. Hot from the oven, the outer surface will be crisp and cracked and the center soft.

STEPS Preheat the oven to 350°F. Grease two large cookie sheets. In a mixing bowl, mix and sift together the flour and baking powder. In a second bowl, beat the butter with 1¼ cups of the sugar on high until the mixture turns white, about 10 minutes. Now don't fret about beating the butter and sugar for 10 minutes. Relax. Use this time to read the paper, wash the dishes, or do some stretches. With the butter well aerated and on low speed, beat in the vanilla and egg yolks. Slowly stir in the flour mixture, half at a time, and then the walnuts.

Using two soup spoons, drop heaping spoonfuls of the dough into the remaining sugar and roll each into a ball. I roll this in the palms of my hands and roll again in the remaining ¼ cup sugar.

Bake for 13 minutes. Cool on a wire rack.

HEALTHY CHOICE ALTERNATIVE This particular combination of real butter, egg yolks, flour, and black walnuts is so distinctive that any change would be ruinous. I can't recommend any substitutions.

Serve with hot coffee, tea, or fresh cold milk.

DIFFICULTY Moderate. With seven ingredients and one step, this recipe is moderate in difficulty.

INGREDIENTS
2 cups sifted all-purpose flour
1½ teaspoons baking powder
1 cup unsalted butter, at room temperature
1¾ cups sugar
1 teaspoon vanilla
3 egg yolks
½ cup chopped black walnuts

YIELD 30 (3-inch) cookies

Forgotten Kisses

*A*lso called forgotten cookies, meringue cookies, heavenly cookies, chocolate-pecan kisses, earthquakes, and magic cookies, this almost-confection is a meringue cookie. We call them magic cookies because they contain neither shortening nor flour. Making these kisses is so simple that I find teenagers whipping them up and getting really excited by their success.

DIFFICULTY Easy. With just five ingredients and no oven to watch when you bake, these cookies are easy to make.

INGREDIENTS
2 egg whites, at room temperature
1 pinch salt
²/₃ cup sugar
¹/₂ cup chocolate chips
¹/₂ cup pecan pieces

YIELD 24 cookies

STEPS Preheat the oven to 350°F. Cut a piece of waxed paper to cover one large cookie sheet.

Using a high-speed electric mixer, beat the egg whites and salt until they form droopy peaks. Add the sugar 1 tablespoon at a time—allow 5 to 10 seconds between each spoonful—and continue beating. Using a rubber scraper, stir in the chips and pecans. Drop by teaspoonfuls onto the waxed paper. Allow 1 minute for the heat to come back to 350°F, and turn off the oven. Do not open it.

Then, forget about your forgotten kisses. Leave them alone for 4 hours, or overnight, and do not peek. (If I am in a hurry, I bake these kisses for 20 to 30 minutes at 275°F.) Store in an airtight container.

HEALTHY CHOICE ALTERNATIVE Already a low-fat and cholesterol-free cookie, you can cut the fat even further by omitting the pecans. With the pecans, these rather large cookies contain 55 calories and about 2 grams of fat. Without the pecans, you'll have 40 calories and less than 1 gram of fat per cookie.

Serve with milk, coffee, and other cookies such as Christmas Rocks, Pecan Pie Bars, and Scotch Shortbread.

Crisp and Tender Shortbread

For some in Appalachia today, this shortbread is a Christmas tradition, and for others the cookie is called Southern Shortenin' Bread. I've found it baked in home kitchens and sold during the summer in southern Appalachian towns.

Shortbread is a bar or cookie of Scotch and English origin. Containing only three ingredients, shortbread compares to Mexican wedding cakes, Russian tea cookies, and German hörnchen. You can make shortbread with nothing more than sugar, butter, and flour, and it never contains eggs. The most basic recipe calls for 1 cup of butter, 1/2 cup of sugar, and 2 1/2 cups of flour. Those that call it Shortenin' Bread may make it with brown sugar.

Shortbread is "short" because the butter keeps the gluten in the flour from forming strands. Remember, shortening shortens gluten strands. If the shortening is fully mixed, strands do not form.

Traditionally, the English and Scots baked shortbread in a large round mold and sliced it from the center like a pie. I like to copy this pattern by using an 8-inch round cake pan, fluting the edges, and pricking the surface.

Scotch Shortbread

*L*ike fine sand pressed together, this cookie crumbles when you bite it. The fine, crisp, tender, and almost sandy texture results from the combination of flour and cornstarch; the source of flavor is real butter.

DIFFICULTY Easy. Mix, measure, sift, and mix again—and with just five ingredients, this cookie is easy to make.

STEPS Adjust the oven rack to the center of the oven. Preheat the oven to 350°F.

In the bowl of an electric mixer, mix the butter on low. Slowly add the sugar and continue to mix, gradually increasing the speed to high. Depending on the

INGREDIENTS

1 cup butter, at room temperature
1 cup confectioners' sugar
2 cups all-purpose flour, sifted before measuring
1 cup cornstarch, sifted before measuring
35 pecan halves

YIELD 35 square cookies

power of your mixer, beat from 6 to 15 minutes, or until the butter turns white.

Remove the bowl from the mixer, and stir in the flour and cornstarch by hand. When you can bring the dough into a ball, stop mixing. The dough will be dry, almost crumbly.

Press the dough into an ungreased 13x9x2-inch baking pan. To get the dough spread evenly, I divide it into twelve parts, and spread them evenly in the pan. Press the dough flat, and score it with a fork.

Press the 35 pecans into the dough—5 rows across and 7 down. Bake for 30 to 33 minutes, or until the dough starts to brown around the edges. Do not let it brown across the top. Cool for 5 minutes, and cut into 35 squares. Cool another 5 to 10 minutes, and transfer to a wire rack. Store in an airtight container.

HEALTHY CHOICE ALTERNATIVE Don't eat many of these cookies—each one has 110 calories and 6.5 grams of fat.

The Scots and English serve shortbread with candied orange or lemon peel. Coming across the sea, we lost that tradition and tend to serve shortbread with milk or hot coffee. Eat it as a snack on the go, or serve it with vanilla ice cream, fresh fruit, and hot fudge sauce.

Apricot Unbeatables

DIFFICULTY Moderate. With six ingredients, this drop cookie is moderate in difficulty.

INGREDIENTS

1/3 cup (3 ounces) dried apricot pieces
1 cup confectioners' sugar
1/4 cup all-purpose flour
1/4 cup egg whites (from 2 or 3 eggs)
1/4 teaspoon baking powder
1 cup chopped walnuts

YIELD 30 cookies

*N*ot until after I started making this cookie did I find out that mountaineers have an affinity for apricots—fresh, dried, and in cookies. I came across this recipe by chance, leafing through a 1977 book called *The Cookie Cookbook* by Darlene Kronschnabel. I was attracted to the cookie because it has a natural gloss, little flour, no shortening, and the flavor of dried apricots. Here I present my adaptation of Darlene's formula.

Apricot Unbeatables are not typical cookies. First, as the cookies bake, they form a crinkly, glossy surface. Second, the fact that this cookie has no spices separates it from cookies such as gingerbread, lebkuchen, and Christmas rocks. Third, most nut and fruit cookies—for example, oatmeal raisin and applesauce—have much more flour and some shortening. This cookie is a light delight, a kiss of sweetness.

STEPS Preheat the oven to 325°F. Grease two cookie sheets, or cover cookie sheets with parchment or waxed paper. Cut the apricots into 1/3-inch pieces.

In a mixing bowl, combine the sugar, flour, egg whites, and baking powder. When fully mixed, add the nuts and apricots. Continue to stir the batter as you drop the cookies by rounded teaspoonfuls onto the parchment.

Reduce the oven temperature to 300°F, and bake for 15 to 18 minutes, or until the edges brown and the tops turn beige. After the cookies cool for 5 minutes, push the blade of a spatula under the cookies, cutting them from the paper. If you grease the parchment the cookies come up easily, but they spread out too much. When the cookies are fully cool, store in an airtight container.

HEALTHY CHOICE ALTERNATIVE Like the Forgotten Kisses, the only source of fat in this cookie is the walnuts, and the walnuts and apricots will add a bit of fiber to your diet.

Dried-Apple Chocolate Chip Cookies

*M*ountain cooks have always prepared special foods for their families, and with this cookie, they doubled the pleasure. Better than any gourmet, giant, fast-food, or shopping-mall brand-name cookie, this is an example of home-baked goodness. These cookies are loaded. They are a big, blended, all-butter, nut-enhanced, dried-apple, and chocolate chip cookie. Enjoy them—a mountain country Toll House cookie.

STEPS Preheat the oven to 350°F.

In a small bowl, combine the flour and baking powder, and set aside. In a large mixing bowl, combine the butter, sugar, and brown sugar, and beat until creamy and light. Beat in the eggs and vanilla. Gradually add the flour mixture, and stir. Add the chocolate chips, almonds, and apple pieces.

For each cookie, measure 1/3 cup of dough (I use an ice cream scoop) onto an ungreased cookie sheet, 6 cookies per sheet. Bake for 18 to 22 minutes. The cookies should be soft in the center and brown on the edges. Cool on a wire rack.

Prepare the frosting as the cookies bake. In a medium bowl, whisk together the egg white and confectioners' sugar. The mixture should be thick enough to spread. Frost the warm cookies with a brush, pour the frosting from a pitcher, or press the frosting through the fine tip of a pastry tube.

TIP Serve fresh or store these cookies in the freezer and serve softened in the microwave. For a fresh cookie that was frozen, preheat the oven to 350°F, and rebake the cookies for 8 minutes, or until crisp on the outside.

DIFFICULTY Moderate. With twelve ingredients and two steps, this recipe is moderate in difficulty.

INGREDIENTS

FOR THE COOKIES
2 1/2 cups all-purpose flour
1 teaspoon baking powder
1 cup butter, at room temperature
3/4 cup sugar
3/4 cup brown sugar
2 eggs
1 teaspoon vanilla
12 ounces (2 cups) milk chocolate chips
1 1/4 cup whole almonds
1 cup dried apples, cut in small pieces

FOR THE WHITE FROSTING
1 egg white
1 1/4 cups confectioners' sugar

YIELD 20 mammoth cookies

HEALTHY CHOICE ALTERNATIVE At almost 400 calories per piece, these are more than cookies—each is a full dessert. The recipe contains 7,749 calories and 377 grams of fat. If you make 20 cookies, each will contain 19 grams of fat and 387 calories. If you make 80 small cookies, each will contain about 100 calories and 5 grams of fat.

Christmas Rocks
(Fruitcake Cookies)

When I was a boy, my mother made fruitcake. Later, as a young man living in Iowa and Wisconsin, I occasionally ate some fruitcake during the Christmas season. Like many others, I didn't really like fruitcake. Then in 1975 I moved to Pikeville, Kentucky, and mountain cooks introduced me to a derivative of fruitcake. This fruitcake cookie, which we call Christmas Rocks, is crunchy, sweet, soft, chewy, colorful, and not over-spiced or over-fruited. A few years ago Carrie Cinnamond of Pikeville, Kentucky, gave me her recipe for Christmas Rocks, and from her handwritten notes I developed this.

Christmas Rocks are different from other fruitcake cookies in that they have very little candied fruit; the batter contains dates, raisins, and pecans. This recipe is extremely large, but Christmas is a time of giving, and in the years when I make this cookie, it lasts throughout the Christmas season, filling many gift and potluck needs. If you don't want to make 120 cookies, cut the recipe in half.

DIFFICULTY Difficult. With thirteen ingredients and sheet after sheet of cookies to bake, this recipe is difficult because it takes time—the better part of 3 hours.

INGREDIENTS

3 cups all-purpose flour
1 teaspoon ground cloves
1 teaspoon cinnamon
1 pound white raisins
1 pound chopped dates
1 pound pecan pieces
1 cup butter
1 1/2 cups brown sugar
3 eggs
1 teaspoon baking soda
2 tablespoons hot water
8 ounces red candied cherries
8 ounces green candied cherries, halved and cut into 1/8-inch strips

YIELD 120 cookies

STEPS Preheat the oven to 350°F. Grease several cookie sheets.

In a large bowl, whisk together the flour, cloves, and cinnamon, and set aside. In an 8-quart mixing bowl, combine the raisins with 1 to 2 heaping tablespoons of the flour mixture, and use your fingers to separate and mix the raisins.

To chop the dates, place them on a cutting board and sprinkle them with 1 or 2 heaping tablespoons of the flour mixture. Using a chef's knife, cut the dates until they are 1/4 to 1/2 inch in size, and mix the pieces with the flour to keep them from sticking together. Add the dates and pecans to the raisins, and mix well.

In a small bowl, cream together the butter and brown sugar. Beat the eggs, and add. Dissolve the baking soda in the hot water, add to the sugar mixture, and stir. When fully mixed, add to the raisin mixture, and stir until combined. If the dough is too thick to stir with a spoon, wash your hands and plunge them into the dough. Drop the dough by rounded teaspoonfuls onto the cookie sheets.

Garnish each cookie with half a red cherry and two strips of green cherry. Place the cherries in an H-shape so that one green strip is on each side of the red cherry. Bake for 10 minutes, or until the cookies brown across the top. Cool on a wire rack.

TIP Chop the dates as I direct above, or at your market purchase chopped and sugar-coated date pieces.

HEALTHY CHOICE ALTERNATIVE If you are trying to add fruit and fiber to your diet, and if you can eat raisins, dates, and nuts, then this recipe—with only 1 cup of butter and 3 eggs—is healthy. Besides that, the cookies are small, and each cookie has less than a $1/2$ teaspoon of butter and $1/40$ of an egg yolk.

Serve these cookies during the seven-week holiday season from Thanksgiving to New Year's. Offer with Scotch Shortbread, Forgotten Kisses, Savage Mountain Pound Cake, or Chocolate Chip Granola Bars. For a complete dessert, combine with hot coffee and vanilla ice cream.

Chocolate Chip Granola Cookies
Chocolate Chip Granola Bars
(Appalachian Trail Cookies)

*A*t any trailhead along the 2,050 miles of the Appalachian Trail you will see picnickers, day hikers, and through hikers—an elite few who hike the entire trail from the south to the north. They start at Springer Mountain, Georgia, and hike to Mount Katahdin, Maine. If they complete the hike they will have walked almost 10 percent of the earth's circumference.

From the time of the trail's completion in 1937, trail enthusiasts have been eating various kinds of granola and gorp. Granola is flavored and roasted rolled oats. Gorp is a mixture of raisins, nuts, and chocolate chips or M&Ms. Today hikers enjoy Appalachian Trail Cookies and granola bars of all kinds. If you don't bake this cookie before you go hiking, you'll find granola bars sold in small stores along the route of the trail.

This cookie is a cross between an oatmeal and a chocolate chip cookie, and it combines gorp and granola. Using granola instead of rolled oats makes these cookies crunchy and a bit sweet. Because granola varies greatly in sweetness, your choice of granola will make a difference. I like to use a honey-coated, highly sweetened, oats, raisins, and almond granola. Use it in the batter and as a coating outside. I prefer to make these as bar cookies—you don't have to use a

DIFFICULTY Moderate. With ten ingredients and one baking step, this recipe is moderate in difficulty. Rolling each cookie in granola takes about 15 minutes. If you don't want to take the time to drop cookies, make them as bars.

mixer, you don't drop the cookies from a spoon, you don't roll them in granola, and you don't mess up four cookie sheets.

INGREDIENTS

1³/4 cups all-purpose flour
1 teaspoon cinnamon
¹/2 teaspoon baking powder
1³/4 cups brown sugar
1 cup butter, softened
2 eggs
1 teaspoon vanilla
8 cups (32 ounces) raisin and almond granola
12 ounces (2 cups) chocolate chips
¹/2 cup raisin

YIELD 45 cookies

STEPS Preheat the oven to 375°F. In a mixing bowl, whisk together the flour, cinnamon, and baking powder, and set aside. Using a heavy, high-speed mixer, beat together the brown sugar and butter, and add the eggs and vanilla. When the mixture is smooth, add the dry ingredients and then the 3 cups of the granola, the chocolate chips, and raisins.

Roll rounded teaspoonfuls of the dough in the remaining 5 cups granola. Space the cookies about 1 inch apart on ungreased cookie sheets. Bake for 12 to 16 minutes or until baked across the top, soft in the center, and brown (not dark) on the bottom.

Cool on a wire rack. Store in an airtight container.

HEALTHY CHOICE ALTERNATIVE These cookies are for the child in all of us. Relax and enjoy a modern sin—each cookie has only 1 teaspoon of butter. If saturated fat is a problem, replace the butter with canola oil and omit the egg yolks.

Serve for lunch with a cold sandwich. Use this cookie for a full breakfast, a meal on the go, a lunch-box treat, a trail snack, or a dessert topped with ice cream.

Chocolate Chip Granola Bars

I make these bars with melted butter, and they are chewy like brownies. Spread the dough onto a greased 15x10x1-inch baking sheet. It will be hard to spread, but you can leave it a bit uneven. Spread granola evenly over the top, using 5 cups total. Cover with plastic wrap and press the granola into the dough. Bake for 30 minutes. Cool completely, cut into squares, and serve.

Candy

DURING THE CHRISTMAS season, at fall fairs, school reunions, and family celebrations as I travel through the mountains, I see homemade candy: chocolate, vanilla, peanut butter, cream, and caramel. Making candy is a common practice, one that brings the generations together. I know a thirty-five-year-old woman who goes to her mother's house each year several weeks before Christmas, and together they make candy. Her mother is teaching her, she tells me, and yet they have been making candy together for thirty years.

Making candy in our mountains is either a family tradition or a social event. Women's clubs, church bazaars, or youth organizations such as Boy Scouts make candy to sell or to serve at their parties. The large size of these recipes reflects the social nature of candy making.

Cooked sugar candies get their names from the stage to which you cook them. This stage corresponds to the final cooking temperature and the way the candy feels when it cools. For example, my Cream Pull Candy is a taffy because I cook it to the hard ball stage.

When making caramels, fudge, or popcorn candy, the final cooking temperature is critical. To know when your candy reaches that temperature, you have to know how your thermometer reads.

Check the accuracy of your thermometer by placing it in a saucepan of water, turning the heat to high, and letting the water boil for several minutes. Read the thermometer. It should read 212°F. If, when the water boils, your thermometer reads higher than 212°F, subtract that amount from the cooking temperature the recipe calls for. If your thermometer reads lower than 212°F, add that amount to the final cooking temperature.

When I am not familiar with how a candy looks, I watch my thermometer and check the sugar using cold water tests. I find it helpful to distinguish candies based on their cooked temperature as well as their cold water test. To conduct cold water tests, drip a bit of hot syrup into a cup of ice water. (To prevent overcooking during the test, remove the candy from the heat.) When the drop of candy is cold, lift it out of the water with a spoon and squeeze it together in your fingers or try to crack it between your teeth. Note its consistency. Feel it carefully, and compare the candy to these tests.

When you press a cold drop of the candy between your fingers, a *soft ball* quickly loses its shape, but you can pick it up; cook fondant, mint patties, and fudge to the soft ball (234°F to 236°F) stage.

A *firm ball* holds a ball and resists pressure, but you can flatten it out; cook caramels and divinity to the firm ball (242°F to 248°F) stage.

A *hard ball* has lost most of its plasticity and will roll around on a buttered plate; cook taffy to the hard ball (250°F to 265°F) stage.

A *soft crack* syrup will form brittle threads in the water but softens when removed; cook crunches or butter brickle and hoarhound candy to the soft crack (270°F to 290°F) stage.

A *hard crack* forms brittle threads in the water and holds them when removed; cook nougat and brittle to the hard crack (300°F to 315°F) stage.

Above 320°F, the sugar starts to caramelize.

To learn to use these tests, cook some peanut brittle, which is cooked to the hard crack stage, and test it at each stage. If you don't want to use the cold water tests, buy a good quick-response digital thermometer. Its half-inch-high numbers are easy to read.

Cream Pull Candy
(Marble Top Candy)

DIFFICULTY Moderate. If you have experience with candy, this recipe is not difficult. Be patient, and allow about 1 hour to cook, cool, and pull the candy.

*S*old in many stores, talked about in hushed tones, and associated with country cooks who live at a slow pace, this soft, creamy, white candy, when made to perfection, is the mark of an outstanding cook. If you follow my recipe, the candy will taste of cream. For an extra bit of goodness, I occasionally add mint flavoring or coat the candy with chocolate.

Do you remember the old marble-topped water stands and dressers? Perhaps you have seen these thick marble slabs gracing the tops of solid wood night stands. Have you rested your hands on their cool tops? These are the surfaces that cooks of years ago used when they cooled Cream Pull or Marble Top Candy.

Cream pull candy becomes smooth and delicate—almost powdery and not grainy—when you pull and stretch it for as long as 40 minutes. If you don't have some strong cooperative arms supported by friendly people, consider using a candy hook. Using a tool in place of people will get the job done, but the same tool will also turn a social occasion into a solitary process.

Because the candy absorbs moisture and because I live in the humid southern mountains, I wait for a dry winter day to make cream candy. I then boil the sugar and cream to the mid-hard ball stage, 255°F to 260°F, cool it on a cold surface (a marble top), and then start pulling.

INGREDIENTS
3 cups sugar
3/4 cup water
1 tablespoon butter
3/4 cup heavy cream
1 teaspoon vanilla

YIELD 1 1/2 pounds
or 90 pieces

STEPS Clean and lightly grease a cold surface onto which you can pour the cooked syrup. The surface may be a marble slab, cookie sheets on a wire rack, or (as I use), a Corian counter top.

In a large, heavy saucepan over medium heat, mix and stir together the sugar, water, and butter. Bring to a boil, and cover the saucepan for 3 minutes. This washes the sugar crystals from the sides of the pan.

Uncover and boil, without stirring, an additional 15 minutes, or until the syrup reaches 240°F. Slowly, a tablespoon at a time, add the cream. Drizzle it over the syrup so that you do not disturb or slow the boiling. Watch the thermometer and keep the temperature above 235°F.

Continue to cook, without stirring, until the mixture reaches the hard ball stage, 257°F. Pour immediately onto the prepared surface. If the candy is allowed to stay in the saucepan, the temperature will continue to rise.

Hold the saucepan close to your prepared surface and, pouring away from you, pour the mixture in repeated S patterns out of the saucepan. Do not scrape the pan. Allow to cool until you can handle the mixture. Bring the candy into a ball, and fold in the vanilla.

Using greased hands, pull and stretch for up to 40 minutes. Initially the candy will be stringy, but it will come back together. Later, the mixture loses its gloss, turns color to white or pale ivory, and holds ridges. The outside surface starts to dry and crumble.

With three people working together (six hands pulling) you can divide the candy in thirds and get it done faster. When the taffy is ready, twist and pull into six ropes, each about 18 inches long. Using a scissors, snip the ropes into 1- to 2-inch-long pieces the shape of pillows—crimped on the ends and high in the center.

To keep moisture out of the candy, place in a sealed container, and allow from 3 to 24 hours for the candy to cream. This period of curing will soften or cream the candy, changing it from chewy to creamy. If you did not pull the candy enough, it will not cream.

As with other sugar candy, keep this candy dry by wrapping each piece and storing in a sealed container. Or coat it with chocolate. (I like to cover this candy with my Chocolate Coating.)

Peanut Butter Rolls

AT SERVICE STATIONS, flea markets, street festivals, ball games, parades, and county fairs—wherever Highlanders gather—you'll find peanut butter rolls for sale. Before buying a piece, I can see the thickness of the cream, the number of rolls, and the amount of peanut butter. But I cannot tell if the candy will be sharp with potato, grainy with sugar, or smooth with divinity. Sometimes I'll sample. Usually I search in vain for a silky-smooth, divinity-based, creamy peanut butter roll.

A peanut butter roll is white candy filled with peanut butter. When this candy warms and melts in your mouth, the starchy, savory peanut butter contrasts with the sweet cream candy. I make peanut butter rolls two ways—with potato or with divinity. If we make peanut butter rolls without cooking the sugar and use potato as the base, we call this potato candy. Or, we make these rolls with divinity.

Potato and divinity peanut butter rolls represent two different kinds of country cooks. One works systematically, takes time, and uses equipment; the other is in a hurry. One reads a thermometer; the other kneads until smooth. One stirs hot syrup; the other gathers friends to mash, mix, and roll the "dough." Some say the potato candy is old-fashioned. I say it represents casual country living and a laid-back personality.

Potato Candy

DIFFICULTY Easy. Assuming that you make this candy with leftover potato, all you do is mix, spread, and roll the candy—three ingredients, no cooking.

*T*his recipe is easy. A typical potato-based, potato wheel candy recipe reads as follows: Mash one small baked potato and stir in confectioners' sugar, adding sugar until the candy feels like dough and can be rolled out.

The trick is to add enough—but not too much—sugar. The amount depends on the amount of water in the potato. New potatoes, boiled potatoes, and leftover mashed potatoes have more water than old baked potatoes. Add sugar until you can roll the potato candy, and it does not stick to the surface. The candy will be dry.

Unlike the Peanut Butter Divinity Pinwheel Candy that follows, this candy is dry and firm.

HEARTY
Cooking
COUNTRY

STEPS Mash the cooked potato until it is smooth and the lumps are gone. (I use a potato ricer.) Be careful—if you have lumps now, you will have lumps later.

Measure out ¹/₂ cup mashed potato. In a mixing bowl, stir 1 cup of the sugar into the potato. Continue to add sugar, stirring and then kneading the potato and sugar as you would bread dough. Add sugar until the mixture resembles pie dough—dry enough not to stick to your hands, but wet enough to roll out. If you add too little sugar, the "dough" will stick to the rolling surface; dust with confectioners' sugar. If you add too much sugar, the "dough" gets hard or brittle and cracks; add 1 teaspoon of water.

Between sheets of waxed paper or on a surface dusted with confectioners' sugar, roll the candy to a ¹/₈-inch thickness. Try to roll the candy into a rectangle, 12x16 inches in size. To square up the rectangle, cut, moisten, and patch as needed. With a spatula, spread the peanut butter evenly over the candy.

From the long edge roll as you would a jelly roll. Cut the log in half, wrap with plastic wrap, and chill until firm—several hours or overnight. Serve as a roll, slicing off pieces as you eat them, or slice roll into ³/₄-inch pieces. If you slice the pieces, keep them covered. If you smash the pieces a little as you cut them, reshape the pieces to make them round.

TIP Once you have mixed the potato and sugar to make the fondant-like candy, try adding cocoa or mint. Spread coconut, peanuts, raisins, or citron on the peanut butter. Try using sweet potato in place of the white potato. For a giant splurge and to prevent drying, dip the candy in Chocolate Coating (page 296).

INGREDIENTS
¹/₂ cup warm cooked potato
4 to 6 cups (1¹/₃ to 2 pounds) sifted confectioners' sugar
1 cup peanut butter

YIELD 20 pieces

Peanut Butter Divinity Pinwheel Candy
(Peanut Butter Rolls)

*D*ivinity—a smooth, airy, creamy white candy—is a type of fudge. When I think of food families, divinity is a first cousin to marshmallow and a second cousin to nougat. Once you learn to make white divinity, you can make other flavors by adding ingredients such as chocolate, lemon, nuts, small candies, or dried fruits. *The Illustrated Encyclopedia of American Cooking*, by the editors of Favorite Recipes Press, includes seventeen divinity recipes, including one similar to what I give below. Their divinity recipe names—what fun they are!—include rainbow puffs, lemon delight, raspberry fluffs, creamy date, chocolate ripple, and cool Christmas mint. The soft smooth sweetness of this divinity darting around your mouth is worth the effort. Be patient, and, as

DIFFICULTY Difficult. Making this candy takes practice. You also need an accurate candy thermometer, eight ingredients, and about 1¹/₂ hours.

one mountain cook says, "Practice a few times, and it will work."

1 1/4 cups peanut butter
2 egg whites, at room
    temperature
1/4 teaspoon salt
1/4 teaspoon cream of
    tartar
1 teaspoon vanilla
1/2 cup water
2/3 cup light corn syrup
2 cups sugar

YIELD 30 pieces

STEPS Clear and clean a large work surface. Get out your waxed paper, and cut and grease a 24-inch piece. Measure out the peanut butter and set it aside.

Using a high-speed mixer, beat the egg white until frothy. Add the salt and tartar, and beat on high until the egg white forms drooping peaks. Add the vanilla.

In a medium saucepan, combine the water, corn syrup, and sugar, stir, and bring to a boil. Reduce the heat, cover, and simmer for 3 minutes. (The lid creates vapor and washes the sides of the pan.) Remove the lid. Do not stir. Increase the heat to high-medium, and cook the syrup about 15 minutes, or until it reaches the hard ball stage (250°F).

With the mixer at high speed, pour the hot syrup slowly into the egg whites— slowly enough to take 1 1/2 minutes. Do not let the syrup touch the beaters or the side of the mixing bowl. Continue to beat for 5 to 10 minutes, or until the mixture thickens and loses its gloss.

With greased fingers, spread the divinity mixture onto the greased waxed paper. With a greased rolling pin, roll the divinity out to 12x24 inches, cutting and patching as needed. It will be about 1/16 inch thick. With a rubber spatula, spread the peanut butter over the divinity. Using the waxed paper to help you get started, roll the divinity like a jelly roll, starting at the long edge. Cut the roll into three pieces, and cover in plastic wrap. Serve the roll on a cutting board, slicing off pieces as you eat them, or slice into 3/4-inch pieces. If you slice the candy ahead, reshape the pieces so that they are round and then keep them fresh by sealing them. As the knife gets sticky, wash it off with water.

Chocolate Coating

This chocolate coating works well because the paraffin melted with the chocolate raises the chocolate's melting point. Melted chocolate without wax will coat candy, but it melts on your fingers as you eat it. The relationship of one ounce of paraffin to eight ounces of chocolate is low on paraffin, but I want just enough to raise the melting point a little, about 10°F. Too much paraffin prevents the chocolate from melting in your mouth. And more paraffin makes the chocolate stick to your teeth, and robs the chocolate of flavor. Use this to coat Buck-Eyes, Cream Pull Candy, or Roasted Pecans.

This melt-and-mix process takes about 15 minutes.

INGREDIENTS
1/2 pound semi-sweet
    chocolate
1/4 block (1 ounce)
    paraffin (Gulf sealing
    wax)

YIELD 1 cup

STEPS In a double boiler over—not in—hot water over low heat, melt the chocolate and wax. Stir to mix.

Buck-Eyes
Peanut Butter Log

$\mathcal{I}$n the fall on the steep moist banks of our hills, buckeye seeds fall from yellow buckeye trees, a member of the horsechestnut family. Most of the round seed has a dark, polished chestnut brown skin, but the top is a light brown, the color of peanut butter. This peanut butter candy is similar in shape and coloring to the yellow buckeye: We cover most of the ball with dark chocolate and leave the top exposed. Using my recipe, this candy compares well to a Reese's Peanut Butter Cup, but my formula gives a smoother, sweeter, and more peanut-flavored center.

Over the years I've found that some families make this candy with corn syrup and dry milk, and others make it as I suggest below, with margarine. I make peanut butter balls with margarine because it gives a soft, smooth, melt-in-your-mouth candy. More of the soft margarine gives a softer and smoother candy. If you add too much margarine, the candy does not hold its shape; if you add too little, it crumbles.

DIFFICULTY Moderate. Including the two ingredients for Chocolate Coating, this recipe takes five ingredients. With the melting, rolling, and dipping it takes about two hours to make a full batch of this candy.

STEPS Prepare one recipe of Chocolate Coating. Cover two cookie sheets with waxed paper.

In a large mixing bowl, combine the sugar, peanut butter, and margarine, and stir. Knead like biscuit dough. If, at this point, the balls are crumbly and do not hold together in the palm of your hand, add more margarine. If they are too soft and do not hold their shape, add sugar.

Form the mixture into balls a little larger than a quarter, about one-half an ounce. With the help of toothpicks or two forks, coat the peanut butter balls by dipping them in the Chocolate Coating. If you want the candy to look like buck-eyes, leave a small portion of the top without chocolate. For a thin layer of chocolate, keep the coating mixture warm. Place the coated balls on the prepared cookie sheets, and chill until firm. Cut the excess chocolate from around the bottom of each piece.

HEALTHY CHOICE ALTERNATIVE This recipe has 4,910 calories, 208 grams of fat, and no cholesterol. When you divide the recipe into 50 pieces, each has 98 calories and about 4 grams of fat.

INGREDIENTS
1 recipe Chocolate Coating (page 296)
1 pound confectioners' sugar
1 1/4 cups creamy peanut butter
1/2 cup plus 1 tablespoon margarine

YIELD 2 pounds or 50 pieces

Peanut Butter Log
To simplify this candy, turn the Buck-Eyes into a Peanut Butter Log. Mix the sugar, peanut butter, and margarine. Roll it into a log, seal in plastic wrap, and slice the pieces to serve. Omit the Chocolate Coating.

Bourbon Balls

DIFFICULTY Moderate. With six ingredients and two steps, these candies are moderate in difficulty. The recipe requires little cooking skill, but I find it a bit tedious to form, refrigerate, roll, and then dip the balls. Allow about 2 hours.

INGREDIENTS

FOR THE CANDY
1 1/2 cups pecans
5 tablespoons bourbon
1/2 cup melted butter
1 pound sifted confec-
tioners' sugar

FOR THE CHOCOLATE
COATING
1 1/3 cup (8 ounces)
semi-sweet chocolate
pieces
1 ounce paraffin (just
less than 1/4 a block of
Gulf sealing wax)

YIELD 50 to 60 pieces

A tiny treat, an ultimate ending—this candy is soft and it melts quickly in your mouth. As it melts you'll get a tinge of chocolate and a burst of bourbon. Our bourbon balls are soft-centered, chocolate-coated, and liqueur-flavored. In the past fifty-plus years, we have developed three kinds of bourbon balls. First, we make them with corn syrup and vanilla wafer crumbs, and second, like my recipe below, we make them with buttercream centers. Finally, some cooks make bourbon balls with fondant centers—a soft and smooth confection of sugar and water cooked to the soft ball stage and aged.

STEPS Cover two cookie sheets with waxed paper. Using a Salad Shooter or other mechanical grater, grate the pecans and mix them into the bourbon. Add the melted butter and then stir in the confectioners' sugar. Mix thoroughly. Drop by teaspoonfuls (about 1 inch in size) onto the waxed paper. If the candy is stiff enough, roll it in the palms of your hands to shape into balls. Refrigerate for 1 hour.

Prepare the coating: As the candy centers cool in the refrigerator, melt the chocolate and paraffin in a double boiler over hot—not boiling—water. When the candy centers are cool and firm, roll them between the palms of your hands. This rolling step makes the candy round.

When the chocolate mixture has melted, stir it up. Reduce the heat and keep the melted chocolate over low-low heat while you dip the candy. To dip the candy, select a spoon and fork. Select a fork with long and wide tines. If you do not have a wide-tined fork, take an old fork and spread the tines.

Roll the candy centers in the chocolate. Rest the dipped piece on the fork, and tap the fork handle on the edge of the pan, forcing the excess chocolate to drip back into the pan. Return the candy to the waxed paper. Refrigerate another hour or more. Loosen the candy from the paper, and use a long chef's knife to trim the excess chocolate from the bottom edges of each piece. Store covered in the refrigerator. Serve these the second day, after the flavors have ripened.

■ ■

Why Popcorn Pops

Popcorn pops because its kernels have a hard, waterproof outside covering. When you heat popcorn, the moisture inside the kernel turns to steam. The covering "tries" to keep the moisture inside, but just as steam has the power to drive a railroad train, the steam pressures the kernel's covering, causes it to burst, and makes a pop—a noisy explosion that forms soft, light, and white popcorn.

■ ■

Mount Mitchell Popcorn Balls
Sorghum Popcorn Balls

*I*n some regions of the mountains, corn is still a primary food, a dependable staple. Years ago, families grew their own corn, and popcorn was a treat—eating it with salt and butter or sweetened with a homemade syrup or sorghum was a joy.

I like to compare popcorn balls to Rice Krispies treats. Because I cook the syrup to the soft ball stage, my popcorn balls are chewy and sticky. Eating popcorn balls adds fiber to your diet, exercises the jaws, pulls at the teeth, and offers sugar, sugar, sugar.

STEPS Pop the corn, and measure out 3 quarts of popcorn, picking out the unpopped kernels. An easy way to separate the unpopped kernels is to pour the popcorn onto a clean table and spread it out. When you see unpopped kernels, roll them aside. Then lift the popped kernels into a pan, allowing unpopped kernels to remain on the table.

In a large microwave-safe bowl, stir the sugar and corn syrup until fully mixed. Microwave for 6 minutes on high, or until the mixture reaches 242°F to

DIFFICULTY Easy. The slowest part of the process is waiting for the balls to cool.

INGREDIENTS
1/2 cup popcorn kernels
  or 3 quarts popped
  popcorn
1 cup sugar
1 cup corn syrup
2 tablespoons butter
1/2 teaspoon salt

YIELD Twelve 3-inch balls

■ More
Desserts

245°F. Remove from the oven, and stir in the butter and salt.

Pour the cooked syrup over the popcorn, and stir gently to coat. When the mixture is cool enough to handle, with greased hands scoop up portions and shape into balls.

Cool on any flat surface, and wrap the balls individually in plastic wrap.

HEALTHY CHOICE ALTERNATIVE To reduce oil, I pop the popcorn in a hot-air popper. The total calorie count for this recipe is 2,140; total fat is 23 grams. Each popcorn ball has 178 calories and 1.9 grams of fat.

Served as a snack, popcorn balls show up at fairs, carnivals, and Halloween parties. To make them easier to bite into, I like to eat popcorn balls sliced. Take a large butcher's knife and slice them into half-inch-thick slices.

Sorghum Popcorn Balls To make sorghum-flavored popcorn balls, use ½ cup corn syrup and ½ cup sorghum syrup. Because sorghum foams, microwave the syrup in a very large bowl.

■ ■

Mount Mitchell

Named after Professor Elisha Mitchell and standing at 6,684 feet above sea level, Mount Mitchell is the highest point east of the Mississippi River. Just off the Blue Ridge Parkway northeast of Asheville, North Carolina, Mount Mitchell is part of the Black Mountain Range of the Southern Appalachian Mountains. If you are in the area, stop at the Black Mountain Camping area or Mount Mitchell State Park. Hike the Mountain Mitchell Trail (six miles) or the Old Mitchell Trail (two miles) to the top. At the summit, see Dr. Mitchell's grave and take in the view of the Blue Ridge Mountains.

After hiking to the top, drink some water and enjoy a Mount Mitchell Popcorn Ball.

Peanut Popcorn Candy

*J*ust forty minutes from now, you can sink your teeth into this brittle, crunchy, sweet, peanutty, fiber-filled, and caramel-flavored popcorn candy. A Friday night home-video side dish, popcorn candy is a family pleaser and a mountain tradition. The syrup here is cooked until the sugar gets to the soft crack stage, some thirty degrees higher than the firm ball stage used for popcorn balls. Happy snacking!

STEPS Pop the corn, and measure out 3 quarts of popcorn, picking out the unpopped kernels.

Preheat the oven to 300°F. Coat a 15x10-inch jelly roll pan with nonstick cooking spray. Pour the popcorn into the pan and place it in the oven.

Make the caramel sauce. In a saucepan over moderate heat, melt the butter and add the corn syrup and brown sugar. Stir until the sugar is melted and fully mixed. Simmer for 5 minutes, or until the mixture reaches 275°F, the low soft-crack stage. Stir in the peanuts.

Remove the popcorn from the oven, and pour the peanut-caramel mixture over the hot popcorn. Using two large spoons, stir and mix until the caramel gets stiff. To soften the caramel, slide the candy back into the oven for another 10 minutes. Stir and mix again, bringing the caramel to the top and spreading it over the popcorn. Bake another 10 minutes, and stir again. At this point, the popcorn should be sufficiently coated with caramel, but if it is not, stir and bake again. Cool.

HEALTHY CHOICE ALTERNATIVE This recipe contains 2,889 calories and 164 grams of fat. Each one-cup serving has 241 calories and 14 grams of fat. To further reduce fat and calories, omit the peanuts—you'll save 856 calories and 73 grams of fat. Each serving will be 71 calories and 6 grams of fat lighter.

Serve the caramel corn in small dishes or store it in small airtight bags, 1 serving per bag.

DIFFICULTY Moderate. While this recipe calls for just five ingredients, I rate it moderate in difficulty because the process takes three cooking steps.

INGREDIENTS
1/2 cup popcorn kernels
 or 3 quarts popped
 popcorn
1/2 cup butter
1/4 cup corn syrup
1 cup brown sugar
1 cup dry-roasted
 peanuts

YIELD Twelve
1-cup servings

Hospitality Extras

Relish, Pickles, Sweet Sauces, and Snacks

Cheese Grits Bars

Tomato Gravy
Tomato Gravy Hot Tomato Sandwich

Corn Bread Dressing
Oyster Dressing

Chow Chow

Pickled Beets

Light Vegetable Dip

Apple Butter
Spiced Apple Butter (Oven Apple Butter)

Pear Honey
(Pear Conserve)

Green Pepper Jelly

Country Whipped Cream
(Whipped Cream)

White Frosting

Lemon Glaze

Cheese Grits Bars

DIFFICULTY Moderate. With seven ingredients and two steps, this recipe is moderate in difficulty.

*W*hile I usually make these bars with instant hominy grits, sometimes I use barley or corn grits. I recommend my Healthy Choice Alternative because these bars don't need all the egg yolks and cheese used in the traditional recipe. Popular as an appetizer, serve this grits dish in place of a zucchini bar or sausage ball. I make the bars ahead, arrange them on a platter, and reheat them at serving time.

INGREDIENTS

FOR THE BARS

1 2/3 cups water
1/2 cup instant grits
1/2 pinch ground red (cayenne) pepper
6 tablespoons butter
6 ounces (1 1/2 cups) grated sharp Cheddar cheese
2 eggs

FOR THE TOPPING

1 ounce (1/4 cup) grated sharp Cheddar cheese
1/3 cup crumbled saltine crackers

YIELD 8 appetizers or 16 bars

STEPS Preheat the oven to 350°F. Grease an 8x8x2-inch baking pan.

In a saucepan over medium heat, bring the water, grits, and pepper to a boil. Stir, and simmer slowly for 2 to 3 minutes. Add the butter, cheese, and eggs, and mix well. Pour into the baking pan, and bake for 30 minutes.

In a small bowl, combine the 1/4 cup grated cheese and the cracker crumbs. Spread over the baked grits, and broil to brown. Cool, and cut into bars.

HEALTHY CHOICE ALTERNATIVE Grease the pan with nonstick cooking spray. Omit the egg yolks, using only the whites. Finally, you can reduce the cheese to 3/4 cup and the butter to 2 tablespoons. For flavor, add 3/4 teaspoon salt. I like this recipe better than the traditional one because it holds together better and does not have a greasy texture.

Serve reheated. Serve as an hors d'oeuvre with squares of Cheddar cheese, radishes, carrots, and celery. I like the contrast between the warm bars and the cold cheese and raw vegetables.

Tomato Gravy
Tomato Gravy Hot Tomato Sandwich

*T*omato gravy is a mild tomato-based cream gravy. It is not the same as tomato sauce, but rather is a white sauce, a cream sauce, or a milk gravy. This mountain tomato gravy is also a breakfast food, and we serve it over fried green tomatoes.

I am familiar with two kinds of mountain-style tomato gravy. Below I give the recipe for a cream gravy made like a cream of tomato soup, with tomato juice as the primary ingredient. To make the second style of tomato gravy similar to Chicken Cream Gravy, I use the pan drippings left from making fried green tomatoes. I add flour to the drippings in the pan, deglaze the pan with milk, and cook until thick.

STEPS In a small saucepan over medium heat, melt the butter and whisk in the flour. Add the tomato juice, cream, and salt, and boil for 1 minute. Add salt and pepper to taste.

HEALTHY CHOICE ALTERNATIVE Replace the cream with ½ cup evaporated milk. When using instant flour, I whisk the flour directly into the cream and juice, and I omit the butter. As I whisk it in, instant flour melts into the milk.

Tomato Gravy Hot Tomato Sandwich For a miracle lunch,
use Tomato Gravy on an open-faced tomato sandwich: On a large oval plate arrange sliced bread, sliced fresh tomatoes, meat loaf, and Mashed Kennebec Potatoes. Moisten the sandwich with Tomato Gravy, and add a garnish of chopped country ham. Serve with a light side salad and iced tea.

DIFFICULTY Easy. With five ingredients, this boiled sauce is easy to prepare.

INGREDIENTS
2 tablespoons butter
3 tablespoons all-purpose flour
1½ cups tomato juice
½ cup heavy cream
½ teaspoon salt

YIELD 2 cups or 4 servings

Corn Bread Dressing
Oyster Dressing

*I*n our markets, you can buy corn bread stuffing mix. The sterile-looking mixture is factory-flavored, -colored, and -sized. If you follow the directions on the package, you get a respectable stuffing, one that will fill a spot on your dinner table. But rather than a joy to make, a pleasure to serve, or a special treat you call your own, making stuffing-mix stuffing is a production, a chore. I prefer this recipe. For this stuffing, I start by opening my freezer. That's where we keep

DIFFICULTY Difficult. Including three different giblets, this recipe has thirteen ingredients. I rate it difficult because of the large number of ingredients and the need for corn bread, not because any of the steps are difficult.

Hospitality
Extras

leftover corn bread, and while frozen corn bread does not reheat very well, it makes some "terrible fine" stuffing. If you have to bake corn bread specially for this stuffing, I suggest Simple Corn Bread or Buttermilk Corn Bread.

Turning old corn bread into stuffing is an amazing transformation. Years ago, when I first diced frozen corn bread, I was surprised at how it crumbled and I thought that the stuffing would be a bust. But the steaming corn bread emerged from the roast turkey soft and moist, melded wonderfully together.

If I stuff and press this dressing into a turkey, I call it corn bread stuffing, but if I bake it in a dish, I call it dressing. Whether you bake it in a dish or a turkey, serving this dressing is like putting hand-tooled silver on your table. Corn Bread Stuffing adds dignity to the meal.

This recipe will stuff a 12-pound turkey, or it will fit nicely into a 9-inch round casserole dish. The dressing is fully flavored and soft. Unlike traditional bread stuffing, corn bread stuffing is smooth and crumbly. If you use the giblets and oysters, you'll hardly notice them, but, my my, how they add flavor!

INGREDIENTS

5 cups cubed fresh corn bread

3 cups cubed fresh bread

Giblets (liver, heart, and gizzard) from one turkey, about 3/4 cup diced

1/2 cup butter or turkey fat

1 cup diced onions

1 cup diced celery

3 cloves garlic, minced

2 teaspoons poultry seasoning

1 teaspoon salt

1 teaspoon sage

1/4 teaspoon pepper

YIELD 12 servings

STEPS The day before serving, dice the corn bread and bread into 1/2- to 3/4-inch cubes. Allow them to air-dry for 24 hours. As they dry, they shrink—make the dressing with 4 cups dry corn bread and 2 cups dry bread.

Preheat the oven to 350°F. Select and grease a 9-inch round casserole dish, or have a 12-pound turkey thawed and ready to bake.

Chop the giblets (liver, heart, and gizzard), and in a skillet over medium heat, fry them in the butter for 1 minute. Add the onion and celery, and fry an additional 4 minutes, or until the celery is soft. Remove from the heat, and add the garlic, poultry seasoning, salt, sage, and pepper. Mix fully. In a large bowl or pot, combine with the dried corn bread and bread cubes.

Pack and press the dressing into the neck and main cavities of the turkey, or spread it into the casserole dish. If using a casserole, stir in 2 eggs and bake 45 minutes. The eggs hold the stuffing together.

HEALTHY CHOICE ALTERNATIVE Replace the butter or fat with 1/2 cup chicken broth.

If you are not preparing turkey and don't have any giblets, use the oysters, and serve the dressing as a side dish with beef or pork. Round out the meal with green beans, mashed potatoes, and gravy.

Oyster Dressing To the above, add an 8-ounce container of fresh oysters or, if you don't use the giblets, two 8-ounce cans of oysters. Chop the oysters in half and add them, with their liquor, to the dressing.

HEARTY Cooking COUNTRY

Pickles, Relish, and Chow Chow

Years ago, and today, mountaineers made all sorts of pickles—
bread-and-butter pickles, dill pickles, dilly beans, mixed pickles,
watermelon rind pickles, pickled beans, pickled corn, pickled eggs,
pickled grapes, pickled onions, and pickled pears. Today pickles
are a treat, and we often give them as gifts.

Also called chowchow, chow-chow, and chou chou, the following
mixed-vegetable preserve is a relish of great importance and popularity. Many think that Chinese laborers introduced it into this
country about 1850 when they worked on our railroads. Its
Chinese origin is suggested, not only by its name, but also by the
seasonings that include a mixture of turmeric and various mustards.

A chow chow is any mixed vegetable relish. While most recipes
call for five or more vegetables, an exception is the recipe published
in 1879 by Marion Cabell Tyree in *Housekeeping in Old Virginia*.
This simple recipe includes onions and cabbage. Another simple
Tyree recipe, one of six chow chow recipes that she presents in
Housekeeping in Old Virginia, includes onions, green tomatoes, and
cucumbers. More typically, recipes for chow chow include all of
these—onions, cabbage, green tomatoes, and cucumbers—as well
as a few of the following: celery, hot red peppers, green beans, lima
beans, ripe tomatoes, apples, and corn.

Every edition of the Boston Cooking School cookbook, the
Fannie Farmer Cookbook, starting in 1896 and through to the new
thirty-second edition of 1990, includes a chow chow recipe. The
recipe published in 1896 calls for 2 quarts small green tomatoes,
12 small cucumbers, 3 red peppers, 1 cauliflower, 2 bunches celery,
1 pint small onions, and 2 quarts string beans. To these vegetables

they add seven flavorings including mustard seed, turmeric, all-spice, pepper, and cloves. Vinegar is the pickling ingredient. By 1990 the number of ingredients had grown to sixteen. My recipe is simpler.

■ ■

Chow Chow

I developed this chow chow for the modern cook. The recipe is small in quantity and easy to prepare. It is an authentic recipe, but I have reduced the amount of vinegar so that I can serve it when I prepare it—most relishes must be aged before serving.

DIFFICULTY Moderate. With ten ingredients and two steps, this recipe is moderate in difficulty.

INGREDIENTS
2 cups cabbage or 1 large green tomato
1 red bell pepper
1 medium onion
1 cucumber
2 tablespoons salt
¹/₂ cup sugar
1 teaspoon ground mustard
¹/₂ teaspoon turmeric
¹/₃ cup white vinegar
¹/₃ cup water

YIELD 3 cups or a small garnish for 12

STEPS Chop, grate, dice, or julienne the cabbage (or green tomato, if using), pepper, onion, and cucumber. Reduce them to 4 cups of tiny pieces, and mix with the salt. Cover and let stand overnight.

Drain the vegetables. Stir in the sugar, mustard, turmeric, and vinegar. In a large saucepan over medium heat, simmer with the water for 15 minutes.

HEALTHY CHOICE ALTERNATIVE This highly flavored pickled vegetable is fat free.

Drain and serve hot or cold as a condiment, garnish, or vegetable. Offer Chow Chow with Soup Beans, Corn Bread, and buttermilk, spread over hamburgers or crackers, or use as a garnish on a lettuce leaf to accompany Chicken and Dumplings, Fried Pork Chops, or Daniel Boone Beef Stew.

Pickled Beets

 $\mathcal{T}$ he beet family is a diverse group of vegetables that include table beets, swiss chard, and sugar beets. Farmers grow sugar beets for sugar, and mangels or mangolds, another beet, for cattle feed. The most common table beets are called red ball or dark red. Another variety, golden beets, do not bleed, and the tops are succulent and tasty. We harvest red and golden beets either when they are half grown or fully mature. These varieties mature in fifty to sixty days. An old variety known as long beets, which matures in 180 days, is sweeter and has superior flavor. I prepare beets with sauces that contain lemon or vinegar because acid helps the beets retain their red color. An orange sauce has the same effect.

We sometimes make pickled beets hot and spicy by cooking them with allspice, garlic, celery seed, dry mustard, or peppercorns. For a sweet spicy flavor, we add sugar, cloves, and cinnamon. Occasionally we pickle beets with onions and green pepper.

DIFFICULTY Moderate. With five ingredients, the process is moderate in difficulty.

STEPS In a glass or stainless-steel saucepan, heat the beet juice, vinegar, sugar, and salt to the boiling point. Add the prepared beets, and return to a boil. Remove from the stove. Serve.

TIP Pack hot beets into hot canning jars, cover with boiling syrup, cap the jars, and process for 30 minutes in a boiling water bath. Or, place the beets in plastic containers, cover them with the syrup, and freeze.

HEALTHY CHOICE ALTERNATIVE This pickled beet recipe is healthy, and if you are trying to improve your diet, substitute Pickled Beets for pastries and chips.

Serve these hot or cold, as a condiment with Soup Beans or Highlander Corn Bread Pie. Enjoy Pickled Beets cold as an appetizer or a diet snack, and eat them with coldcuts or as part of a plate salad.

INGREDIENTS
1 1/2 pounds (2 cups) peeled, cooked, and chopped beets
1 cup beet juice
1/4 cup cider vinegar
1/4 cup sugar
1/2 teaspoon salt

YIELD 4 servings

Light Vegetable Dip

I've made a lot of light salad dressings, but none are as good as this. This dip, dressing, or mayonnaise substitute is thick, creamy, and salty. Now, when I want a tasty vegetable salad with a thick creamy dressing—and when I am watching fat intake—I make this dip.

INGREDIENTS
8 ounces Kraft Fat-Free
  Philadelphia Cream
  Cheese
1/4 cup nonfat buttermilk
1 (.4-ounce) pack
  Original Hidden
  Valley Ranch
  Buttermilk Salad
  Dressing Mix

YIELD 1 1/4 cups or
10 servings

STEPS Scrape and pour the cream cheese, buttermilk, and dressing mix into a large bowl, and, using a wire whisk, whisk until smooth. At first you'll find the ingredients stiff, but if you keep working them, they become smooth. Whisk until you have mixed in the smallest lumps. Refrigerate.

HEALTHY CHOICE ALTERNATIVE This dressing is fat and cholesterol free. The recipe contains about 250 calories and 3,410 milligrams of sodium. Each of ten 2-tablespoon servings contains 25 calories and 341 milligrams of sodium. The dressing mix contains 2,240 milligrams of sodium. If you like a salt substitute, try it in place of the dressing mix.

Serve this as you would any salad dressing, or offer as a substitute for sour cream vegetable dip or chip dip.

Apple Butter
Spiced Apple Butter (Oven Apple Butter)

DIFFICULTY Moderate.
With directions that call
for peeling and coring,
four ingredients, two
cooking steps, and a
blender, this recipe is
moderate in difficulty.

*H*appily, when colored leaves fall from trees and blow through the air, we gather to make apple butter. At our fall festivals, civic groups work as teams to peel, cook, and bottle their favorite apples. From the back of a pickup truck, club members stack bushels of fresh apples high in their vendor tent. Over small fires and in giant cauldrons, using wood stirrers with handles that may be eight feet long, they simmer the apple butter, evaporating the water to make a concentrate. The boiling takes days, and the stirring is continuous. Small groups work around the clock; large groups sit on folding chairs and talk. Later, crowds gather to watch and group members pack the apple butter in pint jars and sell it from under the tent. The apple butter sells faster than the water evaporates. The demand is great, and the supply is limited.

Sugar sweetens and thickens apple butter. Today, some cooks use little sugar, others use a lot, and still others use sweet sorghum. My recipe is light on sugar. The sweetness and flavor in my Apple Butter come from tart apples.

The Apple Butter recipe yields a sweet but mild-flavored butter. My Spiced Apple Butter recipe that follows is a bit more exciting, but for my taste buds its flavor is right. When I eat it straight from the jar, it satisfies me like a piece of candy.

STEPS Wash, peel, core, and dice the apples to make about 10 cups.

In a large saucepan, combine the apples and cider. Cook until soft, about 30 minutes. (I use a pressure cooker, and cook for 10 minutes.) Stir to make applesauce. Blend in the sugar and cinnamon.

At this point, you can thicken the puree either on the stovetop or in the oven. I prefer using the oven because, even though it takes longer, I don't have to stir the apple butter as frequently. Pour the sauce into a china crock, glass casserole, or stainless-steel roasting pan, and bake at 275°F for 4 to 5 hours, stirring every hour or two.

To test for doneness, try one of these three methods: Drop a tablespoon of apple butter on a saucer, let it stand, and a watery ring *does not* form around the edges; a tablespoon of apple butter dropped onto a saucer and then inverted clings to the saucer; or the apple butter is stiff enough to spread with a knife. Refrigerate or pour into pint jars and seal with paraffin.

HEALTHY CHOICE ALTERNATIVE Omit the sugar.

Serve on Gingerbread, biscuits, toast, pancakes, waffles, muffins, sweet potatoes, roast pork, pork chops, sugar cookies, graham crackers, or ice cream. When I am in the kitchen alone, taking a break from my morning chores, I eat Apple Butter like I eat candy: with milk, coffee, or tea—straight from the jar.

Spiced Apple Butter Increase the cinnamon to 2 teaspoons, and add
1/2 teaspoon ground cloves and 1/4 teaspoon allspice. As you stir the spices into the cooked apple, watch it change color from light to deep amber brown. The spices, though not strong, perk up the Apple Butter and give it a slight smack.

INGREDIENTS
8 tart apples
1 cup apple juice
1 cup sugar
1 teaspoon cinnamon

YIELD 4 cups

Pear Honey
(Pear Conserve)

DIFFICULTY Easy.
With three ingredients and about 1 hour of stovetop cooking, this recipe is easy.

xplore this double-miracle: Heat turns a pot of dry-looking julienned fruit into a pot of liquid. Then, this pot of liquid becomes a stiff jam.

Is it honey? No—this conserve is a pear jam, a sweet spread, and a preserve that we call pear honey. Some mountaineers say that pear honey is as good as honey. I hope you agree.

The cookbook *Smoky Mountain Magic*, compiled by the Junior League of Johnson City, Tennessee, offers two recipes for ginger pear honey. They use orange and lemon juice and orange and lemon peel to thicken the conserve. Other cooks, like I do here, thicken pear honey by cooking the fruit and sugar for a long time. If you cook it too long, it will get too thick—but you can thin it down with water.

INGREDIENTS
2 pounds (5 cups quartered) pears
1 pound (2 cups) fresh pineapple
4 cups sugar

YIELD 5 cups

STEPS Sterilize 6 jelly jars, and have the lids and rings ready.

Peel and core the pears. Then, dice, shred, grind, or julienne them. Peel, core, and dice the pineapple. A food processor facilitates this chopping.

Pour and scrape the shredded pears, pineapple, and sugar into a large saucepan. Stir until mixed, and, over low heat, simmer for 1 hour, or up to 1 1/2 hours.

When the honey is ready, it will thicken in the pot, and it will have boiled down to 4 1/2 to 5 cups. To test for doneness, spread 1/2 teaspoon of the conserve on a chilled dinner plate, and refrigerate. When cold, the test sample should be a jelly-like thickness, not thin like a sauce. If the honey is not thick enough, cook an additional 15 minutes.

Fill the jars to within 1/8 inch of the top, seal with lids and rings, and invert the jars for 5 minutes, to help create a seal.

Serve on biscuits, pancakes, or waffles, or spread over ice cream and add to banana splits. If sugar crystals form, add a bit of water and boil them away.

Green Pepper Jelly

*T*he first time I tasted this jam the sweet and sour flavor surprised me. It is a peppery sweet that I enjoy with cream cheese and salty crackers. Because this jelly contains small pieces of green pepper and the pepper peeling, this preserve is technically a jam. However, most cooks call it jelly.

STEPS Wash and sterilize four 1-cup jelly jars.

Wash, quarter, and seed the peppers. In a food processor, process until almost smooth—the pieces should be the size of a grain of rice. Measure 2 cups of the green pepper puree into a saucepan, and add the sugar and vinegar. Bring to a boil, reduce the heat, and simmer for 5 minutes. Add the pectin, return to a boil, and boil for 1 minute. Add the food coloring. Pour into the sterilized jars, filling them to 1/8 inch of the top. Cover with lids, and invert for 5 minutes to form a seal.

HEALTHY CHOICE ALTERNATIVE This jelly has no fat, and I use it in place of butter. If I use it with cream cheese in place of butter (oh, the combination is so good!), I also save fat grams. One ounce (2 tablespoons) of light cream cheese has 5 grams of fat, while the same amount of butter has 23 grams of fat.

Serve this with real butter or cream cheese, spread on Buttermilk Biscuits or salty crackers.

DIFFICULTY Easy. With five ingredients and 5 minutes of simmering, this recipe is easy to prepare. Like most jams, once you have the fruit and jars ready, making the jam is easy.

INGREDIENTS
2 medium (1 pound) green bell peppers
3 3/4 cups sugar
3/4 cup white vinegar
1 1/2 ounces fruit pectin
1 drop green food coloring

YIELD 3 1/2 cups

Country Whipped Cream
(Whipped Cream)

*F*or full rich flavor, I make this topping a day ahead and store it in the refrigerator. In your market, look for heavy cream or heavy whipping cream, which contains at least 36 percent butterfat. For a tempting mix of flavors and temperatures, serve this cold whipped cream on the warm Prune Cake.

DIFFICULTY Easy. With three ingredients, this recipe is easy to prepare.

INGREDIENTS
1 cup heavy whipping cream, chilled
¼ cup sugar
1 teaspoon vanilla

YIELD 6 servings

STEPS Place the bowl and beater of an electric mixer in the refrigerator. When they are thoroughly chilled, add the heavy cream, sugar, and vanilla. Beat on high until the mixture thickens, falls in globs, and has a slight gloss.

Serve this on Sweet Potato Pie, Cushaw Pie, Stack Cake, and Dried Apple Pie. Use it to smother fresh strawberries, blueberries, or peaches. Drop a dollop on your hot coffee, cold cereal, or breakfast waffles.

White Frosting

I make this frosting because it is sweet, decorative, and quick. If your egg white is extra large, use just part of it. When mixed, the frosting should pour in a thin line.

DIFFICULTY Very Easy. With two ingredients and no cooking, this frosting is easy to prepare.

INGREDIENTS
1¼ cups confectioners' sugar
1 egg white

YIELD ½ cup plus 2 tablespoons, or enough to frost 24 cookies

STEPS Sift the confectioners' sugar into a large mixing bowl, and whisk a well in the center. Drop the egg white into the well, and continue to whisk until fully mixed. If the mixture is too thick, add a bit more egg white; if it stirs up too thin, add sugar. Pour and scrape the frosting into a small pitcher, and then drizzle it over cookies, pies, or cakes. Spread it on cookies using a pastry brush.

HEARTY
Cooking
COUNTRY

Lemon Glaze

*T*his glaze is powerful. Use it sparingly, or it may add too much lemon to your desserts.

STEPS In a mixing bowl, whisk the sugar, 1 cup at a time, into the lemon juice.

HEALTHY CHOICE ALTERNATIVE Use this sweet but fat-free topping in place of butter- or egg-based frostings.

I like to pour this glaze into a small pitcher so that I can drizzle it over cakes, pastry, or cookies. I use it on Savage Mountain Pound Cake and Gingerbread.

DIFFICULTY Very Easy. Once you have squeezed the lemon juice, you just stir.

INGREDIENTS
2 ²/₃ cups confectioners' sugar
¹/₃ cup fresh-squeezed lemon juice

YIELD 1 ¹/₄ cups

Eleven

Beverages

Cider, Coffee, and Cocoa

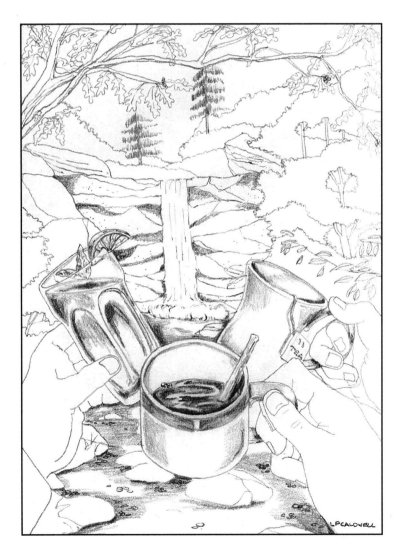

Mulled Cider
(Hot Spiced Cider)

Old-Fashioned Lemonade

Coffee
*Black Coffee, Light Coffee, Sweet Coffee,
Cinnamon Coffee, Chocolate Coffee, Moonshine Coffee,
and Southern Comfort Coffee*

Hard-Times Coffee
*Bran Coffee, Dandelion Coffee, Chicory Coffee,
and Acorn Coffee*

Tennessee Eggnog

Boiled Custard
(Floats, Soft Custard, and Crème Anglaise)

Hot Cocoa

Thick Hot Cocoa

MULLED CIDER, SASSAFRAS Tea, and Lemonade are mountain drinks; too often we take them for granted. We shouldn't. A beverage can be the touch that sets the tone for a Sunday dinner, a warm visit, or a grand afternoon. Beverages may define the setting, the cook, or the dish. Although coffee is still our number one homemade beverage, I am also attracted to sweet, carbonated, and sour beverages. I like them spiced, and I savor drinking them slowly with friends and conversation.

We serve beverages hot, cold, or frozen. We make them dairy and nondairy, fruit or chocolate, carbonated or flat. We boil beverages on a stove, mix them with a spoon, or puree them in a blender.

You are familiar with the basic beverages: tea, coffee, cocoa, and punch. You may also know coolers, shakes, smoothies, drizzles, and floats. But have you heard of pink ladies, orange delights, or Swedish glogg? Do you know our Percolator Punch and Tennessee Eggnog?

Think first of the beverage base—the primary ingredient—which may include water, milk, fruit juice, ice cream, or ice. With so many options, let's clarify some beverages, including waters.

Waters

Don't forget the many bottled waters available in our markets. You can buy them sweetened, carbonated, or flavored. Drink them as they are, or add them to punch.

Punch

Once you invest in a punch bowl, you are ready for holiday entertainment or a summer lawn party. While a punch may contain alcohol, it is a beverage made with two or more fruit juices, carbonated drinks, sugar, flavorings, and ice or sherbet.

Coolers

Common cooler ingredients include fruit juices, soda, fruit garnish, and alcohol. Serve coolers in a tall glass.

Frappés

As you would slushies, smoothies, or Hawaiian ice, serve frappés with crushed ice. Frappés are strong fruit drinks, appetizers, or desserts made by using a blender or food processor to combine frozen fruit, sherbet, or ice.

Wassail

The Norse word *wassail* means "to be in good health." Wassail is a toast, and a spicy drink made of ale, wine, fruit juices, and, most often, apple cider. Serve this brew in a wassail bowl. It is like Mulled Cider.

Garnish

A garnish makes beverages attractive and gives a clue about the ingredients or the occasion. Beverage garnishes, like other garnishes, should match or complement the ingredients. For example, garnish Lemonade with sliced lemon, Mulled Cider with spiced apples, and Hot Chocolate with mini-marshmallows. A garnish can be as simple as a wedge of fruit or a scoop of sherbet or as complicated as a punch-bowl ring.

Punch-Bowl Ring

Also called an ice ring, a punch-bowl ring is made by filling a ring mold half full of fruit punch and freezing it. When frozen, add fruit and additional punch and freeze it again. To unmold, dip the ring in hot water. At Christmas make a holly-wreath ring with cranberries and lime wedges, or with red and green maraschino cherries.

Mulled Cider
(Hot Spiced Cider)

DIFFICULTY Moderate. With nine ingredients, the following recipe is moderate in difficulty. You can make it ahead and reheat.

*T*his sweet and fully-flavored hot drink has many names: spiced cider, hot apple punch, hot cider punch, hot apple cider, spiced apple punch, hot mulled cider, Lou's Wassail, and holiday apple sipper. The word *mull* is a verb, and it means to heat, sweeten, and flavor with spices. With this recipe that is exactly what we do.

While hot spiced cider is usually made by simmering cider in a pot, some cook the spices in the top of an electric percolator and serve the drink in a cup as they would coffee. Others put the spices in a tea ball or cheesecloth. I like to strain the spices out at the end.

The following is strong in flavor, but my friends say it is the best hot cider they have ever had. The only spice common to this drink that I have omitted is nutmeg.

INGREDIENTS

8 cups apple juice or cider

6 ounces frozen orange juice concentrate

1/2 cup packed brown sugar

1 tablespoon whole cloves

1 tablespoon whole allspice

Four 3-inch cinnamon sticks

2 teaspoons sliced fresh ginger root

1 whole orange

8 whole cloves

YIELD 8 servings

STEPS In a large pot over high heat, bring the apple juice, orange juice concentrate, brown sugar, cloves, allspice, cinnamon sticks, and ginger to a slow boil. Reduce the heat, and simmer for 20 minutes. Let stand for 1 hour or more.

As the mulled cider steeps, prepare the garnish. Cut the orange into 4 wedges, and cut the wedges in half. After using an ice pick to make a hole in the peeling, insert a clove into each piece.

Reheat the cider, and strain out the spices. Serve garnished with the orange sections.

HEALTHY CHOICE ALTERNATIVE This fat-free recipe contains 1,600 calories, or 200 calories per serving.

Serve this on a cold winter afternoon in place of hot tea, before dinner, during a card game, or for a drop-by visitor. Serve with rice cakes, snack mix, and salted or unsalted nuts, or with North Carolina Roasted Pecans, Christmas Rocks, Cheese Grits Bars, cheese-filled celery sticks, or orange and apple wedges.

Old-Fashioned Lemonade

I make basic, homemade, do-it-yourself, special-treat lemonade with fresh-squeezed lemon juice, sugar, and water. In the market you can buy fully prepared lemonade or make it from lemon extract, frozen lemon concentrate, or bottled lemon juice. You can, and often we do. But none of these is as good as fresh-squeezed. A simple rule is to use one medium-size lemon per serving. The recipe I give below is rather strong—just the way I like it.

I make this drink one glass at a time, and I "serve" it to myself. Perhaps this joy is egocentric, but sometimes that's the way with food. Food can be private. I indulge myself with lemonade. I sit alone, and I sip it under a shade tree. If you are not alone, you can make any number of servings. The formula is simple: Use equal volumes of lemon juice and sugar.

STEPS Squeeze the lemon. Pour the juice, sugar, and water into a glass. Stir until the sugar is dissolved, and add the ice. Serve.

HEALTHY CHOICE ALTERNATIVE Lemons are high in vitamin C, with the juice of a medium lemon providing about 65 percent of your daily requirement. If you store the juice more than a day, though, you lose the vitamin C.

Add lemon wedges, crushed mint leaves, rosemary, or maraschino cherries frozen in ice cubes. To feast your eyes and create pink lemonade, add grenadine, cranberry juice, or red food coloring. To create an old-fashioned lemon shrub, add brandy. You may also want to frost the glasses: fill heavy, thick glasses two-thirds full with ice and place them in the freezer for at least 30 minutes. Take them from the freezer, particularly on a humid day, and they will gather frost.

DIFFICULTY Easy. With four ingredients and no cooking, the following recipe is easy.

INGREDIENTS
1 medium lemon or
1/4 cup lemon juice
An equal volume of sugar, or 1/4 cup sugar
3/4 cup water
6 ice cubes

YIELD 1 serving

Coffee

*O*n the trail, in the barn, or deep in a coal mine, coffee is a warming companion. Today, coffee fits our fast pace of living: We drink as we travel, and we drink in front of a TV screen or computer monitor. Coffee time is all the time.

Waverley Root and Richard de Rochemont, authors of *Eating in America*, report that, "In the year 1725, coffee houses, a social phenomenon of considerable importance, were booming. There were nearly two thousand of them in London. . . ." I suspect that the Scots and English who settled the Southern Highlands brought coffee with them.

Music, food, and coffee are kind. They comfort the soul, the heart, and the spirit. They give focus to a morning, and they ease the pain of life. They create rituals. Over a cup of coffee we talk, or we sit in silence and share feelings.

We value coffee for its flavor and the fact that it speeds the heart, digests food, quickens reactions, and sharpens our focus. Hot coffee warms us up, but caffeine also helps us endure cold weather.

Mountaineers like coffee with a good aroma, fresh flavor, and full body. We know the difference between instant and brewed, fresh-perked or reheated, and quality beans versus the supermarket specials.

Black Coffee Boiled, percolated, or filtered, black coffee ranges from a light, tea-like drink to deep black brew almost as thick as used motor oil. To make black coffee, use 1 to 2 tablespoons of ground coffee per cup of water.

Once you have made black coffee, use it as a master recipe for the following:

Light Coffee To black coffee, add milk, cream, or evaporated milk to taste.

Sweet Coffee To black coffee, add sugar, honey, molasses, or sweet sorghum.

Cinnamon Coffee Also called Mexican coffee, I like to make this in a percolator. I use one 3-inch cinnamon stick for every 3 tablespoons of coffee and 2 cups of water. Let the coffee and cinnamon perk for 10 minutes, and sweeten to taste.

Or, pour black coffee into a cup, and add 1 cinnamon stick. You may use the same stick for several cups of coffee.

Chocolate Coffee To a cup of black coffee, add a piece of Mexican coffee chocolate, $1/2$ teaspoon cocoa, or 1 envelope of instant hot cocoa mix.

Moonshine Coffee To a cup of black coffee, add 2 tablespoons moonshine.

Southern Comfort Coffee To a cup of black coffee, add 2 tablespoons of Early Times, Jack Daniel's, or Maker's Mark sour mash or bourbon whisky. Lighten with cream.

Hard-Times Coffee

*W*hen money was short, mountain cooks replaced coffee with a variety of flavorings—chicory, bran, dandelion roots, and acorns—but the process they used to prepare coffee remained the same.

Bran Coffee As you would roast coffee beans, roast 2 cups wheat bran and $1/2$ cup cornmeal. To 2 cups of boiling water, add $1/2$ cup of the roasted bran mixture, 1 egg, and 2 tablespoons of 100% pure sorghum. Boil for 5 minutes, filter, and serve.

Dandelion Coffee Gather and clean about 1 pound of dandelion roots, and allow them to dry. Roast the dry roots at 500°F until they get brittle and turn brown, about 6 to 15 minutes. Pound them with a mortar, or process in a food processor. Use as a coffee substitute or additive, adding the dry ground roots to coffee in a ratio of 1 part dandelion to 4 parts coffee.

Chicory Coffee Chicory is a plant with a blue flower and, like the dandelion, is a member of the composite family. We refer to the plant as blue-sailors, and you may know coffee made with some chicory as New Orleans or Luzianne coffee. Dried ground chicory root is a popular addition to coffee because it counteracts coffee's caffeine. I use a 1-to-4 ratio of chicory to coffee. Community Kitchens of New Orleans sells a coffee-chicory blend (see Community Kitchens in the Mail-Order Sources).

Acorn Coffee Hull 2 cups of white oak acorns, and mix with ½ cup cracked wheat. Roast at 500°F as you would coffee beans. When cool, pound with a mortar or process in a food processor. Boil ¼ cup of the mixture in 2 cups of water, and strain through a coffee filter. This makes a reddish-brown coffee.

■ ■

Eggnog and Boiled Custard

"Boiled custard and eggnog may not be native to the South, but they've been here long enough to belong," says John Egerton in *Side Orders*. "If they're not identical twins, they're certainly fraternal, or at least siblings—and whether they're served together or separately, they hold traditional places of honor at festive Southern tables. . . ."

It is said that George Washington used brandy, whisky, sherry, and rum in his eggnog. Washington's old recipe was like the Tennessee Eggnog recipe I present here.

Eggnog is a chilled holiday drink made of milk, cream, eggs, sugar, nutmeg, and, perhaps, liquor. It is available without alcohol in the dairy section of your market from mid-October through New Year's, but don't be tempted. Your home mix will be far superior to anything you can buy.

Boiled custard and eggnog are similar: light, creamy yellow, thick to pour, rich, and flavorful. Eggnog, however, uses raw eggs and whisky. Boiled custard is a cooked custard.

HEARTY
Cooking
COUNTRY

■ ■

Tennessee Eggnog

*J*ust as the Civil War divided North from South, eggnog and boiled custard divide mountaineers into two groups—the saved from the sinner, and the religiously conservative from other mountaineers. You may find that those who drink whisky and bourbon will sip eggnog, and those who do not drink alcoholic beverages enjoy boiled custard.

STEPS In a mixing bowl, whisk together half the sugar, the egg yolks, milk, and heavy cream. Add the bourbon and rum, and stir. In a grease-free bowl and using an electric mixer on high, beat the egg whites till frothy. One tablespoon at a time, add the remaining sugar to the egg whites. When the mixture is thick like a meringue, whisk it into the milk mixture. Refrigerate.

HEALTHY CHOICE ALTERNATIVE Use just 3 eggs and ½ cup cream. Further cuts of cream, sugar, or bourbon will make this drink more healthy but will weaken the eggnog so much that you may as well serve another drink, such as cranberry punch or carbonated water.

With this procedure the egg whites rise to the top. To keep the eggnog mixed, whisk and stir as you serve it. Serve in cold tumblers with a sprinkle of ground nutmeg. Serve this during the seven-week holiday period between Thanksgiving and New Year's. Offer crackers, cheese, and salted nuts, or serve with North Carolina Roasted Pecans or Cheese Grits Bars.

DIFFICULTY Easy. With six ingredients and no cooking, this recipe is easy.

INGREDIENTS
¾ cup sugar
6 eggs, separated and at room temperature
3 cups milk
1 cup heavy cream
1 cup bourbon
¼ cup rum

YIELD 8 servings

Boiled Custard
(Floats, Soft Custard, and Crème Anglaise)

*B*oiled custard is a cooked sauce or drink. We call it float or soft custard, and it is thick, rich, and sweet. The French call it crème anglaise and use it for floating islands. We make boiled custard with milk, eggs, sugar, and vanilla. There is wide variation in the number of eggs and amount of sugar used. My recipe is fairly light, but you can make it lighter, as I suggest in the Healthy Choice. Most recipes call for yolks only, using from four to as many as twelve yolks per quart of milk. You can make your custard richer by using cream or half-and-half.

DIFFICULTY Easy. With just five ingredients and one cooking step, this recipe is easy. Prepare in advance, allowing time to cool.

■ Beverages

Call it what you must and make it how you like, my Boiled Custard is a quick and easy sauce or a smooth, mild-flavored, and full-bodied non-alcoholic beverage.

INGREDIENTS
4 cups milk
4 eggs
1 cup sugar
1 whole vanilla bean, sliced down the center, or 2 teaspoons vanilla extract
Ground nutmeg

YIELD 8 servings

STEPS Prepare well in advance of serving, to allow enough time to cool.

In a saucepan over medium heat, heat the milk. If using a vanilla bean, simmer it 3 minutes and then remove, scraping the seeds into the milk.

In a mixing bowl, combine the eggs, sugar, and vanilla. Pour half of the hot milk into the egg mixture, blend, and return to the saucepan. Over medium heat, cook to 175°F on a candy thermometer, or until the custard thickens and coats the back of a wooden spoon. If it curdles, blend or strain. Cool until serving time.

HEALTHY CHOICE ALTERNATIVE As a substitute for cream, Boiled Custard is a light choice. Lighten it further by using skim milk and omitting 2 egg yolks. Reduce the sugar to ½ cup.

Serve in small juice glasses, and garnish with a pinch of ground nutmeg on the top. I like to serve Boiled Custard as a cold non-alcoholic drink before dinner with salted nuts, chips and dip, or sausage balls. To make a special occasion custard float, pour the boiled custard into a crystal mug and drop a dollop of Country Whipped Cream on the top. Traditionally, mountain gourmets serve Boiled Custard or Custard Floats with cake. As a dessert sauce we pour it over coconut cake, chocolate cake, Savage Mountain Pound Cake, or Persimmon Pudding.

Hot Cocoa

When winter arrives, the fog hangs low. The sky stays gray for days. The hills are even more gray with their covering of leafless trees. The mountains press in against our houses, and the light is low. Moisture seeps through our walls and fills every room. If the winter dulls your spirit, you can brighten the day with a hot fire and a cup of cocoa.

While coffee is a fast-track, everyday drink, hot cocoa is for slow winter Saturdays. Coffee quickens the pace; cocoa slows it down. Coffee bites the tongue; cocoa softens it.

When I lived in Pau, France, my French "mother," Madame Desrat, often served hot cocoa for breakfast. It was the summer of 1964, and I was treated kindly. I recall sitting at a tiny kitchen table for breakfast. Madame Desrat prepared hot cocoa and served it in a large cereal bowl. With the hot cocoa, she served French bread, butter, and anchovy paste. Now, on an occasional Saturday morning in the winter, I take the anchovy paste from the refrigerator and make the same breakfast. I savor the contrast between the hot sweet cocoa and cold salty anchovy paste combined with cold butter and crusty bread.

If you are making cocoa in your kitchen, don't bother with the specialty commercial cocoa mixes. I once bought a box of Swiss chocolate truffle mix, and while I'm attracted to Swiss things and I crave chocolate truffles, this was not Swiss, and it was not good. I made it according to the directions on the package, and it was bland and tasteless. So I fixed the box formula. First, I added more mix. Then I added cocoa. With the additional cocoa, it had a decent chocolate flavor, but it wasn't sweet, so I added sweet sorghum syrup. I spiced it up with a pinch of cinnamon. Finally, I had a good drink, but I may as well have made it from scratch—it would have been faster and less expensive. To make hot cocoa you don't need a package. Follow my recipes, and start with sugar and real cocoa.

Hot Cocoa

*W*hile I often make hot cocoa in a heavy pot on the stove, sometimes I prefer the microwave. Because cocoa does not combine easily with liquid, carefully follow my directions for mixing the milk with the dry ingredients.

When you mix your own hot cocoa, you can add sugar, or you can sweeten cocoa with sorghum, molasses, maple syrup, or honey. You can mix cocoa with water, Pepsi, milk, evaporated milk, or heavy cream. Then, you can add flavorings: orange rind, vanilla, mace, cinnamon, sherry, or salt. Add sassafras tea concentrate or instant coffee. Thicken your drink with eggs, flour, or ground nuts. Top your mix with whipped cream or marshmallow cream. Take the time. Have the pleasure. Create your personal drink.

DIFFICULTY Easy. With three ingredients and one cooking step, this recipe is easy to prepare.

INGREDIENTS
1 tablespoon Dutch processed cocoa
2 tablespoons sugar
1 cup milk

YIELD 1 serving

STEPS In a large mug, mix the cocoa and sugar. Add ½ tablespoon milk, and stir until absorbed. Add a second ½ tablespoon milk, and stir again. Repeat until the mixture is the thickness of cream, and then stir in the remaining milk. Microwave on high for 1 minute 40 seconds.

Do not let it boil, or it will bubble over the top.

Garnish your hot cocoa with miniature marshmallows or a large dollop of marshmallow cream. Top hot chocolate with whipped cream, and dust the cream with cocoa or cinnamon. For a real treat, place a scoop of chocolate or vanilla ice cream on top of your hot brew.

HEALTHY CHOICE ALTERNATIVE Let's distinguish chocolate from cocoa. Chocolate has about 9 grams of fat per ounce. Ounce for ounce, cocoa has about half the fat of chocolate. When you make a cup of cocoa with 1 table-spoon ($\frac{1}{25}$ ounce) of cocoa, it is about 50 times less fatty than hot chocolate made with 1 ounce of chocolate.

Serve with buttered toast, butter cookies, or Pecan Short Bread. Serve for breakfast, serve for a morning snack, or serve at night in front of a blazing fire.

Thick Hot Cocoa

*S*erved hot or cold, this Swiss-style formula makes a good dessert or a strong, chocolaty drink. My favorite style of hot cocoa, it is thick like sauce and creamy with chocolate. This drink is one step away from Chocolate Gravy. For variety, add 1 teaspoon instant coffee. For a richer drink, replace the cocoa with 1 or 2 ounces of sweetened chocolate. Omit the flour and reduce the milk by $\frac{1}{4}$ cup, adding $\frac{1}{4}$ cup heavy cream. Flavor with $\frac{1}{4}$ teaspoon cinnamon and a small pinch of salt.

STEPS In a large mixing bowl (at least 8-cups volume) mix the cocoa, sugar, and flour. Add $\frac{1}{2}$ tablespoon of the milk, and stir until absorbed. Add a second $\frac{1}{2}$ tablespoon milk, and stir again. Repeat until the mixture is like cream, and then stir in the remaining milk. Microwave on high for 1 minute, and then whisk. Microwave for another 2 minutes. Whisk in the sorghum, and serve.

HEALTHY CHOICE ALTERNATIVE To reduce fat, use skim milk. As compared to hot chocolate or cocoa made with eggs and cream, this recipe is light.

DIFFICULTY Easy. With five ingredients and one cooking step, this recipe is easy.

INGREDIENTS
1 tablespoon Dutch processed cocoa
1 tablespoon sugar
2 teaspoons all-purpose flour
1 cup milk
1 heaping tablespoon 100% pure sorghum

YIELD 1 serving

Glossary of Food Terms and Expressions

APPLES, DRIED Home-dried apples are very dry, and the flavor is concentrated. For Dried Applesauce, Dried Apple Stack Cake, and Fried Apple Pie, traditional mountain cooks use dried apples. Roy Mullins of Mullins' Orchard at Wise, Virginia, says that a bushel of fresh apples yields about three pounds of dried apples. Order from Mullins' Orchard.

BEANS

Fall Beans With the arrival of October shellies, October reds, greasy cut shorts, and fall white half-runners, our green bean season renews itself. We call these fall beans, and like our summer green beans, we cook them with pork until they split open and turn to a drab olive color. Order the seed from Henry Fields or Gurney's Seed and Nursery.

Green Beans Robust green beans—varieties such as Kentucky Wonder, Romano, white half-runners, white McCaslans, and contender—are thick, full seeded, and meaty. Green beans are a common mountain vegetable, and they are different from the small, soft, uniformly shaped bean bought frozen or canned. Our mottled beans are neither a tender snap bean nor a tiny French *haricot vert*. Order the seed from Henry Fields or Gurney's Seed and Nursery.

October Beans A fall green bean.

Shuck Beans Shuck beans, shucky beans, and leather britches, as we call them, are mature dried green beans. We dry and sell them on strings three to four feet long. To cook shuck beans, we soak them twelve or more hours, and then boil them with a piece of salt pork or ham hocks. Today, mountaineers prize shuck beans for their concentrated flavor. Order from Floyd Skean's Happy Mart.

Soup Beans Soup beans is another name for dry pinto beans and the name of a common bean soup. In the store we buy soup beans, and at home we cook them with pork flavoring.

BEECHNUTS The American beech tree—also called the "lovers' tree" because young people carve their initials on the smooth gray bark—produces the beechnut we use in cooking. Beechnut trees are part of the beech family, with about one hundred species native to North America, including the chestnuts, oaks, chinkapins, and tanoaks.

We eat beechnuts raw or cooked, and we use them in any recipe that calls for pecans. They are especially good when substituted in pecan pie. Beechnuts are available in the shell in the fall from Louisiana Forest Seed.

BLACK-SEEDED SIMPSON LETTUCE A popular early-season leaf lettuce.

BLACK WALNUTS Black walnut trees grow from New England across the northern states to Minnesota and south from Texas to Florida. In the mountains they prefer cool damp valleys, but they also grow in the open. Black walnuts are a strong-flavored, oily nut. The fruit is almost round, with a green husk and a strong, corrugated nut shell. I use black walnuts in Black Walnut Sugar Cookies, Raw Apple Cake, and the Black Walnut Cake. Order black walnuts from Sunnyland Farms.

BLADES Blades are onion or corn leaves. We eat onion blades in the spring, and during the summer we sit outside and watch the fireflies flicker as the corn blades reflect the moonlight.

BOLTED CORN Bolted corn is ground corn or cornmeal that has been processed to remove the hull.

BUTTERNUTS Closely related to black walnuts, butternuts are also called oilnuts, yellow walnuts, and white walnuts. They do not grow much south of Tennessee. They are available in the shell in the fall only from Louisiana Forest Seed, and shelled from American Spoon Foods (listed in their catalog as wild butternut meats).

BUTTERS Apple, peach, or pear butters are a thick, concentrated fruit conserve. We spread them on buttered toast and use them in Stack Pies or Stack Cakes. Order from Gallery Crafts.

CAST-IRON COOKWARE Saucepans, Dutch ovens, camp ovens, fryers, skillets, kettles, stove broilers, griddles, biscuit, and muffin pans are made of cast iron, a durable alloy of iron, carbon, and other elements. Cast-iron cookware is heavy, and it improves with use. Order from Lodge Manufacturing Company.

CAST-IRON SKILLET This heavy frying pan is made of thick cast iron. These skillets are standard cookware in country kitchens. Mountain cooks use them to fry, blacken, and bake, and in doing so are part of a tradition that goes back four thousand years. Cast-iron skillets are available with or without covers in six-, eight-, eleven-, and fourteen-inch diameters. Order from Lodge Manufacturing Company.

CHICKENTOE Also called Tanglegut, this is the common name for spring beauty, *Claytonia virginica*—a wild early-spring green that we use in salads and serve with soup beans.

CHOW CHOW Chow chow is a mixed-vegetable relish made with cabbage, onions, green tomatoes, green beans, corn, and cucumbers.

CHUCKWAGON Chuckwagon is a beef sandwich made with hamburger or cubed steak, served in mountain restaurants.

CORN CUTTER AND CREAMER Use this tool, with its two settings, to cut corn from the cob or to cut and cream corn. When you pull the corn across the blades, they cut, shred, and scrape the kernels, resulting in creamed corn. To set up the corn cutter, I mount the tool to my workbench; I can then pull the corn across the blades using both hands. This tool is available from the W. Atlee Burpee Company.

CORN DODGERS Dodgers are cornmeal dumplings cooked in water.

CORN, ROASTING EARS Roasting ears are young, not-filled-out fresh sweet corn. John Parris in *Mountain Cooking* says, "If you can get some roastin' ears, you've been to the garden and picked some fine corn." Mountaineers look forward to the corn season, and at the post office or in church, if you listen closely, you'll hear them comment, "It's roastin' ear time."

CORNMEAL Ground from white or yellow corn, mountain millers make cornmeal in fine, medium, or coarse grinds. If the meal is not labeled "stone-ground," the miller has degerminated and hulled it. Order from White Lily or The Old Mill.

Mix, Self-Rising Self-rising cornmeal mix is a combination of cornmeal, flour, salt, and leavening. Unless labeled otherwise, the mix is usually made with enriched, degerminated, and bolted cornmeal. These mixes are all a bit different, but the one I like most is made with 1 cup cornmeal, $\frac{1}{2}$ cup all-purpose flour, $1\frac{1}{2}$ teaspoons baking powder, and 1 teaspoon salt. Order from White Lily or The Old Mill.

Stone-Ground Millers make stone-ground cornmeal in a water-powered grist mill with whole kernel (not degerminated or bolted) corn. Millers reduce the corn kernels to meal when they roll them between two round stones. If the meal is labeled bolted, the hull has been removed. The Old Mill makes some of my favorite stone-ground white cornmeal.

CORN PONE Corn bread batter.

COUNTRY HAM Country hams are dry cured in flaked salt, sodium nitrate, sugar, and seasonings. (If we use a brine, we call it a wet cure.) After dry curing the ham, the salt is rinsed off and the ham is smoked from 1 month to 1 year. Order from Callaway Gardens or The Smithfield Companies.

CRACKLING CORN BREAD Corn Bread made with cracklings.

CRACKLINGS Cracklings or cracklins are crunchy, fibrous morsels. When we render or boil lard from pork fat, we end up with two products: lard and cracklings. The cracklings are a snack eaten out of hand or used as an ingredient in Crackling Corn Bread or Crackling Dumplings. For about $1.40 a pound, I can buy Hormel Pork Cracklings "Processed from Fried-out Pork Fat with Attached Skin" at the supermarket. Look for them displayed with the salt pork or smoked ham hocks. Ask your grocer, butcher, or sausage maker, or order from Poche's Meat Market.

CREAM Fresh milk separates into two parts: cream, or top milk, and fat-free milk. Heavy cream, which I use for Country Whipped Cream, has from 36 to 40 percent butter fat. Here in the mountains, we use the word *cream* to refer to evaporated canned milk. A popular and health-choice ingredient is evaporated skim milk, which is high in calcium.

CUSHAW SQUASH Also called green-striped cushaw, this smooth-skinned, hard-shelled, and striped green-and-white winter squash is shaped like a yellow crookneck summer squash, only larger. Cushaw squash weigh from ten to twenty-five pounds, and they ripen in the fall with pumpkins. We use cushaw like other winter squash. Order seed from Gurney's Seed and Nursery or Henry Fields Seed and Nursery; order the squash in the fall from Floyd Skean's Happy Mart.

White White cushaw squash is smooth-skinned, hard-shelled, and off-white in color, and is similar in texture and taste to green-striped cushaw. This winter squash is shaped like a pumpkin, but larger and more squat, weighing up to thirty pounds. The squash is not common, and we use green cushaw in its place. (I have no mail-order source.)

DANDELION GREENS, CANNED Canned dandelion greens are available from W. S. Wells & Son and sold under the label Belle of Maine.

DELIGHTS Delights are layered portable casserole desserts with a bottom crust. The layers consist of fruit and puddings as suggested by the names: Blackberry Delight, Raspberry Delight, Chocolate Delight, and Dirt Pudding Delight.

DIPPY See Soppy.

DIRT We use the word *dirt* to describe some chocolate desserts, such as Dirt Pudding. Mud also means chocolate, as in Mississippi mud pie.

DRIED APPLES See Apples.

DRIED GREEN BEANS See Beans, Shuck Beans.

FIDDLEHEADS When ferns first sprout from the ground in the spring, they send up coiled shoots we call fiddleheads. The ostrich fern is a popular variety, dark green and nearly as thick as a pencil. Order from New Penny Farm in late April for May shipment.

    Canned Canned fiddleheads are available from W. S. Wells & Son and sold under the label Belle of Maine.

    Freeze-Dried Freeze-dried fiddleheads are available from W. S. Wells & Son.

FLOUR

    Instant Also called quick-mixing flour or sauce-and-gravy flour, this granular flour absorbs hot moisture. When sprinkled over boiling liquid, the liquid absorbs the flour. Instant flour does not form lumps.

    Self-Rising Self-rising flour contains about 1 teaspoon of baking powder and $^{3}/_{4}$ teaspoon salt per cup. Order from White Lily Foods.

FOXFIRE A term from late Middle English referring to the organic luminescence from a widely distributed fungi, some of which we find in Appalachia. Also the name of an educational organization located in the mountains of northeast Georgia and established by Eliot Wigginton.

GOOBER PEAS Goober peas are raw peanuts. Ask your grocer, or order from Gallery Crafts.

GREEN TOMATOES Hard and green, these tomatoes measure two to three inches across. They are available all summer, but are most common in the fall. I've eaten green tomatoes pickled, as part of a relish, in green tomato pie, and, of course, as fried green tomatoes.

    Toni Neeley of Volunteer Produce (615-525-7078) in Knoxville, Tennessee, is a tomato wholesaler serving the chain-store market, and he says he tries to keep green tomatoes all year, "But sometimes in storage, they turn red." Order from Oakwood Market.

GRITS Grits are any coarsely ground or cut grain such as corn, rice, or barley, but in the mountains we make grits with ground whole white corn. Order whole kernel white corn grits from Callaway Gardens Country Store.

    Hominy Grits Corn grits made from white corn hominy are the most common type of grits used in the mountains. They are sold in our markets as Quaker Quick Grits.

GRITTED CORN We cut gritted corn from over-ripe corn on the cob. The corn is too mature to eat fresh but not too old or too dry for gritted corn. We make gritted corn by grating the corn on a grater.

HEARTY
Cooking
COUNTRY

GRITTED CORN BREAD Made with gritted corn, this corn bread is a moist, pudding-like corn bread with a solid crust.

GRUBBING We grub for poke, which means we dig the roots from the ground with a heavy maddock. Why? We grub poke either to plant the roots in the basement so that we can harvest the stems in the winter, or to remove the plant when it is growing out of place.

HICKORY NUTS The hickory nuts most often used in cooking are shellbarks, shagbarks, nutmeg hickories, and mockernuts. Shellbarks are as large as walnuts and rather sweet. Hickory trees are part of the walnut family and include twenty or more varieties, most of which are edible. Many of them grow in the Appalachian Mountains. Green hickory wood chips are a favorite for barbecue and smoking; we make tool handles and sports equipment from dry hickory wood. Louisiana Forest Seed sells shagbark, nutmeg, and shellbark hickory nuts in the shell. Shagbark hickories are available shelled from American Spoon Foods (listed in their catalog as wild hickory meats).

HIGHLANDERS While you may associate the name with the harsh mountains of northern Scotland, Appalachian scholars use the term Highlander to refer to people who live on the Appalachian plateau.

HOMINY Hominy is tender cooked corn, one of the first foods Colonists learned about when they came in contact with Native Americans. Years ago mountain cooks made hominy at home with dried yellow or white corn, cooking it with lye or lime and removing the hull and germ. Today, we serve hominy as a breakfast grain or side-dish vegetable. Millers make hominy grits from hominy.

HOMINY GRITS See Grits.

LARD Lard is rendered pork fat. While 1 tablespoon of butter contains 100 calories and 31 milligrams of cholesterol, 1 tablespoon of lard has 115 calories and 12 milligrams of cholesterol.

LEAN Lean is the name for the thin strips of red meat in pork side meat or bacon.

LIKKER Likker is vegetable broth. See Pot Likker.

LINN HONEY Linn honey is made from the fragrant flower nectar of the July-blooming American basswood trees, in the Linden family. Also sold as basswood honey, it is light in color, runny, and mild. It also offers a fast, immediate sweetness—without any sharpness or aftertaste. Order from Mountain State Honey Company.

LOOSEN Loosen is a term meaning to thin. For example, we loosen both mayonnaise and breakfast gravy with milk.

MIDDLING MEAT A meat cut from pork, middling meat—also called salt pork or smoked side meat—is mostly fat.

MOLASSES Molasses is a colloquial term for sorghum syrup, 100% pure sweet sorghum. Molasses is a by-product of cane sugar production. See Sorghum Syrup.

MORELS Also called dry-land fish or hickory chickens, this pitted, spongy, cone-shaped mushroom pushes up from the soil in late spring. Related to the popular French truffle, morels are treasured for their nutty, fish-like flavor. Purchase dried black and white Michigan morels from American Spoon Foods. Imported and domestic morels, as well as other mushrooms, are available from Aux Delices des Bois.

MUD Chocolate.

MUSH Also known as polenta, mush is made with boiled fine-, medium-, or coarse-ground corn.

OIL CAKES Oil cakes, like my Prune Cake or Pumpkin Layer Cake, are cakes made with corn or safflower oil, rather than butter, lard, or another solid shortening. Oil makes cakes smooth and moist. When you reduce oil, your cake becomes drier and less tender.

PAWPAWS A sweet wild fruit similar in texture and diameter to bananas, but shorter and with large seeds. Pawpaws ripen in the fall on small understory trees. They are well adapted to our cool, moist creek banks, and the fruit is most flavorful after the skin turns brown.

PEANUTS, FRESH OR GREEN (RAW) Called goober peas, raw peanuts are available from Gallery Crafts.

PECANS Pecans are a soft, native Southern nut. While pecan trees grow in open fields, on fence lines, and as far north as northern Kentucky, they prefer a warmer climate and grow well in low, damp areas. Order pecans from Sunnyland Farms.

PERSIMMONS Persimmons are a fruit that ripens in the late fall. Unlike the foreign imports, domestic persimmons have seeds—you'll find ten or more, the size of pumpkin seeds, in each small fruit. If you gather your own persimmons, look for ones that are orange, and wait until after a good frost, one that goes down to about 25°F. When the persimmons have frozen hard, they are sweet, and you can stand under the tree and enjoy them just like the possums do. To remove the seeds and skin, cook the fruit and press it through a food mill. Purchase canned persimmon pulp from Dymple's Delight.

POKE A wild perennial potherb that sprouts in the spring from a large tuber, poke has a short season, as we eat only the young tender shoots. Poke berries, roots, and the mature plants are poisonous. Writers who compare poke to asparagus fail to recognize poke's special tenderness, succulent texture, and mild flavor. While I prefer to gather poke fresh in April and May, Allen Canning of Siloam Spring, Arkansas, cans it as "poke sallet" and sells it in many grocery stores. Order from Oakwood Markets.

PONE A pone or corn pone is a "loaf" of corn bread baked in a round skillet and cut into wedges, like pieces of pie. A corn pone is also a small round piece of corn bread much like a biscuit.

POT LIKKER Pot likker, also pot liquor, is the broth left after boiling cabbage, turnips, greens, or potherbs. We usually boil these vegetables with pork, and we serve the likker with corn bread.

POULTRY Order wild turkey, duck, goose, pheasant, quail, and grouse from International Home Cooking.

RACCOON A smooth, sweet wild game. Order from Millard's Turtle.

RAMPS Ramps are wild leeks (*Allium tricoccum*). Depending on where you live, ramps are in season from January through May. Similar to garlic but not as strong, ramps are good fried, boiled, dried, salted, and in jelly. In fact, we have almost as many ramp preparations as mountain cooks who prepare them. Order fresh in March and April from Donaldson Food Center; order dried and as jelly from Ramps, From the Seed to the Weed.

RED-EYE GRAVY Red-eye gravy is a broth similar to *au jus*. After frying country ham, deglaze the pan with coffee, Pepsi, or water to make red-eye gravy. Order country ham from The Smithfield Companies.

ROLLED DUMPLINGS See Slick Dumplings.

SALT PORK Also called fat back, white bacon, fat pork, side meat, middling meat, and sowbelly, salt pork is salt-cured pork fat. It may be streaked with lean. Fat back and other cuts of pork fat may or may not be salt cured. Bacon is smoked, but salt pork is not.

SASSAFRAS TEA Sassafras tea is made from the roots and root bark of sassafras. In the early history of this country, people drank the tea as a tonic, but today the FDA requires that safrole, the active ingredient, be removed. Order the tea in concentrate form from H & K Products, Inc.

SELF-RISING CORNMEAL MIX See Cornmeal Mix, Self-Rising.

SHUCK The shuck is the outside covering of corn or beans. With corn shucks, we make dolls, and with the shucks of beans, we prepare shucky beans.

SHUCK BEANS OR SHUCKY BEANS See Beans.

SKILLET CORN BREAD Corn bread baked in a skillet.

SLICK DUMPLINGS Like a large flat noodle, these dumplings are usually unleavened. To make them, we roll the dumpling dough out like a pie crust, cut the dumplings, and cook them in a sweet or savory broth.

SLURRY A slurry is a suspension, a mixture of solid particles and water. If you keep the mixture moving, the solids will stay mixed with water. If you don't keep it moving the solids will settle. In our coal fields we move mined coal in a slurry, mixing the coal with water and keeping it moving. In our cooking, a cold roux is a slurry. We mix solid particles of flour with water so that we can add the flour to a hot broth, such as chicken and dumplings, without getting lumps.

SMOKED RAINBOW TROUT See Trout.

SOPPY Also Dippy. A colloquial term for milk gravy, squirrel gravy, or sausage gravy, soppy is made with milk, flour, and pan drippings. We sop up the soppy with biscuits.

SORGHUM SYRUP We refer to this sweetener as sweet sorghum, pure sorghum, or sorghum. It is important to distinguish between sorghum syrup (100% pure sweet sorghum) and sugar cane molasses. Both sorghum syrup and sugar cane molasses are liquid sweeteners made from tall, corn-like plants. Molasses, however, is made from cane sugar plants; sorghum syrup is made from sweet sorghum plants. Here in the mountains, we use the term molasses to refer to sorghum syrup. While molasses is a by-product of sugar production, sorghum is an end product made by pressing the juice from sweet sorghum and boiling it into a concentrate. While sorghum syrup has a sweet, distinct, and slightly burned flavor, molasses is stronger in flavor, bitter, and less sweet. Order from Flag Fork Herb Farm or Townsend's Sorghum Mill. When buying sorghum syrup, be sure to ask for 100% pure sweet sorghum, a syrup that does not contain any corn syrup.

SOUP BEANS See Beans.

SOURWOOD HONEY This honey is gathered from the flowers of sourwood trees and prized by mountain cooks. A good keeper, sourwood is ready in mid-July. Order from Gallery Crafts.

SOUSE Also known as head cheese, this gelatinous coldcut, served sliced, reminds me of a terrine. We make souse from the pig's head and feet, and we mold it in a loaf pan.

STACK CAKE Stack cake is an apple-ginger cake with from four to fifteen layers. The layers are like big ginger cookies, and we cover them with dried apple applesauce, apple butter, or peach butter. After we assemble the cake, we let it sit for a day to absorb moisture from the filling.

STACK PIES Made with fresh fruit or apple, peach, or pear butter, these double-crust pies are perhaps half an inch thick. I compare them to fig or apple newtons. We call them stack pies because years ago we stacked them in a basket and took them to community gatherings.

STONE-GROUND CORNMEAL See Cornmeal, Stone-Ground.

SUCCOTASH Succotash is a starchy vegetable dish made with corn and lima beans.

TROUT, SMOKED Smooth, salty, and full-flavored, this trout has a flavor and texture between fresh baked trout and smoked salmon. Order from Salmolux, Inc.

TURTLE While old-time mountaineers used box, snapping, soft, or hard-shell turtles, today we can buy boneless, ready-to-eat trimmed snapping turtle meat. Order from Millard's Turtle in two- or five-pound packs.

WHITE CUSHAW SQUASH See Cushaw Squash, White.

WILD GREENS Wild greens are picked in the spring. When the temperatures rise to seventy degrees and I am itching for a good walk in the hills, I'll go out and pick poke, chickentoe, fiddleheads, and other edible wild plants.

YARD BIRDS Yard birds are chickens, ducks, and geese that live and grow in the yard. For ducks and geese, the range area includes a creek. Country people who keep chickens around their house enjoy free-range chicken but may not know that city chefs charge a premium for fresh yard-raised poultry.

YELLOW WALNUTS Yellow walnuts are also known as butternuts or white walnuts.

Mail-Order Sources

WHEN EXPLORING A new food, it helps to pick up the telephone and have a conversation with someone who knows it. Ask a few questions, and allow time for a chat. Relax and enjoy the relationship. The suppliers of our special foods are my friends, and they can be your friends too. These are your mountain shopkeepers, and with your telephone, you can make a trip to the country and share our culture.

Some hard-to-find, slowly disappearing, indigenous foods are a traditional part of Appalachian cooking, and this book would not be complete without a list of sources. In your stores I know that you can buy apples, sweet potatoes, and tomatoes. But can you buy green tomatoes, cracklings, cushaw squash, or black walnuts? Can you buy ramps, turtle, or sweet sorghum syrup? If you are like me, you don't want to go from market to market searching for ingredients. I prefer to get on the phone or send a fax to order special ingredients.

Wherever I could, I listed sources from the mountain region, but in some cases that was not possible. Reading through this list, you'll find that I have located some of our special foods in Michigan, South Dakota, Iowa, or Washington.

Because the demand for many of these products is small, some of the companies are also small. Rather than efficiency or fast service, be prepared to enjoy the owner's care and concern. In the following sections, I point out some of the characteristics or history of the business that will help put you in touch. Thanks to Joni Miller for her wonderful book, *True Grits: The Southern Foods Mail-Order Catalog.* Her book is a mail-order treasure for all of the South. The sources I list are specific to our mountain foods.

AMERICAN SPOON FOODS, INC.

Justin Rashid
P.O. Box 566
Petoskey, MI 49770
Orders: 800-222-5886
Information: 616-347-9030
Fax: 800-647-2512

American Spoon Foods, Inc., was founded in 1982 by Justin Rashid and Larry Forgione to encourage the use of native American foods. In the early years, Rashid foraged for mushrooms and marketed many natural wild foods. American Spoon now sells a full line of native American foods including nuts, dried fruits, preserves, sauces, marinades, relish, morels, butters, and dressings that my contact, Will Langmeier, says support the American Food Movement. Their trademark product, Spoon Fruit, is a line of about a dozen different spoonable fruit preserves made without added sugar. Request their four-color, thirty-page catalog.

Forgione, co-owner of American Spoon Foods, is the chef at An American Place, located at 2 Park Avenue, New York, NY, 212-684-2122.

W. ATLEE BURPEE COMPANY
Warminster, PA 18974
Phone: 215-674-4900
Fax: 215-674-4170

The Burpee Gardens' 160-page color catalog is a standard vegetable and flower seed resource and supplier. The company also sells plants, bulbs, seed tapes, and other specialty garden supplies. I include the company in this list because they sell a corn cutter and creamer, a tool I use to cut or cream corn from the cob.

A. M. BRASWELL FOOD CO., INC
P.O. Box 485
Statesboro, GA 30459
Phone: 912-764-6191
Fax: 912-489-1572

For the lowest prices on jams, jellies, preserves, butters, relishes, pickles, and chutney, ask for a Braswell's price list. The minimum order is ten jars. Visa, MasterCard, or personal check accepted.

AUX DELICES DES BOIS
Thierry and Amy Farges
14 Leonard Street
New York, NY 10013
Phone: 212-334-1230; 800-666-1232
Fax: 212-334-1231

Thierry Farges grew up in France, and as a boy he hunted mushrooms with his father. His wife, Amy, attended La Varenne cooking school in Paris, and in 1984 they met in New York. He was a busboy. She spoke French. Since 1988, Thierry and Amy have operated their business, Aux Delices des Bois, selling fresh, dried, seasonal, cultivated, and wild mushrooms. Their list includes morels, portobellos, oysters, chanterelles, black trumpets, shiitakes, and many more. Order by mail, fax, or phone. Visa and MasterCard accepted.

CALLAWAY GARDENS COUNTRY STORE
Pine Mountain, GA 31822-2000
Phone: 706-663-5100
Fax: 706-663-5058

Located in the foothills of Georgia's Appalachian Mountains, Callaway Gardens is a large family vacation resort complete with cottages, lodges, and seven restaurants. The resort includes pools, lakes, ponds, golf courses, gardens, a butterfly center, circus, horticultural center, and biking and hiking paths. Callaway Gardens is also an educational and horticultural organization, a subsidiary owned and operated by the Ida Carson Callaway Foundation. It serves as the southern location for PBS's *The Victory Garden*. Visit Callaway Gardens (1½ hours southwest of Atlanta) to sample their old-fashioned full-flavored

Speckled Heart Grits, or you can order them by mail.

COMMUNITY KITCHENS
P.O. Box 2311
Baton Rouge, LA 70821
Phone: 800-535-9901
Fax: 504-381-7940

Almost eighty years old, the Community Coffee Company is among the largest family-owned coffee processors in the world. In their slick fifty-page color catalog you'll find Coffee and Chicory, The New Orleans Blend. Through their catalog you can also buy the popular Dark Roast Community Coffee. Visa, MasterCard, and American Express are accepted.

DONALDSON FOOD CENTER
Bruce Donaldson
Cherry River Plaza
Richwood, VA 26261
Phone: 304-846-6238
Fax: 304-846-4351

Owner Bruce Donaldson sells ramps when they are in season. He sells them by the pound, peck, half bushel, or bushel, and he is dead serious about quality. Donaldson is a major supporter of the annual Richwood Ramp Feed, held each April, that serves a ramp dinner to about 2,000 people. From January through May, Donaldson's Food Center ships ramps throughout the continental United States. Early in the season the plants have fewer greens and more bulb; later, the greens are more dominant.

DYMPLE'S DELIGHT
Dymple and Vernon Green
Route 4, Box 53
Mitchell, IN 47446
Phone: 812-849-3487

Located between Bloomington, Indiana, and Louisville, Kentucky, Dymple's Delight is a one-product business. Since 1970 Dymple and Vernon Green have owned and managed this 98-acre, 250-tree persimmon farm and pulp processing plant. The Greens, who are approaching seventy years of age and thinking about retiring, still produce 3,000 to 4,500 cans of persimmon pulp and 6,000 pints of frozen pulp per year. They use both their own persimmons and buy from local jobbers.

The Greens' canned pulp is ideal for my Persimmon Bread, Persimmon Cookies, Persimmon Pudding, and other persimmon recipes. In many recipes, I use it in place of paw-paw pulp or applesauce. Keep in mind that the Greens sweeten their pulp—it is half sugar.

Send a self-addressed stamped envelope for a brochure and price list. When ordering, enclose a check or money order, paying in advance. No fax, phone, or credit card orders.

FLAG FORK HERB FARM, INC.

Mike and Carrie Creech
900 North Broadway
Lexington, KY 40505
Phone/Fax: 606-233-7381

Located on one acre on the north side of Lexington's downtown historic district, Flag Fork Herb Farm is an enchanting herb, flower, and plant source. Their 400 products include plants, rural crafts, country furnishings, and mountain foods, such as 100% pure sweet sorghum syrup and chow chow. My favorite craft is their slab-bark bird feeder.

FLOYD SKEAN'S HAPPY MART

571 N. Lake Drive
Prestonsburg, KY 41653
Phone: 606-886-0630

Floyd Skean's Happy Mart is a one-stop deli market, service station, and produce stand. Manager Betty Fyffe says they sell poke, plum grannies, pawpaws, creasy greens, and green tomatoes, but that she cannot ship perishable foods. She will, however, during the fall season, mail cushaw squash and shuck beans. Skean's is not a mail-order service, but Fyffe is helpful and will mail nonperishable foods. I asked Betty about poke and she said, "Sure we sell it—both stems and leaves—but it will not ship. Stop by during May." Then, laughing—it sounded funny to her, too—she added, "I'll sell you a poke of poke."

GALLERY CRAFTS

Box 7-570 Brevard Road
Asheville, NC 28806
Phone: 704-251-9692

For relishes, butters, pickles, jellies, jams, preserves, and conserves, Gallery Crafts is hard to beat. I am fond of their apple, peach, apple-cherry, pear, and pumpkin butters. With thirty-six different flavors of jelly and twenty-eight preserves, Gallery's price list is a valuable source for special items. You can also order moonshine, onion, sassafras, or hot mustard jelly. Gallery also sells jellies called bottled hell, damson plum, corncob, and honey mustard. Starting in July, Gallery sells sourwood honey and, later in the fall, raw peanuts. Call for a price list. Visa, MasterCard, and Discover cards accepted.

GURNEY'S SEED AND NURSERY COMPANY

110 Capital Street
Yankton, SD 57079
Phone: 605-665-1930
Customer Service: 605-665-1671
Fax: 605-665-1671

Since 1866 Gurney's has been delivering seeds, plants, and nursery stock. During the early years, the company's success was bolstered by its location at Yankton, South Dakota, the halfway point on the Missouri steamboat line. Today's success is due at least in part to its catalog, mailed to 17 million customers. Gurney's full-color seed catalog offers thirteen different winter squashes, one of which is green-striped cushaw. They also sell seed for Romano green beans and Kennebec seed potatoes.

H & K Products, Inc.

10246 Road P
Columbus Grove, OH 45830
Phone: 419-659-5110

H & K Products is a family-operated manufacturing business that has been selling sassafras tea—their only product—for more than thirty-one years. Owner Don Nordhaus says he makes tea concentrate from select heavy outside bark and the cambrian layer of sassafras roots. If you like to gather root bark, call Don and he will purchase it from you. H & K sells Pappy's Sassafras Concentrate Instant Tea by the case only, twelve 12-ounce bottles for $22.32 to $28.67 per case, depending on the cost of UPS shipping. Each bottle makes about 12 cups of hot tea.

Henry Field's Seed and Nursery Co.

415 North Burnett
Shenandoah, IA 51602
Phone: 605-665-9391
Customer Service: 605-665-4491
Fax: 605-665-2601

With full color photos of green beans and sweet corn, the seed catalog from Henry Field's has appeal. Here you'll find the solid, robust white half-runners, Romanos, contenders, and Kentucky wonders that we love.

International Home Cooking

Earl and Janice Peck
305 Mallory Street
Rocky Mount, NC 27801
Phone: 800-237-7423
Fax: 800-237-7421

Earl and Janice Peck are enthusiastic purveyors of rare and exotic meats. Write for their extensive black-and-white catalog. This company is a source for venison, rabbit, raccoon, frogs' legs, turtle, alligator, trout, salmon, wild turkey, duck, pheasant, quail, partridge, grouse, guinea, and goose. In addition, this source for the home chef sells meats that are not part of our tradition: bison, lion, bear, kangaroo, emu, ostrich, and elk. If the Pecks don't have it, they'll find it.

LODGE MANUFACTURING COMPANY

P.O. Box 380
South Pittsburg, TN 37380
Phone: 615-837-7181
Fax: 615-837-8279

Since 1896 Lodge Manufacturing has been making cast-iron cookware in the hills of eastern Tennessee. Joseph Lodge settled in the Sequatchie Valley because he appreciated the beauty and found the valley to be the perfect place to build a home and raise a family. Today Lodge makes about 140 different cast-iron products, including skillets, chicken fryers, oval casseroles, Dutch ovens, drop biscuit pans, and corn bread pans shaped as wedges, muffins, cornsticks, and cacti. Ask for a price list and color brochure.

LOUISIANA FOREST SEED CO., INC.

L. D. Delaney, Jr.
303 Forestry Road
Lecompte, LA 71346
Phone: 318-443-5026
Fax: 318-487-0316

Louisiana Forest Seed is in the business of supplying foresters and nurseries with seed for about seventy different trees, including pecans, hickories, beeches, and black walnuts. Their nuts and seeds arrive clean and untreated in the shell; you will have to crack them.

L. D. (Derwood) Delaney, Jr., has served foresters for thirty-five years, and his sons Gary and John—the ones who answer the phone when I call—now work in the business. If you don't want to go into the hills to collect nuts, call Louisiana Forest Seed. The Delaneys are helpful and will supply nuts to any mail-order gourmet.

MILLARD'S TURTLE

Fred Millard
Rural Route 1
Birmingham, IA 52535
Phone: 319-498-4364

When Fred Millard was a boy, he played with turtles—now he raises 45,000 a year. Fred is the world's largest snapping turtle skinner, packer, and shipper. Millard's Turtle is a family-owned and -operated business. Fred's daughter, Sheila, keeps the books, and his son, Sam, is a skinner. In fact, according to proud father Fred, Sam is the world's fastest turtle skinner, and he is trying to get recognition in *Guinness Book of World Records*! During the last two weeks of August, Millard's has a free open house, and you can visit the turtle ponds and watch baby turtles hatch.

HEARTY
Cooking
COUNTRY

MOUNTAIN STATE HONEY COMPANY

Paul and Alisa Poling
Route 1, Box 46
Hambleton, WV 26269
Phone: 304-478-4004

Paul Poling tends nearly 300 bee hives. During a good season, and with close management, he and his wife, Alisa, are able to rob the hives of about nine tons of honey. The Polings collect tulip poplar, linn or basswood, sourwood, golden rod, and sometimes apple or wildflower honey. You will have to ask specifically for linn honey, and remember that because of changing conditions, this delicacy is not available every year. The Polings sell their honey in various containers: salt shakers, honey bears, mugs, squeeze bottles, pint jars, and quart jars. They sell their honey mixed with nuts, in honey mustard, in the comb, and as sticks or straws.

MULLINS' ORCHARD

Roy Mullins
Route 2, Box 644
Wise, VA 24293
Phone: 703-328-3575

Roy Mullins tends forty acres of apples, which he sells fresh and dried. In the winter when orchard work is slow, Roy, his mother, and his aunt dry apples, and they sell thousands of bags each year. Roy couldn't imagine drying apples outside in the fall. He says the flies, yellow jackets, and dust would be disastrous. Rather, his family does the work in large chambers that sit over the heat register in the floor of their homes. As heat rises, it dries the apples. This method requires no extra fuel and is convenient. The apples dry on four or five stainless steel screened racks, and the process takes 24 hours.

In the apple drying business, Roy says he is "on halves" with his aunt and mother. "On halves" means that the money is split half and half—half for the apples and half for the drying.

You can order half-pound bags of dried apples for $2, but Roy cautions that the apples are not available all year. Depending on the season, he sells them for nine months. Roy delivers dried apples to produce markets up and down U.S. Highway 23. He is not in the mail-order business, but if you send a check or money order in advance, he'll ship to you. Be sure to add postage and handling.

NEW PENNY FARM

Chris Holmes
P.O. Box 448
Presque Isle, ME 04769
Orders: 800-827-7551

New Penny Farm specializes in certified organically grown potatoes. Chris Holmes mails out a small but beautiful eight-page catalog, which describes each of his nine or so varieties.

Choose from Green Mountain, Kennebec, Irish Cobbler, Atlantic, Belrus, Bintje, Yukon Gold, Russian Banana, Carola, and others. New Penny Farm is also my source for fresh fiddleheads.

OAKWOOD MARKET

Robert Bishop
1189 Eastman Road
Kingsport, TN 37664
Phone: 615-247-1131
Fax: 615-247-1135

This five-store grocery chain keeps Allens' canned Cut Leaf Poke Salet Greens on the shelf in the spring of the year. Though not a mail-order company, they will mail poke and green tomatoes, depending on availability, if you call for a price and send a check, including postage, in advance. Oakwood buys Allens' poke through Flemming Foods, a warehouse and wholesaler in Johnson City, Tennessee, 800-352-0664.

THE OLD MILL

Kathy Simmons
P. O. Box 146
Pigeon Forge, TN 37868
Phone: 615-453-4628

Located on the Little Pigeon River in Pigeon Forge, Tennessee, this mill was built in 1830. Among the Mill's twenty-eight products are flours, meals, grits, and biscuit and pancake mixes. Today, tourists flock to The Old Mill. The water-powered mill produces high quality white stone-ground cornmeal, much as it has for 165 years. Call for the one-page price sheet.

PENZEYS, LTD. SPICE HOUSE

Bill Penzey
P. O. Box 1448
Waukesha, WI 53187
Phone: 414-574-0277
Fax: 414-574-0278

Penzeys is a family business, and through their catalog they keep me in touch with world politics that affect the spice trade. From Penzeys I order arrowroot, sesame seeds, single-strength vanilla, and ground extra-fancy China Tunhing cassia cinnamon. With a full page describing thirteen different cinnamons, two pages devoted to curry powders, a supply of fresh ground ginger, and the best spice prices I know, the Penzeys free thirty-six-page catalog keeps fresh spices in my kitchen.

POCHE'S MEAT MARKET

Floyd Poche
3015-A Main Highway
Breaux Bridge, LA 70517
Phone: 318-332-2108; 800-3POCHES

Poche's Meat Market and Restaurant makes and sells pork cracklings, white pork sausage called boudin, and churice, an unsmoked marinated pork sausage. They also make andouille, tasso, crawfish boudin, chaudin, and stuffed beef tongue. When the store opened in 1962, boudin and cracklin' were the only items served. Poche's cracklin' is what we call fried pork rinds, because it includes fat fibers, skin, and meat. I use them like other cracklings. Floyd Poche supplements his sixteen-item price list with a booklet of recipes, a history of Poche's, and descriptions of many of the products. Poche's does not accept COD orders and has a ten-pound minimum order.

RAMPS, FROM THE SEED TO THE WEED

Glen Facemire, Jr.
P.O. Box 571
Richwood, WV 26261
Phone: 304-846-4235

Glen and his wife, Norene, offer the most complete line of ramp products and the best of mountain courtesy in West Virginia. In Richwood, wild ramps take center stage. And why not? Richwood claims fame as the ramp capital of the world. At the peak of the West Virginia ramp season in March and April, Glen sells fresh ramps, processes them, and sells them dried and pickled. You can also order ramp jelly, ramp salt, bulbs, seeds, and post cards. Call or write for his brochure price list or his ramp cookbook. Glen accepts mail orders only, and you must pay in advance by check or money order.

SALMOLUX, INC.

Steve Hobson, National Sales Manager
P.O. Box 23910
Federal Way, WA 98093
Phone: 206-874-2026
Fax: 206-874-4042

German-born George Kuetgens founded this value-added seafood processing company in 1988. In 1994 the company moved to a state-of-the-art processing plant, and they hope to process five million pounds of seafood in 1995. Most of their products are raised on Scottish and Norwegian fish farms and shipped to Federal Way, Washington.

Salmon is Salmolux's primary product, but the company also sells trout, halibut, baby coho, whitefish, patés, fish salads, chowders, salmon mousse, and salmon hams.

THE SMITHFIELD COMPANIES
Peter Pruden
P.O. Box 487
Smithfield, VA 23430
Phone: 800-628-2242; 804-357-2121
Fax: 804-357-5407

This company, formed in 1925, prepares and sells Amber Brand Genuine Smithfield Hams (aged 12 months) and Joyner's Red-Eye Country Style Hams (aged 70 to 90 days). Both styles are dry-cured, but Joyner's is less salty and less dry. Order a whole ham or as little as two pounds. The company boasts a beautiful thirty-two-page color catalog and accepts major credit cards.

SUNNYLAND FARMS, INC.
Jane and Harry Willson
Albany, GA 31706-8200
Orders: 800-999-2488
Inquiries: 912-883-3085

Sunnyland Farms sits in the middle of a 14,000-acre pecan grove. The family-operated business has a beautiful forty-eight-page catalog featuring pecans and other nuts and fruits. With more than one hundred different products, the Willsons sell nuts such as black walnuts, peanuts, cashews, and pecans. They sell pecans in the shell, raw, toasted, sugared, spiced, and salted. This catalog is fun—it contains family stories, employee introductions, detailed product descriptions, and color pictures. When you order, Jane and Harry will send you a free thirty-two-page Nut & Fruit Booklet packed with recipes and information.

TOWNSEND'S SORGHUM MILL
Danny Ray or Judy Townsend
11620 Main Street
Jeffersonville, KY 40337
Phone: 606-498-4142

Danny Ray Townsend is the fifth generation of Townsends to make sweet sorghum, and for the last seventy-five years he and his family have made it on their farm in Montgomery County, Kentucky. The Townsends grow and process thirty acres of sorghum using both mules and a tractor to power the mill. Then, using a continuous evaporator, they reduce the juice to sorghum syrup over a wood or natural gas-fired furnace. Danny Ray is president of the Kentucky Sweet Sorghum Producers Association and past president of the National Sweet Sorghum Producers and Processors Association. Danny Ray, who says he could not do everything without help from his wife, Judy, makes sorghum with wood fuel and a mule when he demonstrates old-fashioned sorghum making. The Townsends sell sorghum by the pint, quart, and five-pound tin. They also sell a 300-recipe sorghum cookbook, *Sorghum Treasures*, published by the National Sweet Sorghum Producers and Processors Association. Order by phone or request a price list. No fax orders or credit cards.

W. S. WELLS & SON
P.O. Box 109
Wilton, ME 04294
Phone/Fax: 207-645-3393
Home phone: 207-645-2117

For more than one hundred years the Wells family—Adrian, his wife Jeanne, and their son Adrian, Jr.—has been canning dandelion greens. They raise the greens on half an acre, and from this farm each year they produce 12,000 to 16,000 pint-size cans of dandelion greens. The Wellses also produce canned fiddleheads, freeze-dried fiddleheads, and pickled fiddleheads, and dilly beans (dilled green beans). Adrian advertises his company as "the only company in the world canning dandelion greens and the only company in the U.S. canning fiddleheads"; they sell under the brand name Belle of Maine.

The family cuts dandelion greens three times during the summer and cans them in water. If you live in the area, you can buy them fresh, but otherwise you'll have to place an order. Request a price list and recipe brochure. Phone orders are accepted; you may pay by check before or after you receive the greens. No credit cards.

THE WHITE LILY FOODS COMPANY
P.O. Box 871
Knoxville, TN 37901
Phone: 615-546-5511

When the Williams-Sonoma Catalog started to carry White Lily products, I worried that something unfortunate might happen to this quality mill. Then almost at the same moment, I was heartened by the thought that perhaps cooks outside the South were beginning to appreciate some of the world's finest baking ingredients. White Lily was established in 1883 and is still producing flours and meals in downtown Knoxville. Company literature calls White Lily "the staple of the South." Call or write for an order form. No phone orders or credit cards accepted. Pay in advance with a check or money order.

Bibliography

American Home All-Purpose Cook Book: Your Complete Guide to Successful Cooking. New York: M. Evans and Company, Inc., 1972.

Anderson, Jean, and Elaine Hanna. *The New Doubleday Cookbook*. Garden City, N.Y.: Doubleday & Company, 1985.

Arnow, Harriette. *The Dollmaker*. Reprinted: New York: Avon Books, 1972.

Bailey, Lee. *Country Desserts, Cakes, Cookies, Ice Creams, Pies, Puddings, and More*. New York: Clarkson N. Potter, Inc., 1988.

Beard, James. *American Cookery*. Boston: Little, Brown and Company, 1972.

Beck, Simone. *Food and Friends, Recipes and Memories from Simca's Cuisine*. New York: Penguin Books, 1991.

Birchfield, Jane. *Words from an Old Wife: Tips and Tales from Great Aunt Jane*. Philadelphia: Possumwood Press, 1991.

Brands, Joy, and Cookie Daugette. *Not Just Another Peanut Butter Cookbook*. Foley, Ala.: Underwood Printing, 1983.

Bryan, Lettice. *The Kentucky Housewife*. Cincinnati, Ohio: Shepard and Stearns, 1839. Facsimile editor: Columbia, S.C.: University of South Carolina Press, 1991.

Bucek, Jay, ed. *Somethin's Cookin' in the Mountains: A Cookbook and Guidebook to Northeast Georgia*. Clarksville, Ga.: Soque Publishers, 1984.

Carson, Sam, and A. W. Vick. *Hillbilly Cookin 2*. Sevierville, Tenn.: D & F Sales, Inc., 1972.

Child, Julia, Louisette Bertholle, and Simone Beck. *Mastering the Art of French Cooking*. New York: Alfred A. Knopf, 1961.

Claiborne, Craig. *Southern Cooking*. New York: Random House, Times Books, 1987.

Connor, Phyllis. *Old Timey Recipes*. Winston-Salem, N.C.: Old Timey Recipes, 1985.

Corn, Elaine. *Now You're Cooking: Everything a Beginner Needs to Know to Start Cooking Today*. Emeryville, Calif.: Harlow & Ratner, 1994.

Dull, Mrs. S. R. *Southern Cooking*. 1928 reprint: The Ladies Home Journal Cook Book Club. New York: Grosset & Dunlap, Inc. 1968.

Dwyer, Louise, and Bil Dwyer. *Southern Appalachian Mountain Cookin*. Highlands, N.C.: The Merry Mountaineers, 1974.

Egerton, John. *Southern Food: At Home, on the Road, in History*. New York: Alfred A. Knopf, Inc., 1987.

Egerton, John. *Side Orders: Small Helpings of Southern Cookery and Culture*. Atlanta: Peachtree Publishers, Ltd., 1990.

Emery, Carla. *Old Fashioned Recipe Book: An Encyclopedia of Country Living*. New York: Bantam Books, 1977.

Escoffier, Auguste. *The Escoffier Cookbook: A Guide to the Fine Art of French Cuisine*. New York: Crown Publishers, Inc., 1969.

Facemire, Norene. *Ramps a Cookin'*. Richwood, W.V.: The Facemires, 1993.

Farmer, Fannie Merritt. *The Boston Cooking-School Cook Book,* Eighth Edition. Revised by Wilma Lord Perkins. Boston: Little, Brown and Company, 1947.

Farr, Sidney Saylor. *More Than Moonshine: Appalachian Recipes and Recollections.* Pittsburgh: University of Pittsburgh Press, 1983.

Finley, John, ed. *Courier-Journal Kentucky Cookbook, The.* Louisville, Ky.: The Courier-Journal and Louisville Times Co., 1985.

Flexner, Marion W. *Cocktail-Supper Cookbook.* New York: Bramhall House, Inc., 1955.

Flexner, Marion W. *Out of Kentucky Kitchens.* Reprint 1949: Lexington, Ky.: The University of Kentucky Press, 1989.

Franey, Pierre, and Richard Flaste. *Cooking in France.* New York: Alfred A. Knopf, 1994.

Frazier, William C., and Dennis C. Westhoff. *Food Microbiology,* Fourth Edition. New York: McGraw-Hill Book Company, 1988.

Fussell, Betty. *I Hear America Cooking: A Journey of Discovery from Alaska to Florida—the Cooks, the Recipes, and the Unique Flavors of Our National Cuisine.* New York: Viking Penguin, Inc., 1986.

Gibbons, Euell. *Stalking the Wild Asparagus.* New York: David McKay Company, Inc., 1962.

Glenn, Camille. *The Heritage of Southern Cooking.* New York: Workman Publishing, 1986.

Green, Dymple. *Persimmon Goodies.* Mitchell, Ind.: Dymple's Delight, no date.

Hayes, Irene. *What's Cooking for the Holidays.* Hueysville, Ky.: The T. I. Hayes Publishing Company, Inc., 1984.

Hayes, Irene. *What's Cooking in Kentucky.* Hueysville, Ky.: The T. I. Hayes Publishing Company, Inc., 1982.

Illustrated Encyclopedia of American Cooking, The. Nashville: Favorite Recipes Press, The Southwestern Company, 1972.

Junior Charity League of Monroe, Louisiana. *The Cotton Country Collection.* Monroe, La.: The Junior Charity League, 1972.

Junior League (Johnson City, Tennessee). *Smoky Mountain Magic: A Superb View of Treasured Recipes.* Johnson City, Tenn.: The Junior League, 1960.

Junior League of Jackson, Mississippi. *Southern Sideboards.* Jackson, Miss.: The Junior League, 1978.

Kellner, Lynda W. *The Taste of Appalachia: A Collection of Traditional Recipes Still in Use Today.* Boone, N.C.: Simmer Pot Press, 1987.

Kimball, Yeffe, and Jean Anderson. *The Art of American Indian Cooking.* New York: Doubleday, 1965.

Kluger, Marilyn. *The Wild Flavor.* 1973. New York: Henry Holt and Company, an Owl Book, 1990.

Kowalchik, Claire, and William H. Hylton, eds. *Rodale's Illustrated Encyclopedia of Herbs.* Emmaus, Penn.: Rodale Press, Inc., 1987.

Kremer, Elizabeth C. *We Make You Kindly Welcome.* Harrodsburg, Ky.: Pleasant Hill Press, 1970.

Kremer, Elizabeth C. *Welcome Back to Pleasant Hill*. Harrodsburg, Ky.: Pleasant Hill Press, 1977.

Lang, Jenifer Harvey, ed. *Larousse Gastronomique: The New American Edition of the World's Greatest Culinary Encyclopedia*. New York: Crown Publishers, Inc., 1988.

Ledford, Ibbie. *Hill Country Cookin' and Memoirs*. Gretna, La.: The Pelican Publishing Co., 1991.

Liles, Glennis Stuart, compiler, and Chuck D. Charles, editor. *The W-Hollow Cookbook*. Ashland, Ky.: The Jesse Stuart Foundation, 1992.

Lundy, Ronni. *Shuck Beans, Stack Cakes, and Honest Fried Chicken: The Heart and Soul of Southern Country Kitchens*. New York: The Atlantic Monthly Press, 1991.

Margen, Sheldon, and the Editors of the University of California at Berkeley "Wellness Letter." *The Wellness Encyclopedia of Food and Nutrition: How to Buy, Store, and Prepare Every Variety of Fresh Food*. New York: Rebus, 1992.

McCulloch-Williams, Martha. *Dishes and Beverages of the Old South*. New York: J. K. Cole Studio, 1913. A facsimile edition with an Introduction by John Egerton, Knoxville, Tenn.: The University of Tennessee Press, 1988.

Mickler, Ernest Matthew. *White Trash Cooking*. Berkeley, Calif.: 1986.

Miller, Joni. *True Grits: The Southern Mail-Order Catalog*. New York: Workman Publishing, 1990.

Mitchell, Patricia B. *Grist Mill Quick Loaf Breads*. Chatham Va.: Sims-Mitchell House Bed and Breakfast, 1991.

Mitchell, Patricia B. *Sweet 'n' Slow: Apple Butter, Molasses, and Sorghum Recipes*. Chatham, Va.: Sims-Mitchell House Bed and Breakfast, 1988.

National Sweet Sorghum Producers and Processors Association. *Sorghum Treasures: A Compilation of Recipes—Old and New*. Audubon, Ia.: Jumbo Jack's Cookbooks, 1991.

Netzer, Corinne T. *The Complete Book of Food Counts*, third edition. New York: Dell Publishing, 1994.

Nickell, Estelle B. *My Favorite Molasses Recipes*. West Liberty, Ky.: Estelle B. Nickell, 1981.

Olney, Richard. *Simple French Food*. New York: Macmillan Publishing Company, 1974.

Page, Linda Garland, and Eliot Wigginton, eds. *Foxfire Book of Appalachian Cookery, The, Regional Memorabilia and Recipes*. Garden City, N.Y.: Doubleday, Anchor Books, 1984.

Page, Linda Garland, and Hilton Smith, eds. *Foxfire Book of Toys and Games, The, Reminiscences and Instructions from Appalachia*. Garden City, N.Y.: Anchor Books, 1985.

Parloa, Maria. *Miss Parloa's Kitchen Companion: A Guide for All Who Would Be Good Housekeepers*. Boston: Estes and Lauriat, 1887.

Parris, John. *Mountain Cooking*. Asheville, N.C.: Asheville Citizen-Times Publishing Co., 1978.

Parris, John. *These Storied Mountains*. Asheville, N.C.: Asheville Citizen-Times Publishing Co., 1972.

Patton, Floy Russell Shain. *Favorite Foods by Floy*. Morehead, Ky.: Floy Russell Shain Patton, 1992.

Picayune Creole Cook Book. Compiled by the editors of *Picayune*. New Orleans: Picayune Publishing Co., 1900.

Porter, Mrs. M. E. *Mrs. Porter's New Southern Cookery Book: A Companion for Frugal and Economical Housekeepers*. Philadelphia: John E. Potter and Company, 1871.

Preston, Ruth Stambaugh. *Hoop Skirts and Leather Britches: An Autobiographical Cookbook*. Venice, Fla.: self-published, 1992.

Progressive Farmer Southern Country Cookbook, The. Edited by The Progressive Farmer Magazine, Lena Sturges, Foods Editor. Birmingham, Ala.: The Progressive Farmer Company, 1973.

Randolph, Mary. *The Virginia House-Wife*. Washington, D.C.: Davis and Force, 1824. Reprint edition: Columbia, S.C.: University of South Carolina Press, 1984.

Rice, June. *Common Sense Cooking: For the Cook on the Run*. Paintsville, Ky.: Common Sense Books, 1992.

Rombauer, Irma S. *A Cookbook for Girls and Boys*. Indianapolis, Ind.: The Bobbs-Merrill Company, 1946.

Rombauer, Irma S. *The Joy of Cooking: A Compilation of Reliable Recipes with an Occasional Culinary Chat*. Indianapolis, Ind.: The Bobbs-Merrill Company, Inc., 1946.

Rombauer, Irma S., and Marion Rombauer Becker. *Joy of Cooking*. Indianapolis, Ind.: The Bobbs-Merrill Company, Inc., 1973.

Root, Waverley, and Richard de Rochemont. *Eating in America: A History*. New York: The Ecco Press, 1981.

Schneider, Sally. "April in Helvetia," *Saveur, no. 5*. New York: Meigher Communications, March/April 1995.

Sharpe, J. Ed, and Thomas B. Underwood. *American Indian Cooking & Herb Lore*. Cherokee, N.C.: Cherokee Publications, 1973.

Shelton, Ferne, ed. *Southern Appalachian Mountain Cookbook: Rare and Time-Tested Recipes from the Blue Ridge and Great Smoky Mountains*. High Point, N.C.: Hutcraft, 1964.

Simon, Andre L. *A Concise Encyclopedia of Gastronomy*. Woodstock, N.Y.: The Overlook Press, 1981.

Sohn, Mark F. *Education in Appalachia's Central Highlands*. Pikeville, Ky.: self-published, 1985.

Sohn, Mark F. *Southern Country Cooking*. Iowa City, Ia.: The Penfield Press, 1992.

Sokolov, Raymond. *Fading Feast: A Compendium of Disappearing American Regional Foods*. New York: Farrar Straus Giroux, 1981.

Sokolov, Raymond. *Why We Eat What We Eat: How the Encounter Between the New*

World and the Old Changed the Way Everyone on the Planet Eats. New York: Summit Books, 1991.

Stuart, Jesse. *Head o' W-Hollow*. Reprint of the E.P. Dutton 1936 edition. Lexington, Ky.: University Press of Kentucky, 1979.

Sturges, Lena E. *For the Love of Cooking*. Birmingham, Ala.: Oxmoor House, Inc., 1975.

Tannahill, Reay. *Food in History*. New York: Stein and Day Publishers, 1973.

Tates, The [no first name given]. *Hillbilly Cookin: Mountaineer Style*. Sevierville, Tenn.: C & F Sales, Inc., 1968.

Thorne, John, and Matt Lewis Thorne. "The Irish and Potatoes," *Simple Cooking, no. 38*. Steuben, Maine: John Thorne, April 1994.

Tyree, Marion Cabell. *Housekeeping in Old Virginia: Contributions from Two Hundred and Fifty of Virginia's Noted Housewives, Distinguished for Their Skill in the Culinary Art and Other Branches of Domestic Economy*. Louisville, Ky.: John P. Morton and Co., 1879. Reprinted: Louisville, Ky.: Favorite Recipes Press, Inc., 1965.

Ulmer, Mary, and Samuel E. Beck, eds. *Cherokee Cooklore: To Make Bread*. Cherokee, N.C.: Mary and Goingback Chiltoskey and The Stephens Press, Inc., 1951.

Wigginton, Eliot, ed. *Foxfire Book, The*. Garden City, N.Y.: Doubleday, Anchor Books, 1972.

Wigginton, Eliot, ed. *Foxfire 2*. Garden City, N.Y.: Doubleday, Anchor Books, 1973.

Wigginton, Eliot, ed. *Foxfire 3*. Garden City, N.Y.: Doubleday, Anchor Books, 1975.

Yates, Augusta. *Key to the Pantry: Choice, Tried Recipes*, second edition. Richmond, Va.: 1907.

Index

About the Author

MARK F. SOHN is a writer, chef, and teacher. A full-time professor of educational psychology at Pikeville College in Pikeville, Kentucky, Sohn earned his doctorate from the University of Maryland and has lived in the Central Highlands of eastern Kentucky's Appalachian Mountains for almost twenty years.

Sohn started cooking as an eleven-year-old Boy Scout in the hills of western Oregon, and he has been cooking ever since. In 1987, he studied cooking in Paris, completing the École de Cuisine sponsored by Maxim's Restaurant and Pierre Cardin.

Since 1987, various editors have published nearly 300 of Sohn's food-related articles and 450 of his recipes. His writings cover food history, cooking theory, ethnic foods, restaurants, travel, and many, many recipes, and his work always reflects a sense of culture, place, and season. His previous books include *Education in Appalachia's Central Highlands*, *Psychology for Parents and Teachers*, and *Southern Country Cooking*.

Since July 1990, Sohn has been the host and chef for *Classic Home Cooking*, a successful television cooking show that features the foods of central and southern Appalachia. In 1992, the Penfield Press of Iowa City, Iowa, published Sohn's first cookbook, *Southern Country Cooking*, which featured traditional foods from thirteen Southern states.

Sohn has taught some forty different undergraduate and graduate-level courses at six colleges and universities—Iowa State University, Ripon College (Wisconsin), Dundalk Community College (Maryland), Morehead State University (Kentucky), Northern Arizona University, and Pikeville College.

Sohn is from a family of cooks. As a young man, his father, Fred, worked in a German flour mill as a miller, test baker, and cereal chemist. Today, his dad is a meticulous avocational bread baker, and his mom cooks everything else. He also has four brothers who cook. Sohn is married to Katherine Kelleher of Greensboro, North Carolina, and is the father of two grown children, Laura and Brian. They too do a little cooking and sometimes use one of dad's recipes.

HEARTY Cooking COUNTRY ■